Multiculturalism Rethought

MULTICULTURALISM RETHOUGHT

Interpretations, Dilemmas and New Directions

ESSAYS IN HONOUR OF BHIKHU PAREKH

Edited by Varun Uberoi and Tariq Modood

EDINBURGH
University Press

© editorial matter and organisation Varun Uberoi and
Tariq Modood, 2015
© the chapters, their several authors, 2015

Edinburgh University Press Ltd
The Tun – Holyrood Road
12 (2f) Jackson's Entry
Edinburgh EH8 8PJ
www.euppublishing.com

Typeset in 11/14 Sabon by
Servis Filmsetting Ltd, Stockport, Cheshire
and printed and bound in Great Britain by
CPI Group (UK) Ltd, Croydon CR0 4YY

A CIP record for this book is available from the British Library
ISBN 978 1 4744 0188 3 (hardback)
ISBN 978 1 4744 0190 6 (paperback)
ISBN 978 1 4744 0189 0 (webready PDF)
ISBN 978 1 4744 0191 3 (epub)

The right of the contributors to be identified as
authors of this work has been asserted in accordance
with the Copyright, Designs and Patents Act 1988 and
the Copyright and Related Rights Regulations 2003
(SI No. 2498).

Contents

CONTENTS

Acknowledgements

This volume would not have been possible without funding and support from the Economic and Social Research Council (PTA-026-27-2736), Brunel University's Magna Carta Institute, Bristol University's Centre for Ethnicity and Citizenship and the University of Westminster's Centre for the Study of Democracy. They allowed the Bhikhu Parekh Symposium, at which the chapters in this volume were discussed, to occur. Likewise, John Dunn, Anthony Giddens, Chandran Kukathas, Andrew Mason, Susan Mendus, David Miller, Albert Weale and Ziauddin Sardar carefully read and responded to the papers being discussed so as to make suggestions on how to improve them. Raymond Plant was initially going to be an editor of the volume but he became a valuable chapter author and gave feedback on certain chapters too. The publisher's reviewers also made important suggestions that helped to improve the volume. But without Bhikhu Parekh's political thought, such a volume would not have been necessary, so we dedicate this book to him in recognition of how he has stimulated our own intellectual work and that of so many others.

V. U.
T. M.

Preface

Tariq Modood

The essays that constitute the chapters in this volume are explorations of various aspects of the political theory of multiculturalism. Each is freestanding and of value in itself but all except one were presented at a symposium to honour the contribution of Bhikhu Parekh to this subject, the political theory of multiculturalism. Some of the chapters are concerned primarily with facets of Parekh's theory; more are concerned primarily with a substantive topic *within the political theory of multiculturalism*, and in this way engage with his contribution. What unites them is the appreciation that Parekh's work on multiculturalism, in particular his book *Rethinking Multiculturalism* (2000; second edition, 2006) is a significant presence that has helped to make this subdiscipline of political philosophy. In the next chapter, Varun Uberoi introduces Parekh's philosophy of multiculturalism and the contents of the book. I would like to start the book – just as the symposium started – with a few words to honour Bhikhu Parekh.

Parekh is a remarkable political philosopher who has published major books on many philosophers and concepts. Political theorists he has written about include Bentham, Marx, Arendt and Oakeshott; among concepts he has written about are justice, equality, ideology and civil association. Moreover, Parekh has thought seriously and continuously about his discipline, about the nature of political philosophy, about how it should be pursued and what it is capable of. Indeed, his work on multiculturalism is only a fraction of his political philosophy output. Yet there is no doubt that it is his most widely read work on multiculturalism that has stimulated the most response and had the most profound influence. It has played a major role in the intellectual formation of later generations and in creating a sense of where the important issues are and how they should be engaged with. Many of the contributors of this volume said they were keen to participate in this project because of what Bhikhu Parekh meant to them.

To several of us this does not refer to political philosophy alone but has at least two other important aspects. First, there is his example of public service and intellectual public engagement, which has been impressive, and an inspiration and a guide to others. Parekh was a member of some of the earliest British government commissions on racial disadvantage and multiculturalism, initially in relation to schooling, such as the ones known by the reports named after their chairmen, Rampton (1981) and Swann (1985), later becoming Deputy Chair and Acting Chair of the Commission for Racial Equality. Through both such public service and public interventions Parekh has influenced considerably the way in which citizens, intellectuals and policy makers have come to think about and understand racial equality and multiculturalism in Britain and further afield. Parekh was most significant for instance in articulating, stimulating and leading a multiculturalist position at the time of the *Satanic Verses* affair. He was later the Chair of the Commission of Multi-ethnic Britain, which produced what is known as the Parekh Report, one of the most important public documents in its field, and just before its publication in 2000 Parekh was made a Labour member of the House of Lords, a position he continues to serve with distinction. (Parekh has also played a role in Indian public life but I write here of what I have personally observed.)

Second, Parekh's career in political philosophy and as a public intellectual (in challenging orthodoxies, leading new debates and pointing to new conceptions of who we were as a public and as a country) has been as an ethnic minority individual, as a British Asian. This has given him a direct insight into the things that are theorised in this book, meaning that he can speak with some authenticity and authority on the nature and desirability of multiculturalism, but it has also meant an uphill climb to be heard and to be taken seriously, especially in public affairs.

As a political philosopher, a public intellectual and a British Asian he has been a guide and an inspiration to many. While this book is primarily an engagement in political philosophy, each of these elements has played a part in motivating the contributors to this book to be part of this collection.

List of Contributors

Benjamin R. Barber is Senior Research Scholar at the Graduate Center, City University of New York, and founder and President of the Interdependence Movement. He is Walt Whitman Professor of Political Science Emeritus at Rutgers University. His latest book, *If Mayors Ruled the World: Dysfunctional Nations, Rising Cities* (2013), already in ten foreign editions, has engendered a project to establish a Global Parliament of Mayors, whose first sitting will occur in London in late 2015. Among Barber's eighteen books are the classic *Strong Democracy* (1984), the international bestseller *Jihad vs. McWorld* (1996), and the critique of consumerist materialism and push marketing *Consumed* (2004).

Rajeev Bhargava is Senior Fellow and Director, Centre for the Study of Developing Societies, Delhi. He has held visiting fellowships at Harvard, Columbia, Jerusalem, Bristol and Paris. He is on the advisory board of several institutions and programmes and was a consultant to the UNDP report on cultural liberty. His publications include *Individualism in Social Science* (1992), *Secularism and its Critics* (edited volume 1998), *What is Political Theory and Why do We Need It?* (2010) and *The Promise of India's Secular Democracy* (2010).

Joseph H. Carens is Professor of Political Science at the University of Toronto. He published over seventy articles, edited two books, and written *The Ethics of Immigration* (2014), *Immigrants and* *the Right to Stay* (2010), *Culture, Citizenship and Community: A Contextual Exploration of Justice as Evenhandedness* (2000) and *Equality, Moral Incentives, and the Market: An Essay in Utopian Politico-Economic Theory* (1981).

Andrew Gamble is Professor of Politics and a Fellow of Queen's College, University of Cambridge. He is joint editor of *The Political Quarterly* and a Fellow of the British Academy. He has published widely on British politics, public policy, and political economy. In 2005 he was awarded the PSA Isaiah Berlin prize for Lifetime Contribution to Political Studies. His books include *Between Europe and America: The Future of British Politics* (2003) and *The Spectre at the Feast: Capitalist Crisis and the Politics of Recession* (2009).

Peter Jones is Professor of Political Philosophy at the University of Newcastle. He is the author of *Rights* (1994) and editor of *National Rights, International Obligations* (1996), *Human Rights and Global Diversity* (2001) and *Group Rights* (2009). Most of his published work has appeared in academic journals and edited collections and ranges over a variety of subjects, including cultural diversity, toleration, recognition, freedom of belief and expression, value pluralism, political equality, distributive justice, global justice, democracy and liberalism.

Paul Kelly is Pro-director and Professor of Political Theory at the London School of Economics. He is author, editor and co-editor of fourteen books, including *Utilitarianism and Distributive Justice* (1990), *Liberalism* (2004), *Locke's Second Treatise* (2007) and *British Political Theory in the Twentieth Century* (2010). He was joint editor of *Political Studies* (1999–2005) and editor of *Utilitas* (2006–11).

Will Kymlicka is the Canada Research Chair in Political Philosophy at Queen's University in Kingston, Canada, where he has taught since 1998. His research focuses on issues of democracy and diversity, and in particular on models of citizenship and social justice within multicultural societies. He is the author of seven books published by Oxford University Press, including *Liberalism, Community, and Culture* (1989), *Multicultural Citizenship* (1995), *Multicultural Odysseys* (2007), and *Zoopolis: A Political Theory of Animal Rights* (2011, co-authored with Sue Donaldson).

Tariq Modood is Professor of Sociology, Politics and Public Policy at the University of Bristol and is also the founding Director of the Centre for the Study of Ethnicity and Citizenship. His latest books include *Multiculturalism: A Civic Idea* (second edition 2013), *Still Not Easy Being British* (2010); and he co-edited *European Multiculturalisms* (2012), *Tolerance, Intolerance and Respect* (2013) and *Religion in a Liberal State* (2013). He is a regular contributor to the media and policy debates in Britain. His website is www.tariqmodood.com.

Monica Mookherjee is a Senior Lecturer in Political Philosophy at Keele University, UK. Her main research interests lie in feminism, multiculturalism, human rights and the politics of recognition. Her monograph, *Women's Rights asa Multicultural Claims: Reconfiguring Gender and Diversity in Political Philosophy* (2009), explores the tensions between feminism and multiculturalism in contemporary political theory. She edited the volume *Democracy, Religious Pluralism and the Liberal Dilemma of Accommodation* (2010). She has also written journal articles for *Res Publica*, *Critical Review of International Social and Political Philosophy* and *Feminist Theory*.

Thomas Pantham, born in Kerala, is a former Professor of Political Science at the Maharaja Sayajirao University of Baroda, Vadodara. He has been recipient of a Mahatma Gandhi National Fellowship of the Indian Council of Social Science Research, the Visitor's Nominee for social sciences at Jawaharlal Nehru University, New Delhi, and visiting scholar at St John's College, Cambridge, and Princeton University. His publications include *Political Theories and Social Reconstruction: A Critical Survey of the Literature on India* (1995), and *Political Ideas in Modern India: Thematic Explorations* (co-editor with V. R. Mehta, 2006).

Raymond Plant is Professor of Jurisprudence and Philosophy at the Dickson Poon School of Law at King's College London, and Professor in the same field in the University of Tallinn. He is also a Professor of Humanities at Winchester University and Gresham Professor of Divinity at Gresham College in the City of London. He is the author of eight books in these fields, the most recent being *The Neoliberal State* (2010). In 2008 he was Vincent Wright Professor at Sciences Po and he has frequently taught there since. He has been a member of the House of Lords since 1992.

Charles Taylor is professor emeritus of philosophy at McGill University. His writings include include *Hegel* (1975); *Hegel and Modern Society* (1979); *Social Theory as Practice* (1983); *Human Agency and Language* (1985); *Philosophy and the Human Sciences* (1985); *Source of the Self: The Making of the Modern Identity* (1989); *The Malaise of Modernity* (1991, based on the Massey Lectures for the CBC held in 1991); *Reconciling the Solitudes: Essays on Canadian Federalism and Nationalism* (1993); *Multiculturalism: Examining the Politics of Recognition*, (1994); *Philosophical Arguments* (1995); *A Secular Age* (2007).

Varun Uberoi is Lecturer in Political Theory and Public Policy at Brunel University. His research has been published in *Political Studies, Parliamentary Affairs, Political Quarterly* and the *Journal of Ethnic and Migration Studies*. He co-edited *Options for a New Britain* (2009) and *Options for Britain II* (2010). His next book, *Nation-Building Through Multiculturalism*, will be published in 2016.

Introduction – Parekhian Multiculturalism

Varun Uberoi

What are sometimes called 'political theories of multiculturalism' have a complex philosophical and political history.[1] They emerged only after forms of identity politics spread in different countries, along with the intuition that different types of cultural minorities deserve better treatment than they often receive.[2] Political theorists made sense of this intuition in different ways, hence some showed why much of what cultural minorities strive for is compatible with liberal theories of justice.[3] Others claimed such liberal theories of justice focus on distribution when they should focus on the domination and oppression that cultural minorities face.[4] Yet others ventured beyond theories of justice to note how people need parents, partners and close friends to accept, affirm and respect how they see themselves, which must come from within to be 'authentic';[5] but minorities often internalise inauthentic understandings of themselves as inferiors.[6] Similarly, Bhikhu Parekh in *Rethinking Multiculturalism* (*RM*)[7] ventured beyond theories of justice and did so in a way that was immediately noted by authors of alternative approaches to be highly significant. *RM* was said to justify intercultural dialogue in a unique way and could explain, unlike other theories, why cultural diversity is valuable.[8] It was said to avoid 'privileging' liberalism and justice over other ideals;[9] it tackled many hard cases; was 'profound, original and wide-ranging'.[10] As a result of *RM*, some claim Parekh is 'among the greatest figures' in contemporary British political theory[11] while others claim he has influenced how we think about politics.[12]

1

Many thus study Parekh's work.[13] And even those outside the academy who criticise Parekh note how *RM* influenced them and how it should influence others too.[14]

RM was thus significant and this volume continues the project that *RM* began by first helping to fill a gap. Sustained examinations of parts of *RM*[15] do not explore *why* and *how* Parekh offers the theory that he does[16] so I will do so in this introduction. I provide a new way to think about *RM*, its prominent critics and its themes. Subsequent chapters then explore the intellectual history of some of *RM*'s themes, use such themes to explore contemporary dilemmas in multicultural societies and develop these themes in wholly new directions.

I explore why Parekh offers the theory that he does by briefly examining where his philosophical approach and aims in *RM* come from and how Parekh offers the theory he does by examining the nature and structure of *RM*. I then show how subsequent chapters make use of many of the themes of *RM* that I discuss.

The intellectual origins of RM

Others show how Michael Oakeshott's *Rationalism in Politics* influenced his former student, Bhikhu Parekh.[17] But *RM* was also shaped by Oakeshott's early understanding of philosophy in *Experience and its Modes* which is complex. Yet briefly, Oakeshott argued that scholarly enquiries like history or science are 'worlds of ideas'[18] that remain 'abstract' until we examine and relate the presuppositions on which they rest. Thus we might explore how history presupposes conceptions of time and change, or how science presupposes conceptions of regularity and prediction; and philosophy does just this. Philosophy removes abstraction by examining and relating all such presuppositions to present 'a unity of valid ... and *irreducible*' ideas.[19] When presuppositions are examined and related they are no longer presupposed thus philosophy is ideally 'presupposition*less*' enquiry.[20] Parekh endorsed such a view of philosophy even when discussing alternatives from Marx and Arendt.[21] Hence in the year *RM* was published, Parekh argued 'whatever else it may be, philosophy is a relentless ... search for full self-consciousness, a determined attempt to uncover and critically examine all its own basic assumptions . . .'.[22]

Note, however, that *RM* is no example of early Oakeshottian *political* philosophy which, at the time, Oakeshott called 'pseudo-philosophy'.[23] 'Pseudo-philosophy' retains abstraction and Oakeshott used Ethics as an example as it seldom examined how values presuppose understandings of 'morality', 'good', 'right', of 'ought' and 'is'. Similarly, political philosophy seldom avoids abstraction by 'thinking out *to the end*'[24] political life and how, for example, it presupposes human life, life and existence, thus moving *away* from politics which is a 'starting place'[25] 'soon out of sight and out of mind'.[26] Parekh disagreed as he saw how a political philosopher might instead minimise his presuppositions and work in the opposite direction to Oakeshott by moving gradually *towards* political life. For example, a political philosopher might examine the nature of human life and why it is usually shared with many others, why doing so requires a system of authority in which loyalty, obligation, liberty and so on are conceived and related in ways that legitimise some institutions, but not others. This gradually shapes the 'framework' of our 'thought',[27] 'choices'[28] and 'recommendations'[29] for political life and this is the approach to political philosophy that Parekh used in *RM*.

This approach is *not* presuppositionless but it entails a more limited range of presuppositions about, for example, how human life presupposes life or existence and a means to conceptualise both. Exploring all presuppositions on the way to exploring political life may mean never getting to the latter. But a philosopher can be aware that his arguments remain, as Oakeshott later said, 'conditional' and still approximate[30] to the ideal of being 'presuppositionless' by *minimising* his presuppositions and Parekh tried to do just this in *RM*.

Parekh would thus avoid the unquestioned assumptions of other political theories of multiculturalism. For example, Will Kymlicka claims that 'individuals . . . are the ultimate units of moral worth'.[31] But this assumes unspecified understandings of human life, moral worth and a way to justify a hierarchy of moral worth. It also assumes reasons for when, why and how to think of people as individuals as we cannot always do so as they may be dependent children or parents and people use languages and traditions of thought that unavoidably assume and relate them to others.[32] Similarly, Iris Young claimed that 'justice is the primary subject of political philosophy'.[33] But this assumes an unspecified understanding of political philosophy and its various subjects as well as reasons to organise these subjects into a hierarchy in which justice can be plausibly placed in primary position at the top of this hierarchy and other subjects can be plausibly placed beneath it. As Parekh sought to minimise his presuppositions, he avoided these familiar unexplored assumptions and his aims for *RM* did not require them.[34]

Such aims grew out of exposure to a caste system, untouchability and discrimination, which meant that Parekh saw inequality at 'close quarters'.[35] This bred a lifelong fascination for the idea that inequality assumes and that is needed to detect inequality: *equality*. Some liken equality to sameness or uniformity but Parekh's background made it difficult to ignore how *differences* make equality necessary. Parekh thus wrote in 1974 that an 'Indian in England' is 'haunted' by self-consciousness of their differences as these are misunderstood, feared, and are the source of his discrimination and exclusion.[36] In the same book Parekh thus said that such differences can be normalised in countries like Britain if British people 'redefine'[37] themselves as culturally and racially diverse, but in time Parekh saw how differences could be valued too. He studied and critiqued Gandhi's political thought and learned about how Gandhi saw India as 'a community of communities'[38] that is not just 'plural' but 'plural*ist*', as Indians are often 'committed to pluralism as a desirable value'.[39] Parekh's interests in equality had led to an interest in which human differences to value, when, why and how to do so.

Thus by the time Parekh was writing *RM*, he wanted to show why Britain and any culturally diverse polity could be 'a community of communities'[40] that is not just 'multicultural' but 'multicultural*ist*'.[41] Parekh aimed to show why and how the culturally diverse citizens of modern polities should value and welcome, not fear, their cultural differences. He would start to achieve this aim in *RM* by minimising his presuppositions to discuss ways of conceiving human life that conflict with his own way of conceiving it by suggesting that 'only one way of life is fully human and best'.[42]

The nature and structure of RM

Parekh calls the view that only one way of life is fully human and best, 'monism', which is a term he borrows from Isaiah Berlin but uses differently.[43] As different forms of monism may conflict with the way that Parekh conceives of human life in different ways, he critiques classical, Christian and early liberal forms of monism in too many ways to discuss here.[44] But Parekh notes how the human capacity to contemplate, improve, follow God and much else, have long been used to privilege a way of life as 'fully human'. This assumes an understanding of what it means to be human. Hence understandings of human nature are often offered by monists and Parekh showed why these are often derived from the way of life that monists justify and thus their arguments become circular. In such ways Parekh discussed the fragility of monist arguments and moved on to pluralist thinkers like Vico, Montesquieu and Herder who he showed valued the plurality of human life but made other mistakes.

Such pluralists were shown by Parekh to see how our cultures shape how human needs, behaviour and indeed lives are understood. But these thinkers implausibly conceive of culture as a national, organic and as an unchanging, integrated whole, disassociated from legal, political and economic structures.[45] At best, such pluralists show why national and not any other cultures should be valued. But contemporary liberals like Kymlicka and Raz had an important insight. They offer understandings of culture that many question but they build on the earlier works of others[46] to observe how cultures are linked to individual autonomy as the latter assumes choice, but people need something to choose with, which is the beliefs and norms of their culture. This observation is new, but it shows why individuals need a culture while ignoring what individuals can learn from other cultures and it does *not* show why a person who unquestioningly lives a life of *faith* should have access to any culture! Despite identifying such difficulties Parekh learned much from all these thinkers and says so, and devised a position about human life that seems to begin by thinking about human nature.[47]

For Parekh, human nature is merely those properties that people have that are not socially derived and that they possess by belonging to a species.[48] But as our *understandings* of human nature are derived partly from our cultural, social and other experiences, we have no direct access to human nature. There is no 'state of nature' where human nature appears in a pure form, thus claims that it 'inclines' or 'compels' seem suspect as they can universalise the way only *some* conceive of human beings, and must be avoided. Yet the idea of human nature is also not easy to reject without arriving at the bizarre conclusion that members of the same species have nothing in common. Indeed, human beings share a physiological and psychological structure, certain capacities to think and express themselves, as well as certain needs to eat and sleep and certain experiences like maturing or getting old.[49] Those without such properties are thought the exception not the rule and in this minimal sense, these properties comprise human nature, but are interpreted and prioritised differently in different cultures. The latter are patterns of beliefs, and thus meaning, as well as traditions of behaviour, and while Ann Phillips,[50] Seyla Benhabib[51] and others rightly worry about essentialist conceptions of culture, Parekh explicitly avoids them.[52] He shows why cultures have 'no coordinating authority',[53] 'remain complex and un-systematised',[54] 'internally varied' and speak 'in several voices',[55] are 'never settled, static and free of ambiguity'[56] and have 'no essence'.[57] Cultures are fuzzy but discernible. They help people to conceptualise and interpret their own natures, capacities and experiences, and this makes it strange to suggest, as Charles Taylor famously showed, that any culture could have no worth.[58]

But 'thanks to human creativity, geographical conditions', and 'different historical experiences',[59] different cultures adopt different systems of meaning. They thus differ and help some to think that the good life is lived 'from within' and is self-chosen, others to believe it is about following God, yet others, that it is about adhering to nature's limits, and so on. Certain cultures thus favour certain forms of life over others and use certain ideas and judgements of worth, or values, to defend them. But as values and different types of lives conflict, no culture can realise all of them. Each expresses and legitimises a limited range of values and ways to live, but is silent about or delegitimises others. Each culture is thus, in Oakeshottian language, a 'world of ideas', but need not be, as Oakeshott thought, closed to other such worlds. Indeed, just as Parekh once likened ideologies that give people a restricted view of the world to Oakeshott's 'worlds of ideas' but noted how such restricted views can be overcome, he would do the same with cultures.[60] As worlds of ideas, cultures benefit from exposure to other cultures that illustrate different ways to live, think, realise values and satisfy needs. In doing so, a cultural group is alerted to the limits of their ideas and the potential of those of others. Cultural diversity should thus be valued not as Herder, Mill and others thought for being unavoidable, natural, or leading to experiments in living, as these are not reasons to value anything. Instead cultural diversity should be valued as a prerequisite for the intercultural learning that enables what Gandhi called 'a richer view' of 'reality'.[61]

Parekh thus saw what some call the danger 'of *denying* . . . the chance to cross cultural borders'[62] or 'placing' cultures 'beyond the reach of critical analyses'.[63] Hence he notes what can be gained through intercultural learning, but the latter requires intercultural dialogue and Parekh seemingly thought such dialogue was important at four related levels, the first of which is *personal*. Parekh *seems* to accept Taylor's claim that our self-understandings are formed through 'webs of interlocution' with others like parents, partners and close friends.[64] We need others to respect, confirm or confute how we understand ourselves and if these others are culturally different, they see us and can help us to see ourselves in different ways. Parekh thus admires the 'idea of critical engagement' with those who are culturally different and reshaping one's ideas, beliefs, actions and thus oneself accordingly, and called Gandhi an 'icon' for doing this.[65] Gandhi 'freely borrowed what was valuable in other religions and civilisations' and thought this was possible for each religious person to do by first developing knowledge of their religion so as to then discern how it could be improved.[66] While people should certainly not be coerced into intercultural dialogue, it offers them what scholars who disagree with one another experience as through their discussions and through reading one another's work they see their own ideas through the eyes of others. They in turn see what should be reformed, and why, and Parekh suggests that many can benefit from such a process.[67]

People are also part of cultural communities, and the second level at which such intercultural dialogue is important is *communal*. For example, some minorities may have lower expectations for girls, treat them only as wives or mothers in the making. But through dialogue they can discern why many value gender equality and adapt their practices. Yet cultural majorities may also learn something about the restricted way in which they often interpret gender equality when, for example, Muslim women explain why they might *choose* to wear a *niqab* against the wishes of their fathers, brothers and husbands, and do not see it as a sign of domination any more than they see a 'mini-skirt as a sign of liberation'.[68] Intercultural dialogue introduces communities to the limits of their beliefs and practices and helps to illuminate the need to reform them. This for Parekh is a sign, again following Gandhi, not of betraying one's cultural community or undervaluing its history or intellectual resources. Instead it is a sign of cherishing one's community so much that being blind to its limitations is a form of negligence. All groups in a polity should be 'rooted *and open*'.[69]

At a third level that may be thought of as 'societal', intercultural dialogue can alter the values that govern the collective affairs of all those in a polity and that are inscribed in its constitution, laws and norms. Parekh calls these 'operative public values' (OPVs), and they usually come from the culture of a dominant majority whose history they reflect and whose needs they suit most. Such OPVs are never static, and through intercultural dialogue they can come to reflect cultural minorities too. Indeed, this seemed to happen gradually in Britain after debates about whether Salman Rushdie's book, *The Satanic Verses*, should be banned, carry a disclaimer about its portrayal of Islam, not be released in paperback and so on. Minority intellectuals, including Parekh, explored the nature and limits of freedom of expression, and noted that such freedom had never been unfettered in societies like Britain. If it had been, blasphemy, incitement to hatred and libel laws would be inexplicable. Likewise, they noted that it was unclear why existing blasphemy laws could not be extended to Muslims or why, if British libel laws exist to prevent public untruthful comments about people, they should not be extended to the groups people comprise. Regardless of the plausibility of these arguments, these arguments each extend *existing* practices that come from *within* the political tradition of the majority to minorities. This deepens our knowledge of the potential of such a tradition, shows how accommodating minority needs can be consistent with it and thus enables minorities to leave their imprint on OPVs, which is what seemed to occur. Thus during the Danish Cartoon Affair, British newspapers, including tabloids like the *Sun,* chose not to reprint offensive cartoons.[70] Parekh thus showed how what Oakeshott[71] called the 'intimations' of a political tradition can be interpreted in different ways and the advantages of discussing such interpretations, not assuming or asserting them.[72]

At a final level, intercultural dialogue is a means to 'arrive' at *universal* moral values that *may* be part of the OPVs of a polity in its constitution, for example, but are so, as the point above suggests, for reasons particular to that polity. But if universal moral values are what we think *all* humans, everywhere should accord moral worth to, their nature and history within a polity may or may not resonate with others or justify to them why *they* should value them too. For example, the UN Declaration on human rights lists property rights as a human right, but some indigenous groups and communists may disagree.[73] The nature and basis of universal moral values is therefore contested and cannot be derived from some notion of human worth. Thus we might claim humans have worth because they can think, reason, forge visions of the good in ways that other species cannot, therefore, we should all value their right to life. But when life 'begins and ends', and whether this right can be waived by the 'terminally ill', are seen differently in different religious and national communities.[74] 'Procedural devices' like Rawls' 'veil of ignorance' do not help either, as people construe life, humanity, reason itself, and the various means of relating them differently and even if people *should* reason about values as Rawls suggests, this does not mean they will do so.[75] There is a need to 'woo the assent' of others on how universal values should be understood and why they should be cherished, which requires dialogue. Thus Parekh suggests that the 1948 UN Declaration of Human Rights contains *some* values that have a claim to universality and it is a good 'starting point' for future discussion.[76]

But, at the personal level, as Gandhi saw, people need to know enough about their cultures to know what can be added and absorbed easily and what will take time to acquire and reform.[77] People should be willing to learn about their own cultures, but also feel secure enough to welcome and discuss what they can learn from other ones. If then politicians, the police or the media depict some communities as 'suspect', as often happens with Muslims,[78] or as 'backward' as many like J. S. Mill did, or not ready for 'self-rule', this can have a cost.[79] It can help to cultivate closed communities as rather like with wartime coalitions, *internal* discussions must be suspended to cope with an *external* threat and the same is true of a cultural majority, who feel their way of life is disappearing. The intercultural learning that requires intercultural dialogue thus requires a political structure that legitimises differences, so that people are not afraid to explore their own and are secure enough to learn from, and not feel threatened by, those of others. But not feeling threatened by the differences of others also requires a political structure that can foster the unity needed for differences to not *seem* divisive or destabilising. Thus Parekh identifies 'devices' to legitimise differences and foster unity that include 'equal treatment' and national identities, both of which I will now discuss.

Many focus on Parekh's notion of equal *opportunity*.[80] Yet Parekh justifies equal *treatment* in an original way when he recalibrates how it is usually justified by canonical thinkers like Aristotle and more recent ones like Isaiah Berlin and Bernard Williams. Such thinkers argue that human beings are often thought equal as they are also thought to be, fundamentally, the same.[81] Hence, using human uniformities such as their physiological and psychological structure and their needs, human beings are said to be the same or similar and must be treated as such, as 'similar cases should be treated similarly' or reasons given why not to.[82] As human beings are the same, they must then have the same fundamental legal and political requirements or need the same protections. Equal treatment thus predictably safeguards the human uniformities its justification is based on and entails same or similar treatment, but this can favour some cultural groups while imposing higher costs on others. For example, if children are treated the same in public schools that ban religious headdresses, or if a school uniform mandates a cap, this favours those who have no need for a religious headdress. Yet *yarmulke*, turban or *hijab* wearing children incur a cost that others do not when they compromise a religious belief or practice to attend such schools. Critics of Parekh, like Brian Barry, claim 'this is just how things are',[83] but David Miller rightly asks why people are being treated the same or similarly if some are favoured while others incur higher costs.[84] Miller thus suggests there is a problem, but it is Parekh who identifies its cause.

Parekh thus notes what happens when justifications for equal treatment appeal to human uniformities but ignore one such uniformity: that humans are 'cultural beings'.[85] As cultural beings, humans are the same in a way that makes them different as they interpret their physiological and psychological structure as well as their needs through their cultures, such that in one culture sex can be a biological need akin to, as Bentham claimed, 'scratching an itch' and in another it is sacrosanct. To justify equal treatment through fundamental human uniformities, while ignoring the one uniformity that helps people to understand their other ones, is to be inconsistent. But to include this uniformity with the others entails accepting how human beings are both the same *and different*, and thus they have the same *and different* legal and political requirements, or need the same *and different protections*. To ignore the latter is to ignore necessary requirements or protections, which in the case above resulted in some being favoured while others incurred higher costs. But taking account of how people *also* have *different* legal and political requirements and need different protections requires the children in the above case to be treated differently and given exemptions to wear their religious headdress to ensure they do not incur higher costs and thus unequal treatment. Parekh thus showed how *if a justifica-*

11

tion for equal treatment excludes how humans are 'cultural beings', our understanding of equal treatment becomes narrow and unable to address the difficulties with treating people the same. But including how humans are cultural beings in our justification of equal treatment expands our understanding of such treatment to help ensure that cultural minorities do not incur higher costs and differences like religious headdress thus become more legitimate in places like schools.

This is admittedly an 'easy case', in which those wearing a religious headdress are *not* being privileged as they are merely avoiding higher costs than others. Thus students who want to wear a baseball cap or a bandana to school cannot plausibly complain that they are being treated unequally unless they, their parents or we can plausibly think such a cap and bandana stems from a cultural difference that, as above, helps to condition how they see parts of their life.[86] In other 'harder cases', however, as Parekh notes, other conceptions of equality and other values may have to be considered.[87] Yet I do not focus on the harder cases here as I aim not to justify differential treatment, but to show how Parekh reconceptualised a traditional justification for equal treatment so as to show how it legitimises differences.[88] Indeed, just as anti-discrimination laws used equal treatment to help to legitimise racial differences, Parekh is showing how, at times, equal treatment can do the same with other such differences too. But the latter again occurs using the 'intimations' of a tradition of justifying equal treatment through uniformities, and showing the importance of not ignoring one such uniformity.

What about fostering 'unity'? Parekh nowhere in *RM* says what unity is, but he often uses the term in one of three related ways, each of which helps to explain why the members of a polity form a group. First, 'unity is located' in a state's 'constitutionally prescribed structure of authority' as the state and its laws and institutions govern members of a polity as a group.[89] Second, those governed by the state as a group over time can come to see themselves as a group, hence some national minorities fear they will be subsumed, as common legal, political, educational system and a common language increase the likelihood of this.[90] Third, when the members of a polity see themselves as a group, 'bonds' emerge between them like a 'mutual concern' or 'common loyalty' to one another. The unity of a polity thus comes *externally* from the state, *internally* from its members and from the relations *between* them. And people's national identities are thought to *help* to foster such three-dimensional unity as if the members of a polity feel, for example, 'British' or 'American' then, *inter alia*, they feel part of such a group which then encourages the bonds of group membership.

Yet people cannot say they feel 'British' or 'American' without some 'conception' of what Britain and America are, even if it is vague.[91] If this 'conception' entails people sharing an ethnicity or a culture, 'ethno-cultural' minorities can be, and often are, excluded. Thus Parekh thought that polities should be 'defined' in 'politico-institutional' terms instead.[92] Hence, if America is 'defined' using its constitution and bill of rights then it can be understood according to its political structures and institutions. The latter usually reflect a cultural majority's history, language, norms and values. But such political institutions and structures are shared by a cultural majority and minorities alike and can be used to promote conceptions of the polity that include ethno-cultural minorities by declaring the polity multicultural, as Canada and Australia did.[93] These institutions and structures are part of a polity's structure of authority and govern its members as a group, but Parekh wanted these institutions and structures to also constitute people's 'conceptions' of themselves as a group.[94] Contrary then to what Barry claims, multiculturalists can attach importance to the 'civic' national identities[95] that he himself endorses.[96] But scholars sympathetic to Parekh offered a more plausible criticism.

Hence, Tariq Modood asked how a 'conception' of a polity that is only 'politico-institutional' – not 'ethno-cultural' – could include 'ethno-cultural' minority groups within it.[97] Also political institutions and structures can only constitute how people view their polity because these institutions and structures are also a product of their history, language, norms and so on. Were they just any institutions and structures, they would be less meaningful. People don't have conceptions of their polities that are purely 'politico-institutional', and Parekh should not want them to if he wants to include ethno-cultural minorities in them; hence this claim is gradually lost in Parekh's subsequent works. But *RM* had the resources to identify the more plausible understanding of national identities that Parekh discussed in later works like *A New Politics of Identity*.[98]

Parekh would thus later identify *two* familiar but previously *undistinguished* ways of thinking about national identities, between which he and others had unconsciously moved. In doing so, he clarified his claims in *RM* where he was not only discussing how a person might have a national identity that they exhibit when they feel, for example, British or American. He also discussed how political structures and institutions 'define' a polity which we thus may also think has an identity.[99] After all, just as we might think that a 'city' has an identity as certain features define it and distinguish it, enable us to discern that London is not New York, so we might think a polity has an identity as certain features define it, distinguish it, enable us to discern that Britain is not America.[100] Where some think of national identities as the institutions, history, language, values and other features that, for example, make Britain or America what they are, others think national identities are one of many identities that a person has and exhibits when they say they feel British or American.

Yet when discussing Britain or America's identity we are discussing a conception of a polity and as we saw before, when someone says they feel British or American they indicate that they must have some conception of what Britain or America are, even if it is vague. In both senses then, national identities entail a conception of a polity. But one is a conception of a polity that anyone can have, as a travel writer might discuss the features that define and distinguish Britain and America. The other is a conception that usually only members of a polity have and indicate the presence of when they say that they have a British or an American identity or that they feel British and American.

But when the conception of a polity that members have only includes a cultural majority, as phrases like the 'naturally British' suggest, Parekh notes a problem. Such conceptions can reduce the unity that we saw was important as even though all citizens are governed as a group the cultural majority do not see minorities as part of it. This often increases fear of minorities and discrimination against them thus minorities can come to feel like outsiders even though they are often citizens. But members of a polity can develop more inclusive conceptions of it as these conceptions change over time, but how might this happen?

Note what occurs over time when political institutions that once permitted discrimination and exclusion come to prohibit both, declare the polity multicultural, deliver public services in different languages and promote race equality. Such institutions are promoting a conception of the polity that includes minorities but over time members of a polity also come to realise that while discrimination and exclusion were once permissible they no longer are. This realisation can only occur if people's conceptions of their polity have altered and 'multicultural education' in schools aids this too. It explains to children why immigrants and national minorities also shape a polity's history, institutions and norms in ways that were previously often ignored. Thus the sorts of government measures that Parekh had long defended for many other reasons[101] may also aid the members of a polity to have more inclusive conceptions of it and note how these measures collectively comprise what is often called a policy of multiculturalism.[102] The policies that public intellectuals like David Goodhart[103] or prominent scholars like David Miller assume are about minority identities not national ones,[104] may aid the emergence of the inclusive conceptions of a polity that they also seek.[105] Members of a polity with these conceptions of it will see minorities as part of their polity and develop the bonds that we saw accompany people seeing one another as, *inter alia*, part of the same group. Despite its problems, *RM* thus contained the basis of showing how national identities can include minorities so as to legitimise differences while promoting unity as we saw Parekh wanted.

RM is thus best conceived as an attempt to show why and how the culturally diverse people who comprise modern polities should see themselves as diverse, welcome and value their diversity, not fear it and certain steps are taken to achieve this. To be as free of presuppositions as possible Parekh first disturbs monist ways of thinking about human life to replace them with another way of thinking about it and its relation to culture, the value of culture, cultural diversity and intercultural learning. Such learning requires intercultural dialogue and a political structure that uses, *inter alia*, equal treatment to legitimise diversity and national identities to foster three-dimensional unity. No volume can devote chapters to all the themes in these steps, but what can be done is to take some of them and request leading political theorists to explore their intellectual history, to use them to address contemporary multicultural dilemmas and to develop these themes in wholly new directions. I will conclude this chapter by showing how the subsequent chapters in the volume do just this.

Structure of the volume

The volume is divided into three sections and the chapters in the first one are interpretative as they improve our understanding of the patterns of thought from which the themes of *RM* emerge. Paul Kelly thus focuses on Parekh's idea of a 'community of communities', and shows how thinkers whom Parekh has not considered have utilised versions of the idea, if not the term. Hence J. N. Figgis focused on the relationship between religious authority and the state, while G. D. H. Cole advocated 'guild socialism'. Both Figgis and Cole thought a state was comprised and defined by groups, and both are potential unconscious influences on Parekh's thought. Where Kelly examines these and other potential *unconscious* influences, Thomas Pantham explores a *conscious* influence on Parekh. He traces where Parekh discerned the idea in Gandhi's thought of combining ideas from different cultural traditions to aid political reform. I then use many relatively unnoticed writings from Parekh since the 1970s to illuminate the nature of his distinct way of thinking about national identities that we see only glimpses of in *RM*. I show that Parekh avoids the difficulties of what has become known as liberal and conservative nationalist ways of thinking about national identities. I also show how Parekh's way of thinking about national identities can be of use to different types of scholars and politicians who discuss national identities too.

In the next section chapter authors focus on various themes in *RM* to elucidate current multicultural dilemmas while also identifying ways to address them. Monica Mookherjee explicitly uses the insights of Parekh's theory of culture and intercultural dialogue to illustrate why multiculturalism need not, as Susan Moller Okin and others have claimed, legitimise gendered hierarchies or group rights that disadvantage women. Indeed, Mookherjee shows how Parekh's theory helps us to see how to pluralise feminism and feminise multiculturalism. Peter Jones examines whether the idea of equality can be 'subject dependent', as Parekh claims. Jones considers whether the way Brian Barry criticises this claim from Parekh is plausible so as to probe the nature and limits of using equality to accommodate religious differences. Rajeev Bhargava then explores whether Parekh's theory is as hospitable to religious difference as Parekh thinks, and how it ignores the insights to be gained from the Indian experience of secularism which differs from others as there is no 'wall between church and state', as Jefferson thought there was in America, nor is there official 'establishment' of a faith as in the UK. In India the state interferes with religion when doing so promotes equality, freedom and other such values. Raymond Plant then examines Parekh's conception of identity, the political and legal claims that can flow from it and the basis of coercion in Parekh's political thought.

The third section examines themes integral to Parekh's thought from different perspectives to his which enables chapter authors to take these themes in new and different directions. Hence where Parekh, like many others, criticises essentialised understandings of culture; Will Kymlicka elegantly explores whether theories, policies or discourse about multiculturalism are vulnerable to this essentialist charge to discern if a corrective is needed and if so where. Joseph Carens shows why legitimising cultural differences entails much more than focusing on institutions, principles and rights; hence he examines how expectations, incentives and identities must be adapted to include minorities. Andrew Gamble extends Parekh's concern about national identity to show how anxieties about its loss and erosion have helped to generate various public controversies that theorists like Parekh have been involved in. Benjamin R. Barber shows why a 'politico-institutional' identity akin to the one Parekh identifies in *RM* can, if it takes a particular form, foster the unity that democracies require to take and enforce collectively binding decisions. Charles Taylor shows how Quebec's policy of interculturalism suggests how to legitimise diversity in European nations while fostering unity in them too as Parekh suggests. Tariq Modood shows how such interculturalism helps to illuminate issues about cultural majorities that multiculturalists have somewhat neglected, but it differs little from what Modood, Parekh, I and others would call 'multiculturalism'.

Each of the above chapters can hopefully be read both in isolation and with other chapters in its section. When read in isolation, a chapter offers insights particular to its author and his or her influences and concerns. When read with other chapters in its section, the section helps the reader to interpret and understand the intellectual history of some of *RM*'s themes or uses its themes to address current dilemmas or advances these themes in new directions.

Acknowledgements

I am grateful to Andrew Mason, Noel O'Sullivan, Bhikhu Parekh, Raymond Plant, Elise Rietveld and Jonathan Seglow for their comments. Tariq Modood deserves special thanks not only because he gave extended and invaluable comments on this chapter, but also because he has advised me over many years about how to interpret Bhikhu Parekh's work and because he came up with the idea for this volume!

Notes

1. For a succinct and thoughtful overview of this philosophical and political history see W. Kymlicka's (2007), 'The new debate on minority rights (and postscript)', in A. S. Laden and D. Owen (eds) *Multiculturalism and Political Theory* (Cambridge: Cambridge University Press), which has a useful addition (the postscript)

to the earlier version that Kymlicka published in *Politics in the Vernacular*.

2. By 'intuition' I mean what Kymlicka calls a 'gut feeling' that is the basis of more considered judgement, which of course is still imprecise. For a detailed discussion of what intuitions are, see M. Oakeshott (1933), *Experience and its Modes* (Cambridge: Cambridge University Press), pp. 21–6; W. Kymlicka (2002), *Contemporary Political Philosophy* (Oxford: Oxford University Press), pp. 6–7. See also J. Rawls (1971), *Theory of Justice* (Oxford: Oxford University Press) for a discussion on 'intuitionism', pp. 34–40.

3. W. Kymlicka (1989), *Liberalism, Community and Culture* (Oxford: Oxford University Press).

4. I. M. Young (1990), *Justice and the Politics of Difference* (Princeton, NJ: Princeton University Press).

5. This obviously comes from Charles Taylor who is not necessarily an advocate of 'authenticity', but see C. Taylor (1991), *Ethics of Authenticity* (Cambridge, MA: Harvard University Press), pp. 29, 47–8; C. Taylor (1998), *Sources of the Self* (Cambridge: Cambridge University Press), p. 88.

6. C. Taylor (1994), 'The politics of recognition', in A. Gutman (ed.) *Multiculturalism* (Princeton, NJ: Princeton University Press).

7. Bhikhu Parekh (2000), *Rethinking Multiculturalism: Cultural Diversity and Political Theory* (London: Macmillan).

8. I. M. Young (2001), 'Thoughts on multicultural dialogue', *Ethnicities*, 1:1, p. 117.

9. C. Taylor (2001), 'Multiculturalism and political identity', *Ethnicities*, 1:1, p. 125.

10. W. Kymlicka (2001), 'Liberalism, dialogue and multiculturalism', *Ethnicities*, 1:1, p. 129; T. Modood (2001), 'Their liberalism our multiculturalism', *British Journal of Politics and International Relations*, 3:2, p. 246.

11. P. Kelly (2010), *British Tradition of Political Theory* (Oxford: Wiley Blackwell), p. x.

12. T. Brooks (2013), 'In defence of political theory: impact and opportunities', *Political Studies Review*, 11:2, p. 208.

13. P. Kelly (2001), 'Dangerous liaisons, Parekh and Oakeshottian multiculturalism', *Political Quarterly*, 72:4, explores them. See also J. Baggini and J. Strangroom (2007), *What More Philosophers Think* (London: Continuum); R. Jahanbegeloo (2011), *Talking Politics* (Oxford: Oxford University Press); J. B. Priess (2011),

'Multiculturalism and equal dignity – an essay on Bhikhu Parekh', *Res publica*, 17:2.

14. D. Goodhart (2013), *The British Dream* (London: Atlantic Press), p. 208.
15. P. Kelly (2009), 'The Oakeshottians', in M. Flinders, A. Gamble and C. Hay (eds) *The Oxford Handbook of British Politics* (Oxford: Oxford University Press); N. O'Sullivan (2004), *European Political Theory Since 1945*: Basingstoke: Palgrave Macmillan); Jahanbegeloo, *Talking Politics*; Priess, 'Essay on Bhikhu Parekh'.
16. Many note that Parekh is an expert on Bentham, Arendt, Marx and Gandhi's political thought, that he was influenced by Michael Oakeshott, that he was a former Deputy Chair and acting Chair of the Commission for Race Equality, Chair of the Commission for Multi-ethnic Britain and that he sits in the House of Lords. But why and how these parts of Parekh's CV shape *RM* is not self-evident.
17. Paul Kelly was the first to make this observation, see Kelly, '"Dangerous liaisons"' and 'The Oakeshottians'.
18. Oakeshott, *Experience and Its Modes*, pp. 322–3.
19. Ibid., p. 348.
20. Ibid., pp. 81–2, emphasis added; and M. Oakshott (1946), 'A philosophy of politics', *Religion, Politics and the Moral Life* (New Haven, CT: Yale University Press), p. 127. See also J. Alexander (2012), 'Oakeshott as a philosopher', in E. Podoksik (ed.) *The Cambridge Companion to Oakeshott* (Cambridge: Cambridge University Press), p. 13.
21. B. Parekh (1968), 'The nature of political philosophy', in P. King and B. Parekh (eds) *Experience and Politics* (Cambridge: Cambridge University Press), p. 156; B. Parekh (1982), *Marx's Theory of Ideology* (London: Croom Helm), p. 231; B. Parekh (1982), *Contemporary Political Thinkers* (Oxford: Martin Robertson), p. 4; B. Parekh (2000), 'Theorising political theory', in N. O'Sullivan (ed.), *Political Theory In Transition* (London: Routledge), pp. 250–1.
22. Parekh, 'Theorising political theory', pp. 250–1. Here I move from 'presupposition' to 'assumption' without questioning if they are the same thing but only because I think the two are often used by Parekh interchangeably and others also use both interchangeably. See J. Carens (2013), *Ethics of Immigration* (Oxford: Oxford University Press), p. 299.

23. Oakeshott, *Experience and Its Modes*, p. 335, fn 1. Oakeshott never fully rejected this view. Even in *On Human Conduct*, which was Oakeshott's last book, he recognises that the unconditional theorising that he seeks is not possible if political philosophy is to remain focused on political life, so it must remain 'conditional' and aware of its conditionality (pp. 10–18).

24. Oakeshott, 'A philosophy of politics', p. 131.

25. M. Oakeshott, 'Political philosophy', in *Religion, Politics and the Moral Life* (New Haven, CT: Yale University Press), p. 146.

26. Ibid., p. 153.

27. Jahanbegeloo, *Talking Politics*, p. 40.

28. Parekh, *Contemporary Political Thinkers*, p. 117.

29. Parekh, 'The nature of political philosophy', p. 180.

30. M. Oakeshott (1975), *On Human Conduct* (Oxford: Clarendon), p. 11.

31. Kymlicka, *Liberalism, Community and Culture*, pp. 140, 162–3; W. Kymlicka (1995), *Multicultural Citizenship* (Oxford: Oxford University Press), pp. 75, 80. Parekh questions this liberal assumption in several places. See Parekh, *Marx's Theory of Ideology*, p. 40; B. Parekh (1989), *Gandhi's Political Philosophy* (London: Macmillan), p. 24; Parekh, 'Theorising political theory', p. 251.

32. B. Parekh (1976), 'Asians in Britain', *Five Views of Multiracial Britain* (London: Commission for Racial Equality), p. 44. B. Parekh (1992), 'The cultural particularity of liberal democracy', *Political Studies*, XL, p. 161. Note that *RM* is *not* an 'illiberal' or 'non-liberal' theory, and in it Parekh states its 'strong liberal orientation' (*RM*, p. 14).

33. Young, *Justice and Politics of Difference*, p. 3.

34. Note that many senior political philosophers now agree that political philosophy cannot remain only or primarily focused on justice, see for example, J. Waldron (2013), '*Political* political theory – an inaugural lecture', *Journal of Political Philosophy*, 21:1, p. 6.

35. Jahanbegeloo, *Talking Politics*, p. 128.

36. B. Parekh (1974), 'The spectre of self-consciousness', in *Colour, Culture Consciousness* (London: George Allen & Unwin), p. 81, emphasis added. Those who focus purely on Parekh's work on Bentham's idea of equality at this time will miss this point. See B. Parekh (1970), 'Bentham's theory of equality', *Political Studies*, 18:4.

37. B. Parekh (1974), 'Postscript', in B. Parekh (ed.) *Colour, Culture and Consciousness: Immigrant Intellectuals in Britain* (London: George Allen & Unwin Ltd), p. 230, emphasis added. David Miller in *On Nationality* espouses something very similar but unlike Parekh in 1974 has a systematic theory to support his claims: D. Miller, *On Nationality* (Oxford: Oxford University Press), p. 181.

38. B. Parekh (1995), 'The ethno-centricity of nationalist discourse', *Nations and Nationalism*, 1:1, pp. 39–41.

39. Parekh, *Gandhi's Political Philosophy*, p. 39; see also p. 57.

40. Campaign for a Multi-ethnic Britain (CMEB) (2000), *Parekh Report* (London: Profile Books), p. 56; *RM*, p. 340.

41. *RM*, p. 6.

42. *RM*, pp. 1 and 16.

43. Berlin's depiction of monism is not just about illuminating value pluralism as it is also epistemic. Monism for Berlin is about claiming that each question has one and only one true answer. This is not how Parekh uses the term.

44. Some seem to think Parekh's aim is historical, but while he calls these chapters 'historical', his aim is clearly to critique the assumptions, internal logic and structure of monism. See F. Dallmyer (2003), 'Multiculturalism and the good life', *The Good Society*, 12:2, p. 41; *RM*, p. 10; B. Parekh (2003), 'A response', *The Good Society*, 12:2, p. 55.

45. *RM*, p. 78.

46. Kymlicka, *Liberalism, Community and Culture*, pp. 164–5; Kymlicka cites Dworkin extensively but earlier in the book discusses how Taylor too sees culture as a 'context of choice', p. 74. See also J. Raz (1994), 'Multiculturalism: a liberal perspective', *Dissent*, Winter, pp. 70–1.

47. *RM*, p. 114.

48. Ibid., p. 115.

49. Ibid., p. 116.

50. A. Phillips (2007), *Multiculturalism without Culture* (Princeton, NJ: Princeton University Press), p. 14.

51. S. Benhabib, *The Claims of Culture* (Princeton, NJ: Princeton University Press, 2002), p. 4.

52. *RM*, p. 144.

53. Ibid., p. 144.

54. Ibid., p. 144.

55. Ibid., p. 144.

56. Ibid., p. 148.
57. Ibid., p. 175.
58. Taylor, 'Politics of recognition', pp. 66, 72–3.
59. *RM*, pp.
60. Parekh, *Marx's Theory of Ideology*, p. 27.
61. Parekh *Gandhi's Political Philosophy*, p. 27.
62. Phillips, *Multiculturalism without Culture*, p. 14. Emphasis added.
63. Benhabib, *Claims of Culture*, p. 4.
64. Taylor, *Sources of The Self*, p. 82; *RM*, p. 342.
65. Jahanbegeloo, *Talking Politics*, p. 128.
66. Parekh, *Gandhi's Political Philosophy*, p. 84.
67. *RM*, pp. 167–8.
68. Al Hibri (1999), 'Is Western patriarchal feminism good for Third World minority women', *Is Multiculturalism Bad For Women* (Princeton, NJ: Princeton University Press), p. 46.
69. Parekh, *Gandhi's Political Philosophy*, p. 59. Emphasis added.
70. T. Modood (2006), 'The liberal dilemma: integration or vilification', *International Migration* 44:5, 4–7.
71. M. Oakeshott (1962), 'Political education', *Rationalism in Politics* (Indianapolis, IN: Liberty Fund), pp. 57 and 61.
72. Paul Kelly was the first to illustrate the Oakshottian nature of OPVs, and he elaborates this position in relation to Parekh's work in this volume.
73. B. Parekh (1992), 'The cultural particularity of liberal democracy', *Political Studies*, XL, p. 174.
74. Parekh, *Talking Politics*, p. 73.
75. B. Parekh (2008), *A New Politics of Identity* (Basingstoke: Palgrave Macmillan), p. 212; Jahanbegeloo, *Talking Politics*, p. 73.
76. *RM*, pp. 308 and 133.
77. Parekh, *Gandhi's Political Philosophy*, p. 54.
78. V. Uberoi and T. Modood (2010), 'Who doesn't feel British? Divisions over Muslims', *Parliamentary Affairs*, 63:2.
79. J. S. Mill (1991), *Utilitarianism, Liberty, Representative Government* (Oxford: Oxford University Press), p. 431.
80. See Peter Jones' chapter; for other discussions see B. Barry (2001), *Culture and Equality* (Cambridge: Polity), p. 37; S. Caney (2002), 'Equal treatment, exceptions and cultural diversity', in P. Kelly (ed.) *Multiculturalism Reconsidered* (Cambridge: Polity), p. 88; J. Quong (2006), 'Cultural exemptions, expensive tastes and equal opportunities', *Journal of Applied Philosophy*, 23:1. p. 62.
81. *RM*, p. 239; B. Williams (2006), 'The idea of equality', in *In The*

Beginning Was the Deed (Princeton, NJ: Princeton University Press), p. 97; and I. Berlin (1978), 'Equality', *Concepts and Categories* (London: Hogarth Press), p. 82.

82. Berlin, 'Equality', p. 82.
83. Barry, *Culture and Equality*, p. 34.
84. D. Miller (2002), 'Liberalism, equal opportunities and cultural commitments', in P. Kelly (ed.), *Multiculturalism Reconsidered* (Cambridge: Polity), p. 52.
85. *RM*, pp. 239–40.
86. Note how Barry's infamous motorcyclist who wants to ride a Harley Davidson without his helmet seemingly cannot make any of these claims. See Peter Jones' excellent treatment of this in this volume.
87. *RM*, pp. 261–3.
88. See Barry, '*Culture and Equality*, p. 37; Caney, 'Equal treatment', p. 88; Quong, 'Cultural exemptions', p. 62.
89. B. Parekh (1986), 'The new right and the politics of nationhood', in N. Deakin (ed.), *The New Right Image and Reality* (London: Runnymede Trust), p. 39; B. Parekh (1999), 'The incoherence of nationalism', in R. Beiner (ed.) *Theorizing Nationalism* (Albany, NY: State University of New York Press), p. 323; and *RM*, p. 207.
90. *RM*, p. 196.
91. *RM*, p. 230.
92. Ibid., pp. 231–2.
93. Ibid., p. 235.
94. Ibid., p. 230.
95. Barry, *Culture and Equality*, p. 77.
96. Ibid., p. 80.
97. Modood, 'Their liberalism our multiculturalism', p. 249.
98. B. Parekh (2000), 'British national identity', *Political Quarterly*, p. 6; B. Parekh (2008), *A New Politics of Identity Political Principles for an Interdependent World* (Basingstoke: Palgrave Macmillan). In 'Being British', on p. 310, Parekh does suggest that common identity should be 'strictly political', yet by this he means that it should not be defined racially or ethnically.
99. *RM*, pp. 230–1.
100. Parekh, *A New Politics of Identity*, p. 59.
101. Ibid., pp. 90–4.
102. Uberoi, 'Do policies change identities', pp. 406–7.
103. Goodhart, *British Dream*, p. 178.

104. D. Miller (2008), 'Immigrants, nations and citizenship', *Journal of Political Philosophy* 16:4, p. 380.
105. I develop this point at length in Uberoi, 'Do policies change identities'. See also my V. Uberoi (forthcoming, 2015), 'Legislating multiculturalism and nationhood, *Canadian Journal of Political Science*.

Part I

Interpreting Parekh

Situating Parekh's Multiculturalism: Bhikhu Parekh and Twentieth-Century British Political Theory

Paul Kelly

In a revealing passage about his early life and experiences at the London School of Economics (LSE) in his recent book *Talking Politics*, Bhikhu Parekh describes how his 'intellectual life has been the gift of others'.[1] This typically modest and generous claim contains within itself a profound truth about political philosophy. All political theories, however original, remain complex syntheses of ideas that are derived directly or indirectly from others: Parekh's own theory of multiculturalism is no exception. He is simply more generous in acknowledging that fact about his work.

The activity of political philosophy involves identifying and clarifying those influences, just as much as it is concerned with the critical analysis and reconstruction of those ideas and arguments. Regrettably current professional specialisation tends to separate the critical and analytical task from that of identifying and tracing the source of those ideas. Parekh is an example of an increasingly rare breed of political philosopher who is interested in recovering the ideas and arguments of others as well as developing and defending his own distinct theory.[2] He is also one who has spent much of his career reflecting carefully on the nature of the activity of the political philosopher and its distinction from that of the public intellectual.[3] Parekh has managed to occupy both roles with distinction.

The generous recognition of his debt to others for his intellectual formation and his acknowledgement of the subtle and sophisticated ways in which ideas and values are interwoven into

29

complex theoretical positions intimates the difficulties of tracing the sources and elements of his own distinctive political theory. In this chapter I want to contribute to the process of explaining and analysing Parekh's theory by locating it within a reading of some of the main contours of twentieth-century British political theory. As a result the main theme of this chapter is ostensive and interpretative rather than analytical or critical. My point is not to analyse, criticise or defend aspects of Parekh's arguments: instead I propose to draw connections and situate his arguments alongside themes and positions developed by others.[4] The primary task is not to assess the validity of his arguments but to explain and interpret their nature and suggest why the issues that underpin them have the peculiar saliency that they do. This approach is intended to apply and illustrate of Parekh's own dialogical conception of political philosophy, which he summarises as 'taking a view, imagining possible exceptions to it, refuting or accepting some or all of them, imagining possible objections to one's arguments, and so on'.[5]

Locating Parekh within the contours of a British tradition of political philosophy is perhaps paradoxical. He is, as everyone knows, Indian by birth and remains deeply engaged with the land, as well as the political and philosophical culture of his birth: all this despite being an Emeritus Professor of an English University, a Fellow of the British Academy and a Member of the House of Lords.[6] Yet the paradox dissolves once one sees the British political tradition in a Parekhean light: not as a closed tradition or practice with a fixed and final content, but instead as an interpretative or dialogical argument around a changing set of institutions and issues. The point is not to establish a categorical distinction between the political philosophies of Britain, the United States, France and Germany, let alone that of India. Instead it is to show how the concerns of some British thinkers are inflected in Parekh's work and how his arguments reflect a version of arguments, positions and priorities that are distinct from those found in other anglophone states and cultures. These differences are only perspectival and not categorical, but they remain important for all that. It is important to state at the outset that linking Parekh's work to a tradition of British political thinking is not to deny or down play his equally important contribution to and reflection upon Indian political theory and politics. I do not intend this chapter to be a fully exhaustive intellectual biography, and neither do I intend to claim that his contribution to British political theory takes priority over his contribution to the political theory of India. Instead I merely offer this as one of two parallel narratives that are interwoven in his thought but can nevertheless be usefully distinguished to explain and illustrate the ways in which Parekh's multicultural theory and politics differs from that of thinkers whose experience is wholly Indian or else whose politics and theory emerges in other parts of the anglophone world.

One could, for example compare and contrast Parekh's theory of multicultural inclusion with Will Kymlicka's liberal multiculturalism. The latter argument by a prominent Canadian political philosopher is an attempt to absorb a peculiar conception of societal groups within the terms of liberal egalitarianism, and is not unreasonably characterised as the most recent manifestation of the liberal/communitarian debate.[7] Whereas Kymicka's argument is a further move in a post-Rawlsian liberal egalitarian story, Parekh's multiculturalism does not fit easily into that narrative. Indeed Parekh is generally unsympathetic to the dominance of Rawlsian theory in contemporary political philosophy. However, it is important to note that Parekh does not reject egalitarianism as such, although his theory is anomalous from the perspective of much liberal egalitarianism. He rejects liberalism as a universally applicable philosophy of politics and as a domestic political ideology, but he is not 'illiberal' and he defends many liberal values. To normalise Parekh's position within liberal egalitarianism would be to obscure and neglect the ways in which he forces us to consider the terms and scope of liberal arguments and strategies of philosophical justification without rejecting liberal values outright. Indeed a good parallel to draw is between Parekh's work in British political theory and Michael Walzer's work in American political theory.[8] Both are egalitarians and both are committed to political values such as toleration, respect for individual difference and freedom, which are often defined as 'liberal' values. Yet both Parekh and Walzer are also communitarians of a particular kind and both acknowledge the political character of political philosophy and its origins in a political tradition. Indeed it is precisely this idea that I will later identify as part of Parekh's engagement with Michael Oakeshott. Just as it would be misleading to see Walzer as a narrow commentator on American politics it would equally be misleading to ignore the impact of the politics of American pluralism on Walzer's theoretical account of 'complex equality'.[9] I wish to make similar claims about Parekh's multicultural theory in relation to a tradition of British political theory.

A fruitful way of making sense of Parekh's theory is to see it as one of the most recent manifestations of pluralism, a point that has been made by Rodney Barker among others.[10] As we shall see, this pluralist dimension of British political thought is complex and develops into two distinct pluralist discourses. Parekh incorporates elements of each discourse in his multiculturalist theory. In constructing this complex synthesis Parekh confronts one of the central problems of contemporary liberalism, but instead of following the familiar path to contractarianism and proceduralism he turns instead towards the ideas of Michael Oakeshott for insight. Parekh is no simplistic follower of Oakeshott, and he remains a perceptive interpreter and critic of Oakeshott's conservative philosophy, yet he also finds within Oakeshott's ideas insights that are applicable for addressing fundamental political and philosophical matters that are central to his own theoretical works but which are also implicit throughout the Parekh Report on *The Future of a Multi-Ethnic Britain*.[11]

The Parekh Report, as it has become known, is the work of a distinguished committee and its analysis and recommendations was the work of many hands. Yet the vision and the arguments also reflect the peculiar theoretical voice of its chair, so much so, that I will consider the Report and its language and arguments a feature of Parekh's own theory of multiculturalism.

Two stories about pluralism and the state

Beneath the surface of Parekh's multiculturalist theory one can find elements of the English pluralist political theories that flourished in the early twentieth century. It is this tradition and the problems associated with it that illustrate the distinctive character of Parekh's multiculturalism and distinguish his concerns from those of Canadians such as Will Kymlicka or James Tully.

This section of the argument will explore the two distinct aspects of pluralism that have had such an impact on the development of the course of British political theory in the twentieth century and are manifested within Parekh's works, but it will also suggest some problems of which Parekh is aware, that continually face multicultural politics, so illustrating his meta-theoretical claim that interpretation cannot avoid critical engagement.[12]

PLURALISM AS SELF-GOVERNANCE

One of the most striking echoes of the pluralist discourse of the early twentieth century in Parekh's work comes in his Report for the Commission on the Future of a Multi-ethnic Britain, in which he characterises the multicultural vision of Britain as 'a community of communities'.[13] This view of the British state could have been lifted directly from the work of Figgis, Cole or Laski in the early part of the twentieth century. Of course, I am taking a specific formulation from a work that is the Report of a committee, so one might caution that this is at best circumstantial evidence of an affinity between Parekh's own views and those of the early twentieth-century English pluralists. Yet the idea that the public identity of a political institution and culture of the states is negotiated among the cultural communities that constitute it, which is the fundamental presupposition of Parekh's political theory, is well captured by this phrase even if he is not the direct source of it.

Each of the English pluralist thinkers saw the problem of politics as one of securing the conditions of self-government in the face of the unitary state, precisely the form of political community celebrated by British Idealists such as Bernard Bosanquet in his book *The Philosophical Theory of the State* or utilitarians such as Henry Sidgwick in *The Elements of Politics*.[14] Each of these pluralist thinkers approached the problem of the unitary sovereign state from a different perspective but for each the state and its claims is the main problem or political theory. J. N. Figgis was both a significant historian of political thought in the mould of Maitland and Gierke and a substantial political theorist in his own right.[15] His concerns were shaped by the rise of the state in the early modern period and the way in which it usurped the authority and liberty of other communities and associations. One of Figgis' particular interests was the way in which the idea of unitary sovereignty and the divine right of kings was traceable to arguments for Papal supremacy, and could not be traced further back into the medieval period when jurisdiction over territory and over the spiritual and the temporal realms was not consolidated in a single person or institution. Figgis' concern was with a European and not a peculiarly English phenomenon but he was also interested in the way in which this discourse is domesticated and used to legitimise the peculiar character and growth of state power in Britain. Figgis was an Anglo-Catholic whose political pluralism embodied his commitment to a medieval Catholic conception of Christianity and a rejection of Papal supremacy in favour of subsidiarity and collegiality. The modern state with its claims to regulate and arbitrate between groups and associations was usurping the legitimate plural authority of those associations in the same way that the Papacy usurped the traditional responsibility and jurisdiction of local Bishops and churches.

Figgis' pluralism is concerned with the sources and nature of political sovereignty and the rise of the modern state. It might be thought that claiming a parallel between Figgis' pluralism and Parekh's multiculturalism is to commit a category mistake, as Parekh is not denying the idea of state sovereignty but merely challenging the terms of accommodation between cultural groups within the state: for example, he does not countenance claims to sub-state sovereignty by such groups or allow for group secession. These important differences however, mask equally important affinities. One example of the way in which Figgis' pluralism casts an important light on the priorities of Parekh's multicultural theory is in the way both address the political claims of religious authority. Churches and religious communities claim to be governed by a higher law that rivals and limits the scope and legitimacy of political power and authority. How this assertion of higher authority and its political and moral claims determines the fundamental norms of inclusion of groups within that society is a common problem acknowledged by Parekh and early twentieth-century English pluralism which is largely ignored by much twentieth-century British political thought. Most contemporary liberal theories privatise religious commitments in the same way that post-Reformation thinkers such as Hobbes and Locke privatise the claims of religion. Yet this ability to privatise divine law and church authority is a Protestant innovation and is not shared by all religious groups today any more than it was shared by all Christian thinkers, as Figgis was quick to point out. The proper accommodation of the higher law of God and the claims of the political cannot be decided by the state, without simply begging the question; but nor can we simply ignore the problem by asserting the secular character of the modern state as if religion has become an object of purely historical interest. We can detect echoes of this sensitivity to the claims of religion in Parekh's acknowledgement of the need to accommodate and integrate traditional religious authorities rather than simply subordinate them to the claims of the state in cases of conflict between the two. This vision of plural accommodation between different spheres of authority can be seen in Parekh's open discussion of the desire to accommodate the claims of Moslem and other minorities as parallel jurisdictions (within the state), to regulate aspects of marriage and family law, in the same way that these were regulated until very recently by the Church of England. But more fundamental than that simple contingent similarity is Parekh's appreciation of the nature and problem of political theology in the development of modern and contemporary political theory. Much if not all contemporary liberal theory posits the claims of religious authority as a purely private matter within a secular realm dominated by a unitary sovereign political authority. More historically minded liberals can tell an historical story about the rise to dominance of that conception of political authority, drawing on Hobbes and his successors, but most fail to acknowledge that the argument is not so easily settled as a political matter without committing to contestable epistemological claims that contemporary liberals seek to avoid.[16] However, the main point is not that Parekh is open to the possible truth claims of rival authorities to that of the state, but more importantly the way in which the structures and norms of the British state reflect aspects of a particular religious and political history in the structuring of its norms of inclusion and the organisation of its public political culture: the impact of which persists long after the belief structure on which it was originally based has ceased to be widely shared by the body politic. None of this is intended to suggest that Parekh follows the arguments of some religious and cultural conservatives who want to coercively re-establish the claims of religion in public life and the public sphere. What Parekh's work does suggest, echoing the arguments of Figgis, is that arguments about the reasonableness of secularism as a way of accommodating religious and cultural difference need to be aware about the way forms of secularism are embedded with unarticulated views and perspectives about the nature of the groups being accommodated.

One can only speculate about the extent to which Parekh's Indian upbringing and background has made him sensitive to the complexity of secularism and its variety of justifications – he addresses this to some extent in *Talking Politics*[17] – but whatever the cause, Parekh has been able to appreciate aspects of British political culture that are lost to many theorists who assume an unproblematic uniformity in respect of the institutional context in anglophone political thought.

The acknowledgement of subsidiary associations is also stressed in G. D. H. Cole's defence of pluralism as guild socialism.[18] For Cole specialisation is the basis for challenging the monist or unitary state. As modern societies become more complex and functionally differentiated, the idea of the modern state as equivalent to society, as claimed by idealists such as Bosanquet, seems out of place. Thus where Figgis' argument looks back to a time before the rise of the modern state, Cole's pluralism claims to look beyond the outdated structure of the monist state. He does not, however, reject a role for the state as an arbiter and respecter of boundaries between associations, but he does want to reduce the role of state to that of one association among others. Similarly, Parekh does not reject the state out of hand but sees it as a territorial community of communities[19] yet despite his avowed egalitarianism he, like Cole, is suspicious of the simplistic model of the state as the sole provider of all the benefits of social cooperation that is presupposed in much liberal–egalitarian theory. The multiculturalist challenge to the liberal distributive paradigm is based on the idea that liberal conceptions of justice and the welfare state have a homogenising effect, disciplining the claims of groups and subordinating them to hegemonic discourses of need. This challenge to the normalising paradigm of liberal theories of justice is also found in more overtly pluralist conceptions of politics such as the associationalism championed by Paul Hirst in the 1990s.[20] This problem of normalisation is particularly acute in the context of cultural and ethnic difference because the standard sets of liberal welfare rights and opportunities can not only fail to address the concerns of marginalised groups, but they can actually marginalise groups whose claims cannot be translated into the terms of social justice in predominantly liberal societies. Although Parekh does not put it quite like this, his multicultural theory is an attempt to challenge the domination of the unstable combination of Bloomsbury and Fabianism on the British left.[21]

The final dimension of political pluralism that I want to trace to Parekh's multicultural theory is derived from the early works of Harold Laski.[22] Although Figgis and Cole are critics of the modern monistic state, Laski's pluralism gives perhaps the clearest picture of the state as not merely one among a number of associations, but as an association that has an interest apart from the interests of particular groups and associations. This more sceptical perspective on the state gave way in his later writings to a Marxist view of the state as a vehicle for a particular class interest, but even in his earlier works the state was not seen as a benign expression of the common good as Bosanquet and the idealists had claimed. This scepticism about the state reappears in the multiculturalist's critique of the distributive paradigm, but it also explains the persistence of the pluralist model of self-governance and associational responsibility despite the triumph of the welfare state in the mid-twentieth century.

The transformation of the state into the welfare and enabling state of social democracy after Beveridge and the 1945 Labour Government is often taken as a victory of statism over pluralism. The new order is also reflected in T. H. Marshall's conception of social or citizenship rights, which embodied the idealism of the post-war order and the state as the coordinator of a politics directed at the common good. The experience of war and the demands of economic and social reconstruction required more than a functionally differentiated state holding the ring between other social and political associations. For many on the left the state became a source of social citizenship and a guarantor of equality and respect. It is perhaps no surprise that the first generation of theories of social justice were conceived of by thinkers who came of age in the two decades following the war. Once the claims of the state have been settled fundamental political philosophy has nothing left to say and is displaced by political moralism, which can at least provide normative justifications for social policy. One plausible explanation for the long-term dominance of British political philosophy by issues of social justice from the 1970s until the present is that from the domestic perspective there was no challenge to the claims of a particular vision of the unitary state, consequently all political questions were reduced to moral questions about how state power affected the rights and interests of those subject to it.[23]

Yet this liberal vision of the state as a constitutional community, committed to the protection and respect of individual rights and opportunities, presupposed an imaginary homogeneity that was always overstated, but with the arrival of significant postcolonial immigration any pretence at national uniformity was finally dashed and questions about the terms of social inclusion and the ethnic bias of the conception of citizenship rights embodied in the welfare state began to assert themselves in political life and then in the terms of political theorising. The circumstances of multiculturalism arose because the resurgent statism of the mid-twentieth century had masked the very issues that earlier pluralist thinkers had sought to address, namely representation and self-determination in a community of communities. The marginalisation of subsidiary associations and the domination of certain social and economic interest groups that inspired earlier pluralist thinkers had metamorphosed into the marginalisation of identity groups and societal cultures in the circumstances of multiculturalism in the late twentieth century.

Seen in this light it is not implausible to claim that Parekh's multiculturalism is simply the latest version of a dominant discourse in twentieth-century British political thought about the nature, source and scope of political power, and that it is actually liberal egalitarianism and not multiculturalism that is the exception and oddity.

But in extending and updating this pluralist discourse and applying it to new and under-represented or marginalised social groups, multiculturalism also rehearses one of the problems that earlier forms of pluralism could never satisfactorily address. Respect for individual rights and the criteria for accommodating and arbitrating between conflicting associations is also a persistent problem within British political thought. The specification of self-government rights between groups is a constant problem for pluralists, as some form of quasi or partial sovereignty is necessary in order for groups to function as autonomous associations. If church law and practice are constantly challenged by the secular legislation of the state then churches cannot be free associations or communities. But if they are afforded genuine autonomy then they can act in ways that might discriminate against individual citizens and make imperialist claims to dominate over non-members on issues over which they make truth claims. This raises the vexed question of who decides on the appropriate terms of association and the limits of group autonomy. This is one of the challenges faced by early pluralists that the statist version of liberalism sought to answer; it is also a persistent challenge made against Parekh's multiculturalism by liberal critics such as Brian Barry. The point at issue is not only the content of the norms that regulate inter-group cooperation and accommodation, but the source of those norms. The pluralist discourse of self-governance seeks to provide a political answer to the question of the source of authoritative norms, but in so doing it has to address the problem of the unequal bargaining power of those groups and interests. This is precisely the same issue that Parekh faces in appealing to the operative public values (OPVs) of a society as the basis of multicultural integration: who for example is the arbiter of and spokesman for those values? Yet if appeal is made to a non-political method of addressing this question, such as an impartial norm of reason or a natural law, do we not risk abandoning the claim to political pluralism to some objective external authority? One way of seeking to address this meta-ethical problem is to be found in the other main pluralist discourse that has shaped twentieth-century British political theory.

PLURALISM AND LIBERALISM

The second pluralist discourse that forms part of the intellectual backdrop to Parekh's multiculturalism has developed in isolation from the political pluralism of Figgis, Cole, Laski and others. Indeed this alternative discourse of pluralism has only recently been distinguished by the title. That said, meta-ethical pluralism is as old as Aristotle's ethical theory. Aristotle famously characterised the good life in *Nicomachean Ethics* as having a plural structure or many dimensions and the task of living well or realising the good is one of combining and balancing those dimensions through the exercise of *phronesis*. This pluralistic idea of the good life has been central to the development of ethical thought in the West since the time of the ancient Greeks; as such it does not look a particularly British ethical theory. However, the return to Aristotelian ethics has played an important part in developing a modern variant of meta-ethical pluralism that reappears in the arguments for multiculturalism and also for an increasingly important strand of liberal political theory in Britain.

Pluralism as an ethical doctrine can be seen as a response to monistic theories of morality, just as political pluralism is a response to monistic theories of the state as the completion of society. The particular target of ethical pluralism is the dominance of utilitarianism in British moral theory since J. S. Mill and Henry Sidgwick in the late nineteenth century. Sidgwick's *Methods of Ethics* proved a standard work on moral philosophy in English until the rise of logical positivism and ordinary language philosophy undermined substantive moral theorising as a respectable philosophical pursuit and its replacement by meta-ethical analysis in the mid-twentieth century following the aftermath of logical positivism. Although the logical turn in British philosophy has preoccupied historians of the subject, there is a less widely acknowledged movement in the history of ethics which includes intuitionist philosophers such as H. A. Prichard and W. D. Ross among others, who reacted against the monistic tendencies of utilitarianism.[24] It is unsurprising that this problem of moral monism and its connection with a type of governmentality should be imminent within Parekh's theory, as his earliest published works in political philosophy were on the political ideas of Jeremy Bentham.[25] Sidgwick's utilitarian theory is often characterised as a version of 'government house'[26] utilitarianism, and there is a more direct connection between utilitarian moral and political theory and the ambiguous colonialist dimension of utilitarian government reform and policy making that is captured in Eric Stokes' *The English Utilitarians and India*.[27]

Utilitarianism sees the good life as comprising one overriding duty, namely maximising the greatest happiness of the greatest number. The intuitionists argued that this reduced all moral questions to technical questions about welfare maximisation and asserted a crass individualistic moral ontology. In defending a more traditional set of moral obligations they attempted to provide a moral epistemology and account of motivation that allowed for a variety of fundamental moral principles and values. The precise detail of their argument need not concern us here, but what is important is the way in which the intuitionist rejection of monistic utilitarianism is reflected in subtle ways in the re-emergence of moral philosophy from under the shadow of ordinary language philosophy in the 1950s. Important figures in the renewal of moral and political philosophy in Britain such as Isaiah Berlin, Stuart Hampshire, H. L. A. Hart and Bernard Williams have all developed an approach to morality and normative political theory that rejects the monistic character of utilitarianism. However, they also rejected the alternative to utilitarianism offered by the contractarian followers of John Rawls such as Brian Barry.[28] Hampshire, Berlin and more recently Williams, have continued to challenge the rationalistic and monistic utilitarian character of modern moral philosophy. Although each thinker differs in important ways they each support two main theses about values and morality that underpin Parekh's argument. The first thesis concerns the plural nature of the good, and the second concerns the role of practices in morality.

Ethical pluralism has developed in two directions, sometimes, as with Isaiah Berlin, in the thinking of a single author. This can be seen in the question of the nature of the good or final end of life. Berlin is a defender of the idea of value pluralism, but is notoriously ambiguous about precisely what this means. It can mean that there is a single form of the good life but that this has a plurality of dimensions – arguably this is Aristotle's view. Alternatively it can mean that there are a variety of incommensurable goods that can come into conflict with one another: this is the position of Stuart Hampshire and more recently John Gray.[29] A further alternative is that there is a plurality of equally valuable moral schemes and practices that are also incommensurable (a pluralism of monisms): John Gray also endorses this view of pluralism, as does Berlin in some of his essays.[30] The second thesis develops from this third account of value pluralism by claiming that values and ethical principles are derived from moral practices and traditions. It is these practices and traditions that have authority, rather than the appeal to impartial conceptions of reason such as those offered by utilitarianism or contractarianism.

The idea of plural values and moral schemes and a practice-based conception of ethics can be seen to make an important contribution to Parekh's multiculturalism, not simply because it rehearses the communitarian social thesis, but because it returns anthropology and sociology to the centre of moral and ethical enquiry. The conception of ethics advocated by Berlin, Hampshire and Williams is concerned more with analysing and understanding the diversity of moral practice rather than with the moral criticism of practices and norms. Parekh's theory echoes these arguments in his challenge to the false neutrality of liberal egalitarianism as a further local variant of ethical monism. Similarly the idea that group practices embody values and diverse ways of achieving common human purposes has reinforced the imperative to respect cultural practices and their differences. The idea that ethical truth is embodied in diversity and not merely the practices of a particular universal moral culture has reinforced the multiculturalist aspiration to preserve the moral ecology of the human species. Yet Parekh's multiculturalism also offers an immanent critique of the value pluralism of liberal realists such as Berlin,

Hampshire and Williams. As is clear from his discussion of Berlin in *Rethinking Multiculturalism*, Parekh sees these pluralists as already too liberal in terms of their reductionist account of individual values and their failure to see a plurality of systems of the good life embodied in societal cultures. Although Berlin goes on to acknowledge this point under the influence of his reading of Vico, it remains the case that his conception of pluralism remains embedded within a liberal societal culture with its peculiar conception of the state and political authority.

It would be simplistic to see multiculturalism as a direct implication of ethical pluralism, but the fact of ethical pluralism sustains the commitment to moral diversity and the accommodation of difference that animates the political theory of multiculturalism. However, acknowledging ethical pluralism has a large price for multiculturalists, not the least of which is the risk of relativism.

An implication of the practice-based conception of ethics and the theory of value pluralism is that moral principles and values are particularistic, that is, they apply only in particular local circumstances. This looks suspiciously like relativism, with its denial of moral truth. This risk may not matter for sophisticated philosophical pluralists such as Hampshire, Berlin and Williams, who are all essentially sceptical liberals when it comes to matters of personal conduct, but it does matter for multiculturalist theorists such as Parekh, who does not simply assume the conventional moral wisdom of Bloomsbury or North Oxford. First, it matters because it may not capture the self-understandings of the moral and cultural communities that are being accommodated. Islam and Catholicism (to take only two examples) impose a moral law and practices on their members, but they also do this in the name of a universal truth. It is just not true to say that Catholicism applies to Catholics and Islam to Moslems: both presuppose a universal moral community. So the assertion of meta-ethical value pluralism is in danger of distorting the self-understandings of actual moral and cultural communities by characterising them as one among a variety of viable moral perspectives. This is especially problematic if one were trying to negotiate the terms of social cooperation between such groups. The Pope might well endorse the fact of societal pluralism if this entails religious toleration, but he is unlikely to endorse the truth of ethical pluralism. So the threat of relativism is not merely a preoccupation of philosophers, it touches on the political problems that multiculturalists are trying to accommodate. Parekh is certainly not a meta-ethical relativist but his theory must address the problems that meta-ethical relativism poses.

A further problem of relativism takes us back to the problem of pluralism as self-government. There I argued that pluralism needed an external norm of inclusion and accommodation between different associations, communities and cultural groups if pluralist politics was not merely to collapse into interest group bargaining and the manipulation of power. For multiculturalists, addressing this question is fraught with danger as it seems to privilege the liberal idea of social justice, which for multiculturalists merely offers a new form of cultural domination. Ethical pluralism is supposed to offer a way of defending norms of inclusion that are not merely a function of the arbitrary distribution of power among groups in society. However, the practice-based conception of ethics and the thesis of value incommensurability leave us with only two options: either we have locally valid norms pitched against other locally valid norms, or else a return to ethical norms, which are true and therefore universal. As Parekh acknowledges, the return to truth and universalism can limit the obligation to accommodate difference; it can also change the way in which cultural practices are viewed, and thus potentially continue political marginalisation. For if cultural practices are merely local ways of getting along, and do not have a universal claim to recognition, it is unlikely that politicians will want to defend cultural difference as anything more than a temporary measure. However, if we accept the risk of relativism and stick with a particularistic account of morality, then we have no principled grounds for the norms of accommodation that are negotiated between different cultural groups. Parekh tries to address this problem by appealing to the idea of recognition through deliberation and intercultural dialogue. But in order to do this he must provide a perspective from which this intercultural dialogue can take place, and this takes him from the tensions within political and ethical pluralism to a fundamental reflection on the tasks of political philosophy and the influence of Michael Oakeshott.

An alternative approach to political philosophy

Parekh's social and ethical pluralism confronts the spectre of relativism and its concomitants nihilism and indifferentism. While some value pluralists, such as Berlin, argue that relativism is actually a contemporary preoccupation that was not found among the sources of value pluralism in the eighteenth century, the challenge of relativism still haunts value theories that celebrate diversity and particularity.[31] If the argument is that values are local and particular and there is a plurality of value systems, then how does this differ from the claim that values are merely relative? And if we accept that claim, then why should we not merely impose what we happen to value on others? Why should we respect difference? One can see much contemporary liberal political philosophy as a response to the challenge of settling terms of social cooperation between people who do not share fundamental conceptions of the good life.[32] Yet Parekh has always found the liberal solution involving impartial terms of social cooperation question-begging. Despite his scepticism about the viability of a 'thin' ethic of universal impartiality he does not favour as an alternative position a political or *modus vivendi* approach to accommodating difference of the sort advocated by Hampshire or John Gray.[33] Instead he develops his own distinctive account of inter-group accommodation and evaluation that is subtly influenced by the philosophy of Michael Oakeshott.

Oakeshott's influence on Parekh is considerable, profound and clearly acknowledged, but it is not straightforward. As many contemporaries of Parekh who were also students of Oakeshott are quick to acknowledge, he is anything but a straightforward follower of Oakeshott's conception of political philosophy and its conclusions.[34] In *Talking Politics*, Parekh describes how conversations with Oakeshott at LSE had a profound influence on his subsequent career and formation as a political philosopher.[35] It is this engagement with Oakeshott's work that also distinguishes the character of Parekh's work and locates him within a British tradition of political philosophy that has been shaped by Oakeshott's writings and personal influence rather than by the growing dominance of American philosophers such as John Rawls, Robert Nozick and Ronald Dworkin, who have shaped English language political theory during most of Parekh's career.

Oakeshott's political philosophy has changed and developed over a long and distinguished career often involving profound rethinking of earlier positions. So in identifying affinities and influences from Oakeshott on Parekh's work I am acutely aware that some of Parekh's concerns are incompatible with the theory of civil association found in *On Human Conduct*.[36] Parekh draws more heavily on ideas from Oakeshott's earlier work *Rationalism in Politics*, especially the chapter of that name and 'Political education'.[37]

From these chapters we can detect intimations of Parekh's method of intercultural evaluation through the dialogical engagement with the OPVs of a given political society. Before turning to consider Parekh's account of OPVs and its implications for intercultural evaluation and dialogue, I want to rehearse the arguments underlying Parekh's critique of liberalism to show how they reflect the immanent sceptical communitarianism of Oakeshott and his students that distinguishes their approach from that of liberal egalitarians such Brian Barry, who draw inspiration from Berlin and Hart in developing a proceduralist defence of impartiality. Parekh's arguments against the liberal impartialist approach are familiar and involve three related claims, which parallel neo-Hegelian or communitarian criticisms of abstract universalism.

The liberal impartialist solution to multiculturalism requires the justification of universal moral principles that are neutral between conflicting moral claims. Liberalism is supposed to provide an external, neutral perspective from which it can adjudicate between cultures. Without such a perspective contemporary liberalism is merely one tradition or view and, as such, of no greater authority than any other cultural practice or set of beliefs. Parekh claims that this enormously demanding project remains unredeemed, despite the best efforts of Immanuel Kant and subsequent generations of philosophers down to the likes of John

Rawls in the present day. In this he is no doubt right, to the extent that no impartialist theory has as yet received universal assent. But Parekh is not merely pointing to the fact that as yet we do not have a philosophical consensus on the basis for the liberal principle of impartial inclusion. He claims that the impartialist perspective is incoherent in the way it presumes that there must be one correct ordering of human society and the good life, despite the great variety of different views and practices throughout human history. Given the fact of difference, the very presumption that there should be one single right way of doing things needs both explanation and justification.

As we have seen, for Parekh the fact of pluralism tends to suggest a more substantive moral pluralism. But even if we are unconvinced by this consideration and accept the liberal aspiration of universalism, we are, according to Parekh, still left with two other problems that render the liberal project problematic. The first of these considerations is the motivation problem. Even if we could find a philosophical foundation for a universal liberal norm of inclusion, we might still have a problem of providing a motive to act on such a norm that is sufficiently overriding in the face of competition from other, less impartial moral and political commitments. Impartialism conflicts with the facts of our complex and diverse moral experience. Here Parekh rehearses the familiar charge that universal first-order moral principles are simply too demanding for real moral agents with their partial commitments and special obligations.

The third part of the objection to moral universalism follows from the need to interpret universal principles. Parekh's example of a universal moral principle that needs interpretation is 'respect for human life'. Many, perhaps all, cultures can be said to endorse this principle, but on its own it does not entail any single authoritative interpretation. Does it entail merely negative liberty rights, or the positive provision of welfare? Is it something that is the responsibility of the whole community? Such a moral principle can be given substantive content in many ways in culturally diverse societies, such that appeal to the principle of 'respect for human life' will not in itself do any real work. As Hegel and all communitarian philosophers since have been quick to point out,

47

abstract moral principles, because of their abstraction, have to be actualised in a concrete form of ethical life. Liberals acknowledge that claim but still face the constant challenge showing that their conception of liberal values is universal and not merely the local prejudices of Western liberal societies. Such a form of ethical life will always be particular and local; there is no single universal form of ethical life that will satisfy all people, as we can see from the fact of reasonable pluralism.

Because we have no philosophically uncontroversial moral principles, and because they would not in themselves provide much help in facing the problem of multicultural inclusion, we need another approach. It is here that Parekh turns to the idea of operative public values.

The OPVs of a society are the public moral and political rules that bind a particular group of people into a common society. Without such OPVs the different and often conflicting components of a society could not exist as a cohesive body. They have no higher origin than that they constitute the overlapping common bonds of the various different groups, classes and interests that make up a political society. Their only authority is that they have become part of the received structure of social relations. They are, in effect, 'how we do things around here', and their acceptance and broad acknowledgement is their only claim to authority. These values underpin a common form of life among people who otherwise differ; they do not prescribe the final structure or content of a human life, nor a common set of goals towards which a society is progressing. They are merely the unwritten terms of a common practice within which various particular forms of life are pursued and reconciled. This conception of a shared form of life manifests itself in the constitutional framework of a society as well as in its laws, both municipal and moral. It also manifests itself in the 'civic' relations of its members. These informal rules of conduct include the 'good manners' of a particular society: that is, ways of behaving that share a common but unarticulated understanding of how to act. Parekh is to be credited with the focus on OPVs as the basis for a dialogical engagement as the basis of political philosophy that he outlines in *Talking Politics* and 'The nature of political philosophy'.[38]

Yet there is an instructive affinity between this approach and the way in which Oakeshott describes the activity of politics as the 'pursuit of intimations' within a tradition in the chapter 'Political education'. Of course Oakeshott's point is to criticise the rationalism that preoccupied him in the 1940s and 1950s and the ideological politics that follows from it. Yet the crucial point is that politics is a practical activity that is shaped by given circumstances and institutions and that political wisdom acknowledges that context rather than wishing to impose a wholly new and artificial set of circumstances in their place. Attending to those circumstances is very similar to the Parekhean preoccupation with OPVs, which might themselves be seen as the intimations of a tradition.

OPVs constitute and embody a shared form of public life. They are not derived from a thick conception of the moral life or of the human good, but they are inevitably influenced by such a perspective. How do these OPVs help with the issue of multicultural inclusion?

Parekh clearly suggests that we should turn to these OPVs as a means of establishing and negotiating multicultural inclusion. When faced with a claim for the recognition of a practice by a minority group, the wider society does not merely assert its OPVs; indeed it could not do so as they are always in need of interpretation and are not static and beyond reproach. Instead, the wider society uses its OPVs as the basis for opening a dialogue with the minority group. This dialogue involves both a defence of the OPVs through a process of reason giving, and, if necessary, an attempt to explain why the minority practice offends against those values. The minority must try to defend its practices and show why these ought to be recognised by the wider society. This process is supposed to be dialogical in that both parties learn from and transform their understanding of their respective views and values. If we continue the analogy between pursuing the intimations of a tradition and a dialogue about the scope and meaning of OPVs we can see that there is no single direction to the process of accommodation. Oakeshott might well assume a relatively cautious and conservative form of politics to result from this conception of negotiation, deliberation and dialogue, but there is nothing to preclude quite radical constitutional and social change to follow from the pursuit of intimations within a tradition. Similarly, although Parekh's model of intercultural evaluation based on OPVs may seem to privilege the dominant discourse there remains no reason why it should, and furthermore as it is an ongoing societal process there is no obvious point at which the process ends and a final decision is made.

The apparent advantage of the dialogue between the OPVs of the wider society and the beliefs and practices of the minority claiming recognition is that they provide clear terms within which the minority can articulate its position in order to persuade the multifarious views of the broad public. In the absence of OPVs the minority would need to convince each group, interest or individual of the consonance of its beliefs and practices with their fundamental moral views, and this is primarily a political and not a philosophical matter given Parekh's rejection of substantive universal theories such as liberal egalitarianism. There is no other perspective from which we can construct a better way of dealing with group recognition and multiculturalism, just as there is no other perspective from which we can settle questions of philosophical justification.

Conclusion

Bhikhu Parekh's sophisticated multicultural theory is no mere generalisation from personal experience, but was informed by a thorough grounding in the political ideas and theories of the Western tradition being reapplied to the circumstances of a more obviously plural and diverse society than traditional liberal thought from Mill or the Idealists through to Berlin, Hart and Barry, tended to acknowledge. The underlying problem for Parekh was the way in which the norms or conditions of group integration and accommodation, deployed in both public life and in egalitarian liberalism, contained presuppositions that reinforced the discrimination and disadvantage of ethnic and cultural groups. By cultural groups he meant communities that had settled patterns of belief with an institutional manifestation such as a legal authority. The accommodation of such groups could not be achieved by the imposition of universal general laws and sets of rights, as the nature and authority of these laws and rights was often challenged. Instead this process of integration is dialogical and intended to overcome the ultimate dominance of the larger societal culture. Parekh's work draws on ideas that were familiar to early pluralists such as Cole and Laski, with their emphasis on the need to overcome domination through democratisation and political self-determination and not simply through the redistribution of goods and resources in contexts that sustain subordination. In this he attempts to recover a conception of political liberty and political equality that is not merely negative liberty or liberal egalitarianism and all of this is situated within a critique of monistic universalism that draws on strands of criticism advanced by the British Idealists and by Michael Oakeshott. Although undoubtedly, there is more to Parekh than this engagement with and transformation of British ideas and arguments suggests, one could tell a story about the impact of Indian political experience and ideas on his thinking, but it would be a parallel narrative. Just as it would be an error to underplay Parekh's familiarity and engagement with Indian politics and political ideas, so equally one should not underestimate the value of his engagement with these features of the British political tradition. As Parekh has always insisted with respect to cultural practices, we should see them as sites of interpretation and reinterpretation for which there is never a fully exclusive inside and outside. Practices are always the starting points for deliberation, debate and reinterpretation. As such he is never wholly within but neither is he wholly without the context of British political theory.[39]

Notes

1. R. Jahanbegloo (2011), *Talking Politics* (New Delhi: Oxford University Press), p. 28.
2. See for example B. Parekh (1981), *Hannah Arendt and the Search for a Political Philosophy* (London: Macmillan); B. Parekh (1982), *Marx's Theory of Ideology* (London: Croom Helm).
3. B. Parekh (1968), 'The nature of political philosophy', in P. King and

B. Parekh (eds), *Politics and Experience* (Cambridge: Cambridge University Press), pp. 153–207.

4. For a more critical engagement with Parekh's work, see Paul Kelly: P. Kelly (2003), 'Identity, equality and power: tensions in Parekh's political theory of multiculturalism', in B. Haddock and P. Sutch (eds) *Multiculturalism, Identity and Rights* (London: Routledge), pp. 94–110.

5. Jahanbegloo, *Talking Politics*, p. 76.

6. When I included a selection from his work in an edited collection on British political theory in the twentieth century to mark the sixtieth anniversary of the Political Studies Association, he was both generous in his gratitude but also interested in how he could be considered a British political theorist: see P. Kelly (2010), (ed.) *British Political Theory in the Twentieth Century* (Oxford: Wiley-Blackwell).

7. W. Kymlicka (1989), *Liberalism, Community and Culture* (Oxford: Clarendon Press).

8. Interestingly, Parekh links his own multiculturalism with the pluralism of Berlin, Hampshire and Walzer in Jahanbegloo, *Talking Politics*, p. 75.

9. M. Walzer (1983), *Spheres of Justice* (Oxford: Martin Robertson).

10. R. Barker (1999), 'Pluralism, revenant or recessive?', in J. B. Hayward Barry and A. Brown (eds) *The British Study of Politics in the Twentieth Century* (Oxford: Oxford University Press for the British Academy), p. 131.

11. Campaign for a Multi-ethnic Britain (CMEB) (2000), *The Future of Multi-ethnic Britain* (London: Profile Books).

12. Parekh, 'The nature of political philosophy', p. 166.

13. CMEB, *Multi-ethnic Britain*. The idea of a community of communities is a phrase that is familiar in many other contexts in which Parekh engages. For example, it was used by Gandhi and is familiar as a way of characterising the political pluralism of India, see B. Parekh (1995), 'The ethnocentricity of nationalist discourse', *Nations and Nationalism*, 1, pp. 25–52. (I am grateful to the editors for this reference.) That said, the idea is also associated with English pluralism and in particular with rethinking the character of the British state. In light of the colonial connection between the political cultures of both states it is perhaps unsurprising that there is some commonality in the languages used.

14. B. Bosanquet (1920), *The Philosophical Theory of the State* (3rd edn), (London: Macmillan); H. Sidgwick (1891), *The Elements of Politics* (London: Macmillan).

15. His work is discussed in P. Kelly (2003), 'Contextual and non-contextual histories of political thought', in B. Hayward and A. Brown (eds) *The British Study of Politics in the Twentieth Century*, pp. 44–6.
16. Among the few exceptions are R. Plant (2001), *Politics, Theology and History* (Cambridge: Cambridge University Press); and C. Taylor (2007), *Living in a Secular Age* (Cambridge, MA: Harvard University Press).
17. Jahanbegloo (2011), *Talking Politics*, pp. 65–90.
18. G. D. H. Cole (1920), *Guild Socialism Re-stated* (London: Leonard Parsons).
19. A phrase used in CMEB, *Multi-ethnic Britain*, p. 47.
20. P. Hirst (1994), *Associative Democracy: New Forms of Economics and Social Governance* (Cambridge: Polity).
21. An uncharitable reading of the work of Brian Barry might be thought to fit this vision of liberal egalitarianism, see B. Barry (2000), *Culture and Equality* (Cambridge: Polity). For a more nuanced interpretation including replies from his critics, see P. Kelly (2002), *Multiculturalism Reconsidered* (Cambridge: Polity).
22. H. J. Laski (1917), *Studies in the Problem of Sovereignty* (New Haven, CT: Yale University Press); and H. J. Laski (1919), *Authority in the Modern State* (New Haven, CT: Yale University Press).
23. P. Kelly, *British Political Theory*, pp. 20–9.
24. H. A. Pritchard (1949), *Moral Obligation* (Oxford: Oxford University Press); W. D. Ross (1930), *The Right and the Good* (Oxford: Oxford University Press).
25. B. Parekh (1970), 'Bentham's theory of equality', *Political Studies*, 18, pp. 478–95; B. Parekh (1973), *Bentham's Political Thought* (London: Croom Helm).
26. See B. Williams (with J. J. C. Smart) (1973), *Utilitarianism: For and Against* (Cambridge: Cambridge University Press).
27. E. Stokes (1990), *The English Utilitarians and India* (New Dehli: Oxford University Press).
28. Although Barry was initially critical of Rawls' contractarianism in B. Barry (1971), *The Liberal Theory of Justice* (Oxford: Oxford University Press), he reconciled himself to the value of contract theory in B. Barry (1995), *Justice as Impartiality* (Oxford: Oxford University Press).
29. I. Berlin (1990), *The Crooked Timber of Humanity* (London: John Murray); I. Berlin (1998), *The Proper Study of Mankind* (London: Pimlico); S. Hampshire (1983), *Morality and Conflict* (Cambridge

MA: Harvard University Press); S. Hampshire (1989), *Innocence and Experience* (Harmondsworth: Penguin); B. Williams (1986), *Ethics and the Limits of Philosophy* (London: Fontana); and B. Williams (2005), *In the Beginning Was the Deed: Realism and Moralism in Political Argument* (Princeton, NJ: Princeton University Press).

30. J. Gray (2000), *Two Faces of Liberalism* (Cambridge: Polity).
31. I. Berlin (1991), 'Alleged relativism in eighteenth-century European thought', in *The Crooked Timber of Humanity* (London: Harper Collins), pp. 70–91.
32. This is the common point of two of Rawls' major works: J. Rawls (1971), *A Theory of Justice* (Oxford: Oxford University Press); and J. Rawls (1993), *Political Liberalism* (New York; Columbia University Press).
33. See S. Hampshire (1999), *Justice as Conflict* (London: Duckworth); Gray, *Two Faces of Liberalism*.
34. This is especially clear in Parekh's critical appraisal of Oakeshott's late political philosophy of civil association: see B. Parekh (1995), 'Oakeshott's theory of civil association', *Ethics*, 106:2, pp. 158–86.
35. Jahanbegloo, *Talking Politics*, p. 28.
36. M. Oakeshott (1975), *On Human Conduct* (Oxford: Clarendon Press).
37. M. Oakeshott (1962), *Rationalism in Politics* (London: Methuen).
38. For Parekh's account of political theory as a dialogical activity see Jahanbegloo, *Talking Politics*, p. 76; Parekh (1968), 'Nature of political philosophy', pp. 153–207, *passim*, though he does not emphasise the place of operative public values in these more general statements of his position.
39. I am also grateful to John Dunn and to Bhikhu Parekh for comments on an earlier draft of this chapter.

2

Gandhi, Intercultural Dialogue and Global Ethics: An Interpretive Commentary on Bhikhu Parekh's Work

Thomas Pantham

Mahatma Mohandas Gandhi's moral and political thought and practice, and multicultural political theory and global ethics are two broad areas in which Bhikhu Parekh has made original and valuable contributions, which have been widely recognised. His commentators, however, have focused almost exclusively on his contribution to either one or the other of these two main areas of his intellectual work.[1] As a result, the question of any link between his multicultural political theory and his interpretive account of Gandhi's thought and practice has remained unexplored. This is not entirely surprising because the first edition of Parekh's path-breaking book, *Rethinking Multiculturalism: Cultural Diversity and Political Theory* (hereafter *RM*), and its crowning 'sequel', *A New Politics of Identity: Political Principles for an Interdependent World* (hereafter *NP*), explicitly showed insufficient links with his three earlier books on Gandhi's moral and political thought, which in fact continue to be among the best interpretive works on it.[2] In orientation, however, both *RM* and *NP* shared Gandhi's interculturally or intercivilisationally dialogical perspective. Strikingly, moreover, in his *Gandhi's Political Philosophy*, Parekh had pointed out that Gandhi had deep roots in Indian ways of life and thought and intimate familiarity with the West, and that his 'biculturally grounded and bilingually articulated political theory shows one way in which a global political theory required by the increasingly interdependent world might be constructed'.[3]

Parekh's first major discursive interlinking of his multiculturally dialogical ethical-political theory and Gandhi's moral and
political philosophy and practice is his article 'Mahatma Gandhi
and Osama bin Laden: an imaginary dialogue'.[4] That important
work of interlinking is continued and expanded in Parekh's 'A
Response to my critics' in the second edition of RM, in which he
acknowledges that he has been following Gandhi's 'excellent and
little noticed example of intercultural experimentation'.[5] Parekh's
more recent book of conversation with Ramin Jahanbegloo, an
Iranian philosopher, shows a more discursive integration between
his political theory of cultural diversity, intercultural dialogue
and global ethics, and Gandhi's moral and political thought
and practice. In it, too, Parekh acknowledges that Gandhi has
been the centre of his attention and 'an icon, a patron saint of
intercivilizational dialogue'.[6]

The aforementioned texts and inter-texts frame my contribution to the present volume. I present an interpretive commentary on the nature of, and connection between, his multicultural
political theory and his account of Gandhi's thought. My interpretive viewpoint is that Parekh shares Gandhi's intercivilisationally
and inter-religiously dialogical approach to moral and political
thought and practice. To bring out and comment on that perspectival sharing is my objective in this chapter. Moreover, I take
Parekh's Gandhi-influenced multicultural dialogical approach to
political theory and global ethics to be meritorious or beneficial
in that it serves to bridge the cultural and moral division between
the liberal and non-liberal traditions and thereby to avoid or
overcome the limits of the ethnocentric or monist and relativist
approaches to cultural and moral diversity.[7] Accordingly, my
commentary on Parekh's work is appreciatively interpretive of it.

Actually, Parekh's multicultural political theory and global
ethics has its sources partly in his longstanding critical engagements with various traditions of social-religious and political
thought, including, in particular, the Indian and British traditions,
before and since the Gandhi-led beginning of the end of formal
colonisation. Undeniably, his multicultural political theory also
has its sources partly in his concerned activism in the public life
of the multicultural societies of UK and India. Some 'peculiarly'

British concerns and sources of influence in his political theory is the subject of Paul Kelly's contribution to this volume. In the present contribution, as I have indicated above, I attempt to bring out and comment on the presence of an effective Gandhian layer and strand in Parekh's intercultural-dialogical approach to political theory and political ethics.

In order to bring out and explain the perspectival sharing of Parekh's political theory with Gandhi's moral-political philosophy and practice, I need to first introduce Gandhi's thought and Parekh's emotional and intellectual fascination with it. This is needed because Gandhi does not figure in much multicultural political theory or even in general or standard political theory, for example the theories of Rawls and the Rawlsians. Accordingly, I provide in the next section a brief, mostly Parekhean, introduction to Gandhi's thought and practice.

On Gandhi's political thought

Gandhi's life and work have had not only an intellectual influence but also an emotional impact on Parekh. In *Talking Politics*, he recalls the early influences on his life and thought, and points out to the influence of his father, a goldsmith in the village of Amalsad in Gujarat, who had gone to see Gandhi when he had come to a nearby village in connection with a salt satyagraha. Parekh also remembers the help he had received from a few Gandhian teachers in school, college and university, including, in particular, the late Professor Usha Mehta of the University of Bombay, who had heroically participated in the Indian Freedom Struggle. 'They and I and many others', says Parekh, 'jointly shaped what I eventually became. The liberal and romantic idea of each individual being the author of his life, and responsible for what he makes of it, is a half-truth.'[8]

According to Parekh, it is on that half-truth of the atomistic or individualistic ontological reduction of the concrete human being that the social contract tradition of the liberal individualist political theory from Hobbes to Rawls rests. It is the half-truth of that political theory and the big wrongs of the imperialist/colonial political practices legitimised by it that Gandhi's political movement exposed and effectively resisted in the Natal and Transvaal provinces of South Africa and at Dandi and other places through the length and breadth of India. Following Gandhi, Parekh places concrete human beings rather than abstracted atomistic individuals at the centre of his political thought, and considers their general or common well-being to be the highest political value.[9]

For understanding Parekh's engagement with Gandhi's thought in particular and Indian thought and politics in general, it is necessary to give special attention to a three-year phase (1981–4) of his life and work in India as the vice-chancellor of the Maharaja Sayajirao University of Baroda (Vadodara, Gujarat) and as a member of the University Grants Commission of India. Some relevant information on that phase of his life is given in a note.[10] During that period, he wrote two notable chapters: 'Some reflections on the Hindu tradition of political thought'[11] and 'Gandhi and the logic of reformist discourse'.[12] The latter, which is elaborated in his work *Colonialism, Tradition and Reform: An Analysis of Gandhi's Political Discourse*[13] succinctly prefigures Parekh's intercultural-dialogical approach to political theorising (see the following section).

Parekh's intellectual fascination with Gandhi is centred on his intercivilisational and inter-religious moral-political philosophy, which effectively guided (1) a non-violent civil rights movement of the Indian immigrants in South Africa, (2) the final phase of the Indian Freedom Movement in its non-violent struggle for national political unity and independence, and (3) social-religious reform and regeneration of Indian society. In his *Gandhi's Political Philosophy*, Parekh writes: 'He was the first anti-imperialist leader of the modern age . . . and one of the few in history to fight simultaneously on moral, religious, political, social, economic and cultural fronts'.[14]

According to Parekh, Gandhi's greatest contribution was the forging of a moral and political theory and practice from the standpoint of the oppressed and the excluded that does not itself bring about or legitimise a new system of oppression. In Gandhi's *satyagraha*, he sees an effective new way of moral-political resistance through a combination of the civil liberties of liberal political modernity with non-violence and 'suffering love' even towards one's opponents. It is also pointed out that because of their belief in the indivisibility of humanity, the victors of a Gandhian revolution cannot dehumanise themselves by violating the humanity they share with their erstwhile enemies.[15]

Another aspect of Gandhi's political philosophy that Parekh emphasises is its revision of the liberal individualist conception of rights and duties. Gandhi is shown to have maintained that 'rights had to be defined and exercised in a socially responsible manner, and duties defined and discharged in a way that took account of the agent's uniqueness and claims'.[16] Bringing out Gandhi's philosophically deeper explanation of human duties and obligations, Parekh writes:

> He [Gandhi] rightly argues that every man owes his humanity to others, that he is a recipient of . . . indispensable and non-repayable gifts . . . and that his inherently unspecifiable moral duties and obligations extend far beyond those based on consent, promise, contract and the membership of a specific community. . . . The vast bulk of moral relationship stretches out to men and women in the community's remotest past and the most obscure corners of the globe.[17]

Gandhi's conception of human moral duties is also seen to enlarge and enhance the agenda of moral and political philosophy in the sense that it is required to go beyond liberalism's reduction of morality to 'reciprocal egoism and enlightened self-interest'.[18]

Gandhi also redefined religion in terms of spirituality or morality rather than theology.[19] Thereby, according to Parekh, he 'placed the individual at the centre of the religious search, liberated religion from the stranglehold of traditionalism and literalism, encouraged fresh readings of scriptures, and made space for an inter-religious dialogue'.[20] Gandhi's moral and political thought was generated through critical engagements with the Hindu, Buddhist, Jaina, Christian, Judaic and secular Western traditions, which he refused to see as closed and self-contained worlds and whose exclusivist claims he did not accept.[21] Recognising Gandhi's intercivilisational and inter-religious dialogical approach to be a needed corrective to liberalism's non-dialogical political perspective, Parekh writes: 'Gandhi's political theory cuts across several moral, religious and philosophical traditions and rests on an unusually broad philosophical foundation.'[22]

On Gandhi and intercultural dialogue

In his chapter 'Gandhi and the logic of reformist discourse',[23] Parekh analyses Gandhi's reformist discourse in a *satyagraha* campaign in 1925 against a practice of untouchability and unapproachability in the town of Vykkam in the then princely State of Travancore (presently part of Kerala). It was an effective practice of the caste Hindus at Vykkam to prevent the so-called untouchables from using the public roads passing by the sides of a temple. In the course of a *satyagraha* campaign against that practice of untouchability, Gandhi visited Vykkam and in a three-hour-long dialogue with the top leaders of the orthodox caste Hindus, he argued that it was contrary to the true spirit and teachings of Hinduism, justice, reason and humanity to exclude a section of Hindus from the use of the public roads that were used by caste Hindus, non-Hindus, dogs and cattle. When they refused to agree, he proposed arbitration, referendum or an examination of their preferred texts by reputed pundits. These proposals too were rejected. It was also his claim that he was a true *sānatanī* Hindu, in that he believed in the universal and eternal moral principles and values of Hinduism. This too had no effect. As Parekh notes, Gandhi did not hesitate to step out of the Hindu framework and make secular and rational appeals to morality and humanity.[24] So, although Gandhi started the dialogical process by engaging with and questioning the operative value system of the caste Hindus, he did not remain confined within that framework. His follow-up actions included meetings with the Regent Maharani, the young Maharaja and the Dewan of the State, and speeches before vast crowds of people. He also met the great social-religious reformer, Sree Narayana Swami Guru, who was promoting that *satyagraha* campaign. Parekh highlights the fact that Gandhi used a 'mixed mode of discourse', which combined elements of religion, fundamental or universal principles of ethics, critical reason, public opinion and so on. Thereby Gandhi could reach out to 'a very wide audience', which he could not have done if he had relied on a 'wholly rationalist mode of discourse'. As if in anticipation of his later characterisation of Gandhi as a patron saint of intercivilisational dialogue, Parekh writes: 'His mixed mode of discourse was perhaps the only mode of discourse possible in a society that was highly differentiated and deeply divided'.[25]

According to Parekh, mainstream liberal political theory is considerably insufficient for a multicultural society as it monoculturalises the public realm around a political conception of liberal justice, which is freestanding from, but tolerant of, multiculturality in the so-called private sphere of the citizens' lives. This liberal/Rawlsian framework of combining a monocultural, that is, liberal, public realm with a multicultural private realm should, in Parekh's view, be rethought. Otherwise, the dominant or majoritarian, monocultural public realm, given its state power, political respectability and resources, will overpower and marginalise those cultures that are confined to the private realm.

Liberal-individualist political theory errs, he says, by clinging to the flawed assumption that a 'culture helps individuals develop their capacity for autonomy, which then transcends it and views it and the wider world untainted by its provenance'.[26] Such culturally disembedded beings, says Parekh, do not exist anywhere in this world, in which every human being actually lives her or his life as a culturally embedded self. Liberalism's atomistic conception of the individual 'does not appreciate either his social embeddedness or the ontological and epistemological significance of the other'.[27] While rejecting what is untenable in liberalism, for example its atomistic and acquisitive view of the individual, privileging liberty over equality and neglect of human solidarity, he accepts what is valid and valuable in it, for example the values of human dignity, an area of personal privacy, constitutionally guaranteed rights, critical rationality and toleration.

For Parekh, the political imagination of any historical or cultural community of finite human beings has its limits; it represents only a partial realisation of human potentialities and possibilities. It is therefore necessary for every living culture to be in dialogue or interaction with other ways of life. Different cultures can thereby 'correct and complement each other, expand each other's horizon of thought and alert each other to new forms of human fulfillment'.[28] He recognises that even though liberalism privileges its way of life over other visions of the good life, it is considerably hospitable to cultural diversity. His *Rethinking Multiculturalism* is written from within the liberal tradition and, while remaining strongly committed to its great values, it goes beyond it by taking cultural diversity to be 'a vital human good' and calling for so designing our political and economic institutions as to foster dialogical engagements between different visions of the good life.[29] This, he adds, is for the human good of not only minority or denigrated cultural communities but of *all* the members of a multicultural society. He argues that:

> [a] moral and political discourse is conducted in different languages, the public reason is not homogeneous but plural, that the public realm should not be culturally neutral or bland but multiculturally oriented . . . and . . . we might . . . profitably explore a religiously sensitive form of secularism.[30]

In his view, the dialogically constituted public realm of a multicultural society rests on a robust form of social, economic and political democracy, which ensures that its 'constituent communities receive both just recognition and a just share of economic and political power'.[31]

Some of the Gandhian aspects of Parekh's complex, postcolonial multicultural political theory are brought out in the concluding part of the second edition of *RM*. In it, he notes that it was because of Gandhi's inter-religious ideas from Christianity, Judaism, secular Western thought, and so on, that he was led to ask critical questions about his tradition and to reform and regenerate it.[32] He also shows how by integrating the Hindu concepts of non-violence (*ahimsa*) and non-attachment (*anasakti*), the Buddhist notion of compassion (*karuna*) and the Christian concept of *caritas*, Gandhi constructed a novel idea of an active, positive and detached universal love.[33] Thus, although Gandhi was deeply rooted in his own religious tradition, he was also aware of its limitations, which he sought to remedy by learning from other religions. According to Parekh, he was determined to grow from truth to truth and his intercultural dialogue had no final terminus or dogmatism. 'Liberalism', Parekh writes, 'needs to develop a similar spirit of openness and self-criticism if it is to measure up to the moral and intellectual challenges of our globalizing age'.[34]

According to Parekh, intercultural dialogue is necessary in a multicultural society for resolving conflicts over cultural practices, for example polygamy and female circumcision. For the normative guidance of such a dialogue, he feels that it is necessary to begin that process by engaging with the operative public values of the society as a normative standard or framework of evaluation and possible agreement on the issues in question. He clarifies that the operative public values can be criticised, revised and even replaced. This he says is best done dialogically through appeals to universal moral values such as universally recognised human rights or to the core values of the society. In *NP*, as we shall see below, he develops and proposes three principles of global justice.

In the wake of the abhorrent atrocities of 11 September 2001 in New York, Parekh carried out a thought experiment of an imaginary dialogue between Gandhi and Osama bin Laden. On the basic similarities in their views, he notes that they were both deeply religious, anti-imperialist, critical of the Western pursuit of global hegemony of their own societies, and dismissive of the claim that Western civilisation represents the only or best form of the good life. Concerning their basic differences, Parekh writes: 'Gandhi cherished his religion and thought he had both a right and a duty to enrich it by borrowing the insights of others; for bin Laden, Islam is the definitive and final word of God whose purity he has a duty to safeguard.'[35]

Regarding their views on violence, Parekh states: 'Gandhi rejected violence and trained his followers in the art of non-violent resistance; bin Laden is an uncompromising champion of violence and has set up al-Qaeda camps to train his followers in the dark arts of terrorism.'[36]

Acting as a double role advocate for Gandhi and bin Laden and as an adjudicator between them, Parekh indicates the possibility of a dialogical narrowing of their differences. On terrorist violence and state-religion relationship, he notes that 'differences should narrow, though they would not disappear'.[37] An actual dialogue, he felt, would open up the possibility of self-criticism and self-improvement. He also sees a possibility that they would agree on the need of revitalisation and restructuring of Muslim societies through a prolonged process of education of the masses and work by social activists. He also sees a possibility that they could come to agree that the current US policy has an imperialist thrust and needs to be fought, and also that within the US itself many citizens are deeply unhappy with their government's policy, who, given their democratic set-up, can be seen to be in a position to play a progressive role.

According to Parekh, Gandhi has much to say to contemporary Muslim societies, which are dominated by Western powers with the collaboration of their domestic accomplices. His message to them, Parekh says, would be that the terrorist approach to resistance and liberation is self-defeating as

> [it] creates a legacy of hatred and self-perpetuating cycle of violence, leaves society at the mercy of a coterie of constantly changing masters, does nothing to get the society to take a critical look at itself, and excludes masses from the struggle for their emancipation.[38]

On global ethics and democratisation

In *NP*, Parekh's concern is with the substantive political principles required by our globalised world, in which far-flung societies are becoming parts of a system of interdependence in politics, economics, communications, defence, governance and democracy. This situation, he says, marks a new phase in human history; our feeling of human interdependence and solidarity, and our enlightened self-interest now depend on how people lead their lives in other countries. In this phase of global interdependence, Parekh sees a radical alteration of the context and the principles of the traditional idea of universal morality. Our moral obligations, he says, have now to be partly exercised at the personal/interpersonal level and partly mediated into or through political institutions at the domestic and international levels. We are increasingly required to view the whole of humankind as a moral community and adopt political principles to guide human relations within and between societies – principles that must respect both our common human identity and our different ethnic, cultural and other identities. Bringing out two interrelated aspects of our emerging moral consciousness, he writes:

> We feel, or should feel, concerned about the quality of collective life in other countries, and our efforts should be directed not so much at helping individuals as at assisting struggling societies to cope with their problems. And since we can help them effectively not by individual actions but by acting through our governments, our moral response too takes on a collective or political character.[39]

While acknowledging that individuals will continue to have duties to help others in their need, he emphasises that now those duties 'are also politically mediated and take the form of political communities helping each other directly or through international institutions'.[40] Taking this political mediation of our moral or human duties to be inescapable in our historical context, he argues that we need to recognise the collective nature of our moral life, and that our focus now needs to be 'not so much on the intentions, motives and inner lives of individuals as on the structures of social relations'.[41]

Accordingly, he prefers the term 'global ethics' to the older term 'universal morality', and formulates three principles of the former 'to guide our individual and in particular collective choices, and shape the structure and goals of global institutions'.[42] Those principles are: (1) the principle of equal human worth, which recognises that all human beings have equal claims to the promotion of their fundamental interests in their physical security, meeting their basic needs, having basic rights and liberties, and so on, and which imposes on us the duties not to harm others, to be helpful towards them, to tell the truth, and so on; (2) the principle of human solidarity, whereby humankind as a whole becomes our moral point of reference; and (3) the principle of respect for difference and plurality, whereby we appreciate the ontological and epistemological importance of other cultures, religions, and so on as our conversational partners and as a highly valuable condition of our own growth. These principles of global ethics are, according to Parekh, universally valid and they should guide the actions and choices of individuals and political communities, multinational corporations and international organisations. Striking a note of caution against any overemphasis on rights, he writes: 'A global ethics needs to be as specific in indicating who has what duties to whom, as it is in listing rights'.[43]

Even though there are only a couple of explicit references to Gandhi in *NP*, its perspectival interlinks with his moral and political philosophy are much in evidence. Notably, Parekh's principles of global ethics include such Gandhian norms and principles as the duty not to harm others, to tell the truth and to take the whole of humanity as an indivisible moral whole. That perspectival interlink also explains the common humanity and violence-reducing orientation of Parekh's ethical-political approach to democratisation in the world. Democratic governance, he maintains, is a universally valid political good that needs to be promoted not only outside the West but also within it.[44] The economic and political conditions of democracy also need to be generated or developed within each country for which a supportive international milieu is required. He finds the West's neo-liberal agenda and, in particular, the Bush Government's brazenly self-serving approach unacceptable. 'Promoting democracy', he points out, 'would have a greater chance of success if the West saw it not as an export but rather as a co-operative global project to be pursued in the spirit of partnership'.[45] Rejecting the hegemonic promotion of democracy currently favoured by the dominant groups in the West, he advocates what is basically a Gandhi-inspired approach to redefining the project of promoting democracy in the world 'as an expression of our shared humanity and the duties arising from it'.[46]

This Gandhian idea of 'our shared humanity and the duties arising from it' is explained in Parekh's books on Gandhi. For instance, he explains Gandhi's intercivilisational thinking on universal human moral duties in the following words:

[H]uman beings were necessarily interdependent . . . according to Gandhi. Individuals . . . realized their potential in a stable and peaceful society, made possible by the efforts of . . . anonymous men and women . . . In short, every human being owed his humanity to others, and benefited from a world to the creation of which he contributed nothing. . . .

Given that the debts could never be repaid . . . all that human beings could do was to 'recognise the conditions of their existence', and continue the ongoing universal system of interdependence by discharging their duties and contributing to collective well-being.[47]

It is this Gandhian conception of the universal system of human interdependence and its concomitant idea of the inseparability of right and duty that frame Parekh's violence-reducing ethical-political approach to democratisation. The present forms of global interdependence, he says, should heighten our sense of shared humanity, whereby we see other human beings not in their 'generalised otherness' but in their 'concrete particularity', who too, like us, have concerns, worries, pains, joys, struggles, and so on. In his view, our sentiment of humanity and affirmation of human identity have to find expression in our love or compassion for other human beings and in our recognition of their equal human worth.

Resuming my discussion of Parekh's political theory of global ethics, an aspect of its distinction from the traditional conception of universal morality may be taken note of here. With regard to the former, he writes that in the present context of global interdependence, the significant differences between political life and personal and interpersonal life need to be taken seriously, and that 'Political philosophy needs to do its own moral philosophy, addressing questions arising from within political life and developing appropriate concepts'.[48]

This conception of the specificity of political life and political philosophy appears to be problematic; specificity could mean either the separation or only a relative autonomy of political life from basic or common human morality. Actually, however, Parekh provides to avert any such separation or detachment; he not only includes basic principles of human moral conduct in the first of his aforementioned principles of global ethics but also stipulates that those principles are addressed to both individuals and the collectivities through which they act, for example political communities, international institutions and multinational corporations. He further clarifies that his principles of political ethics are also concerned with the virtues and qualities of character that human beings need to develop for coping with the challenges of globalisation. Humanity, he feels, has to be constituted as 'a single moral world with overlapping and mutually limiting concentric circles'.[49]

He endorses Gandhi's view that the personal and the political, though distinct, are inseparable.[50] Extending this view, Parekh states: 'A well-worked-out moral philosophy should respect both the relative autonomy of, and the necessary interdependence between, different areas of moral life.'[51] It is along this line of thought that he espouses Gandhi's ideal of a non-detachable relationship between basic human morality and political-institutional ethics.[52]

Accordingly, the individual-level or interpersonal human morality, which Gandhi emphasised, has to be seen now as having the added task of generating and sustaining the political mediation of the collective or institutional ethics, which, as shown by Parekh, has now become utterly indispensable.

Pertinently, in Parekh's critical remarks on the war on Iraq by the American and British governments, he raises the issues of a deficit in impartial and truthful information as well as the lies and half-truths that were told to justify that war of killing and destruction.[53] It seems to me that, against the backdrop of this calamitous deficit in collective ethics in government or, in other words, a tragic disconnect between the government and human morality in its society, Parekh's Gandhi-inspired principles of global ethics are highly relevant. Those principles, as we saw above, impose on governments, business, peoples and so on the duties not only not to harm, to render assistance and to tell the truth but also to take the whole of humankind as their moral point of reference. To show that those principles are not lacking in political realism, Parekh invokes Gandhi, who, according to him, thought of his moral vision not as an ideal to realise but 'as a moral compass with which to navigate one's way through life'.[54]

Conclusion

On 18 May 1908, speaking in a debate at the YMCA in Johannesburg on interracial relations in the British Empire, Gandhi distinguished the disruptive or dividing mode of encounter between civilisations and races from the uniting or combining mode of interactions between them. The latter mode, he said, is not only mutually advantageous to the combining parties but also good to the whole of humanity. Advocating the latter mode, he went on to say: 'If we look into the future, is it not a heritage we have to leave to posterity, that all the different races commingle and produce a civilisation that perhaps the world has not yet seen?' In the conclusion to that speech, he referred to the claims made on behalf of the so-called Mission of the Empire and raised the question, 'is it not as well that the millions of human beings should be trained for self-government?'[55]

Echoes of this Gandhian message of intercultural or cross-cultural commingling and democratisation occur in Parekh's work. For instance, he states that his dialogically constituted multicultural society 'sees itself both as a community of citizens and a community of communities, and hence as a community of communally embedded and attached individuals'.[56] He adds that for a non-coerced cooperative life in any multicultural society, its public institutions and public policies should find ways of recognising both the cultural embeddedness of individuals *and* their human interdependence and solidarity through and across cultural boundaries.

Almost all societies today, says Parekh, are multicultural and they face conflict over the values (and the practices based on them) of different forms of the liberal and non-liberal cultural traditions. While acknowledging that liberal political theories of multicultural societies are hospitable to cultural diversity, he notes that they are morally flawed in that they have a commitment to or tendency towards liberal monism, which abstracts away cultural differences.[57] He also rejects relativism because of its static and ghettoising nature. His preferred alternative to moral monism and relativism is a 'pluralist form of minimum universalism' of human values and principles, which can serve as universally valid normative standards for guiding intercultural dialogues, evaluations, judgements, agreements and cooperative living.[58]

For the cooperative life of multicultural societies, they, according to Parekh, require institutionalised dialogue between liberal and non-liberal cultures. This is indicated in his introductory statement (and reaffirmed in his concluding chapter) in which he points out that liberalism's theoretical basis for a multicultural society is morally inadequate, and goes on to add: 'We need to rise to a higher level of philosophical abstraction. And since we cannot transcend and locate ourselves in a realm beyond liberal and non-liberal cultures, such a basis is to be found in an institutionalised dialogue between them'.[59] His dialogically constituted multicultural society is formed and sustained not by any particular political doctrine but by 'the culture and morality of dialogue'. It includes such institutional preconditions as 'freedom of expression, agreed procedures and basic ethical norms, participatory public spaces, equal rights . . . and empowerment of citizens', and the political virtues of 'mutual respect and concern, tolerance, self-restraint . . . love of diversity . . . and a heart open to others' needs'.[60] Some of these institutional preconditions and political virtues were the main concerns in Gandhi's political discourses and struggles. They are also incorporated, as we saw in the previous section, in Parekh's three principles of global ethics, which constitute a normative framework for multicultural political-institutional dialogues, interactions and coming to mutual agreements.

Its perspectival continuity and limited sharing of substantive human values with Gandhi's moral and political philosophy and practice seem to contribute significantly to the compassionate, violence-reducing, truth-valuing and 'human solidarity' orientation of Parekh's political theory of intercultural dialogue and global ethics. Thereby Parekh's political theory is admirably geared to avoid or overcome the limits of ethnocentrism and relativism.[61] Equally importantly, his Gandhi-influenced, unusually knowledgeable and multiculturally commingling perspective on democratic governance and global ethics seems to be oriented to taking us, in a newly needed way, beyond Gandhi's time and his immediately contextual problematic and strategies.[62] Parekh maintains that his multicultural conception of 'global ethics' is not just a new name for the old 'universal morality', but its 'historically novel form in the unique context of our times'.[63] It is indeed a compassionate cross-cultural normative framework to guide the political-institutional mediations of some of our human responsibilities or duties under the present forms and institutions of global interdependence in economics, communications, environmental matters, governance and democracy.

Notes

1. In writing this contribution to this volume in felicitation of Bhikhu Parekh, I have drawn freely from T. Pantham (2001), 'Liberal multiculturalism reconsidered' (review of Bhikhu Parekh (2000), *Rethinking Multiculturalism: Cultural Diversity and Political Theory*, London: Macmillan), *Economic and Political Weekly*, 3–10 February: 462–4; and T. Pantham (2011), 'For a global ethic of pluralist universalism' (review of *Talking Politics: Bhikhu Parekh in Conversation with Ramin Jahanbegloo*, New Delhi: Oxford University Press), *Book Review*, 35:6 (June, 2011), pp. 3–5.
2. B. Parekh (2000, reprinted in 2006), *Rethinking Multiculturalism: Cultural Diversity and Political Theory* (abbreviation: *RM*), (2nd edition) (Basingstoke: Palgrave Macmillan); B. Parekh (2008), *A New Politics of Identity: Political Principles for an Interdependent World* (abbreviation: *NP*) (Basingstoke: Palgrave Macmillan).
3. B. Parekh (1989), *Gandhi's Political Philosophy* (Basingstoke: Macmillan), pp. 4 and 195–6.
4. B. Parekh (2004), 'Mahatma Gandhi and Osama bin Laden: an imaginary dialogue', in A. Lannstrom (ed.) *The Stranger's Religion: Fascination and Fear* (Notre Dame, IN: University of Notre Dame Press).
5. *RM*, p. 370.
6. Jahanbegloo, *Talking Politics*, pp. 91 and 107.
7. *RM*, pp. 126–7.
8. Jahanbegloo, *Talking Politics*, p. 32.
9. Ibid., p. 92.
10. Prior to his advanced studies at the London School of Economics, Parekh had taught for a couple of years in the Maharaja Sayajirao University of Baroda, Vadodara (hereafter MSU), where he became a regular member of a discussion group, the Renaissance Club,

led by Raojibhai Patel, a mathematician at the University, a fellow thinker, with M. N. Roy, in radical humanism. Patel was an intellectual catalyst, and was affectionately addressed as *Mota* (the respected elder). In 1981, Parekh interrupted his teaching career at the University of Hull to return to MSU as its vice-chancellor for a three-year term. During those years he, along with Raojibhai Patel, revived the dormant discussion group and kept it going in high gear with regular meetings held mostly at his official residence. Indian thought, in a very broad and open sense, was the theme of the discussions. Parekh's work *Gandhi's Political Philosophy* is dedicated to Raojibhai Patel. See also U. Baxi and B. Parekh (eds) (1995), *Crisis and Change in Contemporary India: Essays in Honour of Raojibhai Patel* (New Delhi: Sage); the latter's moving 'Foreword' to *Collected Works of Raojibhai Patel*, in which he proudly claims to be *Mota*'s *manasputra* ('intellectual son').

11. B. Parekh (1986), 'Some reflections on the Hindu tradition of political thought', in T. Pantham and K. L. Deutsch (eds) *Political Thought in Modern India* (New Delhi: Sage), pp. 17–31.
12. B. Parekh (1987), 'Gandhi and the logic of reformist discourse', in B. Parekh and T. Pantham (eds) *Political Discourse: Explorations in Indian and Western Political Thought* (New Delhi: Sage), pp. 277–91.
13. B. Parekh (1989), *Colonialism, Tradition and Reform: An Analysis of Gandhi's Political Discourse* (New Delhi: Sage Publications).
14. Parekh, *Gandhi's Political Philosophy*, p. 4.
15. Ibid., pp. 149 and 199.
16. B. Parekh (2001), *Gandhi: A Very Short Introduction* (Oxford University Press), p. 63.
17. Parekh, *Gandhi's Political Philosophy*, p. 197.
18. Ibid., p. 197.
19. B. Parekh (1989), *Colonialism, Tradition and Reform: An analysis of Gandhi's Political Discourse* (New Delhi: Sage Publications), p. 95.
20. Parekh, *Gandhi: Very Short Introduction*, p. 48.
21. *RM*, p. 371.
22. Parekh, *Gandhi's Political Philosophy*, p. 195.
23. Parekh, 'Logic of reformist discourse', pp. 277–91.
24. Ibid., p. 287.
25. Ibid., p. 289.
26. *RM*, p. 110.
27. Jahanbegloo, *Talking Politics*, p. 59.
28. *RM*, pp. 167 and 338–9; Jahanbegloo *Talking Politics*, p. 63.

29. *RM*, pp. 369–70.
30. Ibid., p. 370.
31. Ibid., p. 340.
32. Ibid., p. 370.
33. Ibid., pp. 370–1.
34. Ibid., p. 372.
35. Parekh, 'Gandhi and bin Laden', p. 54.
36. Ibid., p. 54.
37. Ibid., p. 73.
38. Jahanbegloo, *Talking Politics*, p. 109.
39. *NP*, p. 206.
40. Ibid., pp. 206–7.
41. Ibid., p. 207.
42. Ibid., p. 227.
43. Ibid., p. 226.
44. On Parekh's views on problems of democratisation in India, see B. Parekh (2006), 'Limits of the Indian political imagination', in V. R. Mehta and T. Pantham (eds) *Political Ideas in Modern India: Thematic Explorations* (New Delhi: Sage); Jahanbegloo, *Talking Politics*.
45. *NP*, p. 277.
46. Ibid., p. 278.
47. Parekh, *Gandhi: Very Short Introduction*, pp. 51–2; Parekh, *Gandhi's Political Philosophy*, pp. 149 and 197.
48. Jahanbegloo, *Talking Politics* p. 42.
49. *NP*, p. 238.
50. Parekh, *Gandhi: Very Short Introduction*, p. 28.
51. Jahanbegloo, *Talking Politics* p. 43.
52. In this connection, see also T. Pantham (1983), 'Thinking with Mahatma Gandhi: beyond liberal democracy', *Political Theory*, 11:2 (May), pp. 165–88; reprinted in T. Pantham and K. L. Deutsch (eds) *Political Thought in Modern India* (New Delhi: Sage, 1986), pp. 325–46; and T. Pantham (1995), 'Gandhi, Nehru and modernity', in U. Baxi and B. Parekh (eds) *Crisis and Change in Contemporary India*, pp. 98–121; A. Parel (2011), 'Gandhi and the state', in J. Brown and A. Parel (eds) *The Cambridge Companion to Gandhi* (Cambridge University Press), pp. 154–72.
53. *NP*, p. 277.
54. Parekh, *Gandhi: Very Short Introduction*, p. 115.
55. See M. K. Gandhi (1962), *Collected Works of Mahatma Gandhi* (New Dehli: Publications Division, Government of India), 8, p. 246.

56. *RM*, p. 340.
57. Ibid., pp. 11–12.
58. Ibid., p. 127; *NP*, p. 207.
59. *RM*, pp. 14 and 369.
60. Ibid., p. 340.
61. See T. Pantham (1987), 'Habermas's practical discourse and Gandhi's Satyagraha', in B. Parekh and T. Pantham (eds) *Political Discourse: Explorations in Indian and Western Political Thought*, pp. 292–310 (reprinted from *Praxis International*, 6:2, July, pp. 190–205); T. Pantham (1996), 'Post-relativism in emancipatory thought: Gandhi's *Swaraj* and *Satyagraha*', in D. L. Sheth and A. Nandy (eds) *The Multiverse of Democracy* (New Delhi: Sage), pp. 210–29.
62. On a valuable distinction between the thematic and problematic levels of Indian nationalist thought, including Gandhi's thought, see P. Chatterjee (1986), *Nationalist Thought and the Colonial World: A Derivative Discourse?* (New Delhi: Oxford University Press), Chapters 2 and 4. For a critical examination of his reading of the problematic of Gandhi's intervention, see T. Pantham (1995), *Political Theories and Social Reconstruction: A Critical Survey of the Literature on India* (New Delhi: Sage), pp. 83–7 and 105.
63. *NP*, p. 207.

3

National Identities and Moving Beyond Conservative and Liberal Nationalism

Varun Uberoi

Many now note how national identities are controversial when used to justify secession, dangerous when equated with race, but valuable when used to foster unity among citizens otherwise unknown to one another.[1] Such identities are thus difficult to ignore due to their controversial nature, difficult to endorse due to their dangers and difficult to oppose due to their value. It is thus unclear what we should think about national identities and while some political theorists show us how to reduce their dangers and realise their value, other political theorists disagree with them.[2] But theorists on either side of this debate do not examine Bhikhu Parekh's work on the Indian and English 'character', British identity, nationalist discourse and much else, and in this chapter I argue that they should. I will show that the way that Parekh thinks about national identities is distinct, as the way he depicts how these identities should be conceived, given importance and related to other ideas of nationhood such as 'nations' and 'nationalism' differs from other thinkers, and has benefits as it avoids the difficulties that other thinkers encounter. Indeed, I will also show that many thinkers can use Parekh's way of thinking about national identities, and British politicians who discuss such identities can too.

But how could this distinct and beneficial way of thinking from Parekh go unnoticed? Three factors interlink to help to explain this. First, this way of thinking begins to appear in texts by Parekh in the 1970s when, *inter alia*, membership of the European Economic Community, minority nationalism and mass immigration led Parekh and others to question what Britain now was, and whether its identity could be 'preserved'.[3] Second, Parekh's work on national identities continued over many decades but we only see glimpses of it in his well-known books like *Rethinking Multiculturalism* and *A New Politics of Identity* as they were about other subjects and thus said only small amounts about national identities. Third, these books focus on why it is implausible to think only one way of life is fully human and best, why cultural diversity and intercultural dialogue are valuable and much else that makes Parekh a well-known 'multiculturalist'. And despite the value that many 'multiculturalists' explicitly attach to national identities political theorists, politicians and journalists suggest otherwise.[4] Those interested in national identities may thus assume that a 'multiculturalist' like Parekh has not written much that is positive about national identities, and thus they can ignore the small sections on this topic in his well-known books and need not search beyond these books either.

Yet when searching for Parekh's texts relating to national identities we find that many are book chapters, review articles, essays, pamphlets and published lectures. These texts contain arguments that Parekh was 'trying out' and examples that provoke thought and suggest insight but were never fully developed. These texts thus require some interpretation to illuminate the significance of their contents more clearly than Parekh did, so as to avoid the danger of dismissing ideas until we have been presented them in a more defensible form. To do so I will, at times, clarify Parekh's arguments using my own terms and examples, develop and extend distinctions in new ways, connect arguments that he did not connect and make them more consistent than he did himself, so as to also make them more defensible. Similar techniques are explicitly used by Parekh himself[5] and by others.[6] This is because such techniques enable us to see the nature and significance of a thinker's ideas had they the time, inclination and energy to be clearer or more consistent, or to circumvent and anticipate criticisms. I will thus use Parekh's texts to distinguish the benefits of how he conceives, gives importance to and relates national identities to other ideas of nationhood from how other thinkers do so.

As there is no need to distinguish the benefits of Parekh's way of thinking about national identities from those thinking about something else, the other thinkers are *not* Isaiah Berlin, Elie Kedourie or Ernest Gellner. Such thinkers focused on the intellectual, psychological, functional and other sources of nationalism.[7] They mention national identities but say little about how these identities *should* be conceived, given importance and related to other ideas of nationhood. This is also true of Jürgen Habermas who seeks to substitute ideas of nationhood with his own ideas[8] and Maurizio Viroli, Martha Nussbaum and Seyla Benhabib who do the same but using older traditions of political thought, such as republican patriotism or cosmopolitanism.[9] Instead, those examining how national identities should be conceived, given importance and related to other ideas of nationhood are political theorists who are often referred to as 'conservative nationalists', like Roger Scruton,[10] or 'liberal nationalists', like David Miller and Yael Tamir.[11] I will thus distinguish Parekh's ways of thinking about national identities from those of conservative and liberal nationalists. But these two types of thinkers will be shown to address the same subject as Parekh so differently that distinguishing their ideas from his requires no detailed exegesis of conservative and liberal nationalist works. And for this reason, I need say only a little to introduce such nationalist thinkers here.

The presuppositions, philosophical approaches, arguments and thus political positions of each conservative and liberal nationalist thinker usually differ. But as we might expect, such thinkers usually refer to themselves as conservatives or liberals and these traditions of thought shape how they think about ideas of nationhood.[12] For example, the Burkean idea of polities being a 'partnership' between the living, the dead and the unborn[13] shapes the way a conservative like Scruton understands nations, as he describes them not only as those who share territory, history, and institutions, but descent and fate too.[14] Likewise, the liberal ideal that comes from Kant, J. S. Mill and others of an individual who 'chooses' his life 'plan for himself'[15] makes Ernest Renan's notion of nations constituted by 'consent' and a '*desire* to live a common life'[16] attractive to liberals like Miller or Tamir who endorse it.[17]

Once shaped by conservative and liberal traditions of thought, ideas of nationhood are endorsed by these thinkers too, so much so that Scruton, Miller and Tamir argue, in different ways, that nations should be preserved through forms of 'self-rule' and by them constituting states.[18] In doing so, these conservative and liberal thinkers advocate forms of what many call 'national*ism*'[19] and are thus classified, and often classify themselves, as conservative or liberal national*ists*.

I will thus consider the ideas of conservative and liberal nationalists alongside Parekh's and I do so in order first to distinguish the benefits of how Parekh conceives of national identities and how he relates them to ideas of nation and nationalism. Second, I do so to distinguish the benefits of how Parekh discusses the importance of national identities. Third, I conclude by discussing how Parekh's way of thinking about national identities can be used by various other thinkers who write about such identities, and by British politicians too.

What are national identities?

There are, at least, two ways in which we think and talk about national identities. First, as the identity of a political community and thus, for example, Britain, France, Canada or America's identity and second as an identity of a person that they might exhibit when they say they feel 'British', 'French', 'Canadian' or 'American'.[20] Conservative and liberal nationalists do not distinguish between the two, and the former also ignore that whatever else national identities are, they are identities. Liberal nationalists do not make this mistake, but they often do not say what identities are even when they discuss them.[21] In comparison, Parekh's work suggests that we cannot be clear about what national identities are in these two senses until we are clear about what identities are; thus he begins with how he conceives of identities.[22]

Parekh's understanding of identities is complex and is summarised in other chapters.[23] But briefly, it would be rare and strange to ask about the 'identity' of a vegetable, of a table, of history or of a garden. We might ask what these things are and what defines them, but we seldom use the term 'identity' when we do so as we reserve this term for human beings. We thus ask about the identity of a person or of the racial, religious, national and other groups they often comprise and, when we do, we are asking what they are.[24] To know this is to know what constitutes them, which in turn can allow us to discern how they differ from others. The differences between two people or groups of people may also help to illuminate what each of them is. Yet either way their differences are logically distinct to what they are and when we ask about the identity of a particular *person*, we often do so in two ways.[25]

First, we might ask about their 'overall identity' and what they are as a whole, yet we have trouble knowing this about a person.[26] Self-reflection seldom prevents us surprising ourselves and others, and what we are also changes. But while we and others have trouble knowing what we are as a whole, we and they often know parts of what we are hence we discuss, for example, our racial, religious and sexual identities. But being a commuter or a reading group member may also be part of what we are, and it is odd to claim our identities include being a 'commuter' or a 'reading group member'. This is because our identities usually depict only those parts of us that we think help to constitute us, as without them we could not be what we are. Hence, if someone ceases to be heterosexual, a Muslim, a man or an artist they might think themselves to be a different person. Others might too and we seldom think this of being a commuter or of being part of a reading group as these are not parts of us that constitute us.[27]

Everything that we are does not constitute us, and what we think does will change and is not the same for everyone. Thus a religious person may think their faith constitutes them until they lose it and become like those who never thought this about themselves. A person might find it hard to judge what does or could constitute them. But others may not, hence one friend may say to another that he is really a 'writer' not a journalist and a state might make history classes mandatory so as to encourage children to see themselves as 'British'. Our identities need not only be what *we* think constitutes us, but also what others think does or should.

Something similar is true when we discuss the identity of Britain, France, Canada, America and so on. National identities here depict the people that make these political communities what they are. As such an identity focuses on people it can refer to features like their race or culture, which can shape their political concerns, for example, about immigration.[28] But the people of a political community would also not be what they are without the history in which they created their political institutions, their political ideals, the traditions of political thought and behaviour that they use to pursue collective goals and conduct their collective affairs.[29] Such features help us to conceptualise what makes the members of a political community what they are just as people's religious beliefs, types of liturgy, notions of God and so on help us to conceptualise what makes them the religious community that they are. Thus despite, at times, emphasising solely 'politico-institutional' features, Parekh came to note how we use many features to discern what the members of a political community are. In doing so, we achieve a 'more or less coherent conception' of them,[30] and such a conception can be held by those who are not members of a political community; thus de Tocqueville offered a conception of America and Rousseau had one when writing about Poland.

Likewise, when a person says they have, for example, a British, French, Canadian or American identity they are saying that their political community helps to shape and constitute what they are thus they may also say they *are* 'British', 'French', Canadian' or 'American'. And they might feel shaped and constituted by their political community as its legal, political and educational institutions regulate their behaviour and help to shape their understanding of what is normal and acceptable. They are partly, yet unavoidably, shaped and constituted by their political communities. Thus we might say that while people constitute political communities, political communities also constitute people. Hence, when someone says that they feel British they are not just saying that they feel part of a political community, but that they also sense how it influences what they are thus they may discuss 'their Britishness' too.[31]

But people cannot say that they feel British, French, Canadian, American and so on without some conception of Britain, France, Canada and America. This conception is often more vague than clear thus politicians, journalists, philosophers and historians often try to clarify it. Again, this conception may focus on the race, culture and history of a political community, their political ideals, institutions, norms and so on, all of which are often interpreted in different ways. Thus some may see Canada as 'bicultural' others as 'multicultural' and some equate England with Britain; others do not. Thus these conceptions are often shared with only some other members of a political community and not as we share a cake by dividing it, but as two or more people share an opinion. But if conceptions of Britain, France, Canada or America are unavoidable when people say that they feel British, French, Canadian or American and so on, then the two ways in which we think and talk about national identities are not mutually exclusive.[32] National identities in both of the senses that Parekh distinguishes between entail a conception of a political community.

But such a conception need not be of the relatively morally, ethnically and culturally uniform political communities that we call 'nations'.[33] Those political communities that once could have been much more morally, ethnically and culturally uniform often no longer are and have become what Habermas calls 'post-national'[34] and Parekh refers to Britain in this way.[35] Liberal nationalists often suggest that nations need not be so uniform, as nations are merely those who share a history, traditions, a willingness to live a collective life and language institutions, norms and values that help to govern their collective affairs.[36] But this seems like a description of a political community in general that could easily refer to the Athenian *polis*, the Roman *civitas* or medieval kingdoms,[37] none of which are usually thought of as nations.[38]

Liberal nationalists may note that something must make an identity 'national' and this is surely a nation, which is seemingly why liberal nationalists also often clarify what national identities are by first defining and defending what nations are.[39] But 'national' need not imply a 'nation' when we refer, for example, to 'national negotiations' over a trade treaty or a 'national representative' like a prime minister. In such examples 'national' can refer simply to a political community and the same seems true of what we usually call national identities. This is why so many can disagree about whether America, Canada and Britain are 'really' nations[40] but this does not deter discussions about these political communities' identities or people in them having American, Canadian and British identities. When we refer to national identities, 'all we have in mind'[41] is the identity of a political community – and, for example, America's identity – or the identity its members have when they recognise that their political community helps to shape them and make them, for example, American.

Unlike conservative and liberal nationalists then, Parekh sees the two ways that we usually think and talk about national identities as, for example, the identity of Britain and someone having a British identity. He also sees how specifying the nature of both requires some understanding of identities, but not of nations. [42] Yet Parekh also saw how the 'national' in 'national identities' misled many to link the latter to nations, thus Parekh toyed with not using the term 'national identity'.[43] He thus wrote about replacing this term with other ones, yet he had also written about how few understood those, like Michael Oakeshott, who in his later work replaced familiar terms with unfamiliar ones to convey exactly what he meant.[44] And Parekh also studied how people were often convinced using 'idioms' that they were familiar with. Unfamiliar terms carried dangers, and retaining but explaining familiar ones like 'national identity' had benefits, but this does not make Parekh a nationalist in the sense I referred to earlier. We saw above that Parekh does not suggest that people *should* constitute nations. Nor does he advocate the 'self-rule' of nations and them constituting states as Scottish and Welsh nationalists, for example, do.[45] Parekh does not advocate the national*ism* that is usually necessary to be seen as a national*ist* and is thus not what we would usually call a 'nationalist'. Yet he suggests national identities are important in a distinct way that I will now examine.

The importance of national identities

Parekh does not accord importance to national identities as conservative nationalists might. Thus Parekh does not claim that conceptions of a political community are an 'eternal' view of it that its living members *have* just as its unborn members *will* and its dead members *had*.[46] What members of a political community are, and what they think they are, changes over time, thus Britain is not what it was a century ago and few British people today would deny this. Parekh also rejects the conservative nationalist view that such identities convey 'life's meaning' as it is unclear how they make sense of life's 'contingencies' and 'tragedies',[47] or how they can, in Hegel's famous terms, reconcile a person to the world.

However, liberal nationalists are right to claim that choice pre-supposes something to choose with. But liberal nationalists also suggest that national identities aid our choices[48] yet they refer to the norms, values, traditions of thought and behaviour of a national culture as doing so. It is obvious how the norms, values, traditions of thought and behaviour of, for example, an English culture might be what a person uses to make choices but it is not obvious why their English identity is used in this way, and Parekh does not make such claims.

Further, for Parekh, national identities need not foster the 'soli-darity', 'obligation' and 'trust' that enable people to redistribute their income as liberal nationalists hope.[49] This is because whether national identities foster these things is an empirical issue and liberal nationalists accept this thus they show how national identi-ties must be conceived to examine this empirical issue.[50] But they do *not* specify what 'solidarity', 'trust' and 'obligation' are, what forms of them are needed, what our indicators for them are and how we disaggregate national identities as stimulating them from other stimuli. Thus unsurprisingly, evidence to support this empiri-cal claim is inadequate, as liberal nationalists themselves admit.[51] At times, some liberal nationalists thus appear to avoid this claim as they may well see its difficulties, and Parekh does the same.[52]

Instead, for Parekh, the importance of national identities stems from the fact that they are identities that people exhibit when they say they are 'British', 'French', 'American' or 'Canadian' and so on. A person acknowledging such an identity aids their self-under-standing of why, at times, they think and behave as they do. Such an identity also helps them to describe themselves to others.[53] But we saw how those who say they are 'British', 'French', 'American' and 'Canadian' and so on sense they are shaped by their political community and this makes these identities politically important for the following reason.

Many in a political community will sense they are shaped by it as its legal, political and educational institutions seldom focus on just a few of them.[54] Many in a political community will thus also say they have national identities and see themselves, for example, as 'American'. Such people will have differences and disputes but those who see themselves, for example, as 'American', see themselves as a group just as those who share a religious identity as, for example, being 'Muslim', or a sexual identity, as being 'gay' might. And the members of a political community must see themselves as a group if they are to conceive collective goals and accept collectively binding decisions.[55] Most political communities require this from their members and national identities *help* to meet this need.

Other things also help the members of a political community to see themselves as a group and Parekh discusses them.[56] But as I am focusing on Parekh's discussion of national identities we can note a similar political importance if such identities are conceptions of political communities. This is because people cannot say, for example, that they feel 'British', 'French', 'American', 'Canadian', and so on without some conception of Britain, France, America and Canada. Thus people have such conceptions, but these conceptions are often vague. Yet when a person's conception of their political community is clear it helps them to discern which aspects of it they wish to improve, celebrate or 'live up to',[57] as they can visualize a group they are part of. This again *helps* them to conceive collective goals and accept collectively binding decisions with other members of their political community.

But if members of a political community do not see themselves as 'British', 'French', 'American', 'Canadian' and so on then being part of such a group is less important to them as is having a clear conception of their political community. Yet the members of a political community still need to see themselves as a group and as national identities aid this, those who govern political communities often now ask how such identities can be encouraged.[58] But no government can force people to see themselves as 'British, 'French', 'American', 'Canadian' and so on without an 'unacceptable level of coercion' and 'perhaps' not even then.[59] Likewise, no government can promote a single conception of a political community without running the risk of it seeming artificial and imposed to those who think about their political community differently. Members of a political community will have different conceptions of it as they unavoidably interpret it using their experiences, religious and political views and other forms of knowledge all of which vary greatly between people.[60] This cannot be prevented and can be beneficial. Differing conceptions of a political community may contain different insights and the presence of those with different conceptions as well as discussions between them can improve people's knowledge of their political community.

Governments can, however, use education curricula to teach children that it is difficult to avoid being shaped by their political community's legal, political and educational institutions. It is thus more than likely that there will be something 'British', 'French', 'American', 'Canadian' and so on about them. Governments can also use publicly funded education, media and the arts to promote the various different ways that, for example, Britain is seen by British people. This differs to a government simply offering a single conception of a political community and discussing it as instead many different conceptions of it are being promoted. This helps those with vague conceptions of their political community to find ones they agree with or that they can combine parts of so as to arrive at their own conception. It shows those with clearer conceptions of their political community that their conception of it is not the only one, may exclude much and illuminates what they can still learn about their political community.

But conceptions of a political community in which it is, for example, solely 'White' and 'Christian' must also be discouraged as unsurprisingly racial and religious minorities are thus seen as outsiders even though they are citizens. Such conceptions exacerbate the discrimination and exclusion of racial and religious minorities and are discouraged by anti-discrimination laws, the promotion of race-equality and multicultural education in schools. This is because such measures, over time, help to change people's impressions of what is permissible in a political community which means their conceptions of it must have altered. Likewise, such conceptions are discouraged by giving 'public status' to the languages, norms and values of minorities.[61] Legal and political institutions cannot operate without language, norms and values and as these must come from a group, such institutions cannot be neutral between groups. But if legal and political institutions declare the political community to be, *inter alia*, multicultural, as Canada did, and if they deliver public services in different languages, more inclusive conceptions of it are encouraged and ones that exclude minorities are discouraged.

Conservative nationalists do not discuss such government measures and while liberal nationalists subtly discuss how to discourage conceptions of a political community from excluding minorities, they do not discuss the measures above as doing so.[62] Liberal nationalists also do not discuss government explicitly promoting the various ways a political community can be conceptualised or showing children that they will be shaped by their political community. Parekh's reasons for national identities being important thus avoid the more questionable claims of conservative and liberal nationalists and can help us to justify government measures to encourage national identities that such nationalist thinkers do not discuss. Thus Parekh's discussion about why and how national identities can be important is again distinct and beneficial, as was, we saw, his discussion about what these identities are.

Conclusion

Parekh's distinctive way of thinking about national identities means that unlike conservative and liberal nationalists he identifies two ways in which we talk and think about national identities. He sees how specifying the nature of both requires some understanding of identities but not of nations and says little about the importance of nations having 'self-rule' or constituting states. He thus does not advocate what many call national*ism* which is usually necessary to think of someone as a national*ist*. Uniquely, Parekh advocates national identities without nations and nationalism and does so without attaching the questionable forms of importance to such identities that conservative and liberal nationalists do. He thus provides a way to think about national identities that scholars who focus on them should not ignore.

But scholars who might want to make use of Parekh's work are unlikely to be conservative nationalists, as there are fewer of them than there once were. However, there are many political theorists who call themselves liberal nationalists and, like them, Parekh agrees that national identities are important and can be inclusive. But he is clearer about what these identities are and can show more plausibly than liberal nationalists why they are important. Liberal nationalists may thus benefit from expanding upon Parekh's political thought to address the relationships between national identities, citizenship, national and global justice, what rights immigrants are entitled to and so on.[63] Parekh has said less about these issues. But as national identities are central to what liberal nationalists say about them they need clear ways to describe what such identities are and why they are important, and Parekh may provide these.

Parekh's work may also be important for critics of liberal nationalists. Such critics seek to escape the need for national identities and can argue that citizens only need to 'possess a sense of belonging to a polity' in the sense that they 'identify with *it*' and see it as 'theirs'.[64] But a citizen sensing he belongs to a polity presupposes he has some conception of it and thus perhaps a national identity in Parekh's sense. And if citizens should 'identify' with their polity and see it as theirs,[65] then this might occur if they are shaped and constituted by it which is what Parekh thought fostered a person's national identity. Escaping national identities in the senses that Parekh discusses seems difficult. Similarly, those criticising liberal nationalists who are interested in Habermas's notion of the 'post-national' may benefit from Parekh's work.[66] After all, Parekh agrees that political communities that were once seen as nations often no longer are, but he shows why we need not take the next step of rejecting national identities by showing why the latter are not as connected to nations as some think.

Social scientists may also benefit from studying the aspect of Parekh's political thought that I have focused on in this chapter. After all, social scientists often agree with much of what political theorists of multiculturalism argue, but not with their discussion of national identities[67] which can be unclear or can defer to liberal nationalist ideas.[68] Likewise, such social scientists might associate homogeneity and nationalism with national identities, and are often scared of being seen as nationalists. Yet I hope we can now see a clearer way to think about national identities than political theorists of multiculturalism have provided to date. It neither defers to liberal nationalists nor is it associated with homogeneity or national*ism*, hence endorsing it need no more make a person a national*ist* than it does Parekh.

Similarly, politicians in Britain may also want to study and learn from Parekh's work. It can justify, as we saw, policies that promote both the importance of people's national identities in Britain and different conceptions of Britain too. Likewise, Parekh's work also helps to justify goals that British politicians now advocate. This is because, as Tariq Modood and I have shown elsewhere, many leading politicians today talk about 'reimagining' 'Britishness' so that it is more inclusive.[69] They do so, just as the Canadian Federal Government once sought to promote a more inclusive conception of Canada[70] and just as Parekh once advocated in the Commission for Multi-Ethnic Britain that he chaired.[71] Of course, the fact that such politicians can also talk about more 'muscular forms of liberalism' may mean they endorse inclusive forms of 'Britishness' for liberal nationalist reasons just as some public intellectuals explicitly claim they do.[72] But if this is occurring, it is unclear how these politicians avoid the difficulties of liberal nationalist ways of thinking I have discussed, and if this is not occurring, Parekh's work offers such politicians a more plausible basis upon which to advocate 'Britishness' being more inclusive that avoids such liberal nationalist difficulties.

Acknowledgements

I am grateful to Andrew Mason, Tariq Modood, Bhikhu Parekh and Elise Rietveld for their comments on this chapter. I presented a draft at the University of California Berkeley and I am grateful for Mark Bevir and Jonathan Seglow's incisive questions and to Richard Ashcroft for inviting me.

Notes

1. D. Miller (1995) *On Nationality* (Oxford: Clarendon Press). Miller's pioneering book begins with just this claim as does Yael Tamir's (1993) *Liberal Nationalism* (Princeton: Princeton University Press). See also T. Modood (2013), *Multiculturalism* (Cambridge: Polity), pp. 136–7.
2. Tamir, *Liberal Nationalism*; Miller, *On Nationality*. For criticisms of such thinkers' works, see A. Abizadeh (2002), 'Does liberal democracy presuppose a cultural nation? Four arguments', *American Political Science Review*, 96:3; A. Mason (2012), *Living Together as Equals* (Oxford: Oxford University Press); and A. Mason (2000), *Community, Solidarity and Belonging* (Cambridge: Cambridge University Press).
3. See J. Plamenatz (1974), 'Preserving the British way of life', in B. Parekh (ed.) *Colour Culture Consciousness* (London: Allen & Unwin).
4. B. Barry (2002), *Culture and Equality* (Cambridge: Polity), p. 77. See also V. Uberoi (2008), 'Do policies of multiculturalism change national identities?' *Political Quarterly*, 79:3.
5. See the second unnumbered page of the introduction of B. Parekh (1982), *Marx's Theory of Ideology* (London: Croom Helm).
6. G. A. Cohen (1978), *Karl Marx's Theory of History: A Defence* (Oxford: Oxford University Press), p. xvi.
7. See I. Berlin (2003), 'The bent twig: on the rise of nationalism', in *The Crooked Timber of Humanity* (London: Pimlico); E. Kedourie (1998), *Nationalism* (Oxford: Blackwell); E. Gellner (1983), *Nations and Nationalism* (Oxford: Blackwell).
8. See the short discussion by J. Habermas (1998), 'The European nation-state: on the past and future of sovereignty and citizenship', in *The Inclusion of the Other* (Cambridge: Polity), pp. 107–110, 117–20. See also Andrew Mason's important recent book, A. Mason (2012), *Living Together as Equals* (Oxford: Oxford University Press), pp. 178–83.
9. None of these thinkers are opposed to national identities but to nationalism and they say little about national identities specifically. See M. Viroli (1995), *For Love of Country* (Oxford: Oxford University Press); S. Benhabib (2008), *Another Cosmopolitanism* (Oxford: Oxford University Press); M. Nussmaum (1996), 'Patriotism and cosmopolitanism', *For Love of Country* (Boston, MA: Beacon Press).

10. R. Scruton (1990), 'In defence of nation', in J. Clark (ed.) *Ideas and Politics in Modern Britain* (London: Macmillan).

11. Miller, *On Nationality*; Tamir, *Liberal Nationalism*. For those referring to these scholars as liberal and conservative nationalists see Miller, *On Nationality*, pp. 124–30; B. Parekh (1999), 'The incoherence of nationalism', in R. Beiner (ed.) *Theorizing Nationalism* (Albany, NY: State University of New York Press), pp. 296–308. T. Soutphommasanne (2012), *The Virtuous Citizen* (Cambridge: Cambridge University Press), p. 9.

12. Miller, *On Nationality*, p. 1; Tamir, *Liberal Nationalism*, p. 1; R. Scruton (2003), *The Meaning of Conservatism* (Basingstoke: Palgrave Macmillan (2001), p. 4.

13. E. Burke (1996), 'Reflection on the revolutions in France', in D. Wootton (ed.) *Modern Political Thought: Readings from Machiavelli to Nietzsche* (Oxford: Hackett), p. 572.

14. Scruton, 'In defence of nation', pp. 305–6.

15. J. S. Mill (1990), *On Liberty* (Oxford: Oxford University Press), p. 65.

16. E. Renan 'What is a nation?' in V. Pecora (ed.) (2001), *Nations and Identities* (Oxford: Blackwell), p. 175. Emphasis added.

17. Miller, *On Nationality*, pp. 22–5; Tamir, *Liberal Nationalism*, p. 33.

18. Miller, *On Nationality*, p. 81; Tamir, *Liberal Nationalism*, p. 57. In Scruton, *In Defence of Nation*, he seems to reject nationalism: see p. 304 and R. Scruton (2006), *Arguments For Conservatism* (London: Continuum), p. 16. But throughout the latter although he accepts the importance of nation-states, he endorses the importance of nations having states, explicitly on pp. 21 and 25, and is thus a nationalist in the sense described.

19. Here I follow Kedourie, *Nationalism*, p. 67. But Gellner (*Nations and Nationalism*), who disagrees with parts of Kedourie's work, defines nationalism in a similar way on p. 1 of his famous book, as does A. Smith (2002), *Nationalism* (Cambridge: Polity), p. 9.

20. B. Parekh (2008), *A New Politics of Identity* (Basingstoke: Palgrave Macmillan), p. 56. These two ways of discussing national identities can also be seen in. B. Parekh (1974), 'Postscript', *Colour, Culture Consciousness* (London: George Allen & Unwin Ltd), p. 230.

21. Yael Tamir is the exception here, but Kymlicka does not say what identities are when discussing national identities, nor does Miller. See W. Kymlicka (1995), *Multicultural Citizenship* (Oxford: Oxford University Press), p. 189; W. Kymlicka (2002), *Introduction to*

Political Philosophy (Oxford: Oxford University Press), p. 265; Miller, *On Nationality*, pp. 43–5.

22. B. Parekh (1995), 'The concept of national identity', *New Communities*, 21:2, pp. 256–7. B. Parekh (2000), 'Defining British national identity', *Political Quarterly*, p. 5.

23. See Raymond Plant's chapter in this volume for an excellent summary of Parekh's position on identities.

24. Parekh, 'Defining British national identity', p. 6.

25. Parekh, 'Concept of national identity', p. 256.

26. Parekh, *New Politics of Identity*, p. 9.

27. Ibid., p. 8.

28. Parekh, 'Defining British national identity', p. 7.

29. Ibid. Parekh, 'Concept of national identity', p. 256. Parekh, *Rethinking Multiculturalism*, p. 230.

30. For references to national identity as a 'conception', see Parekh, 'Discourses on national identity', p. 492. For Parekh's over-emphasis on political features, see his *Rethinking Multiculturalism* but this position was altered after Tariq Modood's insightful criticism. See my introduction to *Multiculturalism Rethought* (Edinburgh: Edinburgh University Press, 2015).

31. Parekh finds the term 'Britishness' vague but I think the way I have used it here seems intuitively plausible. See. B. Parekh (2008), 'Being British', in A. Gamble and T. Wright (eds) *Britishness* (Oxford: Wiley Blackwell), p. 33.

32. Ibid., p. 56.

33. Parekh, 'Reporting on a report', p. 695.

34. J. Habermas (1998), *The Inclusion of the Other* (Cambridge, MA: MIT Press), p. 219.

35. Parekh, 'Reporting on a report', p. 695.

36. See Kymlicka, *Multicultural Citizenship*, p. 189; Kymlicka, *Introduction to Political Philosophy*, p. 265. W. Kymlicka and M. Opalski (eds) (2001), *Can Liberal Pluralism Be Exported?* (Oxford: Oxford University Press), p. 19; Miller, *On Nationality*, pp. 22–7; D. Miller (2001), 'In defence of nationality', *Citizenship and National Identity* (Cambridge: Polity), pp. 27–31.

37. These are examples that Parekh used to describe a polity but I use these examples in a different way to him. See B. Parekh (1996), 'Citizenship and political obligation', in P. King (ed.) *Socialism and the Common Good* (London: Frank Cass), p. 263.

38. This liberal nationalist way of conceiving nations also often *seems* 'thicker' than they claim as moral and cultural differences are

seen as threatening and as something to limit, tolerate, and not value. Hence all prominent liberal nationalists suggest that immigration should be restricted, as it is a source of such differences. D. Miller (2005), 'Immigration: The case for limits', in A. Cohen and H. Wellman (eds) *Contemporary Debates in Applied Ethics* (Oxford: Wiley-Blackwell), p. 200; W. Kymlickla (2001), *Politics in the Vernacular* (Oxford: Oxford University Press), p. 219; Tamir, *Liberal Nationalism*, p. 74.

39. Miller, *On Nationality*, p. 18; Kymlicka, *Introduction to Political Philosophy*, p. 265; Soutphommasane, *Virtuous Citizen*, p. 71; Scruton, *Arguments For Conservatism*, pp. 16–17.

40. See Miller, *On Nationality*, p. 141; F. Bechhoffer and D. McCrone (2007), 'Being British: A Crisis Over Identity', *The Political Quarterly*, 78:2, p. 253.

41. Parekh, 'The concept of national identity', p. 255.

42. Miller, *On Nationality*, p. 18; Kymlicka, *Introduction to Political Philosophy*, p. 265, Soutphommasane, *Virtuous Citizen*, p. 71; Scruton, *Arguments For Conservatism*, pp. 16–17.

43. Parekh, 'Concept of national identity', p. 255.

44. M. Oakeshott (1975), *On Human Conduct* (Oxford: Clarendon Press), p. 108.

45. It is not that Parekh is unconcerned with ideas of self-rule, but it is unclear what rests on a political community being a nation to be granted it. For those who want 'independence' from a colonial master Parekh noted that they may need no better reasons than a person may need to give as to why they should not be a slave. They can cite a history of mistreatment and exploitation and a long history of their own in which they governed themselves and national minorities like some Quebecans may perhaps do the same. Liberal or conservative nationalists have not proved that the arguments about self-rule required political communities to be nations and the arguments for self-rule are more plausible if political communities are nations. See B. Parekh (1989), *Gandhi's Political Philosophy* (Basingstoke: Macmillan), p. 191.

46. Parekh, 'Discourses on national identity', p. 503; Parekh, 'Concept of national identity', p. 264.

47. B. Parekh (1999), 'The incoherence of nationalism', in R. Beiner (ed.) *Theorizing Nationalism* (Albany, NY: State University of New York Press), pp. 309–10.

48. D. Miller (2006), 'Nationalism', in J. S. Dryzek, B. Honnig and A. Phillips (eds) *The Oxford Handbook of Political Theory*

(Oxford: Oxford University Press), p. 535; Kymlicka, *Multicultural Citizenship*, pp. 89–90.

49. Miller, *On Nationality*, pp. 83, 91, 92; D. Miller (2013), *Justice for Earthlings* (Cambridge: Cambridge University Press), p. 90; Tamir, *Liberal Nationalism*, p. 110.

50. D. Miller and S. Ali (2014), 'Testing the national identity argument', *European Political Science Review*, 6:2.

51. Miller and Ali, 'Testing the national identity argument', pp. 240, 254; A. Abizadeh (2002), 'Does liberal democracy presuppose a cultural nation? Four arguments', *American Political Science Review*, 96:3, pp. 495–509.

52. Kymlicka, *Politics in the Vernacular*, pp. 209, 212.

53. *RM*, pp. 219, 230.

54. Parekh, *A New Politics Of Identity*, p. 56.

55. Parekh, *Rethinking Multiculturalism*, pp. 219, 230.

56. See *RM*, pp. 196–238.

57. Ibid., p. 231.

58. V. Uberoi and T. Modood (2013), 'Has multiculturalism in Britain retreated?' *Soundings* 53:1; Uberoi, V. and Modood, T. (2013b) 'Inclusive Britishness: a multiculturalist advance', *Political Studies*, 61:1.

59. Parekh, *Rethinking Multiculturalism*, p. 196.

60. Parekh, *A New Politics of Identity*, p. 60.

61. B. Parekh (1990), 'Britain and the social logic of pluralism', in Commission for Racial Equality (ed.) *Britain: A Plural Society: Report of a Seminar* (London: Commission for Racial Equality), p. 70.

62. Miller, *On Nationality*, p. 142; D. Miller (2008), 'Immigrants, nations and citizenship', *The Journal of Political Philosophy*, 16:4, p. 380. See the excellent chapter by W. Kymlicka (2001), 'Western political theory and ethnic relations in Eastern Europe', in Kymlicka and Opalski (eds) *Can Liberal Pluralism Be Exported?*, pp. 54–8. W. Kymlicka and K. Banting (2006), 'Immigration, multiculturalism and the welfare state', *Ethics and International Affairs*, 20:3, p. 301 come close though their claim remains different.

63. D. Miller (2007), *National Responsibility and Global Justice* (Oxford: Oxford University Press); Soutphommasane, *Virtuous Citizen*.

64. Mason, *Living Together*, p. 181, emphasis added; see also A. Mason (2000), *Community, Solidarity and Belonging* (Cambridge: Cambridge University Press), p. 127.

65. Ibid.

66. Abizadeh, 'Cultural nation? Four arguments', pp. 495–509.
67. Modood, *Multiculturalism*, pp. 135–9.
68. W. Kymlicka (2001), 'From enlightenment cosmopolitanism to liberal nationalism', in *Politics in the Vernacular* (Oxford: Oxford University Press), pp. 210, 219; Kymlicka and Opalski (eds), *Can Liberal Pluralism be Exported?*, p. 21; Modood, *Multiculturalism*, p. 196.
69. Uberoi and Modood, 'Has multiculturalism in Britain retreated?'; Uberoi and Modood, 'Inclusive Britishness'.
70. V. Uberoi (2008), 'Do policies of multiculturalism change national identities?' *Political Quarterly*, 79:3.
71. T. Modood (2014), 'Multiculturalism and Britishness: provocations, hostilities and advances', in R. Garbaye and P. Schnapper (eds) *The Politics of Ethnic Diversity in the British Isles* (Basingstoke: Palgrave Macmillan), pp. 21–37.
72. Goodhart, *British Dream*, p. 285.

Part II

Elucidating and Addressing Multicultural Dilemmas

4

At the Borders of Otherness: Tracing Feminism through Bhikhu Parekh's Multiculturalism[1]

Monica Mookherjee

Introduction

The last twenty-five years have witnessed important shifts in the relationship between feminism and multiculturalism. Broadly, the 1990s saw 'Third World' and post-colonial feminists such as Uma Narayan,[2] Chandra Mohanty,[3] Gloria Anzaldua[4] and Gayatri Spivak[5] raising incisive criticisms of the failure of liberal multiculturalism to make sense of gender relations across different cultures and nations.[6] Drawing attention to the reliance of 'metropolitan' liberal theories on old colonial notions of cultural difference, post-colonial feminists contested what they viewed as this tradition's essentialist view of culture, or its tendency to view non-Western traditions as 'objects of consumption in a pluralist intellectual marketplace'.[7] Liberal multiculturalism could only support token representations of women in cultures outside the mainstream, they seemed to warn. Yet, to reject liberal humanism altogether appeared an extreme and destructive measure; and the question persisted as to whether a more productive relation between feminism and multiculturalism could be conceived. Fortunately, at this time, radical democratic feminist writer Iris Young offered some hope. In a significant challenge to the uniform rights and interests assumed by modern political thought, Young reconceptualised the public domain to attend to the voices and experiences of diverse groups. Her groundbreaking essay, 'Polity and group difference',[8] and subsequent works,[9] recommended a shift from universal citizenship laws to a differentiated model, in which groups were encouraged to express their unique identities, while still upholding the common good. Briefly, Young believed that a feminist challenge to traditionally 'masculine' political values, such as militaristic honour, competition and a lack of emotion, would respond to the need to respect all forms of diversity, including those relating to gender and culture.

While Young's insights were evidently crucial, by the end of the decade the prospect of an alliance between feminism and multiculturalism again appeared at risk. This time, a notable challenge came from liberal feminist Susan Okin,[10] who argued that differentiated citizenship, with its special minority rights and exemptions, threatened feminist ideals. Thus, liberal feminist commitments to gender equality would often, she argues, involve rejecting cultural claims. While Okin resisted assuming an inevitable conflict between multicultural and feminist claims,[11] she drew attention to forced marriages, female circumcision and restrictive dress codes in immigrant groups to illustrate her fears. Yet Okin's seemingly combative tone appeared to many to confirm earlier post-colonial concerns about liberal humanism; and in the years since her essay numerous feminists have endeavoured to reconceptualise the feminism–multiculturalism relation. Some have drawn on deliberative democracy,[12] others on autonomy,[13] and others still on ideas of power sharing.[14] Thus, the creative research of recent years highlights the fact that the contested relationship between these movements poses difficult questions with no simple solution. The post-colonial concerns of earlier times endure as essential problems to confront.[15]

In the context of this wealth of recent scholarship, it is surprising not to find sustained examination of how Bhikhu Parekh's multicultural thought may act as an intellectual resource for feminism, suggesting how the two movements may be integrated. In particular, it is surprising that feminists have not drawn upon his emphasis on reflective dialogue to negotiate the feminism–multiculturalism relation in a way that would speak to the tensions in this debate. In this chapter, I attempt to fill this gap by explaining how Parekh's commitment to an intercultural dialogue might inform an approach that I label 'border-tracing' feminism. I aim to show that Parekh's illuminating claims in *Rethinking Multiculturalism*[16] respond to some of the unresolved post-colonial concerns about liberal humanism noted here, by showing how feminism and multiculturalism need not exist in inevitable tension, but in a dynamic mutual dialogue. The key claim is that, while multiculturalism may pluralise feminism, feminism may limit multiculturalism and humanise it; and that these projects might be pursued in tandem. The idea of such an integration of feminism and multiculturalism may be developed by focusing on Narayan's[17] concerns about the problematic borders that are often assumed in debates about minority women, the nature of which will be clarified fully as the chapter unfolds.

It suffices to note for now that problematic distinctions and borders are often drawn in the existing feminism–multiculturalism debate: borders between cultures; between cultural insiders and outsiders; between cultural and women's rights; and between well-being and harm. In this regard, the danger is that feminist voices within minority groups are too readily dismissed as 'Westernised', and that certain harms are viewed as 'cultural' rather than as matters of politics or economics.[18] Parekh's path-breaking project to rethink simple accounts of multiculturalism, I argue, encourages thinking across these borders. His approach promotes a conception of the feminism–multiculturalism relation that takes knowledge about human interests, goods and rights as dynamic, provisional and shaped by cultural interactions. Avoiding harmful cultural stereotypes, he contends instead that 'each culture carries bits of the other within itself and is able to conduct a critical dialogue with itself, a necessary condition for a meaningful dialogue with "the other"'.[19] Feminism without tracing borders would lose this dynamic, provisional and progressive ability to learn from the encounter with cultural diversity. It would fail to forge an alliance with multiculturalism that enhances social justice for women and men alike, and rejects 'hierarchies of oppression'.[20]

With these points in mind, this chapter proceeds as follows. The first section identifies the concerns motivating border-tracing feminism, and the resources that Parekh's multiculturalism offers in this respect. The three substantive sections that follow draw more deeply from Parekh's thought to present two complementary dimensions of border-tracing feminism, which establish feminism and multiculturalism as mutually transformative movements. The first dimension of this approach involves a commitment to expanding an understanding of rights to well-being, by exploring Parekh's idea of a bifocal dialogue in the context of debates such as the Muslim veil. The second dimension draws from Parekh's theory of 'pluralist universalism' to highlight how this expansion of rights might be pursued in tandem with the search for intercultural understanding of the issue of oppression. In this sense, for Parekh, the feminist focus on vulnerability and oppression sets humanist limits on the cultural diversity that may be tolerated. These limits are understood by tracing – that is, recognising and investigating – unstable borders of (actual or presumed) cultural difference.

Tracing borders? Women's rights, cultural rights and Parekh's intercultural dialogue

In attempting to highlight the role of border questioning in this debate, it is worth opening by considering a recent account that appears to engage in this task. Sarah Song's compelling book *Justice, Gender and the Politics of Multiculturalism* (2007)[21] considers how cultures often inter-penetrate to reinforce patriarchy. While her insights are significant, they also reveal the need to question borders more comprehensively than even she proposes. For, as Lamont and Molner observe, borders or boundaries often define insiders and outsiders.[22] The assumption of a border can exclude certain people, or it may include them in problematic ways. In doing so, such a border may be highly misrepresentative. Narayan drew attention to this problem in relation to dowry killing many years ago.[23] She argued that these deaths are often represented by Western feminists as violations peculiar to Indian society, in a manner that diverts attention from their similarity to 'Western' domestic violence.[24] Similarly, Gayatri Spivak describes the tendency to conceive other cultures as absolutely different as part of the 'silencing of the subaltern', the figure marginalised from the dominant perspective and language of justice.[25]

While Song is highly ready to question cultural borders, the difficulty is that her account may remain prone to some such issues of silencing and misrepresentation. For instance, she contends that, in the USA, majority cultures have at times reinforced gender injustice in minorities by allowing cultural defences for domestic violence.[26] The problem that she notes is not only that of cultural stereotyping,[27] but also that the deep rationale for these stereotypes is often more complicated than meets the eye. In the case of the cultural defence, one has to consider liberal society's own covert tolerance of private sphere violence. Song thereby counters the tendency to hold minorities uniquely responsible for gender injustice, by arguing that 'what constitutes gender subordination and how best to address it will not be self-evident'.[28] Now, while Song seems to raise urgent questions about the 'inside' and 'outside' of cultural groups in an era of intense global migration, her judgements appear to depend on assuming further borders between cultural rights and women's rights. Notably, her belief that the values of democratic participation and autonomy provide clear reasons to challenge injustice[29] may appear questionable in this regard. For, in supporting the 'qualified recognition of Mormon polygamy',[30] she contends that, if women have freely chosen to remain in polygamous marriages, and if they are free to leave, the state should recognise their unions. While appearing an equitable solution, her account raises the question of why the values of autonomy and free association should decide the issue of state intervention.

My suggestion is that, if we wish truly to integrate feminism and multiculturalism as allied movements, it is necessary to question not only the identity of the group but the values that inform our judgements. The matter is complex, not only because it will often be impossible fully to specify any group's values, which are likely to be vague and conflicting. The problem is equally that feminist judgements in an age of multiculturalism cannot involve a simple attempt to discover empirically what cultural 'insiders' believe.[31] Rather, it is necessary critically to question and contest the borders noted above. As Narayan explains:

> We need to move away from a picture of … cultural contexts as
> sealed rooms … with a homogenous space 'inside' them, inhabited

by 'authentic insiders' who all share a uniform account of their institutions and values. Third World national and cultural contexts are as pervaded by plurality, dissension and change, as are their 'Western' counterparts. Both are often replete with unreflective and self-congratulatory views of 'their' culture and 'values' that disempower and marginalise the interests of many members of the national community, including women.[32]

Taking these problems seriously promises a politically and culturally relevant form of feminism. Such a feminist approach would for instance concede that, while the secular culture of British law recognises abstract, gender-neutral rights promoted by international norms,[33] alternative cultural conceptions of gender may sometimes justify different rights.[34] Of course, feminists have long debated whether women's rights should oppose or recognise gender differences,[35] even before de Beauvoir so compellingly argued that norms and ideals of femininity tend to cast women outside authentic humanity.[36] The issue is all the more complex in today's multicultural settings, as images of the 'Exotic other female'[37] are often associated with women's subjection to fundamentalist regimes.[38] A multicultural, border-tracing feminism would therefore ask how far multiculturalism supports gender justice, and how far feminist insights may enrich multiculturalism. In other terms, how may multiculturalism pluralise feminism? And may feminism in turn limit multiculturalism in a critical but mutually productive encounter?[39]

Bhikhu Parekh's illuminating thought offers a key resource in this respect.[40] His revision of multiculturalism as a critical, open-minded dialogue supports a creative integration of feminism and multiculturalism by showing that these movements need not conflict, but may enrich one another. This is not to say that tensions will not arise; but that there is scope for each movement to prompt the other to reshape its self-understanding. This is so on account of two features of Parekh's philosophy. The first is his *theory of culture* and the other his *theory of intercultural evaluation*. As we shall see, Parekh opposes a simple understanding of cultural difference; and the open-minded dialogue that he recommends to render cross-cultural judgements counters the tendency to assume a fixed scheme of cultural and women's rights. By discussing these two aspects of Parekh's thought in this section, I emphasise the importance of Parekh's philosophy to the border-tracing project developed in this chapter.

In regards to theorising culture, although Parekh holds that our shared condition generates common capacities and emotional dispositions that may ground universal rights, these capacities only acquire meaning, he claims, through cultural traditions that organise the significance of such rights differently. A culture's morality emanates from a complex historical experience, which inevitably includes interaction with other traditions as well as internal debates. Each culture is thus unique, and cannot be compared with another on a single scale; but this does not mean that cultures are absolutely opposed. Each tradition must recognise its own limitations and seek engagement with others to inspire and expand itself. Going beyond the liberalism of, say, Isaiah Berlin,[41] owing to his experience as an immigrant in Britain and his knowledge of Indian traditions of thought, Parekh charges liberalism with failing to reflect on the limitations of its own world-view. Such reflection is necessary because liberalism does not 'represent the last word in human wisdom'.[42] Connectedly, it is crucial owing to the need to question the absolute truth of charters like the Universal Declaration of Human Rights, as they were generally not formed through a fair dialogue between cultural groups.[43]

The second aspect of Parekh's thought that seems promising in relation to this debate is his *theory of intercultural evaluation*. According to this account, practical judgements may be made only through a 'bifocal' dialogue, which encourages deliberation on contentious issues in multicultural societies both within and between cultural groups.[44] Parekh charges many writers in the feminism–multiculturalism debate with a failure to highlight such a dialogical approach. Okin,[45] according to Parekh, ignores the different levels of cultural interaction; and by concentrating too heavily on extreme cases, fails to engage with the real challenges of intercultural evaluation and judgement.[46] Shachar's[47] approach, based on power sharing between minorities and the state (notably, 'transformative accommodation'), fails equally to envisage the state's greater power to define the right and the good,

and thus does not ask how its power might be mitigated by dialogue.[48] In contrast, Parekh wishes to encourage both minorities
and the state to expand their self-understanding through deliberation. It is not sufficient to offer cultural rights to disadvantaged
groups so long as they adhere to contentious liberal values like
autonomy.[49] Rather, what is necessary is a dialogical questioning of fixed borders between liberals and non-liberals; between
members and non-members; between cultural and women's
rights; and between well-being and harm, as we shall discover in
more depth shortly.

For now, I supplement my account with a few crucial obser-
vations about Parekh's views on gender justice. First, and in
line with his theory of cultural diversity, he is unconvinced that
gender justice is reducible to liberalism, because different cultural
forms organise gender relations differently. 'It is one thing to say
that women should enjoy equal dignity and rights', he writes,
'but an altogether different thing to say that they should also be
equally autonomous, free to challenge their social roles, uncon-
strained by the subtle controls of patriarchal cultures'.[50] Yet this
is not to say that a culture's views about gender are set in stone,
because through dialogue one might question dominant liberal
approaches to sex equality, *and* scrutinise the meaning of gender
relations within minorities. To insist on a fixed realm of women's
rights would therefore be as limited and unreflective as dismissing
these rights entirely for their historically masculine or 'Western'
bias. In effect, while Parekh believes that universal judgements
about gender oppression can be made, feminism's dynamic
engagement with multiculturalism may inspire and expand its
horizons. Intercultural dialogue, Parekh believes, 'is likely to generate radically novel ways of conceptualising and structuring
intergender relations that cannot but deepen and broaden the
hitherto somewhat parochial feminist sensibility'.[51] Thus, the aim
is to multiculturalise feminism, and to 'feminise' multiculturalism, by 'transform[ing] the universally hegemonic and boringly
homogenous patriarchal culture that damages both women and
men alike'.[52]

As a final preliminary, it is worth emphasising that, in Parekh's
understanding, both feminism and multiculturalism appear to be

critical projects, in that neither involves simple deference to exist-ing beliefs and practices. While he is not explicit about the nature of feminism, multiculturalism is an open-minded but deeply moral project, which rejects all forms of 'monism', or narrow single-mindedness about the good life. In this regard, Parekh's pluralism seems to draw from aspects of the Indian tradition, such as Gandhi's social thought. Specifically, Parekh's empha-sis on intercultural learning seems to reflect Gandhi's advocacy of non-violent engagement with those who contest one's own truth.[53] While the connection between the Gandhian notion of non-violence (*ahimsa*) and intercultural dialogue is too complex fully to explain in this chapter, it seems true that Parekh, like Gandhi, wishes to claim that each tradition may contain a frag-ment of truth, but always requires engagement with others in order to respond to new dilemmas of the age. If this is right, it is easier to understand his thought that non-Western, non-liberal societies may contain accounts of women's well-being from which the liberal tradition could learn. For instance, Parekh observes that, in some cultures, women 'are treated as inferior when young or unmarried but are revered and enjoy superiority when they reach a certain age, become grandmothers, lead virtuous lives, or display unusual qualities'.[54] Given these insights, it seems promis-ing to draw from Parekh's thought a possible integration of femi-nism and multiculturalism as mutually sustaining projects. The door appears open to a form of feminism that might build 'com-munities of resistance' across class, race, culture, and ethnicity,[55] and a form of multiculturalism that seeks insight into the nature of gender justice and injustice.

Multiculturalising feminism across borders: towards a positive expansion of women's rights

As we shall see, the border-tracing feminist approach proposed here includes two interactive 'strands'. I begin by introducing the first of these in this section, by examining Parekh's *bifocal* multicultural dialogue for a means to relocate the borderline between cultural and women's rights. This repositioning is ethi-cally important, because it expands a shared understanding of women's rights to well-being through a positive engagement with cultural difference.

The two levels of Parekh's dialogue, namely debate *within* a community and *between* communities, encourage participants to engage with the values of different cultures, while also examining their own. Feminists are prompted to question their own understanding of gender justice, while asking: 'How am I naming [the other woman]? How does she name me?[56] Bifocal dialogue is supposed, in effect, to challenge old stereotypes of 'ancient patriarchy versus modern sex equality'.[57] Yet it is controversial too; and indicates that the task of multiculturalising feminism, while potentially enlightening, will not be a straightforward matter.

For consider Parekh's bifocal dialogue in relation to issues like the Muslim veil. The recent debates on this issue in secular European countries revealed tensions not only between different groups, but should, according to Parekh, also trigger conversation between group members over key human interests, goods and rights. The internal dialogues that ensue are important, as they inform collective conclusions on sensitive issues in the wider society. Parekh's analysis here shows how, in France particularly, the constitutional debates about the veil might have drawn more from the perspectives of French immigrant women, some of whom adopted the symbol while their mothers had abandoned it. 'The widely shared belief that the *hijab* reinforces female subordination', Parekh writes, 'ignores its complex cultural dialectic'.[58] Dissent in this case reveals that 'traditional at one level, the *hijab* is transgressive at another'.[59] The varied meanings that Muslim women attribute to this symbol reflect different understandings of the individual rights and cultural goods at stake in assessing this practice.[60]

While recognising this point does not in itself establish a particular conclusion about the veil, it emphasises that the different positions taken by Muslim women may reflect the conception of justice and the good life found in their traditional gender identity. While it would be impossible fully to survey all Islamic approaches to gender relations in this chapter, it is significant that they are internally diverse: some Islamic feminist views are inward looking, focusing on sacred texts, and others are influenced by external (secular or liberal) sources. To this extent, a definite borderline between Islamic and other feminisms is difficult to locate, as Islam has interacted with different traditions over time.[61] Fatima Mernissi,[62] a well-known Islamic feminist scholar, challenges male dominance in the history of the Middle East to contend that Islam favours parity and gender-neutral rights, not equality by separation, by focusing on Islamic figures like Sukayna, who campaigned against the *hijab* and for monogamous marriage.[63] While the textual reinterpretation (*itjehad*) suggesting that the veil is unjustified, as well as that by scholars who support the veil,[64] may appear rather intellectualised,[65] the views about women's rights that it yields demonstrates the plurality of 'insider' perspectives, which are useful for feminism in that they may disclose insights about gender justice in a religiously appropriate way, without alienating traditional group members. It can also encourage communication between cultural insiders and outsiders, and thus encourage fresh debates about the location of the borderline between cultural autonomy and women's rights to well-being.[66]

A further example on which Parekh focuses, namely arranged marriage in British Asian communities, reinforces the ethical value of the overlapping inter- and intracultural dialogues that he recommends. While governments are, he claims, justified in restricting marriage contracted 'under duress as defined in a culturally sensitive manner',[67] uncompromising defences of women's rights to autonomy in this debate risk mischaracterising many women as misled or as victims. These assumptions fail to take seriously those who sincerely find autonomy self-indulgent, or connected with sexual promiscuity and loss of dignity.[68] Parekh's apparent commitment to the deep aims of both feminism and multiculturalism recognises Bhabha's insight that 'Asian and Middle Eastern feminists ... have been deeply engaged in those contradictions of the liberal tradition that become particularly visible in colonial and post-colonial contexts, and carry over into the lives of diasporic or migratory communities'.[69] Since Parekh views feminism as 'perspectival' rather than cultural diversity,[70] as it challenges a society's biases from within, the dialogue he recommends highlights the internal contestations that occur in most cultures over gender roles, which are rarely insulated from external influences.

Of course, some traditional members would inevitably find such a dialogue troubling, and may ask whether the focus on 'women's rights' is not an alien concept, or whether it is necessarily liberal and Western and therefore inauthentic. The clearest response to this point is to emphasise Parekh's view of multiculturalism as a movement for justice, rather than uncritical celebration of all norms. That is, Parekh may be interpreted to mean that, if all cultures change and adapt, and if there should be no 'hierarchy of oppressions', multiculturalism might recognise, and interact positively with, feminism.

Multiculturalising feminism through well-being rights: three areas of moral learning

I would suggest three specific ways, on examination, in which Parekh's bifocal dialogue may pluralise feminism, and critically expand collective insights about rights to well-being and human flourishing. First, while Western feminists have long disagreed over the rights necessary to address gender disadvantage,[71] Parekh's dialogue promises to raise greater feminist awareness of the different ways that cultural traditions might *prioritise* particular aspects of well-being. To return to the issue of arranged marriages, one might concede that many women do not fully and freely consent to their unions in the robust sense required by the defence of autonomy in Article 16(1) of the Universal Declaration of Human Rights. However, rather than dismiss the value of their unions,[72] and claim that the women involved are misled for not valuing autonomy, it is plausible to think that women in arranged marriages use their traditional status to exercise a certain agency or control over their lives.[73] Moreover, while they may not *prioritise* a life of autonomy, they often act in ways that sustain the values that they do rate highly, such as privacy and family life.[74]

To be sure, strong forms of autonomy conceived as 'self-authorship' or 'self-creation' may be rejected by some conservative traditions.[75] However, without understanding how values are balanced, prioritised and traded off in different societies, feminists would fail to appreciate the well-being that women might gain through their traditional practices.[76] The issue is obviously complicated, however. For instance, veiling often enables women to earn an independent income and to pursue employment and education; and it is therefore important to question the stereotyped notion that the practice necessarily *denies* well-being. However, it is also true that women's choices to reject their inherited traditions can be seriously limited by economic burdens and domestic responsibilities. Furthermore, women's voices might be manipulated within intracultural dialogues; and we shall return to the issue of oppression and domination presently. The point is therefore controversial, but hope remains that engaging with cultural diversity can bring to light the particular priorities that women place in different aspects of well-being, which might lead to an expanded understanding of their rights to a good, flourishing life. Considering these priorities in a morally serious way questions the idea of 'patriarchal tradition versus progressive modernity'.

A different feminist benefit of Parekh's bifocal dialogue lies in its potentially creative expansion of cultural *interpretations* of well-being. The possibility of uncovering alternative interpretations of positive rights serves to destabilise assumed borders between cultural autonomy and women's rights, and between well-being and harm. This is not to say that multiculturalism is only valuable insofar as it pluralises feminism, as there may be many reasons for valuing diversity aside from its potential for feminism. However, the point emphasised here is that Parekh's dialogue integrates feminism and multiculturalism, as two important movements for justice, by demonstrating how alternative traditions could be more progressive in their interpretation of some important rights, such as to labour and autonomy, than Western liberal discourses.

A good example here is the notion of gender complementarity, which is central to Hindu and Christian thought, but which has been perhaps most debated recently within Islam. Gender complementarity is the admittedly controversial idea that men and women operate in harmony because their skills dovetail, and that, as such, they inhabit separate but equal spheres of activity.[77] While this idea seems anathema to some Western feminists,[78] who believe their battle for sex equality is still to be fully won, it could be suggested that complementarism supports extensive rights of women to life choices outside the home, and to dignity within it, and, thus, that it has socially progressive implications. For instance, the fact that men in Islam have financial responsibility for the home is thought by some scholars to yield a more substantive right than women enjoy in Western democracies to choose between a career or domestic responsibilities. That is to say, if women's traditional role as caretakers of the household leads to valuing domestic work and women's contributions to the economy through 'home-working', the norm may redefine the meaning of labour rights to incorporate both motherhood and the home as legitimate arenas of economic activity.[79] Therefore, however controversial it may seem initially, women's rights to labour and employment under Islam may be conceived as more radical than those conferred by Western constitutions. In the latter, rights are typically gained by contributing to the public economy, in which women still do not participate equally. On this socially progressive interpretation, Islamic conceptions of women's rights to well-being transcend the Western public/private dichotomy in productive ways. In Katherine Brown's words, this interpretation of their rights promises to 'transform the patriarchal bargain as formulated in advanced capitalist states'.[80]

Border-tracing feminists would need to consider these claims critically, however. While they seem at first to redraw the borderline between cultural autonomy and women's rights, Brown concedes that the claim that Muslim women enjoy extensive rights to labour and autonomy may overlook the fact that many immigrant households struggle to fulfil their basic needs.[81] A broader difficulty may be that secular Islamic feminists ultimately tend to support a strong public–private distinction. While seeming to endorse women's access to the public sphere, they defend norms of complementarity in the home. These ideals, Karin van Nienwkerk argues,[82] depend on notions of male dominance and female dependency that are not genuinely liberating, as the routes they provide for women's entry to the public sphere are comparatively restrictive. This point highlights the complexity of border-tracing feminist dialogues. The project would have to assess in which cases asserting the legitimacy of traditional gender roles is largely strategic, that is, in decentring unhelpful stereotypes; and when they genuinely redefine the moral border between cultural autonomy and women's rights.

The final way in which Parekh's intra-cultural dialogue 'multi-culturalises' feminism focuses on how, through dialogue, it may be revealed that traditional gender roles possibly enhance *concrete protection* of women's rights. For it is plausible to think that social support for traditional gender roles may enhance women's dignity as the necessary psychological condition of liberation or non-domination. This idea has a long history. Women have historically invoked the female virtues central to their cultures, including intellectual strength, truth seeking, tenacity, integrity, commitment and intelligence, to contest their oppression.[83] In this sense, some Islamic feminisms share much in common with womanist discourse in African–American theology,[84] in drawing on norms of femininity that, by highlighting stories of strength, endurance and courage, enhance women's own self-understanding as rightholders. In this sense, different cultural conceptions of gender assist to 'decolonise [women's] minds and affirm their heritage'.[85]

Yet feminists should be mindful that such notions could be used in oppressive ways to justify gender segregation and seclusion, which would be controversial,[86] and probably not conducive to feminist projects in any community. Accordingly, the dialogue inspired by Parekh would scrutinise claims to enhance dignity through such images for their political risks. For instance, a dialogue about gender relations in contemporary Indian society might highlight the fact that traditional images of women played a key role during the pre-Independence period, where women linked their cause to anti-imperialist struggles and the search for an authentic national identity, invoking ideals of Hindu womanhood, including duty, caring, tolerance and non-violent struggle,[87] in ways which were genuinely beneficial to women. However, as Rajeswari Rajan warns,[88] the more recent 'goddess-oriented' Hindu feminisms, which draw on cultural icons like Kali, Laksmi and Durga, have been taken up by aggressive fundamentalist movements that are not progressive for women. Rather than accept gendered cultural images uncritically, then, border-tracing feminism would examine them for their specific strategic investments.

To summarise: on the approach proposed here, debates about the priority, interpretation and protection of women's rights to well-being would be considered during the intercultural dialogue, in an effort to expand feminism's horizons through the engagement with cultural diversity. If multiculturalism is taken as a critical rather than a complacent project, the border-tracing project drawn from Parekh's commitment to the two-level dialogue would combine his commitment to rethink the conditions for intercultural coexistence with an open-minded search for the well-being of all members, including women. This integration unsettles received ideas of cultural outsiders and insiders; and it strives creatively to redraw the border between cultural and women's rights to positive well-being. The result would be a politically relevant and mature feminism, which cautiously recognises diverse conceptions of gender relations in different locations. Rather than leading to conflict, insecurity and reactive culturalism,[89] minority group members would be encouraged to see, to quote Parekh, that 'every tradition can be read in different ways, none of them definitive and final'; and that, 'a culture cannot survive unless it addresses the issues and aspirations of the age'.[90] Although the project necessarily presupposes values of respect and tolerance for diversity, which implies the reform of the world's most dogmatic or authoritarian cultures, this would not be reform that absolutises liberalism. Rather, the ideal is a modest reform; and the requirement that liberals partially suspend assumptions about the absolute priority of their hallowed rights to autonomy and negative freedom, in an effort to understand what, for the world's women, well-being and flourishing might entail.

Pluralist universalism and oppression: tracing feminism's dialogical limit on multiculturalism

So far, I have argued that the border-tracing project inspired by Parekh's thought seeks to expand its understanding of well-being rights. Yet, although it integrates feminist and multicultural ideals in this important way, the project remains incomplete if it focuses only on positive well-being, without also concentrating on issues of oppression and harm. Given that many cultures of the world do justify modes of dominating weaker members, and given that for feminist projects around the globe the problem of oppression is central, the approach developed here must also engage with different cultural forms of suffering, including the frequent and disproportionate lack of access to food and material resources by vulnerable members, their formal and informal marginalisation in the labour market and their susceptibility to violence. Accordingly, I now highlight a complementary, and equally important, aspect of border-tracing feminism, which draws again from Parekh's multiculturalism. This dimension explains how feminism may sometimes critically limit multiculturalism and, through its challenge to harmful oppression, may humanise it. In this further respect, Parekh's thinking offers a meaningful integration of feminism and multiculturalism, rather than assuming incompatibility and conflict between the movements. The dialogical approach is important, because a single (Western, liberal) conception of harm should not be forcibly imposed on those who might contest it morally and politically; and because feminism's preoccupation with vulnerability may humanise multiculturalism as a critical movement of justice.

Here Parekh's intriguing concept of 'pluralist universalism'[91] enables border-tracing feminism to combine a positive expansion of well-being rights with a dialogue about minimal norms that protect against harm. Explaining the interdependency of feminism and multiculturalism in this second sense leads to the possibility that feminism and multiculturalism may exist, in tandem, in a productive dialogue. One must question cultural borders, as we shall see, in order to avoid homogenising women's experiences of oppression, or simply labelling women purely as victims of 'cultural' violence. Both of these options fail to produce a politically progressive and culturally relevant understanding of oppression, which accounts for the different forms of suffering in human life.

Moreover, Parekh's insight seems to take seriously the longstanding feminist controversies over how harm or oppression should be understood. While there have been rather one-dimensional feminist interpretations of oppression as, for instance, 'an enclosing structure of forces and barriers which tends to the immobilisation and reduction of a group',[92] other feminist scholars like

Iris Marion Young[93] define it more fluidly as a relationship with one or more of five 'faces', namely exploitation, marginalisation, powerlessness, cultural imperialism and violence. This is apt, as feminists need to account for the fact that oppression manifests itself in different physical and psychological ways. In this regard, Marnia Lazreg seems right to complain that feminists have been slow to engage with the full complexity of this problem, and that: '[g]eneralisations and stereotypes still flourish . . . There is resistance from the faceless and nameless women who do not write about themselves to reveal their innermost . . .'.[94] Parekh's pluralist universalism addresses this problem by reemphasising what Anne Phillips[95] calls the 'close family relationship' between feminism and multiculturalism, as movements for social justice equally mobilising against suffering and harm.

Parekh's idea of pluralist universalism may be understood, first of all, through a brief examination of his critique of Walzer's famous theory of 'thin minimalism'.[96] This account views universal moral values as regulative principles that 'impose constraints on the permissible range of cultural diversity'.[97] Briefly, Walzer believes that prohibitions against brutality, torture and gratuitous killing arise repeatedly within different cultures. On his account, the global empirical consensus on these norms lends them legitimacy. Yet Parekh rightly questions this claim. While it is tempting to believe that no society could justify torture, much depends on how this term is understood. Also, the legitimacy of baseline moral principles, claims Parekh, does not arise from the fact that they are endorsed, but through human beings' reasoned debates about them.[98] Finally, Walzer's approach is problematic according to Parekh because minimal notions of harm cannot be invoked as 'mechanical yardsticks' to measure injustice. This is because harm takes different forms, and what it means unacceptably to reduce and marginalise, and thereby 'oppress', a human being is always a contextual matter. Taking these insights seriously, the border-tracing approach accepts that the meaning of even negative, minimal moral norms is shaped by pluralism.[99] Thus, while insisting on the universality of norms against slavery, gratuitous killing or degradation,[100] Parekh rightly recognises different ways they should be understood and balanced. In this regard,

Parekh's critical multiculturalism seems productively allied with the insights of post-colonial feminists, who have also been concerned to expose the different dimensions of gendered harm, such as cultural imperialism and sexual violence. They have insisted, in line with Parekh's insight, that these harms combine in particular circumstances to produce discrete experiences of injustice, some of which can never be fully recounted. The point is made most provocatively by Gayatri Spivak in relation to the 'silent female subaltern'. On account of her subjection both to colonialist representations and masculine dominance, she is 'doubly effaced' or 'even more deeply in the shadow'.[101]

As the language of these post-colonial writers can often seem obscure, however, it is worth explaining pluralist universalism's minimal notions of harm more practically, by turning back to the examples provided earlier from British Asian communities and rapidly modernising societies like Pakistan and India. While these contexts obviously differ in important ways, they raise common questions about how minimal universal moral norms may be understood in conditions of rapid globalisation and intercultural penetration. In relation to forced marriage, pluralist universalism would recognise that 'duress' is a culturally variable notion, which should be defined in dialogue with the parties affected.[102] However, feminism's preoccupation with harmful oppression would critically limit and humanise multiculturalism by refusing to classify forced marriages as a pure expression of 'culture'. For, while there are likely to be cultural and religious influences at play, feminism necessitates a reflective dialogue about the causes behind such an aggressive expression of culture, and would accommodate other (political, economic and social) explanations. Narayan's thought on dowry murders in India, as noted earlier, challenges the assumption that women are 'killed by culture' as an unhelpful account of human suffering, if it deflects attention from the greater number of Indian women who suffer violence unconnected with dowry.[103] Therefore, pluralist universalism brings feminist goals to bear on multiculturalism, recognising that different forms or sources of harm often combine to affect human beings differently, and that, at the extreme, these harms should be condemned. Accordingly, Parekh's intercultural dialogue would assist to integrate feminism and multicultural-ism, bringing the former critically to bear on the latter.

A domestic violence case from Pakistan further emphasises the importance of pluralist universalism in this chapter's proposal to integrate feminism and multiculturalism. Ratna Kapur[104] recounts the situation of a Pakistani woman at the 1993 Vienna Tribunal on Violence against Women, who spoke of her husband's attempt to kill her by dousing her with kerosene. While one might, at first, simply view this case as cultural or religious violence, similar to *sati* and other dramatic acts associated with Orientalist construc-tions of 'the East', closer attention to the woman's story does not permit 'multiculturalism' to be used to justify this violence. What becomes relevant through reflective dialogue, it seems, is that the woman was a Christian, whose Muslim ex-husband reacted after she petitioned state courts for child custody. By identifying her as a minority woman challenging dominant Islamic prop-erty laws in a post-colonial state, a more realistic account of the nature, context and causes of gendered violence come to view. The Christian woman's status as a minority, the prevalent norms of child custody and the political assertion of state Islam may have all combined to shape her experience. By tracing – that is, recognising and investigating – the borders of cultural norms and perceived differences, a contextually relevant account of harm comes into view, and renders feminism a resource for critically limiting and humanising an unreflective multiculturalism.

Ultimately, engaged dialogue within and between cultures is necessary because of the difficulties of knowing exactly when feminism may legitimately limit multiculturalism, without under-mining its inherent impulse to respect, protect and nurture diver-sity. In Parekh's words, 'how much leeway a society should have in its reinterpretation [of this moral threshold] and how we can ensure that we do not interpret [these minimal values] out of existence'[105] is a continual challenge for both feminism and multi-culturalism in an age of global diversity and increasingly interde-pendent lives. The point is not only that different cultures contain their unique moral visions of flourishing and well-being, but also that they yield different understandings of harm, oppression and domination. Intercultural conversation concerning gender justice and injustice thus creates perpetual ambiguities at the margins and borders of different communities.[106] Multicultural border-tracing feminists must inquire why certain harms are deemed 'cultural' or 'religious', and which further harms these classifications hide.[107] The problem is that the post-colonial critique of 'Western' historical narratives of progress and the good life does not, in itself, deliver a contemporary moral project. In search of such a project, the chapter has turned to Parekh's thought. Without his moralised, dialogical account of the feminism–multiculturalism relation, feminism risks the unsatisfactory alternatives of a crude cultural relativism, on one hand, or, on the other, an unreflective and potentially alienating form of universalism. Equally, without the focused debates about vulnerability and harm, multiculturalism risks dehumanising itself.

This final section has defended Parekh's dialogical, pluralist universalism as means to bring feminist concerns to bear on multiculturalism. While the economic hardship and deprivations of women in immigrant and post-colonial settings today surely support a defence of high priority rights,[108] knowing what these rights are, and how to support them, involves combining feminist and multicultural movements in a critical border tracing encounter. For, even if one minimally views both feminism and multiculturalism as defences of rights to equality, that is where the dialogue should begin, rather than where it concludes. For equality itself must be conceived '*as a site of discursive struggle, a place where different visions of the world are fought out*, and a struggle in which we do and must engage'.[109] This final section has attempted, by drawing on Parekh's substantial insights, to extend that discursive work to a mature and sensible understanding of how feminism might temper, limit and humanise multiculturalism.

Conclusion

The integration of feminism with multiculturalism through 'border-tracing' defined in this chapter is inspired by Bhikhu Parekh's critical and reflective multicultural thought. It suggests a productive alliance between two social and political movements that have a deep history of tension and conflict. The approach engages respectfully with the complex female identities emerging in immigrant and post-colonial contexts today, for whom experiences of rapid globalisation emphasise the contestability of borders between cultural differences. While, as we have seen, earlier post-colonial feminists like Narayan, Mohanty and Spivak emphasised the contradictions of liberal humanist engagements with cultural difference, Parekh's thought offers a more concrete moral project in response to their enduring concerns. By building on Parekh's fruitful account of intercultural dialogue, the chapter has demonstrated how both a multicultural feminism, and a feminist multiculturalism may arise out of what seemed an antagonistic and conflict-ridden relation. The notion of border tracing proposed here cannot, of course, resolve all the tensions in these debates absolutely. Yet it does reject a 'hierarchy of oppression'.[110] It draws mature and politically engaged conclusions about the complexity of women's and men's lives, seeking to identify the harms of sexism, cultural imperialism and violence that damage us all, as well as the different cultural forms of well-being that might ultimately benefit humanity as a whole.

Parekh's thought is therefore relevant in prompting a re-evaluation of older conceptions of multiculturalism associated with static forms of identity politics. It also decentres stereotypes about women in diverse cultures, and seeks to trace, question and destabilise boundaries between 'us' and 'them', between insiders and outsiders, between cultural and women's rights, and between well-being and harm. It takes seriously the different ways humans prosper and suffer, especially where identity claims are increasingly raised on the basis of controversial notions of femininity and gender. Are these claims progressive or reactionary? Parekh's thought emphasises that there is no easy answer to these questions. Rather, the path to provisional answers involves tracing the borders identified here. To absolutise borders, to take either 'side' as fixed or essential, Parekh seems to insist, denies the critical and transformative impulse of both feminism and multiculturalism. Leading us away from the dangers of *monism*,[111] Parekh affirms that social justice for all may be pursued without presuming a single form of good and evil that may be understood beyond reasoned dialogue and debate.[112]

Acknowledgements

I have benefited enormously from constructive feedback on an early draft of this chapter from participants at the symposium on the work of Bhikhu Parekh at the Magna Carta Institute in London in May 2011, and from illuminating written and oral comments from Lord Parekh in July that year. I would also like to thank Professor Tariq Modood and Dr Varun Uberoi warmly for their kind invitation to contribute to this volume and for their highly valuable and thought-provoking advice on the previous draft.

Notes

1. I have benefited enormously from constructive feedback on an early draft of this chapter from participants at the symposium on the work of Bhikhu Parekh at the Magna Carta Institute in London in May 2011, and from illuminating written and oral comments from Lord Parekh in July that year. I would also like to thank Professor Tariq Modood and Dr Varun Uberoi warmly for their kind invitation to contribute to this volume and for their highly valuable and thought-provoking advice on the previous draft.
2. U. Narayan (1997), *Dislocating Cultures* (Bloomington, IN: Indiana University Press).
3. C. T. Mohanty (1991), 'Under Western eyes: feminist scholarship and colonial discourse', in C. T. Mohanty (ed.) *Third World Women and the Politics of Feminism* (Bloomington, IN: Indiana University Press).
4. G. Anzaldua (ed.) (1990), *Making Face, Making Soul/Haciendo Caras: Creative and Critical Perspectives on Women of Colour* (San Francisco, CA: Aunt Lute).
5. G. Spivak (1993), *Outside in the Teaching Machine* (New York: Routledge).
6. The literature on 'non-Western' feminism, sometimes called 'transnational' or 'global' feminism, is prodigious, and it is impossible to provide exhaustive references. For an indicative cross-section, see G. M. Bottomley de Lepervanche and J. Martin (1991); *Intersexions* (Sydney: Allen & Unwin); G. Ashworth (1995), *Diplomacy of the Oppressed* (London: Zed Books); and Mohanty, 'Under Western eyes'.

119

7. R. Rajan and Y. Park (2000), 'Postcolonial feminism/ postcolonialism and feminism', in H. Schwartz and S. Ray (eds) *Companion to Postcolonial Studies* (Oxford: Blackwell), p. 62.

8. I. Young (1989), 'Polity and group difference: a critique of the ideal of universal citizenship', *Ethics* 99 (January).

9. e.g. I. Young (1995), *Justice and the Politics of Difference* (Princeton, NJ: Princeton University Press).

10. S. M. Okin (1999), 'Is multiculturalism bad for women?', in S. M. Okin (and respondents), *Is Multiculturalism Bad for Women?* (Princeton, NJ: Princeton University Press).

11. S. M. Okin (2005), 'Multicuturalism and feminism: no simple question, no simple answers', in A. Eisenberg and J. Spinner-Halev (eds) *Minorities within Minorities: Equality, Rights and Diversity* (Cambridge: Cambridge University Press), p. 67.

12. M. Deveaux (2006), *Gender and Justice in Multicultural Liberal States* (Oxford: Oxford University Press); and S. Song (2007), *Justice, Gender and the Politics of Multiculturalism* (Cambridge: Cambridge University Press).

13. S. Saharso (2005), 'Sex-selective abortion: gender, culture and Dutch public policy', *Ethnicities*, 5.2: 248–66; and M. Friedman (2002), *Autonomy, Gender and Politics* (Princeton, NJ: Princeton University Press).

14. A. Shachar (2001), *Multicultural Jurisdictions: Cultural Differences and Women's Rights* (Cambridge: Cambridge University Press).

15. See M. Mookherjee (2009), *Women's Rights as Multicultural Claims* (Edinburgh: Edinburgh University Press) for my earlier defence of the two stages suggested in this chapter for integrating feminism and multiculturalism.

16. B. Parekh (2000), (2nd edn 2008), *Rethinking Multiculturalism: Cultural Diversity and Political Theory* (Basingstoke: Macmillan Press) (hereafter *RM*).

17. Narayan, *Dislocating Cultures*.

18. Ibid., p. 27.

19. B. Parekh (2008), *A New Politics of Identity: Political Principles for an Interdependent World* (Basingstoke: Macmillan), p. 176.

20. Audré Lorde, cited in L. Briskin (1990), 'Identity politics and the hierarchy of oppression', *Feminist Review*, 32 (Summer), pp. 102–8.

21. Song, *Justice, Gender*.

22. M. Lamont and V. Molner (2002), 'The study of boundaries in the

social sciences', pp. 167–95 in *Annual Review of Sociology*, 28, at p. 171.

23. Narayan, *Dislocating Cultures*.
24. Ibid., p. vi.
25. G. C. Spivak (1988), 'Can the subaltern speak?', in C. Nelson and L. Grossberg (eds) *Marxism and the Interpretation of Culture* (London: Macmillan). There is much dispute over the meaning of the term 'subaltern'. First invoked by Marxist Antonio Gramsci to signify the proletariat, it has been taken up by postcolonial writers such as Homi Bhabha to refer to social groups whose marginality from the dominant language is crucial to the self-definition of the majority group. Spivak, however, warns that one should not automatically equate 'minority' with 'subaltern' status, as not all who belong to minority groups are excluded in the relevant sense. The definition of this term raises a complicated debate as to whether a multicultural transnational feminism should focus on 'minority' or 'subaltern' women, with which I cannot engage fully in this chapter for reasons of space. I limit the use of the term 'subaltern' because of its contested nature, but when I use it I do so to refer, more generally than Spivak, to a disadvantaged or marginalised group or person.
26. Song, *Justice, Gender*, p. 23.
27. For further discussion of this idea, see R. Rorty (1994), 'The hidden politics of cultural identification', pp. 152–66 in *Political Theory*, 22:1 (February), at p. 148.
28. Song, *Justice, Gender*, p. 171.
29. For example, ibid., pp. 67 and 73.
30. Ibid., p. 160.
31. S. Mullally (2006), *Gender, Culture and Human Rights: Reclaiming Universalism* (London: Hart).
32. Narayan, *Dislocating Cultures*, p. 33.
33. K. Nash (2002), 'Human rights for women: an argument for "deconstructive equality"', *Economy and Society*, 31:4, pp. 413–33.
34. K. Brown (2006), 'Realising Muslim women's rights: the role of Islamic identity among British Muslim women', *Women's Studies International Forum*, 29:4, pp. 417–30.
35. Nash, 'Human rights for women'.
36. S. de Beauvoir (1959), *The Second Sex* (London: Fontana).
37. K. Engle (1991–2), 'Female subjects of public international law: human rights and the exotic other female', *New England Law Review*, 26, pp. 1509–26.

38. M. Moallem (2001), 'Transnationalism, feminism and funda-
mentalism', in E. Castellini (ed.) *Women, Gender and Religion*
(London: Palgrave Macmillan).
39. I am further grateful to Bhikhu Parekh for his generous formulation of these points in personal feedback on an early draft of this
chapter in July 2011. This way of understanding the relationship
between feminism and multiculturalism substantially informed the
development of the argument pursued in this chapter.
40. *RM*; Jahanbegloo (2011), *Talking Politics* (Oxford: Oxford
University Press).
41. Jahanbegloo, *Talking Politics*, pp. 69–70.
42. *RM*, p. 369.
43. Ibid., p. 152.
44. Ibid., pp. 33–4.
45. Okin, 'Is multiculturalism bad for women?'
46. B. Parekh (1999), 'A varied moral world', in S. M. Okin (and
respondents), *Is Multiculturalism Bad for Women?* (Princeton, NJ:
Princeton University Press), p. 761.
47. Shachar, *Multiculturalism Jurisdictions*.
48. B. Parekh (2002), 'Review of A. Shachar, *Multicultural
Jurisdictions*', *American Political Science Review*, 96:4, pp.
811–12.
49. *RM*, p. 106; cf. W. Kymlicka (1989), *Liberalism, Community and
Culture* (Oxford: Clarendon Press).
50. Parekh, 'A varied moral world', p. 72.
51. Ibid., p. 75.
52. Ibid., p. 75.
53. Gandhi, cited in R. Iyer (1987), *The Moral and Political Writings
of Mahatma Gandhi* (Oxford: Clarendon Press); B. Parekh (1989),
Colonialism, Tradition and Reform (New Delhi: Sage), p. 23.
54. Parekh, 'A varied moral world', p. 72.
55. Narayan, *Dislocating Cultures*, p. 45.
56. Spivak, cited in Hardacre and Manderson (1990), 'The hall of
mirrors', paper for the International Workshop on the Construction
of Gender and Sexuality in Southeast Asia, Los Angeles, 9–11
December, p. 17.
57. A. Phillips (2002), 'Multiculturalism, universalism and the claims
of democracy', pp. 115–38 in M. Molyneux and S. Razavi (eds)
Gender Justice, Development and Rights (Oxford: Oxford
University Press), p. 127.
58. *RM*, p. 253.

59. Ibid., 253.

60. Ibid., p. 261.

61. e.g. V. Mogadham (2002), 'Islamic feminism and its discontents: towards a resolution of the debates', *Signs*, 27:4, 1135–71.

62. F. Mernissi (1991), 'The veil and the male elite: a feminist interpretation of women's rights in Islam' (New York: Addison Wesley).

63. Ibid., pp. 193, 195.

64. e.g. L. Abu-Lughod (1986), *Veiled Sentiments* (Berkeley, CA: University of California Press).

65. H. Ahmed-Ghosh (2008), 'Dilemmas of Islamic and secular feminists and feminisms', *Journal of International Women's Studies*, 9:3 (May), pp. 99–116.

66. In an apparently similar vein, Bulbeck notes that white feminists in Australia have remained silent about gender oppression within Aboriginal communities out of respect for the idea of indigenous communities as 'harmonious, peace-loving people living at one with Mother Earth'. Aboriginal women have responded by emphasising that they are not harmonious in the sense of being passive, and have produced a powerful reworking of the 'black matriarch myth' to support their empowerment. In C. Bulbeck, *Re-orienting Western Feminisms: Women's Diversity in a Postcolonial World* (Cambridge: Cambridge University Press), pp. 209–10).

67. *RM*, p. 275.

68. Bulbeck, *Re-orienting Western Feminisms*, pp. 213–14. Bulbeck cites one political refugee in Denmark as follows: 'Will you hear the truth? I do not like your life, your sexual freedom is not good. We think about sexuality in a different way from people in the West. We feel that it is holy.'

69. H. Bhabha (1999), 'Liberalism's sacred cow', in S. M. Okin (with respondents), *Is Multiculturalism Bad for Women?* (Princeton, NJ: Princeton University Press), pp. 79–84.

70. *RM*, p. 3.

71. A. Jaggar (1994), *Controversies within Feminist Social Ethics* (Boulder, CO: Westview Press).

72. A. Brah (1996), *Cartographies of Diaspora* (London: Routledge).

73. Deveaux, *Gender and Justice*.

74. In relation to autonomy, Parekh notes that in Western societies, people are often brought up to choose their marital partners freely but to adhere to tradition in relation to religion or political views (*RM*, p. 170). While a liberal society may provide *greater*

opportunities for the development of autonomy than certain very closed cultures, as Diana Tietjens-Meyers argues, women are often encouraged informally to accentuate caring skills in the domestic sphere. See D. Tietjens-Meyers (2000), 'Feminism and women's autonomy: the challenge of female genital cutting', pp. 469–91 in *Metaphilosophy*, 31:5 (October), p. 485. On these points, see also Mookherjee, *Women's Rights*.

75. J. Waldron (1989), 'Rights in conflict', *Ethics*, 99, pp. 503–19.
76. U. Narayan (2002), 'Minds of their own: choices, autonomy, cultural practices and other women', in L. Antony and C. Witt (eds) *A Mind of One's Own: Feminist Essays in Reason and Objectivity* (Boulder, CO: Westview).
77. Brown, 'Realising Muslim women's rights', p. 424; F. Rahman (1980), *Islam: Ideology and the Way of Life* (London: Muslim Schools Trust); and Bulbeck, *Re-orienting Western Feminisms*, p. 159.
78. S. Wolf (1994), 'Comment', pp. 75–87 in C. Taylor (with respondents), *Multiculturalism and the Politics of Recognition*, edited by A. Gutmann (Princeton: Princeton University Press), p. 76.
79. A. Merali (2004), 'Interview with Arzu Merali of the Islamic Human Rights Commission', with Katherine Brown (no precise date given). See Brown, 'Realising Muslim women's rights', p. 420.
80. Brown, 'Realising Muslim women's rights', p. 426.
81. Ibid., p. 425.
82. K. v. Nieuwkerk (2007), *Women Embracing Islam: Gender and Conversion in the West* (Austin, TX: University of Texas Press).
83. Bulbeck, *Re-orienting Western Feminisms*, pp. 34–56.
84. b. hooks (1990), *Yearning: Race, Gender and Cultural Politics* (Boston, MA: South End Press); and A. Walker (2003), *In Search of our Mother's Gardens: Womanist Prose* (Boulder, CO: Marine Books).
85. Ahmed-Ghosh, 'Dilemmas', p 111.
86. M. Halstead (1991), 'Radical feminism, Islam and the single-sex school debate', *Gender and Education* 3(3), pp. 263–78.
87. D. Chakravarty (1992), 'Postcoloniality and the artifice of history', *Representations*, 37(Winter), pp. 1–26; and S. Thapar (1993), 'Women as activists, women as symbols: a study of the Indian nationalist movement', *Feminist Review*, 4(Summer), 81–96.
88. R. Rajan (1988), 'Is the Hindu goddess a feminist?', pp. 225–32 in *Economic and Political Weekly*, 33:44 (31 October), 34–8; 37.

89. Shachar, *Multicultural Jurisdictions*.
90. *RM*, p. 169.
91. B. Parekh (1999), 'Non-ethnocentric universalism', in T. Dunne and N. J. Wheeler (eds) *Human Rights in Global Politics* (Cambridge: Cambridge University Press).
92. M. Frye (1983), *The Politics of Reality* (Freedom, CA: Crossing Press), p. 10.
93. I. Young (1995), *Justice and the Politics of Difference* (Princeton, NJ: Princeton University Press).
94. M. Lazreg (2002), 'The triumphant discourse of global feminism', in A. Amireh and L. Sudhair (eds) *Going Global* (London: Routledge), p. 33.
95. A. Phillips (2007), *Multiculturalism without Culture* (Princeton, NJ: Princeton University Press).
96. M. Walzer (1994), *Thick and Thin: Moral Argument at Home and Abroad* (Notre Dame, IN: University of Notre Dame Press).
97. Jahanbegloo, *Talking Politics*, p. 74.
98. Ibid., p. 67.
99. Ibid., p. 75.
100. Parekh, 'Non-ethnocentric universalism', p. 152.
101. Spivak, 'Can the subaltern speak?', p. 28. However, with respect to the term, 'subaltern', see my comment at note 24.
102. A. Phillips and M. Dustin (2004), 'UK initiatives on forced marriage: regulation, dialogue and exit', *Political Studies* 53:3, 531–51.
103. Narayan, *Dislocating Cultures*, p. 86.
104. R. Kapur (2001), 'Imperial parody', *Feminist Theory* 2:1, 79–88.
105. Parekh, 'Non-ethnocentric universalism', p. 139.
106. The focus on a 'border', in border-tracing feminism is closely allied, and was also inspired by, a related concept of a 'margin', in feminist theory. Kimberlé Crenshaw's account of 'mapping the margins' of different forms of discrimination to locate problems faced by diverse women is influential in this regard. K. Crenshaw (1991), 'Mapping the margins: intersectionality, identity politics and violence against women of color', *Stanford Law Review*, 43:6, 1241–99.
107. Narayan, *Dislocating Cultures*, p. vi.
108. M. Nussbaum (1999), 'The professor of parody', *New Republic* (22 February), p. 38.
109. Kapur, 'Imperial parody', p. 84, my emphasis.
110. Lorde, cited in Briskin, 'Identity politics'.
111. *RM*, p. 19.

5

Liberty, Equality and Accommodation

Peter Jones

Fifty years ago, polyethnic multiculturalism was a minor feature of European societies; today it is a major subject of public policy. Political theorists were initially rather slow to appreciate its significance for them, but for the last two decades multiculturalism has been firmly lodged at the centre of their concerns. No one has done more to forge the connections between the political philosophy and the public policy of multiculturalism than Bhikhu Parekh. As well as bringing the acute analytical skills of a political theorist and the scholarly expertise of an intellectual historian to the study of multiculturalism, he has brought to it a wealth of knowledge of different cultures, some of it from the 'inside', and the experience of a practitioner who has had to grapple with the details and implementation of public policy. His *Rethinking Multiculturalism* is remarkable for its sheer sweep, scholarship, breadth of vision, grasp of detail and intricacy of argument. It has rightly won recognition as one of a small number of seminal texts on the subject.

In this chapter I want to focus on just one aspect of Parekh's wide-ranging thinking on the issues raised by cultural diversity: his thinking on the issue of accommodation. 'Accommodation' is a term that can be used more or less generously. When a society moves from being largely monocultural and mono-faith to being significantly multicultural and multi-faith, it has to make a variety of changes in its rules and arrangements to provide for its new circumstances. In Britain there have been a multitude of such changes, including changes in the content and administration of law, greater sensitivity to cultural differences in the delivery of health care, efforts to secure greater representation of ethnic minorities in the police, adjustments to the arrangements for and the content of state-provided school education, and so on. Most of these changes might be described as 'accommodation' insofar as they are designed to 'make room' for people whose ethnicity, culture and religion is relatively new to Britain. Here, however, I shall mean by 'accommodation' something more specific: measures that provide differently for different cultural and religious groups. Accommodation in this narrower sense is commonly associated with exemptions, such as the exemptions enjoyed by turban-wearing Sikhs from the law that requires motorcyclists to wear crash helmets and by Jews and Muslims from the law that requires animals to be stunned before slaughter. Accommodation through differential treatment is most conspicuous when, as in these cases, some groups are allowed to depart from a rule with which others must comply. But accommodation includes more than these piecemeal exemptions. It can also be provided through general rules, such as the law on indirect discrimination.

While I want to suggest that accommodation takes in a broader range of measures than is commonly recognised, I do not want to exaggerate its importance for multiculturalism. Multiculturalism as a policy is especially associated with 'difference-sensitivity' rather than 'difference-blindness' and this may lead us to suppose that the issue of whether policy should be multicultural is reducible to the issue of accommodation as I have characterised it. But that would be a mistake. Most measures prompted by sensitivity to cultural difference simply take account of the range of differences present in a society and aspire to provide for them fairly without resorting to arrangements that provide differently for different groups. Certainly, when a society becomes culturally diverse, securing equality among its population will require revisions to its arrangements, but these revisions can move it towards greater equality without the use of accommodation in the narrow sense I have identified. Thus, those, like Parekh, who appeal to equality in arguing the case for accommodation, should not be understood to argue that, in multicultural circumstances, equality *always* requires accommodation of the specific sort that I focus on in this chapter.

Accommodation and opportunity

In *Rethinking Multiculturalism*, Parekh examines a catalogue of cases in which the practices of cultural minorities have clashed with existing societal norms and considers whether, in those cases, the minority practices should be accommodated and, if so, on what grounds. He gives particular attention to the ways in which the principles of equal treatment and equal opportunity bear on the case for accommodation. He does not insist that equality is the only value relevant to accommodation or that it should always be the overriding value. Other values, such as social harmony, the value of diversity, and securing and maintaining a common sense of belonging, should also figure in the assessment.[1] Nevertheless, the demands of equality remain central to his prescriptions for a multicultural society, and much of his argument on accommodation is devoted to determining what equal treatment requires, and how equality of opportunity should be understood, in circumstances of cultural diversity.

One of his principal claims is that, in a multicultural society, we need to consider how cultural differences affect the opportunities available to people. The ideas of 'opportunity' in general, and of 'equal opportunity' in particular, should not be limited to the brute circumstances that people confront. Our conception of people's opportunities should also take account of the cultural attachments they bring to those circumstances:

> Opportunity is a subject-dependent concept in the sense that a facility, a resource, or a course of action is only a mute and passive possibility and not an opportunity for an individual if she lacks the capacity, the cultural disposition or the necessary cultural knowledge to take advantage of it.[2]

By way of illustration, he cites a number of different groups whose cultures or religions can become barriers to opportunities that are available to others.

A Sikh is in principle free to send his son to a school that bans turbans, but for all practical purposes it is closed to him. The same is true when an orthodox Jew is required to give up his yarmulke, or the Muslim woman to wear a skirt, or a vegetarian Hindu to eat beef as a precondition for certain kinds of jobs.[3]

The constraints he is concerned with here are not constraints that are intrinsic to a culture or religion itself. He is not pointing out, for example, that the Sikh is deprived by his culture of the opportunity not to wear a turban or that the Hindu is deprived by his religion of the opportunity to eat beef. Rather he is indicating the way in which a person's culture or religion might close off opportunities that we might think of as 'external' to the culture or religion. If a school has a uniform policy that is inconsistent with the turban, the opportunity to attend that school will not be available to a Sikh; if a department store requires its female employees to wear a uniform that incorporates a knee-length skirt, the opportunity to work in that store will be removed for a Muslim woman; if a Jew can join the army only if he removes his yarmulke, a military career will not be open to him; and so on.

Parekh's characterisation of opportunity as a 'subject-dependent concept' provoked a characteristically robust response from Brian Barry, who argued that, on the contrary, people's opportunities consist in the choice sets objectively available to them. People may have preferences that lead them not to take up a particular opportunity but their preference not to exploit an opportunity does not mean that the opportunity is not genuinely available to them. Similarly, people's cultures or religions may impose constraints upon the opportunities that they are willing to take up, but the existence of those subjective constraints is no reason to hold that the forsaken opportunities are not real opportunities. Nor can subjective constraints justify complaints of inequality of opportunity. For Barry therefore, opportunity is an entirely objective matter and there is no case, on grounds of equality of opportunity, for permitting departures from general rules in order to accommodate the cultural or faith-based wishes of particular groups. On the contrary, such departures are both unequal and unfair.[4]

In this chapter, I want to consider Parekh's claim that

opportunity is a subject-dependent concept. I shall argue that subject-dependent considerations are relevant to a society's response to the way in which people's culture or religion affects their options, but I shall suggest that cultural or religious 'constraints' are different in nature from constraints such as lack of resources or lack of capacity, and that our reasons for taking these constraints seriously should also be different. I also want to consider the relationship between equality and accommodation. It is common ground for Parekh and Barry that the issue of accommodation should turn largely, though not wholly, on the demands of equality. I shall not claim that equality has no relevance for accommodation, but I shall suggest that, in some of its instances, accommodation can find a more compelling justification elsewhere. I shall also suggest that, even when equality is involved, we often need to look to other values to make sense of and to justify accommodation. In making that case, I shall focus on the forms that polyethnic and multi-faith accommodation has taken in Britain, but those forms are not unique to Britain and my argument is intended to apply generally to accommodation in polyethnic and multi-faith societies.[5]

Accommodation and equality

In what form might equality relate to accommodation? In answering that question, I want to make use of the distinction between telic and deontic equality.[6] If we are committed to equality as a *telic* ideal, we shall regard equal outcomes as good simply because they are equal and preferable to unequal outcomes. We may seek telic equality as an intrinsic good, that is, as something to be valued for its own sake. Or we may seek it as an instrumental good; we may seek it, for example, because we believe that a more equal society will be more harmonious and more at ease with itself. If we are committed to *deontic* equality, we shall regard equality as right rather than good and we shall regard it as right, not because we value equal outcomes merely as equal outcomes, but because we value equality for some other moral reason, most commonly because we regard it as a requirement of justice or fairness. When we invoke the ideas of equal respect, equal treatment and equal opportunity – the principles of equality to which Parekh most frequently appeals – we typically do so in a deontic spirit. Certainly, when Parekh mobilises the idea of equality in defence of accommodation, he does so in a way that is implicitly deontic: in a context of cultural difference, accommodation is an instrument of equality and it matters because a more equal society is a fairer or more just society.[7] Accordingly, in considering the relationship between equality and accommodation, I shall focus primarily on deontic equality.

Let us begin with three instances of cultural or religious accommodation in Britain that are particularly well known. Turban-wearing Sikhs are exempted from the requirement to wear a crash helmet if they ride a motorcycle[8] and from hard hat rules if they work on a building site.[9] Sikhs who carry the kirpan, as their faith requires, are exempt from the law that bans the carrying of knives in public.[10] Jews and Muslims are exempt from animal welfare legislation requiring that animals be stunned before slaughter so that they can slaughter animals according to the rites of their religion.[11]

Can we defend these exemptions as instruments of equality? In a simple telic sense, they may seem to make for greater equality. If there were no exemptions, the rules at issue would affect some groups more disadvantageously than others; in precluding that uneven impact, the exemptions remove a potential inequality between the exempted groups and other members of the society. Sikhs become able to ride motorcycles, like others; Jews and Muslims become able to eat meat, like others; and so on. However, the link between exemptions and telic equality is not straightforward. Is subjecting everyone to the same law less consistent with telic equality than subjecting some but not others? The answer depends, of course, on the 'telos' we are seeking to equalise. A defence of exemptions as instruments of telic equality would seem most plausible if we are seeking to equalise people's welfare, but the ideal of equal welfare is notoriously difficult to interpret and operationalise.[12] Moreover, if these exemptions are part of a general endeavour to equalise welfare levels among a society's members, they form a strangely piecemeal, heterogeneous and limited set.

Are they better conceived as instruments of deontic equality?

Do they preclude a potential unfairness? The way that Sikhs, Jews and Muslims would be adversely affected by the relevant laws, in the absence of accommodation, seems more unfortunate than unfair. The laws at issue do not engage in a form of distribution in which Sikhs, Jews and Muslims receive less than others and less than their due. Rather they aim to secure goals whose pursuit has unfortunate side effects for those communities. The laws at stake are not even particularly 'cultural' in character. Seeking to reduce head injuries, knife crime and animal suffering are goals that virtually all cultural communities in Britain would endorse, including Sikhs, Jews and Muslims. In general purpose, those laws do not run counter to the culture of any significant group; they prove problematic only insofar as their pursuit through particular measures clashes with the particular practices of some communities. It is not easy, then, to represent those clashes as arising from a majority's efforts to impose its culture upon minorities who think differently. Nor is it easy to see a requirement that Sikhs, Jews and Muslims should comply with the relevant laws as instances of unequal treatment.

Rather than seeing the exemptions as vehicles for an equality that is either deontic or telic in inspiration, the accommodations are more plausibly seen as efforts to ameliorate the conflicts between cultures and public policies that arise when a society becomes multicultural and multi-faith. Inevitably there will clashes and incongruities between the established rules, practices and mores of a society and the cultures of communities who are relatively new to the society. We then have to ask how, all things considered, those clashes and incongruities are best dealt with. Sikhs have reason not to wear crash helmets and hard hats, and reason to carry knives in public, that other members of the population do not have. Jews and Muslims have reason not to stun animals before slaughter that other people do not have. It is entirely reasonable for a society to notice and to take account of those reasons.

It should also take account of considerations that compete with those reasons, so that what is best done in the particular case will involve an on-balance judgement. So, for example, given the availability of other forms of transport, the loss of the opportunity to ride a motorcycle does not seem a terribly onerous burden to impose on devout Sikhs, particularly by comparison with the very onerous burden they would expérience if they were not allowed to carry the kirpan in public.[13] On the other hand, the potential costs of not wearing a crash helmet are largely borne by Sikh bikers themselves, so that, when these and other relevant considerations are weighed against one another, there is a good on-balance case for exempting Sikhs.[14] The loss of the opportunity to eat meat that devout Jews and Muslims would suffer if the ritual slaughter of animals were not allowed would affect their lives far more centrally. Here again, other factors have to be taken into consideration, particularly the additional animal suffering that ritual slaughter entails. Current policy would seem to reflect an on-balance judgement that any additional suffering that animals may undergo is insufficiently great to outweigh the case for allowing ritual slaughter. If the evidence were to change and to indicate that the additional suffering was much greater than had been supposed, that might tip the balance of considerations the other way. Cases such as these seem altogether too *sui generis* for the idea of equality to contribute very much to their resolution. To question the argument for accommodations in terms of equality is not to suggest that accommodations are unfair or unequal; it is to suggest only that the considerations that bear upon these instances of accommodation lie elsewhere.

The 'balance of considerations' approach that I am proposing here is, in fact, very much in tune with Parekh's own approach to the satisfactory resolution of the conflicting claims that inevitably arise in a culturally and religiously diverse society. In considering how a society should resolve actual or potential conflicts between minority cultural practices and its operative public values, he gives a series of compelling examples of the sort of intercultural dialogue through which majorities and minorities should resolve those conflicts.[15] All of those examples exhibit the sort of on-balance reasoning I have been describing. But even when Parekh makes the case of accommodation by mobilising the idea of equality,[16] the lion's share of his reasoning consists in identifying and weighing the many different and competing considerations that bear on each particular instance of accommodation.

A more general vehicle for accommodation that is present in most European societies, including Britain, is the European Convention on Human Rights (ECHR), particularly Article 9. That Article gives everyone 'the right to freedom of thought, conscience and religion', including the freedom 'either alone or in community with others and in public or private, to *manifest* his religion or belief, in worship, teaching, practice and observance'. The second clause of the Article, however, subjects the freedom to manifest one's religion or belief 'to such limitations as are prescribed by law and are necessary in a democratic society in the interests of public safety, for the protection of public order, health or morals, or the protection of the rights and freedoms of others'. Cases concerning Article 9 that come before the courts are typically cases in which a person claims that his right to manifest his religion in particular circumstances has been interfered with, while others either resist that claim of interference or argue that it is justified by the limitations listed in the Article's second clause. They raise the question of whether someone has the right to manifest his particular religion in particular circumstances and, in resolving that question, courts take account of the specific demands of a person's faith as well as of the specific features of the circumstances in which he wishes to manifest his faith. They are typically, that is, cases in which the issue is whether and how far a person's wish to manifest his religion should be accommodated by others.

Thus, in Britain, such cases have concerned the right of a Christian employee to be exempt from his employer's practice of requiring Sunday working;[17] the right of a Muslim teacher to attend Friday prayers, even though his doing so entailed his being absent from school during teaching hours;[18] the right of a Muslim schoolgirl to attend school wearing a jilbab, rather than the shalwar kameez provided by the school's uniform;[19] the right of a Christian schoolgirl to wear a 'purity' ring contrary to her school's 'no jewellery' policy;[20] and the right of a Hindu on his death to be cremated by open pyre, rather than by the enclosed form of cremation currently provided in Britain.[21] In resolving these sorts of case, courts typically engage in on-balance judgements in which they weigh the claims of the religious against the considerations listed in the second clause of Article 9. Here again, it is not a simple matter of reading off what equality requires but of considering whether someone has the right to manifest a particular aspect of their religious faith in the context of all the relevant circumstances. That is why, in these cases, courts frequently insist that their decisions are 'fact-specific', that is specific to the particular facts relating to the particular case. Certainly, the rights at issue in the ECHR are conceived as rights that people possess equally, but that idea of equality contributes little to determining the kind and degree of accommodation to which someone is entitled in virtue of their right to freedom of thought, conscience and religion.

Accommodation, equality and discrimination

There are, however, other instances of accommodation in which equality is much more to the fore. Arguably, the most significant measure now providing for accommodation in Britain is the Equality Act (2010). The Act brought together and harmonised the various anti-discrimination measures that had been enacted in Britain over several decades. It provides against both direct and indirect discrimination. Laws providing against direct discrimination, including racial and religious discrimination, are clearly defensible in terms of equality, both deontic and telic. But, equally clearly, prohibiting direct discrimination is not an exercise in accommodation: it does not attend to, and provide differently for, the different demands of different racial or religious groups, even though, de facto, the protection it provides is likely to be more significant for some groups than for others.

By contrast, laws on indirect racial and religious discrimination *are* exercises in accommodation. They seek to safeguard people from disadvantages that might arise in relation to employment and the provision of goods and services from *particular* features of their ethnicity or religious faith. For the sake of simplicity, I shall focus here on the case of employment. Stated informally, an employer discriminates indirectly against an actual or potential employee if she applies a provision, criterion or practice (PCP) to the employee that, for racial or religious reasons, disadvantages the employee in comparison with other employees.[22] An employer may apply a PCP with scrupulous equality to all of her actual and potential employees, but if, because of their ethnicity or religious faith, it is more difficult for some employees than for others to comply with the PCP, the employer is guilty, prima facie, of indirect discrimination. If, for example, she has a PCP requiring her employees to be clean-shaven, she is guilty, prima facie, of indirect discrimination if she applies that PCP to male Sikhs. However, an employer is not guilty of indirect discrimination if applying her PCP is, in spite of its discriminatory effect, a 'proportionate means of achieving a legitimate aim'.[23] If, for example, she is able to persuade a court or tribunal that her production process requires strict standards of hygiene that are incompatible with facial hair, the application of her PCP to male Sikhs will not be illegal in spite of its disadvantageous impact upon them.[24]

The law on indirect racial and religious discrimination effectively requires an employer to accommodate the demands of an employee's ethnicity or religion up to the point at which doing so conflicts with her use of proportionate means to pursue her legitimate aim as an employer. Suppose, for example, that she has a PCP specifying the particular weeks of the year during which her employees may take time off for holidays. A particular employee wishes to take his 'holiday time' outside of the specified period so that he can celebrate a religious festival. The employer is then legally obliged to accede to his request, unless she could prove to an employment tribunal or a court that yielding to that request was incompatible with her proportionate pursuit of her legitimate aim. The legal wrong of indirect discrimination does not reside in the PCP itself; it consists in applying the PCP to someone who, in respect of a protected characteristic, is disadvantaged by it. Provided she exempts that person, the employer can retain the PCP and she has no obligation to yield to similar requests relating to unprotected characteristics. So, for example, the employer who is legally obliged to allow an employee time off to celebrate a religious festival is not obliged to allow employees time off for other sorts of reason, such as enabling them to attend a party political conference or to go bird-watching during the only two weeks in the year that a rare bird visits Britain's shores.

How does this form of accommodation relate to equality? It may seem that indirect discrimination is another phenomenon that is more unfortunate than unfair. To be disadvantaged as the side effect of an innocently motivated PCP is rather different from being the victim of a deliberate act of discrimination. Arguably, however, considerations of deontic equality are at stake here. If I am an applicant for a job and my chance of success, relative to those of others, is jeopardised unnecessarily by a PCP, I can reasonably complain that I have been deprived of a fair chance of success even though the PCP was not put in place deliberately to disadvantage people like myself. Success in the competition for a post should depend upon the applicants' competence to perform the tasks it entails; if an applicant's chances are prejudiced by other factors, we can deem that unfair no matter how wilfully or unwilfully irrelevant factors have been allowed to prejudice the appointment process. More generally, deploying a PCP in a way that unnecessarily or unjustifiably limits people's eligibility for employment is inconsistent with the deontic principle of equal opportunity in employment. Of course, how far we can understand measures proscribing indirect discrimination in these terms depends upon how straightforwardly fairness maps onto the law on indirect discrimination. 'Proportionate means of achieving a legitimate aim' is not a precise test, and courts and tribunals have interpreted it less generously in some cases than in others. An employer may have a relevant reason and a good reason for her PCP, yet it may still be adjudged to fall short of the proportionality test. But, if, in a particular case, a PCP's failing that test is tantamount to its being unnecessary or lacking reasonable justification, we can say that measures providing against indirect discrimination protect people from unfairness rather than mere misfortune.

Even in the case of indirect discrimination, however, more than equality is at stake. For one thing, the law providing against indirect discrimination still incorporates a balance of considerations: a balance between the interests of the potential claimant and the interests of the employer or provider of goods and services. Claimants are protected up to the point, but only up to the point, at which the employer's or provider's PCP becomes a proportionate means of achieving a legitimate aim. That limit is likely to leave some claimants less well placed than others; it is likely to mean, for example, that niqab-wearers will have fewer employment opportunities than hijab-wearers. We might not think that unfair all things considered, since it would be unfair if people's cultural or religious commitments were allowed to impose costs and disadvantages upon employers or providers without limit. Even so, the presence of that limit indicates that more is at stake than merely ensuring that people's cultural or religious commitments do not result in their having unequal access to employment opportunities and to goods and services.

More fundamentally, provision against indirect discrimination raises the question of why people should be protected in relation to their culturally or religiously based wishes but not in relation to wishes that have other foundations. The law could, but does not, require the accommodation of *any* request that is not inconsistent with an employer's or provider's using proportionate means to pursue a legitimate aim. That would provide comprehensive and apparently even-handed cover against indirect discrimination.[25] So why should people's cultural and religious commitments be 'protected characteristics'[26] when so many other aspects of their lives are not? Why, in the example that I cited earlier, should the employer have a prima facie obligation to accommodate an employee's wish to be away from work at the time of a religious festival but no similar obligation to accommodate another employee's wish to be away at the time of a political rally or a unique bird-watching opportunity, or indeed to deal with a family emergency or to visit a dying relative?

That question returns us to Brian Barry's objection to accommodation: responsibility for coping with the consequences of cultural and religious commitments should lie with those whose commitments they are. Cultural and religious commitments are no different in status from expensive preferences. People who have expensive preferences are liable to find that they suffer lower levels of preference satisfaction than those who have cheaper tastes, but that gives them no claim to additional resources or freedoms that will enable them to achieve satisfaction levels equivalent to those enjoyed by others. And so it should be with cultural and religious commitments. If the bearers of those commitments find them costly, they must bear the costs themselves; they are not entitled to exemptions or other forms of accommodation that relieve them of those costs and shift them elsewhere.[27]

Opportunity: subjective or objective?

In considering how we might meet Barry's objection, I want to return to the specific claim made by Parekh to which Barry took exception. That claim was that opportunity is a 'subject-dependent' concept in that an ostensible opportunity is really no opportunity for someone who 'lacks the capacity, the cultural disposition or the necessary cultural knowledge to take advantage of it'.[28] How are we to understand that claim?

An obvious possibility is as an assertion of cultural determinism. People develop in accordance with, are shaped by, and become the people they are through the culture they inherit. Their outlook on the world and the choices they feel able to make are predetermined by the cultural context in which they have developed. Thus, an option for one person may be no option for another if, for that other, the option has been closed off by the culture that has shaped his very being. People's cultures are as fixed and unalterable features of themselves as their skin colour or gender.

In fact, Parekh rejects cultural determinism of that simple sort. Certainly people find themselves embedded in a culture and none can escape the influence of culture, but that does not mean that they are unable to take a critical view of their culture or to 'rise above its constitutive beliefs and practices and reach out to other cultures'.[29] The degree to which people are shaped by their inherited culture will vary with circumstances and will depend particularly on how far their culture is isolated from others.[30] One of the merits Parekh claims for a multicultural society is that it enables its members to appreciate the limits of their own culture and to become aware of alternative ways of seeing and living in the world. 'They are able to see the contingency of their culture and relate to it freely rather than as a fate or a predicament'.[31]

Parekh's argument does not therefore rest upon the claim that people are helpless constructs of their cultures. If it did, it would seem the wrong sort of argument, as well as one of questionable truth. It matters less how people have come to hold their beliefs and values than how they now regard them. If they now embrace and endorse those beliefs and values (as they normally do), they can hardly present them as disabilities or handicaps with which they have been saddled by their cultures and for which others must make special allowance. If people really did disidentify with their beliefs and values, if they really viewed them as incubi that burdened their lives, they should be willing to shed them.[32] If they found they could not do so unaided, the appropriate solution would lie in therapy rather than indulgence.

The reality of course is that, when people make claims in respect of their beliefs, they do not present them as burdens with which they have been encumbered by culture or circumstance. Quite the contrary, they insist that others must take their beliefs seriously because they take them seriously. It is because they embrace and endorse their beliefs that others must respect their beliefs. Others may not share the beliefs at stake, but it is still incumbent upon them to respect those beliefs out of respect for their holders. So it is the fact that people strongly identify, rather than that they disidentify, with their beliefs that typically grounds the demands that believers make in respect of their beliefs. Rather than suggesting that people are the mental slaves of culture and incapable of thinking beyond its limits, Parekh observes that giving up a cultural norm or practice is hardest for an individual when it is 'constitutive of the individual's sense of identity and self-respect' and when it 'cannot be overcome without a deep sense of moral loss'.[33] That implies a reason for accommodation very different from mere determinism; it implies a reason that appeals to reasons rather than to causes.

A further possibility is that a person may be deprived of an opportunity by constraints imposed by the cultural community to which he belongs. If he were to fail to conduct himself according to the culture or religion of his community, he would incur the opprobrium of that community and might find himself ostracised from it. This account concedes something to 'subjectivity', since incurring the hostility of one's fellows will constitute a constraint only if it is a penalty that a reasonable person would be unwilling to undergo, but, given what we know about human psychology, this would be a sanction that most people would be reluctant to incur. Nor need we be of a particularly communitarian cast of mind to concede the constraining nature of this pressure. It was, for example, a central concern of J. S. Mill's in *On Liberty*.[34]

David Miller argues that this sort of consideration is relevant to the choice set available to a person. Considering the case of *Mandla v. Dowell Lee*, in which a Sikh boy was barred from attending a school because his turban contravened the school's rules on dress and appearance, he argues that:

> if you grow up in a cultural community and identify with it, then violating one of the community's norms in a way that will effectively exclude you from further participation in the life of that community imposes unreasonable costs.[35]

Jeremy Waldron pleads a similar case on behalf of the person who encounters a conflict between the norms of his religion or culture and those of state law:

> His being pulled in the direction of the cultural or religious practice (contrary to state law) has *social* reality; it is not just a matter of subjective conviction. Because of the positive existence of a scheme of regulation rivalling the state law, the person we are considering is already under a socially-enforced burden, established as part of an actual way of life, a burden grounded in the actually existing and well-established regulation and coordination of social affairs afforded by a religious or a cultural tradition.[36]

These arguments stress the pressures that are placed on the members of a religious or cultural community to conform with its norms, and those pressures need occasion neither protest nor regret; we may view them merely as sociological facts of life and an inevitable part of what being a member of a cultural or religious community entails.

The sociological constraints invoked by Miller and Waldron may well be part of the overall picture,[37] but should we make the case for accommodation depend on them? Once again, this argument seems to put the emphasis in the wrong place: it implies that, but for community pressures to conform, a person would be free to set aside his cultural or religious commitments. Moreover, suppose community pressures were absent or ineffective. Would that make a critical difference to our thinking? Would we then think it right not to concede exemptions, or to concede them only to those who were subject or vulnerable to community pressures?

Obligation, opportunity and freedom

Consider again the examples Parekh gives to illustrate his claim that opportunity is subject dependent:

> A Sikh is in principle free to send his son to a school that bans turbans, but for all practical purposes it is closed to him. The same is true when an orthodox Jew is required to give up his yarmulke, or the Muslim woman to wear a skirt, or a vegetarian Hindu to eat beef as a precondition for certain kinds of jobs.

These cases share a conspicuous common feature: they are all cases in which the 'subjects' consider themselves under an obligation that makes it wrong for them either to do what their faith forbids or not to do what their faith requires.[38] Being 'under an obligation' of that sort is quite different from being prevented by legal restrictions or lack of resources or lack of mental capacity. It would not be out of the ordinary for the Sikh to protest that he was 'not free' to dispense with his turban or the Jew to give up his yarmulke or the Muslim woman to wear a knee-length skirt or the Hindu to eat beef. But the freedom at issue here is of a quite different order from the freedom that is removed by sanctions or absence of resources or lack of capacity. It is to be morally or religiously unfree, to be morally or religiously not 'at liberty', to do those things that one has an obligation not to do. Writers on freedom have become suspicious of this sort of usage because of the tricks that might be played by moralising the concept of freedom, but in fact it is entirely commonplace. For example, if you were to ask why I am not 'free' to meet you this evening, my answer could very well be that I have already promised, and therefore am under an obligation, to méet someone else; and, if I should protest that I am not 'free' to go on a blind date, my explanation could be simply that I am married.

While I think it quite in order that we should use the language of freedom in this way, it points to a notion of unfreedom quite different from that which is the staple fare of analyses of negative freedom (nor does it have much to do with the idea of positive freedom). One thing that is common to that staple fare is the notion that freedom and unfreedom are interpersonal conditions. I can protest that I am unfree to do x, only if I can point to someone who is preventing my doing x either by subjecting me to physical restraint or sanctions of some sort, or by withholding from me the means to do x. But in the case of moral unfreedom, there is no one whom I can hold responsible for my condition. I am simply under an obligation. It would, of course, be possible to tell a psychological story about the origins of my sense of obligation, in which I trace that sense to the influence of my parents or my schooling or my community and so to represent myself as having been internally shackled by an external influence. But that would be to switch from an idea of moral unfreedom to one of sociological or psychological unfreedom and, as I have already argued, people do not normally conceive their deepest moral commitments in that way.

My guess is that the unwillingness of commentators like Barry to take account of this sort of unfreedom in describing the opportunities available to people stems from the kind of unfreedom it is. It is internal to the subject. It is not an unfreedom that I can hold anyone else responsible for my being under; nor can I look to others to relieve me of that condition in the way that they might alleviate my poverty or enhance my education. It would also be a mistake to deal with this issue by assimilating being under an obligation to being physically restrained or subject to duress. H. L. A. Hart pointed out long ago that 'having an obligation' is very different from 'being obliged', where 'being obliged' means being coerced or placed under some other form of duress.[39]

Even so, obligations do limit what people are free to do and what they have the opportunity to do. If a society introduces a law requiring all motorcyclists to wear crash helmets, the turban-wearing Sikh finds himself unfree (in the sense that I have indicated) to ride a motorcycle. By contrast, Barry's biker – for whom nothing compares with the thrill of 'riding a Harley-Davidson at full throttle down a deserted freeway' and who protests that 'a bare head is essential to the value of the experience'[40] – is not rendered unfree to ride a motorcycle by legislation requiring him to wear a crash helmet. His *preference* for not wearing a crash helmet does not preclude his donning a crash helmet and riding a motorcycle, whereas the devout Sikh's *obligation* not to discard his turban would, in the absence of an exemption, preclude his riding a motorcycle. In the same sense, the Jew and the Muslim would not be free to eat meat if ritual slaughter were prohibited; the Muslim woman would not have the option to work as a shop assistant if the shop's uniform required her to expose her legs; and the devout Jew would lose the opportunity to join the military if its uniform required him to discard his yarmulke. That, I suggest, is the truth in Parekh's claim that opportunity is 'subject dependent'.

Even if we accept that argument, however, we do not have a full case for accommodation. We might accept that Sikhs and others are governed by obligations and that those obligations affect what they are religiously or morally free to do, but still question why that should weigh with others. Why should the religious not bear the consequences of their beliefs, just as others have to bear the consequences of their tastes and preferences? Why should the Sikh's obligation not to discard his turban count for any more than the thrill seeker's desire to ride a motorcycle bare-headed?

The answer lies, I believe, in the special significance that we give to people's conscientious commitments and to their belief that there are certain things that they are morally or religiously required to do or not to do. That respect for people's sincerely held convictions shows through most clearly in cases when we confront, but recoil from, the option of compelling people to act contrary to their convictions, such as making a conscientious objector fight in a war, or an orthodox Jew testify in court on a Saturday, or a Catholic priest divulge the secrets of the confessional. An example particularly pertinent to accommodation is the exemption granted by discrimination law to 'organised religions', allowing them to discriminate in employment, not merely on grounds of religion but also on grounds of gender, sexual orientation and marital status, provided that such discrimination is required for compliance with the religion's doctrines or to avoid conflict with the strongly held convictions of a significant number of the religion's followers.[41] Controversial as those exemptions have been, without them discrimination law would require some organised religions to defy their own doctrines.

In the forms of accommodation I have focused on in this chapter, the options are not so stark. If the accommodation were withheld, the unaccommodated would face lost opportunities or incur other sorts of cost or disadvantage rather than be obliged to act in ways that, for them, would be morally or religiously wrong. Nevertheless, if we are committed, as far as possible, to allowing people to live according to their own convictions, it is an intelligible extension of that commitment that we should regret clashes between the demands of a religious belief and a society's public or private arrangements that result in believers being 'burdened' in ways that others are not. It is also intelligible that we should wish to mitigate those burdens insofar as we can do so reasonably. The qualification 'reasonably' reintroduces the need to weigh the case for accommodation against other considerations, particularly against the possibility that we might remove costs from the accommodated only to impose them upon others. If accommodation could be bought only at that price, we would have powerful reason to object to it.[42] It is significant, however, that the types of accommodation on which I have focused impose minimal or insignificant costs upon others. The costs of not wearing motorcycling crash helmets or hard hats on construction sites are largely borne by Sikhs themselves, and the costs of allowing Sikhs to carry kirpans are non-existent or minimal;[43] the additional suffering to animals involved in ritual slaughter is assumed by public policy to be too insignificant to warrant prohibition. Courts in interpreting Article 9 of the ECHR have been conspicuously chary of allowing people's religious beliefs to impose costs on others, especially in the area of employment.[44] The law on indirect discrimination is less parsimonious, but still requires accommodation only insofar as it is consistent with an employer's or provider's proportionate pursuit of a legitimate aim.

My thinking here clearly connects with the idea of liberty of conscience, and that may seem too Protestant an idea to be serviceable in multi-faith circumstances. But I intend nothing so specific. It entails no particular theory of morality and certainly none that turns on a theory of conscience narrowly conceived. Rather it draws on the idea, which seems to be widely shared among faiths and not only among faiths, that people attach a special significance to what they believe to be right such that there is something peculiarly wrong about others not respecting their beliefs and something especially wrong about their being made to betray their beliefs. Certainly people across all major faiths seem to respond with much greater outrage, indignation and anguish when they or their fellows face obstacles to complying with the requirements of their faith, than when their other wishes are frustrated or disappointed.

My thinking might also be questioned because of the emphasis it places upon 'obligation'. I have used that term because it readily conveys the notion that people are not at liberty to do this or that. Sometimes, whether a practice is obligatory or discretionary may be relevant to the case for accommodating it.[45] However, I do not mean to make too much of that distinction for two reasons. First, the distinction between the right and the good, or between the wrong and the bad, might not be present in a faith or moral tradition or it may be present only in a very fuzzy way. Second, quite independently of the contingencies of particular faiths, the idea of obligation may set the stakes too high. If, for example, someone wants to live the best possible Christian or Islamic life, should we really discount that commitment because it exceeds the minimum level of conduct that their faith requires, supposing that to be a distinction that we can make?

From religion to culture

So far I have made my argument primarily with reference to religion, making only occasional references to culture. How does that argument transpose to the idea of a multicultural, rather than a

146

multi-faith, society? The answer is very easy in the case of societies like Britain, where cultural differences are caught up so closely with religious differences, especially where those are differences of faith rather than denomination (or its equivalent). But religion is not the whole of culture and our conceptions of, and modes of thinking about, religion and culture can be very different.

In sympathy with Parekh's thinking, my argument has been that the 'subjective' constraints that people are under contribute significantly to the case for cultural accommodation. The case provided by those constraints is a *pro tanto* rather than always an all-things-considered case, but reasons have force even if they are not always conclusive reasons. The constraint of which I have made most, in some measure differently from Parekh, is that of being subject to an obligation or to some other form of normative imperative. The logic of my argument applies therefore as much to non-religious as to religious imperatives, including those that would be appropriately described as 'cultural'. In that respect, the argument comports with Article 9 of the ECHR, which protects 'thought' and 'conscience' as well as religion, and with current British discrimination law which applies to 'religion or belief', rather to religion alone.

If this is so, why does religion figure so much more prominently than non-religious belief in the reality of accommodation? Part of the answer lies in the way in which religion figures so centrally in the cultures of minority communities – communities who are most likely to encounter a clash between their cultures and the norms and practices of the larger society, especially the civil society, in which they reside. But it also lies in the greater propensity of religious than non-religious belief to throw up norms that are likely to clash with the wider society's arrangements, such as norms providing for special forms of dress, diet, religious festivals, holy days, and prayer times.

My argument therefore applies to an aspect of, rather than to the whole of, culture, but that need not be a failing. Given the comprehensive and all-enveloping character of 'culture', at least in idea, and given the impossibility of transposing cultures to a poly-ethnic society in the complete and uncompromised form in which they existed in their societies of origin, we cannot give equal significance to every element of culture. Moreover, we should remember that a person's 'culture' is all that shapes his or her being and mode of existence, not just the 'exotic' features that relate to a person's ancestry. Hybridity is therefore a feature of virtually everyone's real culture, especially in a multicultural society. In that respect too, 'culture' comes too close to absorbing everything to provide an undifferentiated claim to accommodation.

However, I must acknowledge two limits to the range of my argument. First, it does not apply – and it does not aspire to apply – to every legitimate instance of accommodation. Second, it need not be the only justification for cultural accommodation, nor need it apply to every instance of justified cultural accommodation.

The first of these limitations is almost too obvious to need stating and is illustrated clearly by indirect discrimination law in Britain. That law applies to a wide range of 'protected characteristics': age, disability, gender reassignment, marriage and civil partnership, race, religion or belief, sex, and sexual orientation.[46] If we suppose that the accommodation of each of these characteristics is justified, it is clear that their bearers' beliefs about the obligations and normative imperatives to which they are subject will not provide the relevant justification for accommodating most of these characteristics.

The way in which current British law has wrapped up all of the characteristics in a single piece of legislation and protects all of them in largely the same way might suggest that the case for accommodating each should be identical. This, however, is difficult to accept. The approach favoured by luck egalitarians might suggest that it is the choice/chance distinction that provides the common thread: people should be accommodated for features of themselves for which they are not responsible, but not for those that are consequences of their choice. But, aside from the complex case of 'religion or belief', several other of these characteristics are not straightforwardly unchosen.[47]

A more prosaic possibility is that the protected characteristics are simply those that happen, as a matter of contingent fact, to be the most common grounds of discrimination. In principle, it is wrong that *any* characteristic of a person that is not genuinely relevant to a particular form of employment or to the receipt of a particular good or service should affect his or her opportunities.

In practice, *some* characteristics are more likely than others to affect people's opportunities adversely and it is those for which the law provides. This argument can be deployed quite persuasively in relation to the characteristics that are currently protected, or not, from direct discrimination. It can be deployed much less plausibly in defence of the current law on indirect discrimination, given the multitudinous ways in which PCPs can adversely affect people's opportunities. If we are to defend the current law on indirect discrimination, we have to explain why some characteristics merit protection from the adverse effects of indirect discrimination while others do not. Given the heterogeneous nature of the current set of protected characteristics, it is unlikely that our explanation can or should be the same in every case.

Turning to the second limitation, it is often the case that more than one reason can be offered in defence of a public policy and does, in fact, motivate the policy. So, for example, concerns for social cohesion might justify attempts to ameliorate the differential impacts of public policies or PCPs. So too might the wish to mitigate the extent to which religious and cultural disadvantage compounds racial inequality. Parekh rightly insists on the plurality of considerations that bear on multicultural issues and that should receive their due in intercultural dialogue.[48] Consistently with his view, I do not claim that the argument I have made constitutes the only defence that might be offered for cultural accommodation. However, even if we conceive the normative imperatives to which people are subject as cultural rather than religious, the fact that they are imperatives helps to explain why there is a case for their accommodation. As I have already observed, if we set normativity aside, culture merely as such is too inclusive and indiscriminate a phenomenon to be a plausible candidate for accommodation. The law on racial discrimination (direct and indirect) defines race as including 'colour', 'nationality' and 'ethnic or national origins'.[49] It therefore protects claims of culture insofar as those can be represented as claims of national or ethnic identity. But identity is a complex and controversial phenomenon, as Parekh has shown in depth and detail,[50] and it is not clear why the aspects of people's cultural identity that are 'racial' as defined by law should matter more than others.[51] Moreover, as multicultural societies become increasingly intercultural and as lived cultures assume eclectic and fused characters, people's real cultural identities will be less assignable to primordial nationalities or ethnicities that are supposedly theirs.

Conclusion

Like Parekh, and unlike Barry, I have argued that the range of opportunities available to people can be, in part, 'subject dependent'. Parekh traced this subject-dependency to the way in which cultural differences can render people differently able or disposed to take advantage of opportunities that are objectively open to them. I have suggested that we should find the explanation in the different normative imperatives by which people believe themselves to be governed. Morally we are not free to do what we are obligated not to do, nor are we free not to do what we are obligated to do, even when we cannot hold others responsible for those unfreedoms. The lost opportunities that should be a society's concern are not those debarred by the normative imperatives themselves, but those that disappear as a result of the intersection of the demands of those imperatives with the society's rules and arrangements. The imperatives involved in those unfortunate interactions need not be religious in foundation but, in the multicultural circumstances of a society like Britain, they most frequently will be.

The mere loss of options does not, of itself, make the case for accommodation. That case depends upon our finding reason, at least prima facie, why a society should relieve or mitigate the burdens that people incur when their society's arrangements combine with their own imperatives to deprive them of options that remain available to others. Given the difference in the conditions of the burdened and unburdened, we might expect the idea of equality, especially deontic equality, to provide that reason. Equality can indeed contribute something to the case for accommodation but it cannot resolve the issue alone. We have to find reason why we should give people's conscientious convictions, religious or non-religious, a status different from their preferences, whose satisfaction might be no less frustrated by a society's arrangements. We have too to weigh the case for accommodation against the diverse considerations that argue against it. One of the messages running through Bhikhu Parekh's work on multiculturalism, particularly in *Rethinking Multiculturalism*, is that there is no simple template for the proper organisation of a multicultural society. Much has to depend upon context and circumstance, and upon the particular considerations that relate to each particular case. And so it is with accommodation.

Notes

1. B. Parekh (2006), *Rethinking Multiculturalism: Culture Diversity and Political Theory* (2nd edn) (Basingstoke: Palgrave Macmillan), pp. 262–3.
2. Ibid., p. 241.
3. Ibid., p. 241.
4. B. Barry (2001), *Culture and Equality: An Egalitarian Critique of Multiculturalism* (Cambridge: Polity), pp. 48–62. Barry allows that considerations other than equality might bear on the case for accommodation. But he limits those to pragmatic considerations that, for the most part, justify only temporary continuation of an accommodation that is already in place.
5. I follow Will Kymlicka (1995), *Multicultural Citizenship* (Oxford: Oxford University Press), in contrasting 'polyethnic' societies with 'multination' societies. Multination societies include societies such as Canada, Australia and New Zealand, that possess settler populations and indigenous peoples, and in those societies the issue of accommodation takes a rather different form.
6. D. Parfit (2002), 'Equality or priority?', in M. Clayton and A. Williams (eds) *The Ideal of Equality* (Basingstoke: Palgrave Macmillan).
7. Parekh, *Rethinking Multiculturalism*, pp. 132–3, 211, 240–1.
8. Initially by the Motor Cycle Crash Helmets (Religious Exemptions) Act (1976), and later by the Road Traffic Act (1988), s. 16(2). For further details of the law relating to this exemption, see S. Poulter (1998), *Ethnicity, Law and Human Rights* (Oxford: Oxford University Press), pp. 297–301.
9. Employment Act (1989), s. 11. The legal position was complicated

by EU Regulations governing Personal Protective Equipment at Work that came into force in 1992 and that included no exemptions. See Poulter, *Ethnicity*, pp. 313–22, and G. Singh and D. S. Tatla (2006), *Sikhs in Britain: the Making of a Community* (London: Zed Books), pp. 134–5, 137.

10. Criminal Justice Act (1988), s. 139. For my doubts about whether we should interpret permission to carry knives for religious reasons as an 'exemption', see note 13 below.

11. Now under schedule 12 of the Welfare of Animals (Slaughter and Killing) Regulations (1995); but legal exemptions to permit ritual slaughter date back to the nineteenth century. See Poulter, *Ethnicity*, p. 132.

12. R. Dworkin (2000), *Sovereign Virtue* (Cambridge, MA: Harvard University Press), pp. 11–64.

13. There is reason to question whether the right of Sikhs to carry the kirpan in public constitutes an 'exemption'. The law that excepts Sikhs, and others who have religious reasons for carrying knives, also excepts those for whom knives are an occupational tool or part of their national dress (such as Scotsmen for whom Highland dress includes a dirk inserted into a sock). The law aims to prevent the carrying of knives by people who intend, or who are liable, to use them to harm others; the three excepted categories of people carry knives for innocent reasons and fall outside the law's target group. Thus, the law effectively provides that people should not carry knives in public unless they have good reason for doing so. Read in that way, the law as it relates to Sikhs seems much less like an exemption. In particular, it does not run counter to the purpose of the law in the way that exempting Sikhs from crash helmet and hard hat rules, and Jews and Muslims from animal welfare legislation, clearly does run counter to the purpose of the laws from which they are exempt. For the history of the issue of accommodating the kirpan in Britain and elsewhere, see Singh and Tatla, *Sikhs in Britain*, pp. 135–7.

14. It is possible that a court would reduce the compensation claimable by an injured Sikh motorcyclist to the extent that it deemed his wearing a turban rather than a crash helmet to have contributed to the injury he suffered. See Poulter, *Ethnicity*, pp. 297–301. The law is clearer in the case of construction workers and hard hats. The Employment Act (1989) provides that, if a turban-wearing Sikh incurs injury, loss or damage for which another party is liable, that party is liable 'only to the extent that injury, loss or damage would

have been sustained by the Sikh even if he had been wearing a safety helmet' (s. 11(5)).

15. Parekh, *Rethinking Multiculturalism*, pp. 264–92.

16. Ibid., pp. 239–63.

17. *Copsey v. WWB Devon Clays Ltd* [2004] UKEAT/0438/03/SM; [2005] EWCA Civ 932.

18. *Ahmad v. Inner London Education Authority*, Employment Appeal Tribunal: [1976] ICR 461; Court of Appeal: [1978] 1 QB 36; [1977] 3 WLR 396. I examine this case in P. Jones (1994), 'Bearing the consequences of belief', *Journal of Political Philosophy*, 2:1, 24–43.

19. *Begum v. Denbigh High School* [2004] EWHC 1389 (Admin); [2005] EWCA Civ 199; [2006] UKHL 15.

20. *R (Playfoot) (A Minor) v. Governing Body of Millais School* [2007] EWHC 1698 (Admin).

21. *Davender Kumar Ghai v. Newcastle City Council* [2009] EWHC 978 (Admin); [2010] EWCA Civ 59.

22. Equality Act (2010), part 2, ch. 2, para. 19.

23. Ibid.

24. This example is based on *Panesar v. The Nestle Company Ltd* [1980] IRLR 60 EAT and [1980] IRLR 64 CA.

25. Cf. Barry's argument that, if an employer has good reason for a rule, that rule should remain and the employer should be able to make compliance with it a condition of employment; but, if there is inadequate reason for the rule, the employer should be required to dispense with it altogether, so that all employees, and not only those who are adversely affected by it for religious or cultural reasons, would be freed from its restrictions. Barry, *Culture and Equality*, pp. 54–62.

26. Equality Act (2010), ch. 2, para.19.

27. Barry, *Culture and Equality*, pp. 32–62.

28. Parekh, *Rethinking Multiculturalism*, p. 241.

29. Ibid., p. 157; see also pp. 158, 336, 350.

30. Ibid., p. 158.

31. Ibid., p. 167; see also B. Parekh (2002), 'Barry and the dangers of liberalism', pp. 133–50 in P. Kelly (ed.) *Multiculturalism Reconsidered* (Cambridge: Polity), pp. 141–2.

32. Dworkin, *Sovereign Virtue*, pp. 289–96.

33. Parekh, *Rethinking Multiculturalism*, p. 241.

34. J. S. Mill (2006), *On Liberty* and *The Subjection of Women*, edited by Alan Ryan (London: Penguin).

35. D. Miller (2002), 'Liberalism, equal opportunities and cultural commitments', in P. Kelly (ed.) *Multiculturalism Reconsidered* (Cambridge: Polity), p. 53.

36. J. Waldron (2002), 'One law for all? The logic of cultural accommodation', pp. 3–34 in *Washington and Lee Law Review*, 59:3, p. 24.

37. Cf. the example of marriage and duress discussed by Parekh in *Rethinking Multiculturalism*, p. 248.

38. Virtually all the other examples Parekh cites in Chapter 8 of *Rethinking Multiculturalism* are also religious in foundation.

39. H. L. A. Hart (1961), *The Concept of Law* (Oxford: Clarendon Press). Arguably, legal freedom and unfreedom should be understood primarily with reference to obligation. If a law to which I am subject prohibits x, I am unfree to do x in that I am under a legal obligation not to do x, and only secondarily and contingently because I am liable to be punished if I do x. Whether a rule proscribes a freedom is a matter quite separate from whether a punishment is annexed to the rule.

40. Barry, *Culture and Equality*, p. 47.

41. Equality Act (2010), schedule 9, para. 2. In addition, 'organisations relating to religion or belief' are permitted to restrict their memberships and to whom they provide goods and services on grounds of sexual orientation, provided such restrictions are necessary to comply with the organisation's doctrines or to avoid conflict with the strongly held convictions of a significant number of the religion's or belief's followers.

42. For an account of that 'powerful reason', see P. Jones (2015), 'Belief, choice and responsibility: the case of indirect religious discrimination', in G. B. Levey (ed.), *Authenticity, Autonomy and Multiculturalism* (London: Routledge).

43. See notes 13 and 14 above.

44. L. Vickers (2008), *Religious Freedom, Religious Discrimination and the Workplace* (Oxford: Hart Publishing), pp. 86–94.

45. It was deemed relevant, for example, in *Eweida v. British Airways* [2010] EWCA Civ 80, though mainly with reference to the question of whether the disadvantage suffered by the claimant was one that would be suffered by 'persons of the same religion or belief' as the claimant.

46. Equality Act (Act 2010), Ch. 2, para. 19.

47. Marital status and gender reassignment are two obvious such cases. The law also makes no distinction between congenital disability and

disability resulting from culpable risk-taking. For an extensive list of accommodations relating to chosen or semi-chosen features of people, though one focusing primarily on US cases, see S. V. Shiffrin (2004), 'Egalitarianism, choice-sensitivity, and accommodation', in R. J. P. Wallace S. Pettit Scheffler and M. Smith (eds) *Reason and Value: Themes from the Moral Philosophy of Joseph Raz* (Oxford: Clarendon Press). Two celebrated and opposing exponents of luck egalitarianism are R. Dworkin (2000), *Sovereign Virtue* (Cambridge, MA: Harvard University Press) and G. A. Cohen. See Cohen (1989), 'On the currency of egalitarian justice', *Ethics*, 99:4, 906–44; and Cohen (1999), 'Expensive tastes and multiculturalism', in R. A. Bhargava K. Bagchi and R. Sudarshan (eds) *Multiculturalism, Liberalism and Democracy* (Delhi: Oxford University Press), pp. 80–100. Shiffrin, 'Egalitarianism', and J. Quong (2006), 'Cultural exemptions, expensive tastes, and equal opportunities', *Journal of Applied Philosophy*, 23:1, 53–71, provide arguments for accommodation that expressly reject luck egalitarianism. For an analysis and discussion of the choice/chance distinction as it relates to the dispute between Parekh and Barry, see S. Mendus (2002), 'Choice, chance and multiculturalism', in P. Kelly (ed.) *Multiculturalism Reconsidered* (Cambridge: Polity), pp. 31–44.

48. Commission on the Future of Multi-ethnic Britain (2000), *The Future of Multi-ethnic Britain: The Parekh Report* (London: Profile Books); Parekh, *Rethinking Multiculturalism*.

49. Equality Act (2010), Ch. 1, para. 9.

50. B. Parekh (2008), *A New Politics of Identity: Political Principles for an Interdependent World* (Basingstoke: Macmillan).

51. One well-known instance of the uneven protection afforded to cultural identities by racial discrimination law was the way in which the Race Relations Act (1976) secured protection for the religiously based claims of some groups but not others. Unsurprisingly, in 1980, the courts defined Jews as a racial group within the meaning of the Act so that Judaism gained protection as an ethnic characteristic (*Seide v. Gillette* [1980] IRLR 427). A few years later and more controversially, the House of Lords defined Sikhs as a racial group within the meaning of the Act, so protecting Sikhs in respect of features of themselves that were clearly religious in nature (*Mandla v. Dowel Lee* [1983] 2 AC 548). Other religious groups, such as Muslims, were and are denied protection under racial discrimination law because their religion is not definitive of a particular ethnic or national identity, even though it is central to the culture of many

ethnic and national groups. Those groups gained legal protection from religious discrimination in relation to employment only in 2003 and, in relation to the provision of goods and services, only in 2006. In spite of the introduction of laws prohibiting religious discrimination, Sikhs remain able to pursue discrimination cases on grounds of race rather than religion: see, for example, *Sarika Watkins Singh v. The Governing Body of Aberdare Girls' High School* [2008] EWHC 1865 (Admin).

6

Parekh's Multiculturalism and Secularism: Religions in Political Life

Rajeev Bhargava

Introduction

This chapter has three sections. The first maps out and assesses Parekh's pluralist–universalist multiculturalism. The second outlines Parekh's views on the place of religion in political life. The third further analyses these views and offers some friendly criticism. Here its main claim is that Parekh's conceptions of multiculturalism and secularism are deeply at odds with one another. While his multiculturalism shows deep sensitivity to multiple cultural sources, his secularism is surprisingly monocultural.

I

Multiculturalism is the first cousin of nationalism, somewhat diminutive and poorer but equally pervasive and emotionally charged. It is as much a product of modernity as nationalism is. Ernest Gellner, contrasting pre-industrial and industrial societies, makes an interesting observation that while culture had great social significance in pre-modern societies, it had very little political salience.[1] These societies were marked by an extremely complex, nuanced and differentiated cultural domain. Differences in language, rituals, food, clothing and beliefs separated each small group from the other, particularly to mark social hierarchy. The transition to modern industrial societies gradually demolished these minute differences, created larger cultural units and made them politically salient, perhaps for the first time in history. Culture began to provide the criterion of political rule. Thus nationalism was born. And all unfinished, half-articulated or failed projects of nationalism began to carry within themselves the seeds of modern multiculturalism.

I deliberately speak of the incipiency of multiculturalism because in the West the proper articulation of these differences could not have been possible without the arrival of immigrants from former colonies and an intensified globalisation. Given the dominance of Western Europe and America in political theory, it is hardly surprising therefore that multicultural issues remained unexplored till immigrants acquired citizenship rights and began to assert themselves in these societies. The relatively large-scale immigration into Britain of people from the subcontinent provided a fertile ground for the theorisation of multiculturalism by scholars from the same region, such as Bhikhu Parekh and Tariq Modood.

The impetus to such theorisation came from within political theory too. First, communitarian writing emphasised the need for a stable identity and explicitly registered the relevance of cultural communities to the formation of identities. Second, it was belatedly recognised that a culture-relative self-esteem frequently matters as much to people as the fulfilment of material needs. Third, it was recognised that the sense of identity and self-worth of persons derives from cultures that they not only know well but also that they can and may call their own. Therefore, not culture in general, but rather a *particular* culture matters to them. This foregrounds issues of cultural belonging as well as the interest people have in ensuring the survival of particular cultures, even when other cultures may suffice. Fourth, philosophers such as Charles Taylor, drawing upon the work of Hegel, pointed out that identity and self-worth are dialogic notions, and rich empirical work in sociology demonstrated that well-delineated identities as well as well-demarcated cultural communities to which these identities are linked, are formed through dialogic interaction and struggle. A further implication of such work is this: if cultural particularity is pervasive and valuable, and if the number of political communities can never be the same as the number of cultural communities, then it is neither feasible nor desirable to have assimilationist, unicultural polities. Instead, cultural differences must be accepted, respected and publicly affirmed. In short, it is imperative to design multicultural polities.

These theoretical insights provide the background to Parekh's work. He is among a handful of scholars who have developed them and constructed a political theory of multiculturalism and, in my view, is the only theorist in the West to have shaped it by the philosophical and metaphysical premises of the majority of immigrants, at least in Britain. Parekh helpfully points out that the form of cultural diversity situated at the heart of multiculturalism must be distinguished from what he terms 'subcultural' and 'perspectival' diversity. Subcultural diversity exists when specific groups such as gays and lesbians 'broadly share their society's dominant system of meaning and values', and wish to 'carve out within it spaces for their divergent lifestyles'.[2] These groups leave the existing culture as it is, but wish to exempt themselves from it. A second form of diversity exists when some members of a society, 'highly critical of some of the central principles or values of the prevailing culture', wish to 'reconstitute' it.[3] This he calls perspectival diversity, represented for example by feminists or environmentalists. Neither of these two forms is at the centre of multiculturalism, which is characterised by *communal* diversity. Such diversity is 'sustained by a plurality of long-established communities, each with its own long history and way of life which it wishes to preserve and transmit', for example Québécois, Gypsies.[4] They resist assimilation into mainstream national culture, and require a political and ideological movement to do so. The politicisation of group identities flows from the initial premises of multiculturalism.

Implicit in this claim is the view that multiculturalism is a particular response to multicultural societies. Many societies that happen to be multicultural are marked by monocultural political responses. They deny the political significance of cultural difference, refuse recognition of groups that are culturally different from the dominant group and, if they are liberal, grant the same basket of rights to all citizens regardless of their cultural differences. For Parekh, multiculturalism is a normative response to

159

major cultural differences in a society – and one that is morally superior to other monocultural responses.

This necessitates the abandonment or at least a modification of the ideal of equal treatment under common laws. Every law of the land need not be followed by all cultural groups. The demand for a strictly uniform set of laws may unfairly impose great burdens on some groups. It may, for example, be unfair to expect Sikhs to abandon their turbans in order to meet the requirements of a uniform dress code, say, in the army. Fair treatment entails that a slightly different dress code be acceptable if their religion so requires. Such group-specific rights are required by the ideal of equal citizenship. A normatively defensible multiculturalism requires minority rights within specific domains rather than an identical set of rights for all citizens. Parekh gives us a nuanced and detailed defence of these views and takes them further.

Parekh argues that modern states and their institutional structures need to be rethought deeply in a way appropriate to multicultural societies. For Parekh, multiculturalism is not only about the rights and claims of minorities, but concern more significantly 'the proper terms of relationship between different cultural communities'.[5] Such a relationship can only be derived through an open-ended and equal dialogic process between the communities. He thus offers an idea of an institutionalised dialogue between communities, a 'political dialogue':

> [that has] a distinct structure and is not as inconclusive and open-ended as is sometimes suggested. Commitment to it implies a willingness both to accept certain norms, modes of deliberation, procedures, and so on and to live with and act on such consensus as the subject in question allows.[6]

Multiculturalism's three basic insights – that human beings are culturally embedded, that intercultural diversity and dialogue is inescapable and desirable, and that all cultures are internally plural – lead Parekh to a set of conclusions. From the perspective of multiculturalism, the good society cannot be '[committed] to a particular political doctrine or vision of the good life and ask how much diversity to tolerate within the limits set by it'.[7] No political doctrine, whether liberalism, conservatism, socialism or nationalism, can represent the 'full truth of human life', and each is culturally embedded.

Rather, cultural diversity should be the starting point of the dialogue through which the society's political life would be structured. This dialogue:

> requires certain institutional preconditions such as freedom of expression, agreed procedures and basic ethical norms, participatory public spaces, equal rights, a responsive and popularly accountable structure of authority, and empowerment of citizens. And it also calls for such essential political virtues as mutual respect and concern, tolerance, self-restraint, willingness to enter into unfamiliar worlds of thought, love of diversity, a mind open to new ideas and a heart open to others' needs, and the ability to persuade and live with unresolved differences.[8]

Such a political community then sees itself as a 'community of citizens and a community of communities and hence as a community of communally embedded and attached individuals'.[9] The sense of belonging to the community is of a political nature, and does not have an ethnic or cultural basis. Members of the community need not share a common political doctrine or common assumptions about the past/history or common understanding on desired social or economic systems, as these may all be contested among them. The political loyalty towards the community comes rather from a loyalty to the idea of dialogue.

The community must similarly reciprocate to its citizens. For Parekh, equal citizenship is necessary, but not sufficient, in creating a sense of belonging. While he agrees with Charles Taylor's formulations on the necessity of social recognition, he differs on the means required to secure these. Securing recognition by persuasion of the dominant group through rational argument that Taylor appears to advocate, misunderstands the idea of misrecognition, which has both a material and cultural basis, he says. Parekh writes: 'Misrecognition can . . . only be countered by both undertaking a rigorous critique of the dominant culture and radically restructuring the prevailing inequalities of economic and political power'. A multicultural society 'requires a robust form of social, economic and political democracy to underpin its commitment to multiculturalism'.[10]

II

How do these views relate to religion? What is the place of religion in political life? Parekh helpfully distinguishes two questions that are not always made explicit in the literature on the subject. First (1), what is the place of religion in official politics, in the political life of the state. Second (2), what is the place of religion in the broader political life of society, in social and political movements, in democratic politics, in, for instance, the life of political parties, etc?

The standard answer, identified with secularists, is that there should not be any place for religion in either (1) or (2). Religion must be excluded from both. This view bifurcates further. If religion is excluded from (2), from the entire political life of a society, then it is automatically excluded also from (1). There are good reasons to support exclusion from (2). Hence, religion must be excluded from (1). Yet the reasons for excluding religion from the state and from non-state institutions and practices do not depend on each other. But in each case they are better and more convincing than reasons for including religion. Together, though for independent reasons, they entail that religion must be excluded from the entire political life of a society. There is a good case for treating these two claims separately and independently. However, for the purposes of this chapter, I will ignore the difference between these two positions.

What is the mainstream (liberal democratic) secularist reasoning underlying the exclusion of religion from the state? Secular states usually enjoin their citizens to support only those coercive laws for which there is public justification. Why so? Because if others are expected to follow a law in terms that they do not understand and for reasons they cannot endorse, then the principle of equal respect is violated.[11] If other reasonable and conscientious citizens have difficulty in comprehending reasons in support of a coercive law, then this rationale does not count as public justification. Because a particular religious rationale is a paradigmatic case of a reason that other citizens with different religious beliefs or no religious beliefs whatsoever fail to understand, it does not count as public justification; and because it does not count as public justification, a law grounded solely on a religious rationale must never be enacted. In short, purely religious convictions or commitments have no role to play in democratic and pluralist polities. So suppose that a law banning beef eating is proposed by Hindus on the ground that cow slaughter is taboo within Hinduism. Non-Hindus and atheists may understand the sacredness of the cow to the Hindus. They may even understand why Hindus do not eat beef. However, this reason cannot become part of their own motivational structure: they cannot have the motivation to stop eating beef. It is hard for them to understand why they should be made to follow a law banning beef eating. Hence, the rationale offered by Hindus cannot become widely acceptable and therefore there cannot be publicly acceptable justification for the said coercive law.[12]

Parekh challenges this dominant (or perhaps a once-dominant) view and joins a long list of scholars who have argued against secular parochialism and/or for greater accommodation of religion in public and political life. He finds it unpersuasive because though possible to exclude religious reasons, it would be morally unjust to do so. First, secular reasons are not culturally and politically neutral.[13] They presuppose a world-view, for instance, either that the world here and now is the only world there is or that this-worldly affairs are autonomous of the affairs of the other world. The former is a strong secularist belief contested by many and the second is a parochial view shared by some believers, not all. The sloughing off of the transcendental world is a move that occurs exclusively within Western civilisation, a late product of Protestantism and shaped by it.[14] Therefore, the universal pretensions of exclusive secular humanism are perhaps its greatest drawback. Moreover, its links with Christian civilisation are easily forgotten because over time they have silently slid into the background. Christianity allows this self-limitation and much of the world innocently mistakes this rather cunning self-denial for its disappearance.[15]

Second, Parekh agrees that the requirement that religious

reasons be excluded from liberal democratic politics is offensive to religious persons who, like others, wish to support their favoured political commitments on the basis of their conscience.[16] By asking religious persons to exercise restraint and exclude religious reasons in their justification for a coercive law, mainstream secularism forces her to act against her conscience and in doing so it fails not only to respect the moral agency of these persons but also violates its own principle of equal respect. If people believe that their politics must be consistent with their morality then why should they be discouraged or stigmatised for behaving accordingly? There is a third reason that supplements Parekh's. Secularism relies excessively on a rationalist conception of reason that imposes unfair limits on the manner in which issues are to be brought in the public domain. Some issues are constitutively emotive; others become emotive because they are articulated by people who are not always trained to be rational in the way liberals mandate. Moreover, it is mistaken to assume that only religious people bring passion and sectarianism into politics or, as Richard Rorty believes, that only religion is a conversation-stopper.[17] If, as Parekh puts it, political life can cope with multiple secular languages, why can it not deal with a variety of religious languages?

Fourth, the demand that restraint be exercised is counterproductive, because exclusion from the larger public sphere forces the religious to form their own narrow public where resentment and prejudice will flourish.[18] This would lead not only to the freezing of identities but to the building of unreachable walls between the religious and other citizens. Therefore, 'engagement with religious people is typically better than shunning them'.[19] Fifth, secularism does not understand the believer's life as it is lived from the inside. It misses out on perhaps the most significant feature of most religions that they encourage their members to choose to live a disciplined, restricted, rule-bound, and desire-abnegating life. A religious life is not just a life of personal and whimsical attachment to a personal God but one in which one submits to his commands and lives obediently by them. This may be a nightmare for a standard liberal but it gets the constitutive features of most religions rather better than liberal secularism does.

Thus Parekh argues that the secularist requirement that citizens abstract away from their religious beliefs and arrive at or even defend their views on secular grounds is unacceptable. It discriminates against religious persons and violates the principle of equal citizenship. It is undemocratic, impractical, counterproductive and unwise.

Since there are a great many religious people in every society, their alienation from the polity may generate a crisis of legitimacy. For all these reasons, we should recognise, respect and within limits accommodate religion. Furthermore, the secularist is simply mistaken in his belief that religion has little to contribute to political life. In many parts of the world, it has been a source of emancipatory movements – Gandhi, Martin Luther King, liberation theology, the anti-apartheid struggle, communist repression in Eastern Europe to name just a few of examples from the twentieth century. It also provides a counterweight to the power of the state and to the state's claims to being the sole guardian of a society's moral life and ultimate values. Moreover, against the utilitarian bent of modern secular life, it brings a quality of intrinsic worth and principles that are not easily negotiable.

So, Parekh argues that in our imagination of social and public life, greater space must be given to religions. Religious ways of life, including those with marked non-liberal leanings, have moral integrity that mainstream liberal secularism frequently fails to realise.[20] Yet, Parekh is not an uncritical accomodationist. He would agree that in our effort to accommodate religion, we must not ignore the fact that religion also continues to be a source of severe oppression and exclusion. Religion, Bhikhu reminds us, can arouse powerful emotions and create 'a veritable hell on earth'.[21] 'Since it is generally of ancient origin, it is sometimes deeply conservative, insensitive to social change and harbours a deep anti-feminine bias.' All of this is true. To take just two examples of religion's anti-feminine bias: In Pakistan, the religiously sanctioned law of evidence, *Qanoon-e-Shahadat*, holds on par the evidence of two women or two non-Muslims with that of a single male Muslim, thereby establishing the intrinsic superiority of Muslim men over women and minorities and contravening the fundamental principle of equality.[22] In Hinduism, religiously sanctioned customs related to purity and pollution, for example the bar on the entry of menstruating women in several temples in India, continues to exclude women from the affairs of their own religion and perpetuate an institutionalised system of subordination of women.

What does all this show? It demonstrates at least two things. First, that we must be sensitive simultaneously to the moral integrity of liberal and non-liberal religious ways of living and to religion-based oppression and exclusions. Second, states that are strongly aligned to religions may be sensitive to the moral integrity of non-liberal religions but not always to their oppressions. Thus, accommodation of religion has limits. Parekh advocates a limited accommodation of religion, though one that secularists usually resist.

III

What about the relation of religion and state? Parekh spends less time on the weaker thesis. Here, he takes the opposite, equally sensible view. A state should not establish religion or formally endorse it but in general maintain a policy of strict indifference towards religion. Any identification of state with religion must be avoided because this fusion:

> corrupts both, threatens human dignity, restricts liberty of conscience, violates the moral and religious integrity of individuals, denies equal citizenship to those belonging to no religion or to one not officially endorsed by the state, compromises the impartiality of its officials and so on. In short, secularists are exactly right in demanding separation of state from religion.[23]

Their mistake lies in pushing separation further than is warranted – taking it beyond the state to the entire political life.

Parekh's is an eminently sensible view, one with which I have substantial agreement, as long as it located and viewed from within a specific socio-historical context. However, I am not certain that Parekh does so. For what is remarkable about this view is that the unacknowledged descriptive account on which it is grounded and the prescriptive lessons it draws from this background narrative are both profoundly European. Parekh's claims and proposals about the place of religion in political life are almost entirely grounded in the familiar European opposition between the religious and the secular. Europe's secularists may once have been right in challenging religion, its domination over all other spheres of life and its excesses. But they must not overshoot their goal. They cannot continue to use political power to limit religion without violating some of their own cherished principles of freedom and equality. The need for accommodating a chastened religion springs from the very demands out of which the initial challenge arose. Much the same is true of the epistemic weaknesses of Europe's pre-eminent religion, Christianity. The struggles of an emergent science against religion are vastly different from the arrogant comprehensive claims to truth of a triumphant scientific world-view. Religion can re-enchant the world and can be a source of moral renewal in a world bereft of meaning and moral agency. The need for accommodation and limited respect for religion could not be timelier.

What, however, the standard European account occludes and what remains equally hidden from Parekh's account of religion and political life is that the problematic within which a binary opposition between religion and political life or science made sense could not have arisen without morally dubious settlements and solutions involving the 'religious other'. The so-called conflict between religion and state was in fact a clash between the church of a single religion and a secularising state. The moral imperative of secularism arose when one confession had already eliminated or tamed its rivals. Had Europe turned to or been allowed to turn to more desirable and morally defensible options, the entire narrative of the place of religion in political life or secular state would have been very different. Allow me to develop this point.

The breakup of Western Christendom and the process of competing confessionalisation led virtually to every European polity having a confessional state. Each territory under a sovereign followed the principle: one king, one faith, one law. This meant that large sections of the population were forced to embrace the faith/religion of the sovereign. Religious dissent was tantamount to sedition and dissenters were faced with death or expulsion. Thus, the birth of confessional states was accompanied by massive expulsion of subject-communities whose faith differed from the religion of the ruler. So England became Anglican, Sweden Lutheran, Holland Calvinist and so on. Confessionalisation meant religious homogenisation. With the dissolution of diversity, Europe became an aggregate of predominantly single-religion societies. I use the term 'predominantly' because it is also true that the idea of toleration, or rather a specific conception of toleration, was also born in the same context, at the same time. Some confessions were indeed tolerated but toleration did not mean what the term means today, namely a policy of 'live and let live' under roughly equal conditions and on roughly equal terms. It meant rather an invidious invisibilisation and a deeply negative privatisation. Take Holland, widely considered to be pluralist and tolerant. As Ben Kaplan has shown, in Holland non-Calvinists were not allowed to have churches on the same high street where Calvinists built theirs. Non-Calvinists had their churches tucked away in by-lanes. Moreover, their 'churches' could not look like churches. These places of worship existed in residence halls, ordinary buildings, private gardens, and so on. Calvinists knew that Catholics existed and where they were, Catholics knew that Calvinists knew they existed and where they were, but neither spoke about this fact in public. Even by the lights of that period, this was a deeply humiliating existence of a defeated group.[24]

Issues of radical individual freedom and citizenship equality arose in European societies *after* this process of religious homogenisation had been more or less accomplished. It is not surprising then that European secularism arose in response to what can be called intra-religious domination, but was always blind to inter-religious domination. The liberal–democratisation and the consequent secularisation of many European states have helped citizens with non-Christian faiths acquire most formal rights. But such a scheme of rights neither embodies a regime of inter-religious equality nor effectively prevents religion-based discrimination and exclusion. European secularism replicates and reproduces its originary evasion of inter-religious domination. Indeed, it masks majoritarian, ethno-religious biases.

This went virtually unnoticed for a very long time, but with the migration of peoples of non-Christian faiths from former colonies, these biases have resurfaced and are clearly evident today in different kinds of difficulties faced by Muslims. For example, in Britain a third of all primary school children are educated by religious communities, yet applications for state funding by Muslims are frequently turned down. At one point, there were only two Muslim schools compared to 2,000 run by Roman Catholics and 4,700 by the Church of England. Similar problems persist in other European countries.[25] In neither France nor Germany is a single Muslim-run school subsidised by the state. This is also manifest in the failure of many western European states to deal with the issue of headscarves (France), demands by Muslims to build mosques and therefore to practise their own faith properly (Germany, Italy), discrimination in ritual slaughter (Germany) or to have proper burial grounds of their own (Denmark). In recent times, as Islamophobia grips the imagination of several Western societies (exemplified by the cartoon controversy in Denmark); it is very likely that their Muslim citizens will continue to face disadvantages simply on account of membership in their religious community.

I have tried to argue that one conception of secularism that has world-wide dominance, both in its strong and weak form (in Parekh's senses), arose after other religions were publicly effaced or eliminated. Since dilemmas were squashed rather than resolved, the deep moral problems generated by multiple religions were carried over into the conceptual and normative structure of this secularism. European secularism continues to be afflicted by this moral malaise, which reveals its fangs when European societies are forced to re-examine the issue of profound religious diversity. A secularism that emerges in response to both intra- and inter-religious domination is bound to be different. Given the limitations of this chapter, I can only allude briefly to what these differences are.

For a start, the presence of multiple religions provides a different set of reasons to exclude religion from political life. The motivation for exclusion here comes not from some intrinsic limitations of religion to which secular reason draws attention, but rather from moral demands made by other religions (and other non-religious world-views). In short, the reason for exclusion may come from within religion. I need to exclude my religion from political life not because of an extraneous demand made by secularists but because of moral requirements imposed by the presence of other religions.

It is not by accident that a philosophical treatment of this impulse has come from a philosopher of the United States, more at home with religious diversity, than from Europe. Thus Rawls' overlapping consensus, when appropriately interpreted, gives us a more nuanced conception of secularism. To remind ourselves, the issue before secularists who are committed to equal respect is this: the mere acknowledgement of a concern for each other and the acceptance in turn of the burdens of justification, that we must offer reasons that no one can reasonably reject, does not guarantee the moral legitimacy of the political system. For someone can always claim that the best reasons in favour of the basic structure of society flow from his own particular conception of the good, which by its sheer superiority commands universal assent. If every person follows this chain of argument, it results in permanent value conflict and very likely in an injustice among what Nagel calls first-order impartialities. A different order of impartiality that embodies an appropriate concern for others is therefore required. Principles embodying this impartiality must both show up the partialities of first-order impartialities, put them in their place and then also arbitrate among them. Only this secures the idea of (a truly liberal and egalitarian) secularism. For a theorist defending secularism, the challenge is to identify the best formulation of second-order impartiality, to show that it is a coherent idea and that it can square up with a plausible view of human motivation.

Thus someone keen to develop secularism in a multi-religious society confronts two questions: The first is: how is it possible for there to exist over time a just and stable society of free and equal citizens who still remain profoundly divided by reasonable religious, philosophical and moral doctrines?[26] (to use the classical formulation of John Rawls). The second related question raises the issue of legitimate power: given multiple religious and non-religious world-views, and the potential divisions over conceptions of the good, how can people legitimately exercise power over each other? The core of Rawls' secularist answer to these questions is that the basic structure of society must embody a political conception of justice that 'may be shared by citizens as a basis of reasoned, informed and willing political agreement', that 'expresses their shared and public political reason'[27] and that can 'gain the support of an overlapping consensus of reasonable religious philosophical and moral doctrines in a society regulated by it'.[28]

To repeat, secularism is widely seen as an austere doctrine of excessive self-restraint for which basic political principles must be justified in terms wholly independent of all religions – a view Parekh himself identifies with secularism. On this view, the secular ideal of public reason is so stringent that it gives no place to religions in the justification of political principles. Critics, including Parekh, argue that this carries a wholly unrealistic conception of human motivation. But secularism need not be committed to this radical exclusion of religion from public justification. Secularism can be seen less as radically exclusive of religion and more as a subtle, two-tiered doctrine concerning the relationship of religion and politics, with distinct justifications appropriate at each level.

Let me elaborate. The exposition of this different secularism involves four distinct moves: each successive one marked by greater analytical focus and precision. The first move is to claim that an institutional design that makes living together possible must embody some general abstract, politico-moral principles that all relevant persons endorse. The second move specifies these principles. What principles are acceptable to persons motivated by diverse religious and non-religious views but a shared desire to cooperate and to justify their actions in terms that no one can reasonably reject? The standard secularist answer is that these principles must embody a political conception of justice and include guidelines provided by public political reason with which this conception is defended, discussed, justified, criticised and opposed.

Our third move appears to follow fairly straightforwardly from the second. Here, the new prescription is to avoid reliance on religious and non-religious world-views in the justification of public policies connected with the basic structure in public or official fora. All these moves are found in the more familiar secularism.

However, it is the fourth move that is unexpectedly novel. Now a place is once again found once again for religions. Removed from first-order justification in public fora, multiple religions are brought back, in their role as second-order justification, to support one's commitment to public reason. Given their desire to cooperate and to justify their actions to others, people choose to remove their religions from first-order justifications. This may be viewed as a form of pre-commitment. This deliberate reshaping of the feasible set – certain choices that flow from a direct reliance on religions are excluded – is nevertheless endorsed from within one's own religion. What explains this move?

I believe that in this way the standard secularist acknowledges that he has hitherto insufficiently emphasised the motivational power of religions. People can act or justify independently of religions only when there is a second-order justification from within such conceptions for these actions or justifications. The secularist now acknowledges the insufficiency of the agreement motive to get us to principles governing our basic political structure. But he insists that religious and non-religious views can be self-limiting. When all reasonable doctrines limit themselves, they leave a space that no one can reject. Principles of political justice occupy precisely this space and depend ultimately on the self-limiting capacity of all relevant, reasonable doctrines. This is the primary motivation for new strategy. A secondary reason is the idea that no single route to standards of public reason are necessary and that forms of reasons and evidence on which we converge need not be identical with the entire set of reasons and evidence available from within each religion.

In short, between an exclusive and direct reliance and a total prohibition on any reliance on religion lies the differently secularist idea of an indirect reliance on religions. I have already delineated the structure of this two-tiered doctrine. We eschew reliance, on religions and deploying the resources of public reason arrives at impartial moral principles to regulate the most fundamental political relations between groups and people. However, we rely indirectly on religions because in the last instance the motivation to give up a reliance on one's religion comes from within a person. Each religion discovers an internal motive to live together with other religious and non-religious world-views, and thereby to limit itself and allow for contextual abstraction, because it has rejected other morally desirable alternatives such as extermination, expulsion and outright domination.

This Rawls-inspired secularism largely underpinned the model dominant in America until recently. It is plausible that Parekh's own views are unwittingly influenced by this model. However, a more likely source might have come from the European experience I mentioned. Indeed, in the West, though separation means exclusion, exclusion itself has two meanings: (1) mutual exclusion or (2) one-sided exclusion. In (1), neither the state nor religion is meant to interfere in each other's domains. This mutual exclusion is believed to be the only way to resolve conflicts between different Christian denominations, to grant some measure of equality between them but most crucially to provide individuals the freedom to set up and maintain their own religious associations. Mutual exclusion is necessary initially for religious liberty and then for the more general liberties of individuals. This strict, or 'perfect separation' as Madison termed it, must take place at each of the three distinct levels: of (1) ends, (2) institutions and personnel and (3) law and public policy. Levels (1) and (2) make the state non-theocratic and disestablish religion. Level (3) ensures that the state has neither a positive relationship with religion, for example there should be no policy of granting aid, even non-preferentially, to religious institutions nor a negative relationship with it; it is not within the scope of state activity to interfere in religious matters even when some of the values (such as equality) professed by the state are violated within the religious domain. The Congress simply has no power to legislate on any matter pertaining to religion. This non-interference is justified on the ground that religion is a privileged, private (non-state) matter, and if something is amiss within this private domain, it can be mended only by those who have a right to do so within that sphere. This, according to proponents of this view, is what religious freedom means. Thus, the freedom that justifies mutual exclusion is negative liberty and is closely enmeshed with the privatisation of religion. In my view, this model of secularism encourages on the part of the state a passive respect for religion, and is sensitive only to some aspects of inter- and intra-religious domination.

In (2), the idealised French understanding, separation is interpreted differently. The state is separated from religion at levels (1) and (2), but at level (3) it retains the power to interfere in religion, yet religion is divested of any power to intervene in matters of state. In short, separation means one-sided exclusion. The state may interfere in religion to hinder or suppress it or even to help religion, but in all cases only to ensure its control over religion. Religion becomes an object of law and public policy but only the state's terms. This conception also arose in order to solve the internal problem of Christianity – the excessive domination of the church – and it is clear that it encourages an active disrespect for religion, and is concerned solely with preventing the religious order from dominating the secular. It is somewhat indifferent to aspects of inter-and intra-religious domination.

However, Parekh's idea of limited accommodation of religion is implementable neither with mutual nor with one-sided exclusion of religion. Indeed it is incompatible with his own conception of secularism. It flows instead from his multiculturalism. It follows that Parekh's secularism is deeply at odds with his multiculturalism. The type of secularism that embodies a 'limited accommodation' of religion is found in fact within a different conception of secularism, one that he has not theorised – surprisingly, especially as he cannot have failed to experience it.

This model of secularism, worked out jointly by Hindus and Muslims in the subcontinent, can be found loosely in the best examples of inter-communal practice in India; and in the country's constitution, appropriately interpreted. It meets the needs of deeply religiously diverse societies and also complies with principles of freedom and equality. It responds not only to problems within religions but also to problems between religions.

Seven features of the Indian model are striking and relevant to wider discussion. First, multiple religions are not extras, added on as an afterthought but present at its starting point, as part of its foundation.

Second, the model is not entirely averse to the public character of religions. Although the state is not identified with a particular religion or with religion more generally (there is no established religion), there is official and therefore public recognition granted to religious communities.

Third, it has a commitment to multiple values – liberty or/and equality, not conceived narrowly as pertaining to individuals but interpreted broadly to cover the relative autonomy of religious communities and equality of status in society, as well as other more basic values such as peace and toleration between communities. This model is acutely sensitive to the potential within religions to sanction violence.

Fourth, it does not erect a wall of separation between state and religion. There are boundaries, of course, but they are porous. This allows the state to intervene in religions, to help or hinder them without the impulse to control or destroy them. This involves multiple roles: granting aid to educational institutions of religious communities on a non-preferential basis; or interfering in socio-religious institutions that deny equal dignity and status to members of their own religion or to those of others (for example, the ban on untouchability and the obligation to allow everyone, irrespective of their caste, to enter Hindu temples, and potentially to correct gender inequalities), on the basis of a more sensible understanding of equal concern and respect for all individuals and groups. In short, it interprets separation to mean not strict exclusion or strict neutrality but rather what I call 'principled distance'.

Fifth, this model shows that we do not have to choose between active hostility and passive indifference, or between disrespectful hostility and respectful indifference towards religion. We can combine the two: have the necessary hostility as long as there is also active respect: the state may intervene to inhibit some practices of the religious community, so long as it shows respect for other practices, and it does so by publicly lending support to them.

Sixth, by not fixing its commitment from the start exclusively to individual or community values or marking rigid boundaries between the public and private, India's constitutional secularism allows decisions on these matters to be taken either within the open dynamics of democratic politics or by contextual reasoning in the courts.

Finally, this commitment to multiple values and principled distance means that the state tries to balance different, ambiguous but equally important values. This makes its secular ideal more like a contextual, ethically sensitive, politically negotiated arrangement (which it really is), rather than a scientific doctrine conjured by ideologues and merely implemented by political agents. Thus the constitutive values of this secularism do not always sit easily with one another. On the contrary, they are frequently in conflict. Some degree of internal discord and therefore a fair amount of instability is an integral part of this secularism. For this reason, it always requires fresh interpretations, contextual judgements and attempts at reconciliation and compromise. For instance, the conflict between individual and group rights or between claims of equality and liberty or between claims of liberty and the satisfaction of basic needs cannot always be adjudicated by recourse to some general and abstract principle. Rather they can only be settled case by case, and may require a fine balancing of competing claims.

A somewhat forced, formulaic articulation of Indian secularism then goes something like this. The state must keep a principled distance from all public or private, individual-oriented or community-oriented religious institutions for the sake of the equally significant (and sometimes conflicting) values of peace, this-worldly goods, dignity, liberty and equality (in all its complicated individualistic or non-individualistic versions). Indian secularism then is an ethically sensitive negotiated settlement between diverse groups and divergent values.

Let me elaborate in somewhat greater detail the key feature of Indian secularism, namely, principled distance. Indian secularism admits fairly strict separation at the level of ends – the state has no religious ends, and at the level of personnel and institutions – this is part of what is meant by 'distance'; but at the third level it maintains a flexible approach on the question of the inclusion/exclusion of religion and the engagement/disengagement of the state, which depends on the context, nature or current state of relevant religions. This engagement must be governed by principles undergirding a secular state – that is, principles that flow from a commitment to the values mentioned above. This means that religion may intervene in the affairs of the state if such intervention promotes freedom, equality or any other value integral to secularism. For example, citizens may support a coercive law of the state grounded purely in a religious rationale if this law is compatible with freedom or equality. Equally, the state may engage with religion or disengage from it, engage positively or negatively, but it does so depending entirely on whether or not these values are promoted or undermined. A state that intervenes or refrains from interference on this basis keeps a principled distance from all religions. This is one constitutive idea of principled distance. This idea is different from strict neutrality, that is, the state may help or hinder all religions to an equal degree and in the same manner, that if it intervenes in one religion, it must also do so in others. Rather, it rests upon the idea that treating people or groups as equals is entirely consistent with differential treatment. This idea is the second ingredient in what I have called principled distance.

What kind of treatment do I have in mind? First, religious groups have sought exemptions from practices in which states intervene by a promulgating a law to be applied neutrally to the rest of society. This demand for non-interference is made on the ground either that the law requires them to do things not permitted by their religion or prevents them from doing acts mandated by it. For example, Sikhs demand exemptions from mandatory helmet laws and from police dress codes to accommodate religiously required turbans. Elsewhere, Jews seek exemptions from air force regulations to accommodate their yarmulkes. Muslims women and girls demand that the state not interfere in their religiously required chador. Jews and Muslims seek exemption from Sunday closing laws on the ground that this is not required by their religion. Principled distance allows then that a practice that is banned or regulated in one culture may be permitted in the minority culture because of the distinctive status and meaning it has for its members. For many republican or liberal theories this is a problem because of their simple, some what absolutist morality that gives overwhelming importance to one value, particularly to equal treatment or equal liberty. Religious groups may demand that the state refrain from interference in their practices but they may equally demand that the state interfere in such a way as to give them special assistance so that these groups are also able to secure what other groups are able to obtain routinely by virtue of their social dominance in the political community. It may grant authority to religious officials to perform legally binding marriages, to have their own rules or methods of obtaining a divorce, rules about relations between ex-husband and ex-wife, method of arbitrating civil disputes and so on. Principled distance allows the possibility of such policies on the grounds that to hold people accountable to an unfair law is to treat them as unequals.

However, principled distance is not just a recipe for differential treatment in the form of special exemptions. It may even require state intervention in some religions more than in others, considering the historical and social condition of all relevant religions. For the promotion of a particular value constitutive of secularism, some religion, relative to other religions, may require more interference from the state. For example, suppose that the value to be advanced is social equality. This requires in part undermining caste hierarchies. If this is the aim of the state, then it may be required of the state that it interferes in caste-ridden Hinduism much more than say Islam or Christianity. However, if a diversity-driven religious liberty is the value to be advanced by the state, then it may have to intervene in Christianity and Islam more than in Hinduism. If this is so, the state can neither strictly exclude considerations emanating from religion, nor keep strict neutrality with respect to religion. It cannot antecedently decide that it will always refrain from interfering in religions or that it will interfere in each equally. Indeed, it may not relate to every religion in society in exactly the same way or intervene in each religion to the same degree or in the same manner. To want to do so would be plainly absurd. All it must ensure is that the relationship between the state and religions is guided by non-sectarian motives consistent with some values and principles.

I have argued that Western secularism, in its idealised American or French versions, whether underpinned by a Rawlsian philosophy or not, is not the only one available. Other versions exist for which the presence of multiple religions does not necessarily impose a moral requirement to exclude religion, but involves the obligation to include some or perhaps all religions in political life. In short, political life may exclude or include religion for religiously grounded and non-religious reasons. Secularism requires both engagement with or disengagement from religions, the said engagement may be negative or positive and may even be more in one religion in any given context than in others, depending entirely on which of these is able to reduce morally undesirable options such as extermination, expulsion and domination of some religions. This profoundly different secularism embodying what I have elsewhere called principled distance is conceivable only in societies that take deep diversity of religions as a natural part of their social and political environment. The US gives us a hint of it but in India we find its fuller realisation.

Allow me to reformulate and bring together all the major points in Parekh's discussion of religion and politics that tally with all that I have said above about my own preferred conception. First, religion plays an important part in the lives of many people and religious institutions function in this world like other purely secular institutions. Given this, secularism must be neither servile nor hostile to religion. It must manifest an attitude of neither blind deference nor indifference but one of critical respect towards all religions. Second, those who think that they are emancipated from religion or believe that their own religion is emancipated, but not that of others, should accept with humility that none of the achievements of their own religion are irreversible. They should also not fail to remember the history of oppression within their own respective religions as well as the repressive policies of many secular states. As more and more societies become multi-religious, a sense of the vulnerability of one's own religions, indeed of one's own world-view, will be crucial for a peaceful and just world order. The conclusions to be inferred from these two points but which Parekh does not draw are as follows: first, the state cannot avoid having or endorsing a policy towards religion or religious organisations. So, separation cannot mean excluding religion from the domain of the state. Second, separation of religion and state should also not be interpreted as absolute or strict neutrality. No state can possibly help or hinder all religions in the same manner and to the same degree. Third, the state may interfere with religion and refrain from such interference depending entirely on which of these promotes the values of freedom and equality or undermines inter-religious and intra-religious dominations. Fourth, the values of freedom and equality must be interpreted as both rights of individuals, and wherever required, rights of communities. Community rights are particularly important if religious groups are vulnerable or, because of their small size, they have relatively little power to influence the process of decision-making. Fifth, secularism, which professes principled distance and is sensitive to multiple values, cannot avoid making contextual judgements. Contextual judgements allow for ethically sensitive balancing and compromise. Finally, if secularism is to survive as a transcultural normative perspective, it must be de-Christianised, de-Westernised, de-privatised and de-individualised. In saying so, I do not mean that it must wholly sever its links with Christianity or the West but its ties with them must be loosened. It should be able to accommodate other civilisations and community-based rights. Only with this form of secularism and a state nourished by it, can deep religious diversity be managed.

To sum up, I have argued first, that had Parekh drawn the appropriate lesson from his advocacy of limited accommodation of religion, he would have arrived at a different understanding of separation to mean principled distance. Second, a focus on mainstream Western secularism betrays toleration for highly individualised and privatised religions and a failure to cope with religions that mandate greater public or political presence, or have a strong communal orientation. This group-insensitivity of secularism makes it virtually impossible for it to accommodate community-specific rights and therefore to protect the rights of religious minorities. But if this is so, this 'inherently dogmatic' secularism cannot coexist innocently with other religions.[29] Given the enormous power of the state, it must try to shape and transform them: a clear instance of illegitimate influence, if not outright violence. Thus, with all its claims of leaving religions alone, of granting religions liberty, this secularism is hostile to non-liberal, non-protestant believers.[30] Indeed, it is surprising that Parekh's secularism has been worked out as if the only religion inspiring or shaping it is Christianity.

But it can be argued that Parekh's multiculturalism is subtle and flexible enough to provide ample room for these. Is it justified then to criticise him for omitting community rights from his account of secularism? However, this response is consistent with my critique, which argues precisely that he should extract his secularism from his overall conception of multiculturalism, rather than relying on mainstream Western conceptions and the entire problematique/framework within which Western religion is conceived and thought about. Reliance on the specific European narrative of religion, in particular depending exclusively but implicitly on the historical trajectory of Christianity, prevents him from allowing a different secularism to flow from his own broader conception of multiculturalism.

Notes

1. E. Gellner (1994), *Encounters with Nationalism* (Oxford: Blackwell), pp. 34–46.
2. B. Parekh (2006), *Rethinking Multiculturalism: Cultural Diversity and Political Theory* (New York: Palgrave Macmillan), p. 3.
3. Ibid., p. 3.
4. Ibid., p. 4.
5. Ibid., p. 13.
6. Ibid., pp. 14–15.
7. Ibid., p. 340.
8. Ibid., p. 340.
9. Ibid., p. 341.
10. Ibid., p. 343.
11. R. Audi (1993), 'The place of religious argument in a free and democratic society', *San Diego Law Review*, 30, p. 701; C. Larmore (1996), *The Morals of Modernity* (Cambridge: Cambridge University Press), p. 137; L. B. Solum (1990), 'Faith and justice', pp. 1133–42 in *De Paul Law Review*, 39, p. 1095; S. Macedo (1990), *Liberal Virtues: Citizenship, Virtue and Community in Liberal Constitutionalism* (Oxford: Clarendon Press), p. 249; J. Rawls (1971), *A Theory of Justice* (Cambridge: Belknap Press), pp. 337–8; P. Weithman (1997), *Religion and Contemporary Liberalism* (Notre Dame, IN: University of Notre Dame Press), p. 6.
12. J. Butler, J. Habermas, C. Taylor and C. West (2011), *The Power*

of Religion in the Public Sphere, edited by E. Mendieta and J. VanAntwerpen (New York: SSRC/Columbia University Press).

13. Parekh examines the Rawlsian claim of the neutrality of political liberalism and argues that it presupposes both comprehensive liberalism and cultural monism. Parekh, *Rethinking Multiculturalism*, pp. 86–90.

14. C. Taylor (2007), *A Secular Age* (Cambridge, MA: Harvard University Press).

15. W. Connolly (1999), *Why I Am Not a Secularist* (Minneapolis, MN: University of Minnesota Press), p. 24.

16. Ibid., p. 89; M. J. Sandel (1993), *Freedom of Conscience or Freedom of Choice*, in T. Eastland (ed.) *Religious Liberty in the Supreme Court* (Cambridge, MA/Michigan, MN: Eerdmans Publishing Company), pp. 483–96.

17. R. Rorty (1994), 'Religion as a conversation-stopper', *Common Knowledge*, 3:1, p. 2; C. J. Eberle (2002), *Religious Conviction in Liberal Politics* (Cambridge: Cambridge University Press), p. 77.

18. J. Spinner-Halev (2000), *Surviving Diversity: Religion and Democratic Citizenship* (Baltimore, MD: Johns Hopkins University Press), pp. 150–6.

19. Ibid., p. 155.

20. Ibid., pp. 110–12.

21. Ibid., pp. 330–1.

22. I. H. Malik (2002), *Religious Minorities in Pakistan* (London: Minority Rights Group International), p. 18.

23. Parekh, *Rethinking Multiculturalism*, pp. 322–3.

24. B. Kaplan (2010), *Divided by Faith: Religious Conflict and the Practice of Toleration in Early Modern Europe* (Cambridge, MA: Harvard University Press).

25. V. Bader (2007), *Secularism or Democracy?* (Amsterdam: Amsterdam University Press).

26. Rawls, *Theory of Justice*, p. 47.

27. Ibid., p. 9.

28. Ibid., p. 10.

29. J. Keane (2000), *The Political Quarterly – Secularism* (Oxford: Blackwell Publishers), p. 14; T. N. Madan (1998), 'Secularism in its place', pp 297–320 in Rajeev Bhargava (ed.) *Secularism and its Critics* (New Delhi: OUP), at p. 298.

30. P. Hamburger (2002), *Separation of Church and State* (Cambridge, MA: Harvard University Press), pp. 193–251.

7

Identity, Values and the Law

Raymond Plant

In this chapter I shall look critically at some of the central themes in Parekh's latest work on identity and its political role, which in one absolutely central respect I agree with. What I have in mind here is his general taxonomy of identity.[1] Parekh distinguishes quite rightly between three dimensions of identity: the individual, the collective and the universal. These three dimensions are indispensable. They cannot be reduced to only one. They have to be held in a relationship if our political thinking is to get a grasp on the complexities of modern politics. Mistakes are made when one of these features is neglected, or another is elevated at the expense of others. This neglect of some forms of identity and overemphasis on others accounts for what Parekh sees as some of the defects of modern political thought. So, as we shall see, liberal political thought goes wrong in neglecting the collective forms of social identity and emphasising only the universal in terms of wholly general and abstract principles on the one hand and the individual or particular, usually conceived within the liberal tradition as the bearer of rights, on the other; communitarianism goes wrong in neglecting universal values and forms of identity rooted in our common humanity, or at least in failing to integrate such values into communitarian accounts and not having a clear account of the role of the individual in a communitarian perspective. For Parekh a full account of identity will treat it as being what Hegel calls a concrete universal in his *Science of Logic*,[2] and Parekh explicitly acknowledges the influence of Hegel here. In a concrete universal the various 'moments' (as Hegel would call them) of universality, individuality and specificity (which corresponds to Parekh's collective form of identity) have to be held together in a complex dialectical relationship. This means that we cannot put them into some kind of a priori set of relationships, partly because the forms that these types of identity take are historical and not logical or analytical relationships. To understand the complexity of identity is a matter of understanding how identities have developed in human history and the various cultural forms that this history has created. These will embody the features of individuality, specificity and universality.

There is, however, a very big difference on this point between Parekh and Hegel. For Hegel, history has an end or goal, at which point the various aspects of identity coalesce into an integrated whole so that the claims of the different forms of identity are given their proper and final place. When this point is reached, as Hegel explained in the Preface to the *Philosophy of Right*, reality will confront us in a cut and dried way and, because we have reached the end of history, the Owl of Minerva – Hegel's symbol for philosophical insight – will be able to take flight with this gathering of the dusk. We shall then have some kind of absolute knowledge, some kind of final knowledge about how the various aspects or moments of identity integrate with one another and about the kind of political institutions that can embody and facilitate this. If, however, we leave Hegel's metaphysical views on one side we can still see, as Parekh argues, that this dialectical view of identity does help us to understand complexity in the modern world without expecting that there will be some kind of final resolution of the relationships between the sense of identity that I have as an individual, as a member of different and indeed multiple social identities, and the sense of myself as sharing a sense of common humanity with others, which is the most comprehensive and universal aspect of identity. Because there will be no final resolution of these moments into one final coherent whole there cannot be any final political, social, legal or cultural theory that can be the last word on these aspects of identity and the degrees of integration that they can achieve at any moment in human history. To this extent Parekh's theory sets out the framework for a sort of research programme to which a range of contributions can be made from different perspectives. Parekh accepts that, because of the dynamic nature of these moments of identity, and indeed their interaction with one another, the most that can be said in a wholly definitive way has to do with the framework rather than the substance, because the ways in which the identities are realised is dynamic and subject to change and development. All that we can say is that an account of identity that neglects one or more of these aspects or moments will be defective and that we cannot set up one form of integration of aspects of identity – for example liberalism – as normative for the rest and as a goal to which all others will have to aspire.

It is obviously important to say something about these three aspects of identity, although Parekh has set out their general taxonomy in a very clear and compelling way. All are subject to great complexity in their elaboration but because I want in the more critical part of this chapter to concentrate on their relationship I will not in fact delve into these complexities, which in any case I don't think alter the power of Parekh's case. So I shall give the merest sketch of what he means by these different aspects or moments of identity.

In the case of individual identity we are concerned with the individual person. His or her own conception of themselves, their sense of themselves as agents acting on the world, both natural and human, their sense of values and what matters to them, what they and others take to be their character and the narrative that could be elicited from them about their lives and how they see themselves.

Of course, such individuals with such identities do not just spring up like mushrooms but they derive their values and a sense of what is important in life in their interaction with others, and is heavily dependent on various forms of social and cultural life in which they play a part. Some of these are given forms of cultural, collective or specific identity that have not been chosen by the individual – home and family life being the most obvious one. But while as T. S. Eliot says in 'East Coker', home is where one starts from but it is not where one finishes. But there are forms of identity that are important and indeed controversial when they relate to others. These other unchosen forms of identity include race, ethnicity, gender and sexual orientation. Other forms of identity are more obviously chosen and self-assumed. The contrast between these forms of identity can lead to problems in terms of their relationship, as we shall see later. An individual shares in a wide range of cultural forms and learns values and vocabularies from them – vocabularies in terms of which they can construct the narrative of their own lives. Again, to use Eliot's language, 'We shall not cease from exploration' – and human life has this sense of exploration as a central feature, though it is not some kind of isolated existentialist self-invention but is heavily dependent on the cultural forms that are available to an individual. Sometimes these will have involved autonomous choice – to join this or that cultural community (for want of a better word); others though will be forms into which one is born. Some forms of collective identity will be seen as a matter of choice others are more a matter of fate. The main point just for the moment though is that individual identity is not some kind of given status: it is rather something that we develop and achieve, and the process of this development and achievement depends heavily on the cultural (in the widest sense) context in which an individual is embedded, and some aspects of this will be a matter of choice and other aspects will not. For Parekh, a political theory that neglects or downplays these collective forms of identity and concentrates on the individual alone, as some forms of libertarian political theories do for example, is bound to be blind to the complexities of modern life.

However, we are not just individuals and members, whether by choice or birth, of various groups, communities or forms and collective identity; we also have a sense of the universal in human life. This is a sense of what we share in common with other human beings as members of the same species. These commonalities may well include a sense of common needs and, in a broad and rather thin sense, common human values. These sorts of considerations about the individual and political claims of what might be called humanity are again indispensable for a fully comprehensive account of identity. In the same way, though, as individual or personal identity depends upon a range of cultural forms for its development so too the universality of the claims of humanity do not just appear but are in turned nurtured and exemplified in a range of cultural forms that either aim at some kind of universal message, or address themselves to a universal audience or support in direct or indirect ways such a universalist position. So, just to take two examples from Western culture: despite many contrary aspects, Christianity has played a significant role in providing a basis for a sense of aspects of common humanity and the idea of the inherent dignity of the human person, as has the idea of natural law, whether in its Greek, Roman or Catholic form – as Parekh makes clear. He takes from Hegel the insight, contra Rousseau, that there cannot in general be a leap from the particular or individual to the universal, from the conception of oneself as an individual to a concern with humanity in its universal aspects. This universalist aspect has to be developed and it has to be achieved through the individual's development in his or her participation in cultural forms that broaden the circle of the individual's concern and (as it were) mediate between the individual and the universal.

This latter point is fundamentally important for Parekh's account of identity in the modern world and this is so in various respects. First of all, liberal political theory in his view tends to base itself on an account of the individual and his or her rights and on some universalist account of the type of state that can be made compatible with this view of the individual. Twentieth-century liberalism, unlike that say of T. H. Green and other nineteenth-century idealist liberals, neglects the role of intermediate and mediating forms of relationship within which the individual is embedded either through choice, nature or circumstance, which may help or impede the attachment to universalist principles. A universalist perspective has to be developed, it is not just a given. It is an achievement, and this cannot happen without the role of cultural forms that develop universalist impulses. Second, the link between the forms of social and collective identity and a universal standpoint marks his major point of difference with the communitarians. Communitarians emphasise, in contrast with the liberal individualist, the role of the individual as engaged with and embedded within cultural and community forms as at the very least partly constitutive of an individual's identity. The individual is a 'radically situated self' in Michael Sandel's words.[3] Individuals do not, however, situate their communitarian perspective in a context that can explain the attachment to the universal – that is to say, that is concerned with the nature and requirements of recognising our humanity and the rights and obligations that flow from doing so. In addition, concern with a universal aspect of our identity provides a normative standard for our approach to collective and communitarian forms of identity. For many communitarians, what is normative is embedded in the forms of community and culture that contribute to the constitution of the individual's identity. Any critical stance towards the culture, values and practices of a form of community has to come from the inside, in a form of immanent critique. That is to say, a cultural community can be criticised from within because, for example, it embodies values that it consistently fails to live up to, or is incoherent in how it applies such values. No doubt such forms of cultural and community-based critiques are powerful and indispensable, but they do not exhaust the issue of the normativity of cultural communities because from Parekh's perspective they must also be seen from the standpoint of the universal. Universal concerns to do with human rights and human dignity can and should provide a critical tool for interrogating the claims and practices of such communities. Thus the universal perspective provides a more general normative standard in terms of which to judge cultural communities and, much more radically, a basis for deeming some types of collective identity embodied in cultural communities as illegitimate. This normative role for universal values is very important, because Parekh regards it as a basis in terms of which it is possible to argue for the reshaping of forms of community life in a modern society so that they become compatible with such universalist concerns. In his chapter, 'Global ethics' in *A New Politics of Identity*, he is clear on this point. He believes that such changes and indeed transformations in the attitudes of cultural communities can in fact come through dialogue, presumably in a pluralistic society rather than through the law, which is a point to which I shall return later.

This universalist position also provides the basis for Parekh's rejection of cultural relativism – the view that morality and indeed rationality are in fact relative to culture. He rejects relativism partly on the grounds that it cannot be stated incoherently, as follows: is the thesis of relativism true in a non-relative way? If it is, then it is false because there is one truth, namely the truth of relativism, which is not relatively true. At the same time if it is taken to be relatively true then it might well be false. But his other reason for rejecting relativism is that we do in fact find a universalist perspective in things like the UN Declaration of Human Rights. Again there are some complexities with this position to which I shall return.

Earlier I drew attention to Parekh's own comparison of his position on the complex nature of identity with that of Hegel. As we saw he rejected one aspect of this comparison that Hegel held, which might be seen as an absolutist view – that there is in fact a form of social, political and legal order in which all the complex aspects of identity could be reconciled and the role of the individual, cultural/collective/community and universal identity could all have a clear and allotted part. Parekh rejects this and argues that his absolutist metaphysics and idealist epistemology distort his views and 'lead him to think that respectively that all identities form part of a harmonious hierarchical whole and that conflicts between them arise only from our inadequate understanding of them'.[4] Parekh rejects this in favour of a much more pluralist approach, and as I said at the beginning of this chapter this allows him to argue that he has provided a compelling framework for analysing identity, while allowing that its substance could be provided from a range of perspectives and there would never be some kind of ultimate and complete account of identity in the modern world. Given this view I think, he has to do more to explain the seeming priority that he assigns to the demands of universality and humanity. I am wholly sympathetic to the view that there is this priority, but if in fact this is where the fundamental norms of human life are located so that they can be invoked to provide a critique of and show the way towards a refashioning and indeed delegitimising forms of community and cultural life then it is not clear to me that Parekh doesn't have his own absolutist standpoint, which is provided by his commitment to a global ethic rooted in the idea of humanity, human dignity and worth, human rights and mutual obligation. This view of the role of human as opposed to particular and specific forms of identity is normatively very strong indeed, because he says in *A New Politics of Identity* that while recognising the fundamental importance of cultural communities and individual perspectives and the fact that human solidarity cannot be constructed 'behind their backs', nevertheless 'we should respect these identities but redefine and restructure them in the light of, and bring them into harmony with, the universal human identity. The two are no longer conflictual but complementary.'[5]

This does seem to put the forms of human identity into some kind of hierarchy despite Parekh's disavowal of this. Individual identity depends crucially upon the way an individual relates to cultural communities with which he or she is engaged either through nature, nurture or choice, but those communities must in their turn be compatible with universal values or reshaped and redefined in the light of the more basic normative requirements of humanity in its universal form and in terms of the global ethics that is rooted in this universal form. So where lies the contrast drawn by Parekh between his own position and that of Hegel? It is certainly true that Parekh does not adopt a metaphysical and epistemological position towards the normative priority of humanity to parallel that of Hegel. His position is that in a globalised world we are increasingly engaged with one another at this level rather than at the level of particularistic communities, and that this interaction, which is partly the result of globalisation, leads to a growing consensus about universal, transcultural values. These values can form a kind of bedrock of ideas like rights and obligations, which we all share. They include such things as human worth, rights, common obligations and human solidarity, and respect for difference and plurality.

However, I have a doubt here. As we have seen, the universal claims of humanity, embodied for example in global ethics, can be invoked to reshape the beliefs and practices of particular cultural communities, but the fact is that many of these communities, particularly religious ones, may well resist the claims of universal or global ethics in some particular respect – the most obvious one in the UK at present being gay rights. A right to freedom of sexual orientation and practice may form part of a universal value system (although there are many who would disagree with this and global ethics are supposed to embody consensus). A person from a particular religious perspective may well resist the idea of such a right when it places that person under an obligation to perform an act such as officiating at a gay marriage, or providing a commercial service such as letting a room to a gay couple, as a condition of staying in business as a guesthouse owner. In the view of such a person, these acts performed by that person from their religious perspective would be wrong. Such a view may be rooted in quite deep theological conviction for which they believe they have an epistemological sanction and authority within their cultural community. This theological authority may in fact mean more to them and command their loyalty much more than claims about the requirements of humanity. Parekh believes that over time such attitudes can be changed by dialogue. But what if they cannot: surely then the issue of law and coercion come into the picture. It also comes in if universal values can be used to reshape the beliefs of cultural communities and indeed to delegitimise them. It is difficult to see such delegitimation taking place without the law. Parekh seems to assume that all of these things will follow from consensus on global ethics and dialogue about the reshaping of community values and practices in the light of these. Surely in some situations however there will have to be a role for coercion and the law. Doesn't justifying the role of the law in such circumstances require strong claims about the compelling nature of the universal values? Parekh seems rather ambivalent about this, in that he rejects attempts at what might be seen as some kind of philosophical foundation for such values, and explicitly rejects Kantian and Rawlsian approaches to such values. What matters is the emergence of a consensus in values from pluralistic cultures, coupled with a challenge to those who disagree with them to come up with robust arguments. However in the religious context that I am discussing, while religious arguments may seem to have these characteristics they will almost certainly not be seen in these ways by members of faith and perhaps other cultural communities where there are strongly held and quite elaborate views about what might count as a reason, or appropriate evidence and so on. If universal values are to be invoked to justify coercion, particularly when community-based forms of identity are to be regarded as illegitimate and unacceptable, then we have to be pretty sure of the ground on which we are standing in coercing those whom we regard as unreasonable. This has to do with the content or substance of global ethics, and also with the priority that global ethics have at least implicitly for Parekh, since this ethical stance can be utilised to reshape first-order cultural identities or to delegitimise them. So I would argue that Parekh's normative ordering needs to be based upon an epistemological position of its own. In a sense this is because he thinks that reasonable people considering evidence and so on will come to assent to this view. This falls well short of what one might call a philosophical foundation for prioritising global ethics over cultural identity but is it a strong and compelling enough basis for the use of coercion? Of course if everything happens over time through dialogue that is one thing, but if we go back to the gay rights cases I mentioned earlier it is difficult to see how the global ethical principles at stake here can be secured without the coercive power of the law.

I very much doubt whether the reshaping and redefining of cultural communities, particularly religious ones, can come through dialogue alone. This is because the beliefs of religious adherents are comparable to what Bernard Williams calls 'ground projects', which are forms of belief that give people a sense of identity, worth, belonging and a sense of why life is worthwhile at all. If many forms of religious belief are like this, they may be rather immune to claims about the requirements of humanity understood in a non-adjectival way, that is to say not humanity understood in itself and not from a particular perspective. If this immunity exists and I believe that it does, we have to be able to answer William's point made in his essay 'Moral luck' when he argues:

> There can come a point at which it is quite unreasonable for a man to give up in the name of the impartial ordering of the world of moral agents something which is a condition of having any interest in being around in the world at all.[6]

This is the sharp question of when and how do we justify saying to a religious believer that their value system has to yield to the claims of humanity as a whole, and as embodied in rights (as well as other things for Parekh). I find it difficult to think that the reshaping and restructuring of forms of community life can occur in these circumstances without the use of coercion and the law rather than dialogue. This is indeed what has happened in a whole range of legal cases in the UK and on the continent in respect of the attitudes of religion to gay rights, on religious dress, and on the freedom to manifest religion. If redefining and restructuring cultural communities consisting of ground projects for those who adhere to them can only ultimately proceed coercively through the law then we are likely to need at least some assumed epistemology to tackle the truth claims made by the adherents of such community-based views. In fact at one point in the book Parekh comes close to acknowledging this in his discussion of faith and reason in the chapter 'The pathology of religious identity'. He produces a strong case for reason and a critique of the role of faith. I shall not assess these arguments at this stage. All that I would say is that it seems clear to me that he is in fact claiming some epistemological authority for his position as I believe he has to do to in order to liberalise faith communities (in a broad sense of the word liberalise). If dialogue doesn't work then to fulfil Parekh's programme there has to be a place for the law and coercion, and this means answering the hard question of how do you justify the coercion of those whom you regard as unreasonable; and this is bound to involve at least tacit epistemological claims, particularly since Parekh is explicitly critical of Rawls' much shallower idea of public reason.

What would not work for the Parekh framework with humanitarian claims in the normatively most important position to itself would be regarded as a matter of faith or commitment if it were to be used to challenge, redefine and reshape forms of cultural community that are themselves a matter of faith – because what is it then that privileges the claims of universalist humanity over the claims of cultural community identity if both are based on faith? Clearly Parekh does not think that global ethics does depend on faith or commitment as opposed to consensus arising out of reasoned deliberation, but in order to achieve that he has to have a basis for the conversation. This is secured I think for Parekh by a recognition of the value and importance of pluralism: that if I recognise pluralism, then as an adherent of, say, a faith community I will recognise that other may disagree with me and that it is reasonable for them to do so. The fact that Parekh puts a great deal of weight on the recognition of pluralism can be seen by the language that he uses in Chapter 10 of *A New Politics of Identity* when he says:

> When one appreciates the ontological and epistemological importance of plurality and difference, one sees other cultures, religions and so on, not as threats or rivals but as conversational partners, indeed as the very condition of one's own growth.[7]

However, in the case of religion again I don't think that it is as straightforward as this. As Stuart Hampshire argues in Justice is Conflict: 'One God; one morality', that is that most religions seem to be intrinsically linked to a position which is a long way from pluralism and a recognition of its ontological and epistemological superiority. Parekh argues that a respect for plurality and difference is part of global ethics, which as we have seen can then be invoked for reshaping or even delegitimising cultural communities. However the problem still remains as to how it is possible to convince someone who has a complete belief in a set of religious doctrines to acknowledge that it is reasonable for others to disagree with that position, because this is an important element of pluralism. It is not capable of an easy answer because as Joseph Raz has argued the consequences for the believer's position might be a plunge into incoherence:

> To assume that one believes a proposition (i.e. believes it to be true) while one regards it as no more likely to be true than its contradictory is to allow a radical rupture between belief and belief that one's belief is justified.[8]

So, my conclusion at this point is that more needs to be said about what Parekh calls the epistemological and ontological significance of pluralism and why in some sense it is reasonable or, more strongly, rational to accept it as a guiding principle in understanding the relationship between human values and collective ones. What cannot be the case for Parekh is that pluralism is in a sense underpinned by moral and cultural relativism since he has rejected the relativist position and his own insistence on the role of global ethics shows how far away from relativism he is.

I want now to turn to another issue that has to do with identity: the law and coercion. If cultural communities are to be reshaped then we have to have, as Parekh himself recognises, some account of and conception of the acceptable form of manifestation of identity. This is discussed by Parekh in the context of his idea of 'acceptability' – manifestations of a cultural including religious identity must be acceptable – but he does not really go much further in elaborating this. It seems to me that there are two ways in which one might look at this question. The first is to try to distinguish between ways of manifesting identity that are thought to be intrinsic or essential to the identity in question. If an essential form of manifestation is to be regarded by others as unacceptable, then there is a very considerable problem, particularly in relation to religious belief. The Human Rights Act (HRA) and the ECHR in Article 9 guarantee an absolute right to freedom of religious belief with a more conditional right to freedom to manifest belief. Assume for the moment that a form of manifesting belief is regarded as essential to that belief such as a Muslim praying five times a day facing Mecca. To abridge a right to manifest that belief could be regarded as an interference with the fundamental right to religious freedom, because it is an intrinsic part of the belief in question. So, if the aim is to avoid abridging the right to freedom of religious belief than it looks as though lawmakers and the courts need to have some sense of what is and is not an essential and intrinsic requirement in terms of the manifestation of that belief. This is an example of where there is clear tension between two levels in Parekh's model of complex identity. On the one hand, the universal or the level of humanity might provide a basis for a universal right to freedom of belief that should not be abridged, while at the same time the question will arise as to whether or not a particular form of manifesting the belief is intrinsic to it. That is to say the universal level has to be involved in an account of the collective identity or the cultural community's sense of identity and what are and are not, in the useful terms coined by Anthony Appiah, the normative requirements of identity.[9] This will raise the issue discussed earlier about the relationship between the universal level of human identity and the community-based aspects of identity. If community identities are to be reshaped and redefined in the light of the universal, then it would seem to imply that the only manifestations of identity that could be regarded as being acceptable are those which are compatible with the rights of others understood as part of the universal level or the level of humanity. I have no quarrel with this approach but it is important to see its implications and the potentially very radical consequences that flow from it.

First, what the position essentially entails is that manifestations of an identity must be compatible with the rights of others, and not harm others. This seems to be a distinctively liberal conception, and yet Parekh has been keen in several publications to distance his own project from that of liberalism.[10]

Second, whether the attempt to redefine and reshape cultural identities is pursued through dialogue or through coercion and the law, it seems clear that we need a proper understanding of what constitutes 'identity' and what are its normative requirements' so that it is possible to judge where and when an attempt to abridge the manifestation of an identity in the interests of universal or human identity in fact strikes at the character of the identity itself. This will be a particularly acute problem in relation to religious identity just because in Western states at least, as I have pointed out, there is an absolute right to freedom of belief. So reshaping and redefining an identity may well be seen by at least some with that identity as compromising its very essence. In his discussion of community-based identity, Parekh is not keen on the idea of essentialism: that an identity has an essential nature, that there are joint necessary and sufficient conditions for the ascription of an identity. However insofar as issues of the law and coercion will apply rather than those of dialogue and debate it is very difficult to see that one can avoid the issue of what constitutes the essence of an identity, in that restricting some manifestations of identity will be seen as not infringing religious freedom whereas others would –for example abridging the requirement on Muslims to pray five times a day could be seen to strike at the essence of the identity whereas a dress code would not (or might not as the issue is acutely controversial). In order to answer these questions we would need to have some idea of what is and what is not essential to an identity. These are not just theoretical issues, in that the English courts have been asked to rule on precisely issues of this sort as part of the process of determining whether or not some restraint on the manifestation of belief is a restriction of religious freedom just because that manifestation is regarded by the person with the beliefs as being essential to their belief system.

The only real way of avoiding issues of this sort would be to argue that identity and its essential nature should be left out of the picture and that the issue of which forms of manifestation of identity were to be regarded as acceptable or unacceptable should be seen in terms of the harm principle – that is to say: Does the manifestation of identity harm others or not? Does it infringe their rights or not? If no harm is done then the manifestation should be allowed. What needs to be pointed out here, though, is that in order to address this question we do not need to bring questions of identity and its requirements into the picture at all. Rather we just concentrate on the issue of harm. However, this would make the position quite close if not identical to what has been called 'difference-blind' liberalism, that is to say, a form of liberalism that does not take account of Parekh's second community-based form of identity. While they may be important for individuals, such forms of identity have no political or legal salience for the difference-blind liberal. All that we need to concentrate upon is the claim to harm, not on the identity that is held to underpin or sanction the action which has been called to account in terms of harm. Parekh cannot, however, concede this, since he sees his own position as quite contrary to difference-blind liberalism. Nevertheless, as I have suggested at least in respect of religious identity and at least in respect of the law to avoid difference-blind forms of liberalism, Parekh may have to accept much more about the essential nature of different forms of identity than he seems willing to concede. So the crucial thing at stake here it seems to me is the relationship between the forms of identity at the level of the cultural community and at the universal level of human identity. If these relationships and the modifications to community forms of identification can be resolved by dialogue then that is fine and it is undoubtedly the best and most humane way forward. If, however, there has to be a role for the law and coercion in securing a proper relationship between community-based forms of identity and the universal level on which their reshaping rests then there will be serious questions to answer about the legitimacy of the standpoint of the universal, given that it is going to have the effect of reshaping and redefining people's deepest beliefs.

I want now to take up a further issue about how we are to understand the normative requirements of identity, and again my view is that the questions I shall raise involve metaphysical questions that Parekh wishes to disavow. What I have in mind here can initially be sketched in terms of a rather conventional and well-known argument, which has certainly been deployed with some frequency in controversies between those with religious beliefs or a religious identity and the issue of gay rights. It is frequently argued that being based upon faith and commitment religious belief is a matter of choice, and insofar as we want to talk about identity here it is a matter of a self-assumed identity and it is also an identity that one can disavow. Sometimes this thought is put in terms of religion being a lifestyle choice on a par with other lifestyle choices. This it is claimed contrasts sharply with sexual identity and sexual orientation, which are given forms of identity: they are not matters of choice, they embody things that one finds discovers oneself not things that are chosen. Given such a view it is then argued that it is not legitimate to allow beliefs that are rooted in faith and choice to be a basis of discrimination against those with a given form of identity. Hence the law has to protect those with a given or naturalised form of identity against discrimination by others based on lifestyle choices such as religious beliefs. So the law has to protect gays and lesbians, both of which are forms of natural or given, rather than self-assumed, identity against discrimination by religious people whose beliefs are based upon choice and faith. So the contrast to be drawn is between naturalised identity and choice-based forms of identity.

The first is given and cannot be disavowed; the second is assumed and can. Of course there are parallel arguments in respect of race, gender and ethnicity, which are forms of natural identity, and the beliefs held by those who wish to discriminate against those with these forms of identity, which are not.

However the picture is more complex than this and again has to do with the normative requirements of identity, as Appiah puts it. The normative requirements of identity cannot just be, as it were, read off from the natural account of the identity in question. We cannot just read off from a biological account of identity what sorts of claims such identities sanction, nor can we read off what we owe to those with these identities. To think that we can read off these requirements from just the identity itself is not only a mistake in logic but is also highly conservative. It implies some kind of natural order that corresponds to biological nature: that women, given their nature, should be constrained within certain roles, or that people of different races or ethnicities have a kind of normative framework built around them in respect of such roles. As Simone de Beauvoir argued in *The Second Sex*, a woman's biological nature is not some kind of fate, which lays down some kind of essential type of self-fulfilment. Rather women in a free society can construct for themselves what they regard as important or even essential for their nature. Sartre argues much the same thing throughout his work, but if we take just one example, namely the character Daniel in *The Reprieve*,[11] we can see the point that Sartre is making. Daniel muses to himself that he wants to be a homosexual in the same way as an oak tree is an oak tree. He wants to be what he is. He wants to objectify his nature in some kind of essentialist way. For Sartre this is quite impossible. We are always free to construct our own view about our identity and what we think that this identity requires if we are to live with our own sense of integrity. In his recent book *Joseph Anton* Salman Rushdie makes this point in a pithy way: 'the self is its origin and its journey'.[12] We are not wholly defined by our origin; it is always possible to construct an alternative way of living one's life. Now, if there is truth in this picture then, as Bernard Williams argues in *Shame and Necessity*,[13] there are no necessary social identities in the modern world. There may of course be natural differences, but this does not underwrite necessary forms of social identity. These involve choice and construction. If this is so, then the stark contrast with which we started, of natural identity as a discovered identity in contrast with the self-chosen identity of the religious person, for example, is greatly overdone. If this is so, it seems difficult to argue that the nature of the two sorts of identity can justify two different roles in legislation: one for naturalised identity and one for self-assumed identity. The normative aspects of these identities involve construction and choice in each case and there is nothing necessary about them.

If this is so then a number of things would follow in respect of Parekh's account of collective or cultural community identity within his account of complex identity. Insofar as an adequate form of politics must take account of identity or grant legal recognition to identities it should do so recognising that none of these identities in their normative/social dimensions are in fact necessary or, as it were, logically required or essential to identity. They are not, to use Parekh's very useful term, highly 'scripted' identities. Yet it is in terms of their social and normative 'requirements' that identities enter into the legal and political sphere. These issues enter the public realm in terms of what rights people have to pursue their sense of identity in one way rather than another and what duties others have to respect the normative and social aspects of identity. In many ways this makes the issue of reshaping and redefining identity as Parekh wants much easier to achieve, because it would not then do to argue from within an identity that somehow the normative requirements are natural or essential. They too – as much as say religious identity – involve matters of choice, commitment and construction. No doubt, as Parekh argues, these choices about how to pursue identity are made in relation to the beliefs and practices of cultural communities but they are not in any sense necessary forms of social identity, in the sense that the claimed normative requirements of identity follow from a biological basis for the identity where there is such a basis for its existence. These remarks however lead to a very big issue in political theory which Williams recognises in *Shame and Necessity*, namely about the relationship between the politics of recognition and the politics of social justice and the place of liberalism within this dichotomy. The strongest case for the politics of recognition is that certain forms of identity such as race, ethnicity, gender and sexual orientation have a biological base, and that they are forms of unchosen identity. Political and legal institutions then ought to give some kind of recognition to such forms of identity, and in particular to protect them from forms of discrimination. If however the social dimensions of the identity are matters of choice and construction then it is not so clear as to why politics and the law should give recognition to all the particular forms that a social identity takes. If social identities do not embody some sense of necessity then there is a case for arguing that the politics of recognition should give way to considerations of justice. This immediately raises the issue of the role of liberal political thought from which Parekh distances himself in quite a few respects. For as Williams says: 'A central feature of modern liberal conceptions of social justice can indeed be expressed by saying that they altogether deny the existence of necessary social identities'. Further, 'those who salute the power of modern enlightenment . . . find a liberating force in the recognition that any social role can be held up to human criticism and that no such necessities are dictated to us by nature'.[14] Questions of justice may well be concerned with some of the necessities of human life and with the role of luck, but so far as social identities go these can be considered within a framework of justice that does not have to concede some kind of legal recognition of identity.

Parekh accepts a good deal of this sort of argument. He emphasises the extent to which a social identity is a construction and an interpretation and can be subject to critique. Indeed, it is a central theme of his work that, as we have seen, identities can be criticised in relation to universal values and he is quite prepared to say that some forms of social identity should certainly not be recognised because they are incompatible with these universal values. He also accepts that a politics of recognition can in fact lead to the essentialisation of some forms of identity. Political and legal recognition of identity can only work if the identity is clear and has a certain definite character in the public realm. This process almost intrinsically generates an homogenisation of identity that neglects both the dynamic of identity, the relationship between one identity and another – for example being black and being a woman – and it will also mean that those who have the power to define an identity within a cultural community will have their position underwritten and legitimated by the process of legal and political recognition of the identity in question. So it would certainly be quite wrong to interpret Parekh's work as in some sense sanctioning a commitment to the politics of the recognition of social identity, despite such inferences being drawn by some of his critics. It still remains true though that he does still see a role for the politics of identity as well as social justice and does not want to surrender all the political claims that can be entered at the level of what we saw earlier he calls the collective level of identity. Parekh does this by arguing that the modern liberal concern with justice is inadequate as a full account of a good society. The recognition of identity provides a political and legal basis for something that liberals believe in, namely the pluralism and diversity of a liberal society. However, in Parekh's view the emphasis on social justice may be indifferent to the legal and political basis of diversity, whereas the whole point of the politics of recognition is to provide a legal and political framework for pluralism. It is also his view that the legal recognition of identity may well be of particular help to marginalised and disadvantaged members of society who share common identities. For Parekh, the aim of a diverse society would be one in which individuals can have 'the freedom to explore, reconstitute and express our individual and collective identities in an environment free from obsession with uniformity', and he argues that this position requires that 'the state should, under appropriate circumstances, recognise, respect, cherish and support legitimate identities'. Such legitimate identities will be those that are compatible with, or have been reconstituted to become compatible with, universal values. What is not so clear though is why this is impossible within what might be thought of as standard liberal accounts of the state, with all citizens having equal civil and political rights, equality before the law and some kind of welfare state to ensure that such rights can be protected and exercised. Liberalism recognises the importance of pluralism, and indeed in the view of some people pluralism is essential to the justification of liberalism.

202

Within such pluralism individuals can choose to come together in groups of one sort or another to celebrate what they have in common, and to pursue their interests as members of groups and communities; or they can stand aside as individuals from all of these sorts of identity creating activities. What is not clear is what it is about liberalism that requires, in addition, the legal recognition of identity. No doubt many liberals, at least in the twentieth century, were rather neglectful in terms of failing to incorporate a role for groups and for identity within their theories. It does not seem to me that there is anything intrinsic about that. Indeed, what Parekh says about pluralism (the role of the state in securing the freedom to explore express and redefine identity) it seems to me would be quite compatible with the view of someone like Nozick, a very radical liberal, in the section on 'A framework for Utopia'in *Anarchy, State and Utopia*.[15] Maybe liberals have not been as warm about identities as they might but it is unclear why the role that Parekh wants to see identity (suitably reinterpreted in the light of universal values) play in politics cannot be secure in a strong constitutional framework of civil and political rights that would set out in concrete terms those universal values which could appropriately be turned into rights.

In the final part of the chapter I want to turn to his account of universal values. I am basically in full agreement with him about these values and the role that they could play in reconstituting (liberalising?) identities. What I am concerned about however are two interrelated things. First of all there is the fact that at the level of global ethics in *A New Politics of Identity*, these universal values are rather thin (to use Michael Walzer's terminology). To play a role in politics in a particular society they would have to be thickened and become richer and more determinate. The second issue then comes into play; namely, if we live in a society in which there is a reasonably strong recognition of identity, will not cultural communities want to thicken up such general values by drawing upon their own beliefs, conceptions and practices. This is not just a theoretical possibility in that in relation to something like the UN Declaration of Human Rights, which Parekh sees as both a statement of universal values and as a practical refutation of moral and cultural relativism, the fact is that within nation states there has been resistance, or least reinterpretation of such rights to reflect the cultural values of the nation states themselves. This sort of process has occurred in China and also in Malaysia, where both Prime Minister Mahtir and his then deputy (before they fell out) Anwar Ibrahim wrote at length and powerfully about human rights and what they called 'Asian values'. The aim was both to reinterpret human rights in the context of Asian values and also to insist that a human rights regime did not exhaust the political vision of Asian countries such as Malaysia. If universal values such as human rights have to be enriched by interpretation in the context of cultural traditions as has been claimed, then there is no reason why this should happen only at the national level. It could equally occur within societies against the background of a plurality of cultural groups within that society. If this is so, and if universal values are to be the touchstone for distinguishing between legitimate and illegitimate identities, it seems imperative that a society should share a common view about these values in their thickened form. This is of vital importance because, as I argued earlier, such values may provide the basis for the coercive and legal delegitimisation, or the reconstitution, of an identity. If, however, such universal values need to be enriched before they are useful, will this not engage a struggle over the appropriate interpretation of universal values between cultural communities that are subject to them? This is not at all fanciful. In the UK one could quite easily regard the HRA as giving legal effect to universal values, and likewise the Equality Act. Yet both of these Acts have given rise to intense controversy about how Article 9 of the European Convention on Human Rights, incorporated into UK law by the HRA, should be interpreted, with religious groups and secular groups disagreeing in quite fundamental ways. The same is true of the Equality Act (2010) in relation to sexual orientation. Will any cultural groups in fact respond to Parekh's idea of discussing the reconstitution of identity in the light of universal values if their interpretation of such values is rather different from those of other groups? This cannot be just a matter of dialogue. If as Parekh says the universal values can be used to delegitimise some forms of identity then these values will have to underwrite a form of coercion and their interpretation will have to be clear. In *A New Politics of Identity* Parekh recognises most of these points, but I think that he could have drawn out the implications of his views more fully.

To sum up: I find Parekh's work on identity extremely stimulating and as I said at the start, in terms of the taxonomy of identity, convincing. I also believe that if dialogue can play the role he assigns to it then most of his other arguments go through. If however one is less optimistic than that then the role of the law and coercion has to be considered and here I think that there is more work to be done, as I have suggested. This is entirely to be expected, since Parekh himself always regards his own account of the politics and dialectic of individual, community-based and human forms of identity as a work in progress. This chapter is a small contribution to that task, which has been so perceptively set before us by Bhikuh Parekh.

Notes

1. B. Parekh (2008), *A New Politics of Identity* (Basingstoke: Palgrave).
2. G. W. F. Hegel (2010 [1812–16]), *The Science of Logic* (Cambridge: Cambridge University Press).
3. M. Sandel (1982), *Liberalism and the Limits of Justice* (Cambridge: Cambridge University Press), *passim*.
4. Ibid., p. 2.
5. Ibid., p. 2.
6. Subsequently published in book form as B. A. O. Williams (1981), *Moral Luck* (Cambridge: Cambridge University Press).
7. Parekh, *A New Politics of Identity*, p. 227.
8. J. Raz (1994), *Liberalism, Scepticism and Democracy in Ethics and the Public Domain* (Oxford: Oxford University Press), p. 10.
9. A. K. Appiah (2005), *The Ethics of Identity* (Princeton, NJ: Princeton University Press).
10. Parekh, *A New Politics of Identity*.
11. J.-P. Sartre (1962), *The Reprieve* (Harmondsworth: Penguin)
12. S. Rushdie (2012), *Joseph Anton: A Memoir* (London: Jonathon Cape).

13. B. A. O. Williams (1993), *Shame and Necessity* (Cambridge: Cambridge University Press).
14. Ibid., p. 127.
15. R. Nozick (1974), *Anarachy, State and Utopia* (Oxford: Blackwell).

Part III

New Directions

8

The Essentialist Critique of Multiculturalism: Theories, Policies, Ethos

Will Kymlicka

Since the late 1960s, in response to increasing restiveness and mobilisation on the part of minority groups, a number of Western democracies have engaged in new experiments in the recognition and accommodation of ethnic diversity. These experiments include:

- recognising land rights and self-government rights for indigenous peoples;
- strengthening regional autonomy and official language status for sub-state national groups;
- adopting more accommodationist policies for immigrant groups.[1]

I will describe all of these as experiments in 'liberal multiculturalism'.

While these experiments started to emerge forty years ago, it took a while for political theorists to turn their attention to these developments. It was only in the early 1990s, twenty years later, that we started to get the first scholarly discussions by academic political philosophers aiming to articulate normative theories of multiculturalism, and to explore how these emerging practices relate to liberal democratic values and principles.

Both the policies and the theories have come under sustained attack in recent years, and multiculturalism is widely viewed as in retreat across the Western democracies. To oversimplify, we can place the critics into two broad camps: the 'anti-multiculturalists' and the 'post-multiculturalists'.[2] Anti-multiculturalists, such as Brian Barry[3] and Samuel Huntington,[4] say that multicultural-ist ideas are inherently illiberal – that is, that multiculturalism is based on a repudiation of Enlightenment values of individual freedom, democratic citizenship and universal human rights, and it is precisely this repudiation of core Enlightenment principles that explains why multiculturalists seek to challenge traditional Western models of national citizenship in the name of cultural difference. The post-multiculturalists, by contrast, accept that multiculturalism is rooted in familiar liberal democratic ideals of equality, freedom and citizenship, and indeed aims precisely to address the many ways in which full equality and citizenship are denied to minorities. They worry, however, that multicultur-alist reforms have either failed to solve the problems for which they were intended, or inadvertently created new ones. In Anne Phillips' words, despite its noble intentions, multiculturalism has become a 'cultural straitjacket' rather than a 'cultural libera-tor', and it requires 'radical overhaul' if it is to serve its original emancipatory goals.[5]

In this chapter, I will focus on the post-multiculturalist critique. I have argued elsewhere that the anti-multiculturalists are demon-strably mistaken about the origins and motivations of the rise of multiculturalism in the past four decades. The rise of multicultur-alism in the West, far from repudiating liberal democratic values, has been part and parcel of a broader rights revolution that is intimately linked to processes of liberalisation and democratisa-tion.[6] But the post-multiculturalist critique cannot be so easily dismissed. After all, it is not uncommon for public policies to have unintended, even counterproductive, effects, and there's no reason to assume that multiculturalism is immune to this risk. Moreover, despite forty years of experiments in liberal multiculturalism it is clear that minorities continue to face many forms of exclusion and stigmatisation, some of which may indeed be getting worse. So we need to take seriously the possibility that multiculturalism has become part of the problem, rather than part of the solution, and that it needs overhauling.

I am particularly interested in the role that academic politi-cal theories of multiculturalism are said to play in the post-multiculturalist literature. As we will see, post-multiculturalists do not typically say that multiculturalism is 'good in theory but bad in practice'. On the contrary, they often insist that the flaws of multiculturalism in practice are reflected in, and perhaps even attributable to, flaws in the way political theorists have conceptualised multiculturalism. A few even suggest that multiculturalism has been better in practice than in theory, and that the situation would have been even worse if academic theories of multiculturalism had been implemented more faithfully.

So political theories of multiculturalism have served as an important target in the post-multiculturalism literature. The theories are said to be defective, and these theoretical defects are said to be at least partly responsible for the failings of multiculturalism in practice. I want to challenge this picture. My concern is not primarily to defend theories of multiculturalism, although I do think they have often been misinterpreted. My concern, rather, is with the cavalier way post-multiculturalists link theory and practice. I will argue that much of the post-multiculturalist critique conflates different potential targets, jumping from critiques of academic theories of liberal multiculturalism to critiques of government policies of multiculturalism to critiques of everyday street-level discourses or enactments of ethnic difference. I will argue that we need to more carefully distinguish these different targets, and that once we do, we will find that the criticisms are less damning to liberal multiculturalism than initially supposed. Indeed, we may find that the theories and practices of liberal multiculturalism, far from being the cause of the problem, are still the best remedy to them. But in any event, we cannot make progress on this issue without being more cautious and reflective about the relationship between theories and practices.

To develop this point, I will focus on the issue of 'essentialism', which is one of the most important themes in the post-multiculturalist literature. According to critics, liberal multiculturalism involves essentialising the identities and practices of minority groups. To quote Phillips, multiculturalism

exaggerates the internal unity of cultures, solidifies differences that are currently more fluid, and makes people from other cultures seem more exotic and distinct than they really are. Multiculturalism then appears not as a cultural liberator but as a cultural straitjacket, forcing those described as members of a minority cultural group into a regime of authenticity, denying them the chance to cross cultural borders, borrow cultural influences, and to define and redefine themselves.[7]

This is a widespread concern among the post-multiculturalists – I will cite several similar statements from Anthony Appiah, Seyla Benhabib, Nancy Fraser and Samuel Scheffler below – even among those (like Phillips herself) who have earlier expressed sympathy for multiculturalism.

In one sense, this charge is puzzling. After all, one of the central planks in many defences of multiculturalism is precisely the complaint that national identities have all too often been essentialised in ways that exclude minorities. Opening up space for multiculturalism has typically required challenging these essentialist conceptions of nationhood. We can see this clearly in Parekh's work on nationalism and national identity, where a defence of multiculturalism has been predicated upon a critique of essentialism.[8] It seems implausible that multiculturalist theorists would begin by attacking essentialist conceptions of national identity and culture, and then turn around and adopt essentialist conceptions of minority identity and culture.

But that is indeed what critics argue, and we cannot simply dismiss the objection. No one can seriously doubt that the problem of essentialisation exists, or that members of minority groups often feel that they are confined by cultural straitjackets. What it is less clear, I will argue, is the role that multiculturalism plays in this phenomenon. When critics blame multiculturalism for causing or exacerbating essentialism, they typically conflate political theories, government policies and social practices in a way that makes it difficult to diagnose the real source of the problem, and impossible to identify appropriate remedies. Or so I will argue.

I will start by explaining what I mean by liberal multiculturalism, and how it operates in both theory and practice. I will then consider the essentialist critique, and explore how it relates theory and practice, before concluding with some reflections on the implications of this analysis for ongoing debates.

212

Liberal multiculturalism: an overview

Much of my work over the past twenty years has been motivated by the hope and belief that there is such a thing as a distinctly *liberal* multiculturalism (hereafter LMC). So I should start by clarifying what I mean by 'liberal multiculturalism', and the different senses in which I think it is worth defending.

Both halves of that compound term are important. On the one hand, LMC is a distinctly *liberal democratic* form of multiculturalism, grounded in core liberal values of freedom, equality and democracy, and to be evaluated for its effects on these values. It therefore differs from non-liberal or illiberal forms of multiculturalism, of which there are many historic examples, in which groups agree to terms of peaceful coexistence while remaining indifferent to the freedoms or democratic rights of individuals.

On the other hand, LMC is a distinctly *multicultural* form of liberal democracy, going beyond the familiar list of basic liberties contained in all liberal democratic theories and constitutions to also include policies that recognise and accommodate ethno-cultural minorities. Many features of a liberal democracy provide important protections to ethno-cultural minorities – particularly guarantees of non-discrimination and guarantees of individual civil liberties (freedom of speech, association, religion, and so on). But a multicultural liberalism differs from other forms of liberal democracy by going beyond these generic guarantees to also adopt group-differentiated laws and policies that recognise and accommodate various types of diversity, including the three patterns I mentioned earlier: (1) indigenous land rights and self-government; (2) regional autonomy and official language rights for national minorities; and (3) accommodation rights for immigrant groups.[9]

I have tried to defend LMC on three different levels. The first is *philosophical*: I believe that if we start from the core premises of liberal political philosophy, as articulated by, say, Mill or Rawls, including their accounts of autonomy and justice, we can show that there is no logical or conceptual inconsistency in also endorsing various multicultural laws and policies. Indeed, we can construct arguments in which LMC enhances, strengthens or deepens these liberal premises – for example, it enhances the ability of individuals to exercise Rawls' 'two moral powers', by securing one or more of the conditions needed for personal and political autonomy; and/or enhances society's compliance with Rawls' difference principle, by diminishing one or more forms of arbitrary disadvantage in life-chances. In particular, I have suggested that a liberal concern for autonomy requires a concern for people's cultural 'context of choice', and that this can generate a liberal argument for the adoption of minority rights that enable sub-state national groups to sustain their 'societal cultures', and that enable immigrant groups to have their identities accommodated fairly.[10]

The second concerns *policy goals*. This philosophical argument, if valid, shows that LMC is a theoretical possibility – that is, one could imagine a hypothetical ideal world containing a version of multiculturalism that fits comfortably with liberal democratic values. Some people might accept this, but insist that it has no connection to the actually existing forms of multiculturalism, which are grounded in different sorts of values that conflict with liberal democracy. Real-world multiculturalism, on this view, is grounded in decidedly illiberal views, and indeed is best understood as being inherently 'anti-universalistic in their thrust',[11] 'in its essence anti-European'[12] or even a 'war against the West'.[13]

I have argued, however, that LMC is not just a theoretical possibility. Rather, it exists as a real-world practice. Indeed, most of the real-world experiments in recognition and accommodation adopted in the Western democracies over the past forty years have been inspired by a belief that they contribute to processes of liberalisation and democratisation.[14] These policies have been framed to fit with liberal democratic values, and their principles have been interpreted (for example, by bureaucrats and courts) to preserve that fit.

More specifically, multiculturalism can be seen as part of a larger 'human rights revolution' in relation to ethnic and racial diversity. Prior to World War II, ethno-cultural and religious diversity in the West was characterised by a range of illiberal and undemocratic relations – including relations of conqueror and conquered; coloniser and colonised; master and slave; settler and indigenous;

racialised and unmarked; normalised and deviant; orthodox and heretic; civilised and primitive; ally and enemy. These relationships of hierarchy were justified by racialist ideologies that explicitly propounded the superiority of some peoples and cultures, and their right to rule over others. These ideologies were widely accepted throughout the Western world, and underpinned both domestic laws (for example, racially biased immigration and citizenship policies) and foreign policies (for example, in relation to overseas colonies). After World War II, however, the world recoiled against Hitler's fanatical and murderous use of such ideologies, and the UN decisively repudiated them in favour of a new ideology of the equality of races and peoples. And this new assumption of human equality has generated a series of political movements designed to contest the lingering presence or enduring effects of older hierarchies. We can distinguish three 'waves' of such movements: (1) the struggle for decolonisation, concentrated in the period 1948 to 1965; (2) the struggle against racial segregation and discrimination, initiated and exemplified by the African-American civil rights movement from 1955 to 1965; and (3) the struggle for multiculturalism and minority rights, which has emerged from the late 1960s.

Each of these movements draws upon the human rights revolution, and its foundational ideology of the equality of races and peoples, to challenge the legacies of earlier ethnic and racial hierarchies. Indeed, the human rights revolution plays a double role here: not just as the inspiration for struggle, but also as a constraint on the permissible goals and means of that struggle. Insofar as historically excluded groups struggle against earlier hierarchies in the name of equality, they too have to renounce their own traditions of exclusion or oppression in the treatment of women, gays, people of mixed race, religious dissenters, and so on. The framework of human rights, and of liberal democratic constitutionalism more generally, provides the overarching framework within which these struggles are addressed. We cannot understand the rise of LMC in the West – we cannot understand when, where and why these experiments arose, or how they have been formulated – except as part of this larger human rights revolution.[15]

The third level is *outcomes*. One could accept this claim about the liberal inspiration for multicultural experiments, and yet still think that they have failed in practice. Policies often have perverse effects, and so LMC may have operated in practice to reduce autonomy, limit democratic participation, and/or exacerbate inequalities. As Koopmans puts it, while there are 'legitimate normative reasons' for multiculturalism, 'we cannot simply assume that what is normatively justifiable will also be practically efficient',[16] and indeed he argues that it has been counterproductive.

Yet here again I want to argue that LMC has often worked to enhance liberal democratic values. The evidence on outcomes is not easy to locate: very few multiculturalism policies have been studied systematically. As Reitz puts it, while academic discussions of multiculturalism have been extensive, 'there is no real evaluation. The information base for such an evaluation is simply not there'.[17]

So any conclusions in this field will need to be tentative. Yet insofar as we have preliminary evidence, it suggests that most real-world experiments in LMC within the Western democracies have had beneficial effects on liberal values. Let me briefly review the three main cases:

- Sub-state national groups: the evidence is perhaps clearest in relation to these groups, where the shift to regional autonomy and (where relevant) official language status has enhanced the economic, political and social equality of national minorities, and done so in ways that fully protect individual civil and political rights. Indeed, in many cases, these sub-state national societies have used their autonomy to adopt more liberal policies than in the larger society. So this particular form of liberal multiculturalism is broadly uncontested in the scholarly literature: it is difficult to find anyone who thinks, for example, that it was a mistake for Spain to federalise to accommodate Catalan and Basque nationalism, or that Canada, Belgium, Switzerland, Italy, Finland or the UK should revoke their existing systems of autonomy or bilingualism.
- Indigenous peoples: the evidence regarding indigenous peoples is less clear, since they continue to be the most disadvantaged members of society, and so the adoption of liberal multicul-

turalist models has clearly not been 'successful', in the usual sense of that term. Yet if we compare indigenous peoples across the Western democracies, or indeed within individual countries, those with stronger self-government rights are doing better than those without. And here again there is a broad consensus in support of this approach among scholars and international organisations, reflected in the virtually unanimous adoption of the UN Declaration of the Rights of Indigenous Peoples in 2007.[18]

- Immigrant groups: the most contested case concerns immigrant groups, where there is both greater political contestation and scholarly disagreement about the effects of multiculturalism policies. While many scholars celebrate the benefits of multiculturalism in this or that country, an equal number of scholars have declared it to be a failure. For example, in an influential recent book, Paul Sniderman and Luuk Hagendoorn[19] blame multiculturalism for the high levels of ethnic stereotyping between native Dutch and Muslim immigrants in the Netherlands. But of course ethnic stereotyping is a pervasive problem throughout history and around the world, whether or not multiculturalism policies exist, and they provide no evidence that this stereotyping became worse in the Netherlands after the adoption of multiculturalism than before; or that it is worse in the Netherlands than in countries that have not adopted multiculturalism. In short, they make no effort to identify the differential effect that multiculturalism has on pre-existing dynamics of stereotyping. This is typical of work in the field, which generally lacks either longitudinal or comparative data needed to determine the differential effect of adopting multiculturalism. However, if we look at those few studies that do have a comparative or longitudinal dimension, and hence that attempt to isolate the differential effect of having multiculturalism policies, they generally suggest that multiculturalism has been beneficial in terms of political participation,[20] trust and social capital,[21] prejudice,[22] solidarity,[23] and psychological well-being.[24]

I emphasise again the limits of this evidence: it would be premature to claim that we have conclusive evidence of the merits of LMC. But it would be even more premature to claim we have evidence for its failure. There is a tendency in some quarters to dismiss LMC as an intellectual fad or fashion. But as we have seen, there were LMC practices twenty years before there were academic theorists of multiculturalism, and the best explanation for the emergence of these practices across a wide range of Western democracies starting in the 1960s is that they were part of a larger human rights revolution aimed at addressing the lingering effects of inherited racial and ethnic hierarchies, and thereby contributing to the processes of liberalisation and democratisation. And while these hopes may have been naïve or misguided, there is no evidence I can see that these experiments have generally or systematically eroded liberal democratic values. On the contrary, there is some provisional evidence for their beneficial effects.

And yet it is equally obvious that any such benefits are very uneven across different countries and different minorities. Western societies remain scarred by ethnic and racial hierarchies, by feelings of distrust across ethnic and religious lines, and by anxieties about the future direction of these relationships. Even if on average these policies have had beneficial rather than pernicious effects, they clearly have not achieved the highest hopes of their defenders, and in at least a few high-profile cases, they seem not to have worked at all. Indeed, I have argued elsewhere that there are some situations where they *cannot* work. Successful models of LMC have preconditions that are not always present, particularly outside the context of consolidated democracies, and efforts by international organisations to diffuse models of LMC have had very mixed and uneven results.[25]

A central task is to try to explain the deeply uneven nature of multiculturalism's effects, to look honestly at the failures and limitations, as well as the successes. In this respect, the current wave of sober second thoughts about multiculturalism, represented in particular by the growing post-multiculturalist literature, is welcome and necessary. But as we will see, the usefulness of this post-multiculturalist critique is compromised by a persistent tendency to conflate different levels of analysis, and to move inconsistently between theory and practice.

218

The post-multiculturalist critique of essentialism

According to the post-multiculturalist critique, the emancipatory impulse underlying multiculturalism is being subverted by the 'essentialist' way that cultures or identities are understood. Let me quote a few characteristic examples of this concern:

- Nancy Fraser: '[By] enjoining the elaboration and display of authentic, self-affirming and self-generated collective identities, it [the identity model] puts moral pressure on individual members to conform to group culture. The result is often to impose a single, drastically simplified group identity, which denies the complexity of people's lives, the multiplicity of their identifications and the cross-pulls of their various affiliations.'[26]
- Seyla Benhabib: Multiculturalism involves a 'reductive sociology of culture' that 'risks essentializing the idea of culture as the property of an ethnic group or race, it risks reifying cultures as separate entities by overemphasizing the internal homogeneity of cultures in terms that potentially legitimise repressive demands for cultural conformity; and by treating cultures as badges of group identity, it tends to fetishize them in ways that put them beyond the reach of critical analysis'. . . . 'The culture-based approach 'yields illiberal consequences' including 'acceptance of the need to "police" these [group] boundaries to regulate internal membership and "authentic" life forms'.[27]
- Jane Cowan: 'concerned with the ethical ambiguities of a discourse which may constrain, as much as enable, many of those it is meant to empower, by forcing their expressions of difference into a dichotomous interpretive frame that misrepresents their complex identities' . . . 'This is the central ambiguity of a minority rights discourse; that it must deny ambiguity and fix difference in the realms of identity, or cultural practice, in defence of distinct cultures . . . even when meant to contest claims of national homogeneity, it locks us ever more tightly into precisely the same national logic of purity, authenticity and fixity.'[28]
- Kwame Anthony Appiah: 'we know that acts of recognition, and the civil apparatus of such recognition, can sometimes

219

ossify the identities that are their object ("if pursued with excessive zeal")' . . . 'upholding differences among groups may entail imposing uniformity within them . . . Indeed, when multiculturalists like Kymlicka say that there are so many "cultures" in this or that country, what drops out of the picture is that every "culture" represents not only difference but the elimination of difference: the groups represents a clump of relative homogeneity, and that homogeneity is perpetuated and enforced by regulative mechanisms designed to marginalize and silence dissent from its basic norms and mores'.[29]

- Samuel Scheffler: talk of multiculturalism 'provides an invitation to mischief both by encouraging us to think in unsustainable strong-preservationist terms and by promoting a distorted and potentially oppressive conception of the relations between individuals and cultures'.[30]

This is just a sample – one can find virtually identical statements in Patchen Markell, David Hollinger, Jurgen Habermas, Wendy Brown, and many others. And the general conclusion, shared by all, is that we need a 'radical overhaul' of multiculturalism.[31]

What is striking about this list of authors is that it includes many people who have devoted their careers to exposing the false universalism or false neutrality underlying traditional republican or unitary models of difference-blind citizenship, and who therefore might be expected to be sympathetic to multiculturalism. These are not the anti-multiculturalists who are ideologically opposed to any particularist corruption of the purity or sanctity of republican citizenship. Nor are they conservatives, who are nostalgic for the good old days of homogeneous nationhood or unreflective patriotism. Rather, these are progressive theorists who take seriously the multiculturalist premise that traditional models of citizenship have been unjust and exclusionary, who support struggles for the emancipation of historically excluded groups, and who are committed to listening to their voices.

So, unlike anti-multiculturalists, these theorists are not out simply to score points against multiculturalism, or to ridicule or caricature it. In many ways their instincts are to sympathise with multiculturalist struggles. And yet they have all come to the conclusion that multiculturalism needs a radical overhaul, and in particular an overhaul of its essentialist tendencies.

If so many scholars who are committed to the inclusion and empowerment of minorities have come to this conclusion, then it must be true. But in what sense it is true? Or rather, in what contexts it is true? For example, when Scheffler says that multiculturalism 'encourages' people to think in preservationist terms, or that it 'promotes' an oppressive relationship between individuals and cultures, who or what is doing this encouraging and promoting, in what contexts? Is it philosophical theories of multiculturalism that are encouraging essentialism, perhaps because of the way they conceptualise culture and identity? Is it official public policies of multiculturalism that are encouraging essentialism, perhaps because of the way they define access to rights and entitlements? Or is it rather a more diffuse public ethos or discourse of multiculturalism that encourages essentialism, perhaps by reinforcing or legitimating pre-existing tendencies towards stereotyping?

In order to know *how* to radically overhaul LMC, we need to pin down the source of the problem. As it turns out, despite the apparent similarity in their phrasing, these writers have different targets in mind. Indeed, they actually give contradictory accounts of where the problem lies, in ways that generate different remedies. Once we distinguish these different targets and remedies, what appears to be an overwhelming consensus on LMC's essentialist flaws starts to dissolve into a more disparate and disjointed series of largely unsupported speculations and assertions.

CRITIQUES OF MULTICULTURALIST THEORIES

In some cases, the target of the essentialist critique is philosophical theories of LMC. I will start with these, before moving to those who focus more on public policies or public ethos.

The two writers who most clearly target philosophical theories of multiculturalism are Benhabib and Appiah, who have both extended discussions of the ideas of culture and identity developed either in my work or that of Charles Taylor. Indeed the quotes listed above from Appiah and Benhabib follow directly on from their discussions of my account of 'societal culture'. It is my concept of societal culture, Benhabib claims, that 'potentially legitimises repressive demands for cultural conformity', that puts cultures 'beyond the reach of critical analysis', and that entails 'acceptance of the need to "police" [group] boundaries to regulate internal membership and "authentic" life forms'. Similarly, Appiah argues that my concept of societal culture 'may entail imposing uniformity' within groups, because:

> [W]hen multiculturalists like Kymlicka say that there are so many 'cultures' in this or that country, what drops out of the picture is that every 'culture' represents not only difference but the elimination of difference: the group represents a clump of relative homogeneity, and that homogeneity is perpetuated and enforced by regulative mechanisms designed to marginalize and silence dissent from its basic norms and mores'.[32]

Unsurprisingly, I think these are misinterpretations of my theory, but I don't want to go into that debate here. I do however need to say something about my idea of societal culture, not to defend it, but to help us sort out what follows from their critique of it. As they both note, my account of societal culture was intended to explain and evaluate the claims of sub-state national groups like the Québécois to autonomy and official language rights. In my view, the case of Québécois nationalism clearly exemplifies the goals of LMC, and I was looking for a way to make sense of this conceptually.

In the 1960s Quebec went through what is called the Quiet Revolution, which involved a double transformation. First, it involved a process of internal liberalisation within French-Canadian society, particularly in the form of secularisation, civil rights and gender equality. This is one of the most dramatic examples of liberalisation I know of, resulting in a society that is today the most liberal society in North America, more so than the rest of Canada or the United States.[33] Second, it involved a process of increasing nationalist mobilisation in relation to the rest of Canada, fighting for greater minority rights, particularly self-government and language rights. The result of this nationalist mobilisation has been a significant reduction in inequalities between anglophones and francophones in Canada, whether measured in terms of average incomes, government employment or democratic participation.

Here is a paradigm case of LMC in action, resulting in greater *freedom within groups*, and greater *equality between groups*. And while we can see this analytically as two separate processes, it was seen by the actors involved as two sides of the same process – namely, building a more free, democratic and prosperous Québécois nation. It was not as if there was one group of liberal elites fighting for liberalisation, and another group of nationalist elites fighting for nationalism. It was the same elite involved in both struggles – an elite committed to liberal nationalism.

How are we to make theoretical sense of such a case? It is not explicable in the terms of traditional liberal theory, with its implicit assumptions about unitary and undifferentiated citizenship. We need new concepts to explain how minority rights can enhance liberal values. My suggestion was that self-government and language rights enabled the consolidation and prosperity of a francophone 'societal culture' in Quebec. This societal culture provides a 'context of choice' for its members – that is, it provides the adequate range of options from which individuals are able to choose rationally and reflectively, as required by the liberal commitment to autonomy. Of course, this strategy of empowering Quebec to protect a francophone societal culture carries risks: these very same rights and powers could be used to suppress individual freedom in the name of upholding some vision of an 'authentic' or 'traditional' Québécois culture. To avoid this risk, we need to understand these rights as 'external protections' not as 'internal restrictions'. That is, these rights are intended to diminish the extent to which members of a minority are vulnerable to the external decisions of the larger society, and are not intended to allow the minority to suppress basic civil and political freedoms internally. This principle is reflected in the requirement that a minority's powers of self-government are constrained by the same constitutional requirement to respect human rights as all other levels of government. Since minority rights, on this view, are understood as external protections whose aim is to ensure the flourishing of a societal culture as a context of choice, they provide no justification for exemptions from or limitations on the basic liberties. Of course, once we rule out internal restrictions, this means that individual members will be free to question inherited beliefs and practices, and to adapt, revise or even reject them, as indeed happened during Quebec's Quiet Revolution, with its dramatic collapse of traditional (Catholic, patriarchal) ways of life. It is important, therefore, to distinguish the flourishing of a societal culture from changes to the 'character' of that culture. Minority rights for the Québécois ensured the former, but allowed dramatic change to the latter in response to the exercise of individual autonomy.

That was my way of trying to make theoretical sense of the Quebec case, using a handful of new concepts – 'societal culture' as a context of choice, external protections versus internal restrictions, and so on. As I hope this makes clear, the whole point of the concept of societal culture was that it did *not* provide a justification for imposing 'authentic life forms'[34] or for 'marginalising and silencing dissent'.[35] It was intended precisely to explain how it was possible for a minority society to seek minority rights while disavowing any desire to enforce traditional lifestyles, and instead to liberalise and transform itself dramatically through the exercise of individual autonomy.

So, predictably, I think that Benhabib and Appiah's interpretations are uncharitable. Both authors claim that my use of the term 'societal culture' somehow legitimates denying individuals the right to rationally revise their inherited ways of life, but so far as I can tell, they simply assert rather than argue for this. However, I am not a neutral observer in this debate, and others have found their critiques compelling. And in any event, that is not my main interest in this chapter.

So let's assume they are indeed right, and that my concept of societal culture has these flaws. What implications does this have for the real-world practice of LMC? After all, they both insist that their anxiety is not just about essentialism within the halls of academic philosophy departments. They believe that essentialism is a problem with multiculturalism as a political project, which therefore needs a 'radical overhaul'. But what would this mean in cases of sub-state nationalism like Quebec? Recall that my concept of societal culture was developed to justify and explain claims for official language status and regional autonomy of such groups. Should we radically overhaul the way liberal democratic states deal with such groups? Should we reject their claims to official language status and regional autonomy?

And here, things start to get murky. Benhabib and Appiah hedge their bets. Both immediately deny that they are necessarily opposed to the language and autonomy rights accorded to Quebec. As Appiah says about Quebec's language policy,

> let me be clear that my target is not the particulars of the policy, but its rationale . . . I'm happy to put myself in the position of the proverbial philosopher who demands 'that's all very well in practice, but will it work in theory?'.[36]

The policy may work 'very well in practice', but he thinks that talk about preserving societal cultures misidentifies why it can be a legitimate part of liberal democratic practice. Similarly, Benhabib says that she 'welcomes and supports' movements for 'intercultural justice', including many struggles for regional autonomy, but she too thinks that they can be legitimate precisely because, and insofar as, they are *not* about preserving cultures.[37]

So both accept that this model of real-world LMC – regional autonomy and official language rights for sub-state national minorities – can work well in practice, and may not be in need of a radical overhaul, so long as they are not based on 'culturalist premises'.[38] So what, on their view, does provide the legitimating basis for struggles by sub-state national groups for autonomy and language rights?

In both cases, they respond that the basis for evaluating such movements should be 'political' not 'cultural'. In Benhabib's words, 'intercultural justice between human groups should be defended in the name of justice and freedom and not an elusive preservation of cultures'. Struggles for recognition and identity/ difference should be supported:

> to the degree to which they are movements for democratic inclusion, greater social and political justice, and cultural fluidity. But movements for maintaining the purity or distinctiveness of cultures

seem to me to be irreconcilable with both democratic and more basic epistemological considerations.

In short, movements of minority groups can be progressive 'to the degree that they are motivated by other than conservationist impulses'.[39] And so, in the particular case of Quebec or other movements for autonomy, she says: 'If asked how to evaluate claim for regional autonomy, I would say, "Study their demands and their platform first!"'. For example, we should ask how they propose to treat women, immigrants, democracy, foreign policy. And she insists that this 'political' approach is very different from my argument that is 'based on culturalist premises rather than political evaluations of movements and their goals'.[40]

Similarly, Appiah says Quebec's language policy can be understood and justified not in terms of maintaining a francophone societal culture, but as 'equality of citizenship in a francophone state'.[41] Quebeckers have a democratic right to make French 'the political language', and once they have done so, it is appropriate to ensure that all citizens have equal access to it. This citizenship-based argument, he says, is different from a right to maintain a francophone societal culture, since it operates within a framework of equal citizenship and individual autonomy, not cultural preservation.[42]

I confess I have no idea how to understand this distinction between 'political' and 'culturalist'. The whole point about the Quebec case, as I mentioned earlier, is that these two motivations were fused. Elites during the Quiet Revolution wanted to consolidate their societal culture (*vis-à-vis* the larger society) while simultaneously liberalising and democratising their society internally, improving its treatment of gays, women, immigrants, religious minorities and so on. These were two dimensions of the same underlying motivation – namely, to build a prosperous and democratic francophone society within Canada. They were committed to liberal democratic values, but they were not indifferent to the scale or unit within which those values were operationalised. They wanted to implement those liberal democratic values within the province of Quebec as an autonomous francophone society. And while they were strongly committed to nationalist values, they were not indifferent to the form that nationhood took: they wanted a liberal democratic form of nationalism.

This is not unique to Quebec. It is a characteristic feature of sub-state nationalist movements across the Western democracies since the 1960s. They are simultaneously and intensely both 'political' and 'cultural'. If it is to be useful, any normative political theory of (post)-multiculturalism has to say something about this combination. And yet, so far as I can tell, both Benhabib and Appiah fail in this task.

Indeed, their positions are full of ambiguities. On one interpretation, Benhabib and Appiah are saying that certain political criteria operate as a *constraint* on culturalist political projects. On this interpretation, struggles for minority rights are legitimate so long as human rights norms and individual civil rights are respected. Regional autonomies must, for example, comply with constitutional protections of individual rights, and with international human rights norms. If so, then of course I fully agree, and this simply restates an essential part of any liberal multiculturalist position (and of international norms of minority rights).

But their comments suggest a more radical interpretation, which is that movements for regional autonomy are illegitimate insofar as they have any 'culturalist premises' or 'conservationist impulses'. These movements are illegitimate if ideas of maintaining cultural distinctiveness play any role in their motivations. On this view, it is not enough that minority groups comply with the constraints of liberal norms; they must be solely and exclusively motivated by these norms. They must, in short, be indifferent to the scale or unit of liberal democracy, and have no intrinsic preference for exercising liberal democracy in, say, a predominantly Francophone Quebec rather than a predominantly anglophone Canada.

If this is their position, then it is truly radical. It would involve rejecting all real-world sub-state nationalist movements, since they are clearly not indifferent to the scale or societal/linguistic context within which liberal democracy operates. It would therefore seem to entail abolishing autonomy for Catalonia, Quebec, Flanders, Puerto Rico and South Tyrol, all of which emerged from what, on this view, would be illegitimate political movements.

If this is indeed their view, then I think it is wholly implausible.

It would involve rejecting what are viewed almost universally as successful forms of accommodation, and would do so on the basis of a fetishistic dislike of 'culturalist' motivations. It is also, I think, deeply hypocritical, since it is clear that majorities also operate on these culturalist motivations, and yet Appiah and Benhabib do not suggest that the majority's claims to self-government and language rights should be rejected. Members of dominant groups in England, Spain or Canada are not indifferent to the scale or linguistic context of liberal democratic political life: they want to engage in liberal democratic politics in contexts where they form a majority, and which use their language. Yet Appiah and Benhabib do not suggest that these states should lose their independence because of these culturalist premises. No one thinks that Denmark or the Czech Republic should give up their independence and join a larger German-speaking political unit, on the grounds that their commitment to national independence has 'culturalist premises'. So why should Catalonia or Quebec give up their pursuit of autonomy on the grounds that it involves culturalist premises?

In fact, both Appiah and Benhabib realise that this radical interpretation is untenable, and so back off it. Appiah, for example, says that while Quebec's language law is only permissible if it is motivated by equal citizenship values not cultural survival values, he then acknowledges that these two motivations are not really separable. He acknowledges that sustaining a francophone societal culture is aided by the choice of French as the 'political language' for Quebec, and indeed he accepts that this is *why* that particular language was democratically chosen. Moreover, he says, 'such an aim is a perfectly acceptable consideration in democratic politics', so long as it is pursued within a framework of equal citizenship and personal autonomy.[43] But now we are back to the more modest position that liberal democratic norms constrain the pursuit of culturalist projects – a position that simply restates the LMC he claimed to be criticising.

Similarly, Benhabib says that being motivated by cultural allegiances is after all perfectly legitimate, so long as 'the goal of a public policy for the preservation of cultures must be the empowerment of the members of cultural groups to appropriate, enrich, and even subvert the terms of their own cultures as they may decide'.[44] In short, culturalist projects are legitimate so long as they do not impose internal restrictions. But here again, this is simply a restatement of the LMC she claims to be critiquing. Benhabib claims that her account of 'complex cultural dialogue' differs from mine in that it allows 'democratic dissent, debate, contestation and challenge to be at the centre of practices through which cultures are appropriated'. But any liberal conception of multiculturalism, including mine, affirms rights of democratic contestation and individual rational revisability. So far as I can tell, neither Benhabib nor Appiah provide any conceptual tools or political recommendations that go beyond what is already built into the theory and practice of LMC.

In any event, this is one version of the post-multiculturalist critique. It starts with the claim that academic theories of liberal multiculturalism contain essentialist premises, and while it is implied that these flaws have implications for real-world political practices, the implications are left indeterminate or ambiguous. Interpreted radically as rejecting any political claims that are even partly motivated by culturalist aspirations, it would require rejecting all real-world experiments in LMC, regardless of the evidence of their benefits from a liberal democratic point of view. Interpreted more moderately as simply requiring that liberal democratic constitutional norms be respected, it leaves all real-world practices of LMC untouched. Neither interpretation, it seems to me, adds to our understanding of the uneven successes and failures of LMC.

CRITIQUES OF MULTICULTURALIST POLICIES

Let me turn now to a second version of the post-multiculturalist critique, exemplified by Phillips' work.[45] Recall her central claim that multiculturalism

> exaggerates the internal unity of cultures, solidifies differences that are currently more fluid, and makes people from other cultures seem more exotic and distinct than they really are. Multiculturalism then appears not as a cultural liberator but as a cultural straitjacket, forcing those described as members of a minority cultural group into a regime

of authenticity, denying them the chance to cross cultural borders, borrow cultural influences, define and redefine themselves.[46]

While this sounds similar to Benhabib and Appiah, she explicitly states that her target is not academic theories of LMC. Indeed, she says 'it would be absurd' to blame theorists for these essentialising effects.[47] She acknowledges that theorists of multiculturalism often have relatively sophisticated understandings of cultural activities and identifications, and it would be a case of 'mistaken identity'[48] or even 'polemical diatribe'[49] to accuse theorists of embracing these crude notions.

Her concern, rather, is with the *practice* of multiculturalism, and with the more simplified understandings of culture and identity that inform laws, policies and public discourses. For example, she says that 'one of the biggest problems' with multiculturalism is 'the selective way culture is employed to explain behaviour in non-Western societies or individuals from racialised minority groups, and the implied contrast with rational, autonomous (Western) individuals, whose actions are presumed to reflect moral judgements'.[50] Yet as she notes, this is not a problem with academic theories of LMC. They do not distinguish (non-Western) 'culture' from (Western) 'reason/judgement', but rather attempt to show how liberal autonomy itself has cultural preconditions. This problem of selectivity, then, arises at a different level, in the way multiculturalist ideas get translated into political practices.

So if Appiah says 'that's all very well in practice, but will it work in theory?', Phillips' approach could be phrased as 'that may work in theory, but will it work in practice?'. This is a different target, and it requires different sorts of evidence, and also leads to different conclusions about the sort of 'radical overhaul' that might be required.

So what does Phillips mean by the practice of LMC, and how do we judge whether it is having these essentialising effects, and how would we fix the problem? At first glance, it seems that her concern is with formal laws and policies. The book is essentially a review of a series of British cases in which public officials have had to deal with issues of immigrant diversity, including forced marriages, the cultural defence, dress code exemptions, and so on.

And so when she says that multiculturalism 'appears as a cultural straitjacket . . . forcing those described as members of a minority cultural group into a regime of authenticity', it seems to be public officials, acting upon multiculturalist laws and policies, who are doing this exaggerating, forcing and denying.

And yet, as her book proceeds, it becomes clear that this is not in fact her target. On the contrary, she repeatedly observes that British public officials – whether educators, social service workers, police or judges – often have a fairly sophisticated understanding of the issues. For example, the courts have rejected the view of culture as a straitjacket,[51] and have dealt sensitively with the complexity of rights of exit.[52] This sensitivity is due in part to the fact that public officials typically receive training in handling these issues – training that is itself part and parcel of multiculturalism policies, and that explicitly disavows and warns against simplistic and essentialising ideas of culture.

And so, by the end of the book, her overall conclusion seems to be that the formal laws and bureaucratic regulations and procedures are more or less appropriate, and are not themselves in need of a radical overhaul. She says that on these basic policy questions 'I reach much the same policy conclusions' as liberal multiculturalists,[53] and it is not clear in what ways, if any, she would change the current laws, regulations, jurisprudence, handbooks, codes of conduct, and so on, that are used by public officials to address issues of multiculturalism.

So what then is the problem of essentialism, on her view? If the problem does not lie with academic theories of multiculturalism or with public policies, who or what is encouraging essentialism? If we dig deeper, it seems to me that her concern is with a more diffuse phenomenon, which she sometimes calls a 'public discourse' or 'public ethos' of multiculturalism. For example, she says that even if no formal law endorses or fosters an essentialist view, 'a strongly multicultural public ethos is likely to have some of the suggested effects'.[54] A multiculturalist 'public discourse' or 'public ethos', she fears, is likely to reproduce pre-existing stereotypes and prejudices, such as the assumption that non-Europeans act blindly from cultural compulsion whereas whites act from reason and moral judgement.

In short, the problem seems to be with 'the way we talk' about multiculturalism in public life, and it is this that needs a radical overhaul, not multiculturalist policies per se or academic multiculturalist theories. Her concern seems to be with the way multiculturalism is talked about in the media, in the associational life of civil society, or even among friends and families.

This is an interesting claim, but it requires unpacking. What exactly is a public ethos of multiculturalism, and how do we test whether or not it is having essentialising effects? Her book contains many examples of everyday public discourse that exhibit essentialising assumptions – a phenomenon well captured in Gerd Baumann's famous study of street-level discourses on ethnic difference in Southall.[55] But as Tariq Modood notes, it may be a mistake to read too much into these statements:

> a successful politics of difference-recognition may (or may not) be accompanied by crude, confused unreflective notions of culture, but for theorists to latch on to the reification in the confused or crude accounts that agents give of their activities and beliefs is actually to over-homogenize and essentialize the beliefs that people have . . . The charge of essentialism is itself essentialist. It rightly identifies some elements of essentialism in the political discourses of identity and culture but attributes a false importance to them. It gives them the status of being *the* beliefs that constitute the understanding of culture, identity and so on in multiculturalism, when in fact multiculturalist discourses may be, indeed invariably are, based on a variety of beliefs and assertions about culture.[56]

So there are interesting complexities here about how to describe or measure the extent to which a 'public ethos' does or does not perpetuate essentialist assumptions.

However, for my purposes, the more pressing question is how we would we go about fixing the problem of an essentialising public ethos. Some commentators might think that the best way to change this public ethos is to reject formal policies of multiculturalism. But that is not Phillips' proposal. There is no evidence that public policies are generating the essentialising tendencies in the public ethos. On the contrary, as I noted earlier, insofar as we have comparative data, it seems that the problem of ethnic stereotyping is lower in countries with multiculturalism policies.[57] So it would be another case of 'mistaken identity' to blame multicultural public policies for an essentialising public ethos.

Indeed, it may be that strengthening these policies is the best remedy. It may be that the best way for public authorities to combat an essentialising public ethos is to actively diffuse the more complex and sophisticated understandings about multiculturalism that are currently given to the public officials tasked to implement these policies. This is indeed more or less what Phillips proposes, such as new programmes of community outreach and education. While she describes her book as a call for a 'radical overhaul' of multiculturalism, these suggestions seem to me to be firmly within the family of LMC, as it already exists in countries like Canada, Australia and indeed the UK. Her recommendations seem largely to be a call for strengthening these policies. In short, the answer to the essentialising risks of a 'strongly multiculturalist public ethos' is not to abandon multiculturalist public policies, but to re-commit to them.

CRITIQUES OF MULTICULTURALIST ACTIVISTS

Finally, let me turn to a third version of the post-multiculturalist critique, which is also in a sense about a 'public ethos' of multiculturalism, but which locates the problem in a different place. A good example is Jane Cowan's work on the essentialising effects of the political mobilisation for minority rights among the Macedonian minority in Greece. She shows how, in order to justify their claims for Macedonian language rights, ethnic activists are encouraging people of Macedonian origin to self-identify in public as 'Macedonian', and not to identify themselves as 'Greek'. This has been an uphill battle, in part because for many decades anyone who self-identified in this way was discriminated against by Greek public officials. But it is also an uphill battle because many ethnic Macedonians have, over the years, come to identify with the Greek language, literature and culture, and indeed to take pride in it. Whereas ethnic activists promote a discourse in which 'they' (the Greeks) have a long history of

233

persecuting 'us' (the Macedonians), most ethnic Macedonians themselves do not share this simple us versus them identity. In some contexts, they too feel Greek, and not just in the sense of being a citizen of the state of Greece, but also in the sense of participating in a Greek-language culture, even as they still retain a sense of Macedonian identity, and an attachment to their ancestral language. Whereas activists seek to impose a particular narrative or script in which one must choose between being Greek or Macedonian – a proud Macedonian is someone who resents and rejects what 'they' the Greeks have done to 'us' and our language – most ethnic Macedonians dislike having to make this sort of choice among their multiple identities.

Cowan finds this minority activist discourse to be disturbing. Recall her central claim: she is:

> concerned with the ethical ambiguities of a discourse that may constrain, as much as enable, many of those it is meant to empower, by forcing their expressions of difference into a dichotomous interpretive frame that misrepresents their complex identities . . . This is the central ambiguity of a minority rights discourse; that it must deny ambiguity and fix difference in the realms of identity, or cultural practice, in defence of distinct cultures . . . even when meant to contest claims of national homogeneity, it locks us ever more tightly into precisely the same national logic of purity, authenticity and fixity.[58]

This is a compelling case study, and it is not unique to that particular country or minority. It echoes fears expressed by Fraser and Appiah about minority activist discourses in the United States. Fraser worries that minority scripts:

> put moral pressure on individual members to conform to group culture. The result is often to impose a single, drastically simplified group identity, which denies the complexity of people's lives, the multiplicity of their identifications and the cross-pulls of their various affiliations.[59]

Similarly, Appiah has famously argued that minority scripts exaggerate group homogeneity, and seek to enforce this homogeneity 'by regulative mechanisms designed to marginalize and silence dissent from its basic norms and mores'.[60]

This is a very important issue, but it is different from that in Phillips' work. Phillips' concern (as I have interpreted it) is primarily with how a 'multiculturalist public ethos' can lead members of the dominant group to have essentialist views about minorities – that is, multiculturalism encourages members of the mainstream to treat members of minority groups as prisoners of their exotic cultures, thereby reinforcing their already-existing prejudices. Cowan, by contrast, is primarily concerned with how members of the minority group itself, particularly its self-appointed activist leaders, seek to impose a particular script on co-members. Her focus is on *intra-group* processes of essentialisation, not *inter-group* essentialisation.[61]

Processes of intra-group essentialisation clearly exist. But what does this have to do with LMC? After all, we can find examples of self-appointed leaders of ethnic and religious groups trying to impose 'purity, authenticity and fixity' on their members throughout history and around the world, long before the rise of multiculturalism. This is as old as the Bible – indeed, we might say it is an eternal feature of ethnic and religious life. There are always some people within any group who are telling other members that they need to return to a more original, authentic or pure form of their culture or creed (just as there are always revisers and reformers who are pushing for more open and pluralistic understandings of identity and culture). This has been the stuff of great novels and literature around the world for centuries. It would be bizarre to imply that this phenomenon only emerged when LMC arose in the 1960s.

Indeed, it is particularly bizarre to blame multiculturalism for the essentialising discourses of minority activists in Greece, since Greece has no multiculturalism policy! It is one of the countries in Europe (along with France and Turkey) that has most resolutely opposed any ideology of multiculturalism. Indeed, we might say that this is precisely the problem: Greece has no legal principles or political culture of LMC, and hence has no established traditions within either the minority or the majority for accepting ideas of multiple and complementary loyalties and identities. The Greek government has operated on the premise that ethnic identities are zero-sum and inherently antagonistic, and the minority activists simply replicate this assumption. The solution to this, one might argue, is precisely a good dose of LMC, both in terms of legislation and political culture. Indeed, this is one of the findings of cross-national research on multiculturalism I cited earlier. By ensuring respect and recognition for a minority's identity, multiculturalism policies facilitate minority members adopting dual and complementary identities that bridge to the larger society, thereby enabling better psychological well-being and educational outcomes.[62] Multiculturalism policies can help turn what were seen as zero-sum identities into multiple and complementary identities.

Cowan (sometimes) acknowledges that this tendency towards essentialisation predates multiculturalism, but she nonetheless worries that multiculturalism might exacerbate it. Multiculturalism might, for example, empower activists to force this essentialising script on unwilling group members. This recalls Appiah's concern that the 'civil apparatus' of group recognition can be used to 'marginalize and silence dissent' within a group, or Fraser's concern that multiculturalism can be used to 'impose a single drastically simplified group identity'.

But does multiculturalism really allow activists to 'force' or 'impose' identities, or to 'silence' dissent? How are we to interpret these dramatic claims of 'forcing', 'imposing', 'suppressing', 'policing', and 'silencing'? If it is meant literally – that is, that multiculturalism policies would legally empower minority activists to 'force' members to accept a simplified identity – then it is simply false. In the Macedonian case, minority activists have no legal power whatsoever to compel group members to identify as exclusively Macedonian, and nor would they somehow gain this power if Greece suddenly adopted stronger minority language rights. On the contrary, the right of individuals not to be forced to declare a minority identity is a fundamental principle of both European and international human rights law, which is precisely the law that minority activists are appealing to. It is no part of their agenda – and no part of any possible multiculturalist outcome – that they would gain the power to legally compel people of Macedonian origin to adopt or declare a Macedonian identity.

Of course, one could imagine scenarios in which minority activists would use non-legal coercion or intimidation to force individuals to accept their script. Activists might threaten to assault people, or to burn down their houses, if they do not declare an exclusive Macedonian identity. This surely happens in many cases around the world. But this is not what Cowan has in mind. She gives no evidence that activists use extra-legal coercion against group members. As she tells the story, activists operate fully within the law. Similarly Appiah and Fraser do not recount acts of physical threat or intimidation by minority activists.

So in what sense then do minority activists 'impose' or 'force' their script on unwilling members? To my mind, this is the crucial question for any liberal democratic theory, yet it is sidestepped by all of these authors. After all, it is a foundational right within any democratic society that people can freely state their opinion that (for example) a proud Macedonian should speak Macedonian wherever possible, and should resist the corrupting influences of Greek culture. In a democratic society, people must be free to state this sort of opinion, and to seek to persuade others of it.

In principle, one could imagine attempting to forbid anyone expressing this sort of opinion, but this could only be done by violating fundamental civil liberties. Surely no one thinks that Jewish activists should be prohibited from saying that a good Jew will marry within the faith and avoid the corrupting influences of Christian culture (for example celebrating Christmas), even if this reproduces (in Cowan's words) a dichotomous 'logic of purity, authenticity and fixity'.

So far as I know, no post-multiculturalist would endorse the radical solution of banning speech that involves this sort of essentialist logic. But what then exactly is the problem, and how do we fix it? What is the nature of this 'forcing' and 'imposing' an identity on someone, and how do we distinguish it from, say, 'democratically persuading' someone to adopt an identity? Fraser says that multiculturalism enables group leaders to exercise 'moral pressure' on group members, and that this is how identities are 'imposed'. But what distinguishes moral pressure from moral persuasion? What criteria do we use to distinguish legitimate forms of argumentation and mobilisation from illegitimate 'moral pressure', 'force' and 'imposition', and how can we address these latter problems without restricting basic civil and political liberties?

So far as I can tell, the post-multiculturalists have no answer to this question, and as a result, they offer no guidelines for how to revise the practice of multiculturalism.[63] If the problem is 'moral pressure' within a group, rather than legal compulsion or extra-legal intimidation, what can and should a liberal democracy do, other than firmly insisting on the right of other citizens inside and outside the group to contest that particular script freely and democratically? Post-multiculturalists often conclude by emphasising the necessity of enabling democratic contestation of scripts, but of course that simply restates a core part of LMC.

The right to democratic contestation is crucial, but it's worth noting that there was nothing in the Macedonian case that precluded such democratic contestation by those with alternate understandings of Macedonian and Greek identity. Indeed, this is clear from Cowan's own story: the reality is that the Macedonian activists have been largely unsuccessful in persuading people to adopt an exclusive Macedonian identity, precisely because they are not in a position to 'force' or 'impose' this identity on anyone. Minority activists are trying to peacefully and democratically persuade their co-ethnics to adopt a certain script about who they are as a group, but theirs is just one voice and one narrative in an ongoing democratic process of deliberation and contestation and persuasion. It is unclear what, if anything, Cowan would propose to change in this scenario.

So it is also unclear what implications this version of the post-multiculturalist critique has for the real-world practice of multiculturalism. And so, unsurprisingly, Cowan too ends up hedging on what, if any, changes follow from her analysis. She concludes by saying:

> [T]he only tenable position for the engaged scholar [is] a paradoxical one: to support the demands for recognition of the Macedonian minority, but as a category that is chosen rather than imposed (whether explicitly or de facto), yet at the same time, to problematize rather than celebrate its project, and to query its emancipatory aura,

examining the exclusions and cultural disenfranchisement it creates from within.[64]

She presents this as a critique of LMC, but, so far as I can tell, it is simply a restatement of LMC, both as it is theorised and as it is embodied in public policies and international law. LMC, like Cowan, supports demands for recognition within liberal democratic constraints that do not allow for the involuntary ascription of ethnic categories or for the undemocratic imposition of cultural scripts. So far as I can tell, like all of these post-multiculturalist authors, she offers no tangible recommendations for reform that differ from, or go beyond, a liberal multiculturalist framework.[65]

Conclusion

In this chapter, I have explored what appears to be a nearly unanimous consensus among recent writers that multiculturalism is guilty of essentialism, and that addressing this problem requires a radical overhaul of the multiculturalist project. I have suggested that, despite this seeming consensus, the implications of this critique are in fact indeterminate, in large part because critics fail to make clear their target, and hence the required remedy. While the different versions of this critique all point to legitimate issues – essentialising tendencies clearly exist in society – it is not clear in what ways LMC is contributing to these tendencies, and hence in what ways multiculturalism might need to be reformed. While all of the authors begin with a strong rhetorical commitment to a radical overhaul of multiculturalism, by the end of their analysis, they have all backed away from making any radical proposals for change. Indeed, so far as I can tell, they do not cite a single example of a group-differentiated right that liberal multiculturalists endorse that they would reject on essentialist (or other) grounds.

Ironically, I believe that this post-multiculturalist critique of essentialism is itself guilty of reification. According to critics, multiculturalism reifies ethnic groups as unified agents who speak and act with one unified voice. I would argue that this critique itself involves a reification of multiculturalism, treating it as if it is a single unified force that walks and talks out there in the world. According to critics, multiculturalism actively 'encourages' people to think in essentialist terms, 'pressuring' people to act in essentialist ways, even 'forcing' and 'imposing' essentialist identities and practices on people. But all this talk of multiculturalism doing things out there in the world is hopelessly reified. Multiculturalism is not a single actor or force that speaks with a single voice. It operates at different levels: theorists of multiculturalism say one set of things; laws, bureaucratic regulations and court decisions tell us another set of things; the media tell us yet another; and activists have their own message. We cannot hope to figure out how to improve multiculturalism – or how to build a better post-multiculturalism, if you prefer – without pinning down which actors at which levels are responsible for what effects.

At the end of her book, Anne Phillips pleads for a new version of multiculturalism that puts agency at the centre of the project. I agree with this commitment to agency – as I noted earlier, autonomy is the foundational premise of my approach – but I would say that we need to put agency at the centre of any useful *critique* of multiculturalism. The post-multiculturalist literature is full of agentless processes. According to post-multiculturalists, there is this thing called multiculturalism that is telling people, encouraging people, pressuring people, forcing people – but it is never specified who is doing this talking, encouraging, pressuring or forcing. Is it theorists, legislators, bureaucrats, judges, social workers, educators, activists, media commentators? I believe that if we start to specify the actors, and hence the causal processes, it might turn out that LMC is not after all in need of a radical overhaul.

This is not to say that the early theorists of LMC somehow resolved all the key theoretical issues twenty years ago, and that the only task is to build the political will to implement those theories more fully. For one thing, the early theorists of multiculturalism had important disagreements among themselves, which remain unresolved.[66] Moreover, the world has changed in the past two decades, and new challenges have emerged that were barely even contemplated in the first wave of multiculturalist theories. Let me mention just a few of these issues:

1. Existing theories of LMC implicitly or explicitly operate on the assumption that immigrants are settled permanently in their country of residence, as opposed to being temporary visitors or migrant workers, and are intended to provide new models of inclusion for such permanent residents. Multiculturalism as a model of inclusion only become relevant and meaningful in Europe when it was accepted that post-war immigrants were 'here to stay'. For a period in the 1980s and 1990s, this was indeed the reigning assumption. But today we see a resurgence of programmes of temporary or seasonal migration, both at the low end of the socio-economic ladder (for example, seasonal farm workers) and at the high end (skilled workers on short-term contracts). We also see sizeable numbers of unauthorized migrants and asylum seekers, both of whom face the prospect of being forced to return to their country of origin. This proliferation of migrant statuses, with varying and unpredictable durations of stay, has led to a situation that Vertovec calls 'super diversity'.[67] It is far from clear, in either theory or practice, what sort of multiculturalism is appropriate in contexts other than permanent settlement.

2. Existing theories of LMC presuppose, implicitly or explicitly, that state–minority relations are 'desecuritised' – that is, the governance of state–minority relations is seen as an issue of social policy to be addressed through the normal democratic process of claims making, consultation, and debate, not as an issue of state security that trumps normal democratic processes. States are highly unlikely to accord multicultural rights to minorities who are seen as disloyal, or as potential collaborators with enemies. I have elsewhere argued that the vast bulk of state–minority relations in the West were indeed desecuritised in the post-war period, particularly in the crucial period of the 'ethnic revival' in the 1960s to 1980s. This was true in relation to indigenous peoples, sub-state national minorities and most immigrants, and this made possible experiments in LMC.[68] But today, particularly since 9/11, we see a resurgence of the security framework, most obviously in relation to Muslims. This has led to diminished support for multiculturalism, but also to subtle (or not so subtle) revisions

241

to multiculturalism programmes so that they focus on fighting radicalism rather than on issues of accommodation and inclusion. Multiculturalism, when it persists at all, is being used as a tool for monitoring and policing the behaviour of Muslims suspected of disloyalty. We can bemoan this distortion of multiculturalism, but we cannot behave as if issues of security do not exist. And this raises difficult questions, unresolved in theory or practice, about what we might call securitised multiculturalism, as distinct from the desecuritised multiculturalism theorised in the early 1990s.

In these two respects, some of the preconditions of LMC are eroding. LMC, I would argue, was theorised for situations in which immigrants were seen as legally authorised, permanently settled, and presumptively loyal. In an age of securitisation and super-diversity, these assumptions are put into question.

But even where these assumptions are still valid, there are important issues that were not adequately addressed in early theories of multiculturalism. Let me mention two of them:

1. Critics often claim that multiculturalism is about segregation and 'parallel societies', and say that multiculturalism should therefore be replaced with a 'civic integration' approach, built around things like language requirements and citizenship tests.[69] Theorists of multiculturalism have always insisted that multiculturalism for immigrant groups is not about segregation, but rather is a mode of integration, aiming at fairer terms of inclusion. And so, at a conceptual level, there is no inherent inconsistency between multiculturalism policies and civic integration policies, and indeed countries like Canada and Australia have always had robust integration policies alongside their robust multiculturalism policies. But we do not yet have good theories about the relationship between civic integration policies and multiculturalism policies, and about when the former complement or subvert the latter.[70] And this in turn raises even deeper questions about the relationship between multiculturalism and nationalism. While critics often assume that multiculturalism aims to dislodge the centrality of

national identities, and that is therefore pushes us towards a post-national world, it may well be the case that multiculturalism works best when it is seen as a constituent part of national identities, and when it pushes us towards a more 'multicultural nationalism'. This indeed has been the argument recently made by Varun Uberoi.[71] Yet the conceptual links between multiculturalism and nationhood remain under-theorised.

2. Finally, in retrospect, it seems clear that early theories of multiculturalism did not adequately address the specific challenges that religion raises. This is certainly true of the 'Canadian school' of multiculturalism, reflected in the work of people like Taylor, Tully, Carens and my own work, which was heavily shaped by the claims of the Québécois and Aboriginal peoples, neither of whom mobilise around faith-based claims. Even immigrant groups in Canada have not historically mobilised around religion, at least not until very recently. Multiculturalism in the Canadian context has therefore been theorised in terms of language, territory, race, ethnicity and indigeneity, rather than religion. This inattention to religion has been rightly criticised by many scholars.[72] By contrast, public debates in Europe today around multiculturalism are almost exclusively focused on religion, and particularly on Muslims. This raises a whole host of complex issues, not least about the meaning of secularism and about when multicultural claims framed in the language of faith are or are not consistent with secularism. These issues are rendered even more intractable in many countries by the fact that states have rarely been consistent over time in the way they have interpreted secularism, with the result that there is typically a palimpsest of different accommodations reached at different times with different religious groups. In evaluating faith-based claims, should our goal be to implement what we as a society now take to be the most persuasive interpretation of the requirements of secularism, even if this means that newer religious groups are denied longstanding accommodations that were offered to earlier religious groups? Or should we rather aim to ensure that there is no discrimination between religious groups, and hence ensure that any accommodations negotiated in the past for one group

be offered today to newer groups? In my view, this is not a rhetorical question: it is a genuine moral dilemma, for which again we lack good theoretical tools.[73]

This is just a sample of the unresolved issues confronting theorists of multiculturalism. One could quickly expand the list, particularly if we move beyond the immigrant case to also consider unresolved issues around the claims of sub-state national minorities and indigenous peoples. So there is no shortage of theoretical work remaining to be done, on the proliferating forms of diversity, the securitisation of diversity, the link with civic integration and national identities, and with religion and secularism. On all of these issues and others, early theories of multiculturalism now seem at best incomplete, and at worst outdated, resting on assumptions and preconditions that may no longer apply.

Yet I would argue that on all of these issues, neither the 'post-multiculturalism' nor the 'anti-multiculturalism' literature is of much help. Both have misidentified the nature and goals of multiculturalism, and hence misdiagnosed the challenges we face, and prematurely closed off theoretical and practical options that deserve our attention. In facing up to the challenges of the 21st century, I would still argue that multiculturalism remains a viable starting point.

Notes

1. Keith Banting and I have attempted to measure the spread of these policies across the Western democracies in our 'Multiculturalism Policy Index', available at www.queensu.ca/mcp (accessed 10 September 2014).
2. For this contrast, see S. Vertovec (2005), 'Pre-, high-, anti- and post-multiculturalism' (ESRC Centre on Migration, Policy and Society, University of Oxford); and D. Ley (2005), 'Post-multiculturalism?' (Research on Immigration and Integration in the Metropolis, Vancouver Centre of Excellence, Working Paper Series No. 05–18).
3. B. Barry (2000), *Culture and Equality: An Egalitarian Critique of Multiculturalism* (Cambridge: Polity).
4. S. Huntington (2004), *Who Are We? The Challenges to America's National Identity* (New York: Simon and Schuster).

5. A. Phillips (2007), *Multiculturalism without Culture* (Princeton, NJ: Princeton University Press), p. 16.
6. W. Kymlicka (2007), *Multicultural Odysseys* (Oxford University Press).
7. Phillips, *Multiculturalism without Culture*, p. 14.
8. e.g. B. Parekh (1995), 'The concept of national identity'. *New Community* 21:2; and B. Parekh (1999), 'The incoherence of nationalism', in R. Beiner (ed) *Theorizing Nationalism* (Albany, NY: SUNY Press), 295–325.
9. For a more comprehensive account of the group-differentiated policies related to these three types of diversity, see the Multiculturalism Policy Index (note 1), which distinguishes nine characteristic multiculturalism policies for indigenous peoples; six characteristic policies adopted in relation to national minorities; and eight such policies in relation to immigrant groups.
10. W. Kymlicka (1995), *Multicultural Citizenship* (Oxford: Oxford University Press). In this way, my defense of liberal democratic multiculturalism appeals to distinctly liberal conceptions of autonomy and justice. Parekh, by contrast, tries to defend liberal democratic multiculturalism while avoiding appeal to distinctly liberal values. Indeed, he argues that any theory of multiculturalism rooted in distinctly liberal values is 'structurally ill-equipped to appreciate the specificity of non-liberal cultures and cannot avoid distorting them' (B. Parekh (1997), 'Dilemmas of a multicultural theory of citizenship', pp. 54–62 in *Constellations*, 4:1, at p. 60). He argues that the merit of these liberal values should itself be open for contestation in an inter-cultural dialogue, and that while liberal values may indeed win the day in such a dialogue, they should not be presupposed in advance (Parekh, *Rethinking Multiculturalism: Cultural Diversity and Political Theory* (Basingstoke: Macmillan). This raises a number of complex methodological and substantive issues that I cannot address here, but I have argued elsewhere that Parekh's 'dialogical' defense of liberal democratic multiculturalism smuggles in distinctly liberal values, and that the contrast between a 'monological liberal' approach and a 'dialogical intercultural' approach is not as sharp as he claims. (See my review of Parekh in W. Kymlicka (2001), 'Liberalism, dialogue and multiculturalism', *Ethnicities*, 1:1, pp. 128–37.) In any event, this disagreement is not central to the argument of this chapter, since the essentialist critique has been applied to both of our approaches.

11. Barry, *Culture and Equality*, p. 5.
12. Huntington (2004), *Who Are We?*, p. 171.
13. I. Kristol (1991), 'The tragedy of multiculturalism', *Wall Street Journal*, 31 July, p. 15.
14. The motivations for adopting laws and policies are complex, including the desire to win ethnic votes, or amoral bargaining amongst self-interested groups. But the policies adopted for these complex reasons are framed to fit with liberal democratic values.
15. Kymlicka, *Multicultural Odysseys*.
16. R. Koopmans (2006), 'Trade-offs between equality and difference: the crisis of Dutch multiculturalism in cross-national perspective', Danish Institute for International Affairs, Brief (December), p. 5.
17. J. Reitz (2009), 'Assessing multiculturalism as a behavioural theory', in R. Breton, K. Dion and K. Dion (eds) *Multiculturalism and Social Cohesion: Potentials and Challenges of Diversity* (New York: Springer), p. 13.
18. I discuss the evidence regarding national minorities and indigenous peoples in Kymlicka, *Multicultural Odysseys*, Chapter 5.
19. P. Sniderman and L. Hagendoorn (2007), *When Ways of Life Collide* (Princeton NJ: Princeton University Press).
20. I. Bloemraad (2006), *Becoming a Citizen: Incorporating Immigrants and Refugees in the United States and Canada* (Berkeley, CA: University of California Press); M. Adams (2007), *Unlikely Utopia: The Surprising Triumph of Canadian Pluralism* (Viking, Toronto).
21. C. Kesler and I. I. Bloemraad (2010). 'Does immigration erode social capital? The conditional effects of immigration-generated diversity on trust, membership, and participation across 19 countries, 1981–2000', *Canadian Journal of Political Science* 43:2; A. Harell (2009), 'Minority–majority relations in Canada: the rights regime and the adoption of multicultural values', paper presented at the Canadian Political Science Association Annual Meeting, Ottawa ON; and A. Kazemipur (2009), *Social Capital and Diversity: Some Lessons from Canada* (Bern: Peter Lang).
22. S. Weldon (2006), 'The institutional context of tolerance for ethnic minorities: a comparative, multilevel analysis of Western Europe', *American Journal of Political Science*, 50:2, pp. 331–49.
23. K. Banting and W. Kymlicka (eds) (2006), *Multiculturalism and the Welfare State: Recognition and Redistribution in Contemporary Democracies* (Oxford: Oxford University Press); M. Crepaz (2006), '"If you are my brother, I may give you a dime!" Public opinion on multiculturalism, trust and the welfare state', in K. Banting

246

and W. Kymlicka (eds) *Multiculturalism and the Welfare State: Recognition and Redistribution in Contemporary Democracies* (Oxford: Oxford University Press).

24. J. Berry, J. Phinney, D. Sam and P. Vedder (2006), *Immigrant Youth in Cultural Transition* (Lawrence Erlbaum Associates, Mahwah). I discuss these studies in more depth in Kymlicka (2010), 'Testing the liberal multiculturalist hypothesis: normative theories and social science evidence', *Canadian Journal of Political Science*, 43:2, pp. 257–71, and Kymlicka (2012), *Multiculturalism: Success, Failure and the Future* (Washington: Migration Policy Institute). The main exception to this generalisation is the work of Ruud Koopmans (2010), 'Trade-offs between equality and difference: immigrant integration, multiculturalism and the welfare state in cross-national perspective' *Journal of Ethnic and Migration Studies*, 36:1, pp. 1–26), and E. Ersanilli and R. Koopmans (2011), 'Do immigrant integration policies matter? A three-country comparison among Turkish immigrants', *West European Politics*, 34:2, pp. 208–34), who argue that multiculturalism is responsible for some of the poorer outcomes of immigrants in the Netherlands as compared to neighbouring countries without multiculturalism policies. For doubts about his analysis of the Dutch case, see W. G. J. Duyvendak and P. W. A. Scholten (2011), 'The invention of the Dutch multicultural model and its effects on integration discourses in the Netherlands', *Perspectives on Europe*, 40:2. Even if his analysis holds up, it remains an exception to a growing literature showing that multiculturalism policies have positive effects in cross-national and longitudinal studies.

25. Kymlicka, *Multicultural Odysseys*.

26. N. Fraser (2001), 'Recognition without ethics', *Theory, Culture and Society*, 18:2, p. 24.

27. S. Benhabib (2002), *The Claims of Culture*: *Equality and Diversity in the Global Era* (Princeton, NJ: Princeton University Press), pp. 4, 68.

28. J. Cowan (ed.) (2001), *Culture and Rights: Anthropological Perspectives* (Cambridge University Press), pp. 154, 171.

29. K. Appiah (2005), *The Ethics of Identity* (Princeton University Press), pp. 110, 151–2.

30. S. Scheffler (2007), 'Immigration and the significance of culture', *Philosophy and Public Affairs* 35:2, p. 124.

31. Phillips, *Multiculturalism without Culture*, p. 16.

32. Appiah, *Ethics of Identity*, pp. 151–2.

33. E. Grabb and J. Curtis (2010), *Regions Apart: The Four Societies of Canada and the United States* (Oxford University Press).
34. Benhabib, *Claims of Culture*, p. 68.
35. Appiah, *Ethics of Identity*, p. 152.
36. Ibid., pp. 123, 101.
37. Benhabib, *Claims of Culture*, pp. ix, 65.
38. Ibid., pp. ix, 65.
39. Ibid., pp. ix, 65.
40. Benhabib, *Claims of Culture*, p. 65.
41. Appiah, *Ethics of Identity*, p. 103.
42. Ibid., p. 104.
43. Ibid., pp. 103–4.
44. Benhabib, *Claims of Culture*, pp. 66–7.
45. Unlike most of the other authors being discussed, Phillips does not suggest abandoning the term, 'multiculturalism', and does not describe herself as a 'post'-multiculturalist. However, as her book title *Multiculturalism without Culture* indicates, she seeks a post-culturalist multiculturalism, and this is relevantly similar to the other authors.
46. Phillips, *Multiculturalism without Culture*, p. 14.
47. Ibid., p. 23.
48. Ibid., p. 76.
49. Ibid., p. 73.
50. Ibid., p. 9.
51. Ibid., p. 112.
52. Ibid., p. 144.
53. Ibid., p. 113.
54. Ibid., p. 76.
55. G. Baumann (1996), *Contesting Culture: Discourses of Identity in Multi-ethnic London* (Cambridge: Cambridge University Press).
56. T. Modood (2007), *Multiculturalism* (Cambridge: Polity), pp. 97–8.
57. Weldon, 'Institutional context'.
58. J. Cowan, *Culture and Rights* (Cambridge University Press), pp. 154, 171.
59. Fraser, 'Recognition without ethics', p. 24.
60. Appiah, *Ethics of Identity*, pp. 151–2.
61. While these authors differ in their primary focus, I should note that Phillips also expresses concern about intra-group essentialisation, and Appiah/Cowan/Fraser express concerns about inter-group processes.

248

62. Berry et al., *Immigrant Youth*.
63. This version of the post-multiculturalist critique arguably reproduces the very paternalistic logic that Phillips was objecting to – that is, it assumes that while members of the white majority can safely be trusted to engage in democratic persuasion and deliberation about their identities and cultures, members of minority groups are trapped in cultural scripts that pre-empt or override their capacity for autonomy, and 'we' (the state, the white majority) need to intervene in these intra-group processes to fight the essentialisers.
64. Cowan, 'Culture and rights', p. 171.
65. Nor do I understand why she thinks of this as 'paradoxical' – supporting minority rights within liberal democratic constraints is a wholly consistent, unparadoxical position.
66. For example, see Parekh's critique of my work in B. Parekh (2000), *Rethinking Multiculturalism: Cultural Diversity and Political Theory* (New York: Palgrave Macmillan), Chapter 3, and my critique of his work in Kymlicka (2001), 'Liberalism, dialogue and multiculturalism', *Ethnicities*, 1:1.
67. Vertovec, 'Pre-, high-, anti-'.
68. Kymlicka, *Multicultural Odysseys*.
69. C. Joppke (2004/2007), 'Beyond national models: civic integration policies for immigrants in Western Europe', *Western European Politics*, 30:1.
70. For some preliminary reflections, see Kymlicka, *Multiculturalism: Success, Failure and the Future*; K. Banting and W. Kymlicka (2013), 'Is there really a retreat from multiculturalism policies? New evidence from the Multiculturalism Policy Index', 11:5, pp. 577–98.
71. V. Uberoi (2008), 'Do policies of multiculturalism change national identities?', *Political Quarterly*, 79, 404–17.
72. e.g. Modood, *Multiculturalism*.
73. W. Kymlicka (2009), 'The governance of religious diversity: the old and the new', in Paul Bramadat and Matthias Koenig (eds) *International Migration and the Governance of Religious Diversity* (McGill-Queen's University Press).

9

Beyond Rules and Rights: Multiculturalism and the Inclusion of Immigrants

Joseph H. Carens

A couple of years ago when I was travelling by train in Britain, I was sitting opposite an elderly Pakistani couple and next to their adolescent daughter. When the crowded train pulled out of the station, the parents began to talk in Urdu. The girl felt restless and nervous and started making strange signals to them. As they carried on their conversation for a few more minutes, she angrily leaned over the table and asked them to shut up. When the confused mother asked why, the girl shot back 'just as you do not expose your private parts in public, you should not speak in *that language* in public'.[1]

This story told by Bhikhu Parekh in *Rethinking Multiculturalism* draws our attention to the fact that the inclusion of immigrants involves much more than questions about formal laws and policies. There is no suggestion that the girl in the story thought her parents were violating any formal rule or that they had no legal right to speak Urdu to one another. Rather she apparently believed that her parents' behaviour violated a British social norm that one should only speak English in public (or at least that one should not speak Urdu).[2] Furthermore, given the analogy that she drew between speaking Urdu on a train and public exposure of one's genitalia, she must have internalised this norm herself, experiencing her parents' use of Urdu in public as deeply embarrassing. From her perspective, therefore, immigrants who wanted to fit in and be accepted within the wider British community were expected to keep some aspects of their inherited culture and identity, including their native tongue, behind closed doors.

I assume that most readers will be troubled, as I am and as Parekh was, by the idea that there might be a social norm against using whatever language one wants in conversing with family members or friends on a train. Such a norm seems like an unreasonable intrusion into the sphere of personal freedom that every individual in a liberal democratic state should enjoy.

Of course, we need not take the girl's perceptions at face value. Adolescents in Europe and North America often feel mortified by their parents' behaviour in public spaces for reasons that seem utterly mysterious to the parents themselves.[3] Perhaps no one on the train would have been affronted to hear her parents speaking Urdu. Her parents themselves apparently felt free to speak Urdu to one another. If there was a social norm against this, they must not have learned it, given the mother's puzzlement at her daughter's request. So, the girl may have been mistaken about social norms in Britain regarding immigrants' use of their native languages in public.

On the other hand, one has to wonder how a child would ever develop such a strong view about the shamefulness of speaking Urdu if no one had ever communicated anything to her about the use of languages other than English in public. Moreover, the children of immigrants are often much more attuned to the norms and expectations of society than the immigrants themselves. The girl may have been right about the expectations of others and her parents simply unaware of the disapproval their behaviour was eliciting or was likely to elicit (although not from their fellow passenger Parekh).

Whether the girl was right or not about this particular social norm, the story alerts us to one of many ways in which the inclusion of immigrants in the political communities where they live can depend on things besides the legal status of the immigrants and the formal rules and policies of the state. In this chapter, I want to consider three other factors that affect the inclusion of immigrants: expectations, incentives and identities.

For the sake of simplicity of exposition, I will normally use the term 'immigrants' to mean both immigrants themselves and their immediate descendants, even if the latter are born in the state to which their parents moved and so are not actually immigrants. Similarly, for the sake of simplicity, I will assume that the immigrants have become citizens of the state to which they have moved, or, in the case of the descendants, citizens of the state in which they were born.

My basic goal in the chapter is to show that liberal democratic principles have implications for the kinds of expectations, incentives and identities that a liberal democratic political community should regard as morally acceptable or even morally required in relation to immigrants, even though these expectations, incentives and identities cannot be enforced through formal rules or constructed as legal rights. The underlying presupposition of my discussion is that a liberal democratic community has an obligation to create an ethos of inclusion so that all citizens are seen by others and are able to see themselves as full members of the political community where they live, regardless of their ancestry.

I begin by briefly situating my discussion in the context of the ongoing theoretical debates over multiculturalism. The contemporary concern with multiculturalism in Anglo-American political philosophy first emerged in the late 1980s as a critique of many different forms of exclusion and marginalisation: race, class, gender, ethnicity, religion, sexuality, age and disability among others. Advocates of multiculturalism usually saw themselves as critics of liberalism. Theorists like Iris Marion Young were especially concerned with the ways in which liberal conceptions of freedom and equality disguised the advantages that existing social arrangements created for some groups over others. These critics often focused attention on the informal ways in which power was exercised through school curricula, informal social practices, and unconscious habits of mind and heart.[4] Immigrants appeared occasionally in these early discussions of multiculturalism, but often at the margins.

The publication in 1995 of Will Kymlicka's influential book *Multicultural Citizenship* shifted the framework of the academic debate in three important ways.[5] First, Kymlicka argued that multiculturalism was required by liberalism rather than conflicting with it. Second, Kymlicka framed his discussion almost entirely in terms of legal rules and rights, arguing in favour of 'group-differentiated rights' for minorities. Third, Kymlicka focused his analysis almost entirely on national minorities and ethnic groups (the latter being composed of immigrants) rather than on the wide range of socially disadvantaged groups that had previously been the concern of multicultural theorists.

Parekh's work in 2000 kept Kymlicka's focus on ethnic and national minorities, but like earlier multicultural theorists he paid considerably more attention than Kymlicka to questions about forms of inclusion and exclusion that were not easily captured under the rubric of rules and rights. The opening anecdote illustrates this approach. Parekh uses this story to criticise what he calls the 'civic assimilationalist view', the idea that it is possible to draw a sharp line between the public sphere and the private sphere, permitting wide diversity in the private sphere while demanding conformity, including cultural conformity, in the public sphere.[6] That approach, Parekh argues inevitably fails to provide adequate respect for diversity. At the same time, Parekh acknowledges that democratic societies do need some cultural commitments that are common to most members of society. He also thinks that immigrants normally want to belong to the political community in which they live. They want to be, and to be seen as, full members, on a par with others. In this chapter I would like to pursue this line of enquiry, probing a bit further into the question of what sort of democratic ethos is compatible with the social realities of a multicultural society, and how democratic states ought to pursue the inclusion of immigrants.

Expectations

Let's start with expectations. An expectation, in the sense in which I use the term in this chapter, is an informal public standard or a social norm. In other words, it is prescriptive. It is important to distinguish this sort of expectation from one that is predictive or empirical. An empirical expectation is simply a prediction about what will happen. It carries no necessary implication about what anyone ought to do. For example, if a social scientist says that she expects that most of the grandchildren of immigrants will not be able to speak their grandparents' native language, she is simply making a prediction about likely developments, not communicating any view as to whether this development is desirable. By contrast, the expectations that I am concerned with in this chapter impose a certain kind of demand upon those to whom the expectation is addressed. If a child's parents say 'We expect you to learn your grandparents' language', they are trying to tell the child what they think she ought to do, not simply make a prediction about what she will do. In this chapter, unless otherwise specified, I am using the term 'expectation' to refer only to prescriptive expectations.

Most social interactions are shaped in part by expectations about roles and relationships – what it is to be a good parent or friend, how to behave responsibly as a colleague or supervisor, and so on. Expectations operate at many different levels, from highly particular expectations in a workplace to widespread social norms and the broad expectations that citizens have of one another.

To see more clearly what expectations are and why they matter, it may be helpful to contrast them with rules. A rule is a formal requirement, imposed by some authority and backed with some explicit sanction. A law passed by a legislature is obviously a rule of this sort, but rules include a much wider array of phenomena. Like expectations, rules operate at many different levels. Almost any policy or regulation to which some formal sanction is attached is a rule in the sense in which I am using the term. For example, if a business requires its employees to wear a uniform, that is a rule. Rules impose duties but also often create corresponding rights or formal entitlements.

The key difference between rules and expectations is that the consequences that greet a failure to meet expectations are informal social sanctions and often unspecified. Also, expectations are often implicit, though they can sometimes be made explicit. Like rules, expectations have a coercive dimension. They are supposed to govern the behaviour of those subject to them. Expectations can play a crucial role in supporting rules. Few rules work effectively if people are constrained only by the consequences they will face if caught breaking the rule. Rules work better if those subject to them feel the rules ought to be obeyed. At the same time, the creation of rules can affect what people think. They can generate expectations. For example, rules against discrimination may be difficult to enforce unless most people accept the idea that the prohibited discrimination is actually wrong, but having a rule against that kind of discrimination may contribute to people seeing it as wrong. So, rules and expectations can interact with and reinforce one another.

Sometimes expectations do not reinforce rules but substitute for them. It may be impractical to use formal rules in some contexts but possible to rely on expectations to regulate social interactions. The norms of polite behaviour are a good example. It may also be against our principles to use a rule for something but acceptable to construct a social norm about it. For example, it is difficult and often morally problematic to construct rules about values, attitudes, dispositions and feelings, but it may be both possible and acceptable to have social expectations about such matters.

Many of the conflicts related to immigration are concerned not with what people do but with what they think and feel, things that are normally not subject to rules. That is why it is so important to pay attention to expectations. Expectations can be general norms adopted without immigrants in view, though sometimes having a differential impact upon them, or they can be norms specifically connected either positively or negatively with immigrants. Some of the most crucial questions relating to the inclusion of immigrants are about the reasonableness and defensibility of the expectations that other citizens have of immigrants and vice versa.

Like rules, expectations can be subject to moral evaluation. Some expectations would clearly be unjust from a liberal democratic perspective. An expectation about what religion an individual should adopt would be morally unacceptable, even if there were no formal rule to enforce it, because that sort of expectation conflicts with the liberal democratic commitment to freedom of religion. That freedom requires more than the absence of legal constraints. It also entails informal social respect for the religious commitments of individuals. Thus, for example, it would be wrong to treat being a Christian as an informal prerequisite for acceptance as a full member of the political community or being a Muslim as a barrier to acceptance.

As I noted above, expectations are often implicit. Recently, a number of democratic states have tried to address some of the challenges posed by immigration by constructing social or moral contracts with immigrants.[7] The presupposition underlying such contracts is that it is not good enough to make sure that immigrants understand the formal rules to which they are subject and the formal rights and duties that follow from those rules. If it were, there would be no need to construct contracts with immigrants. It would be sufficient to provide them with information about the rules. At bottom, these contracts are attempts to make explicit the expectations that the receiving society feels entitled to have of the immigrants and also the expectations that the society thinks immigrants are entitled to have of the receiving society. Sometimes these contracts emerge as part of a wider political current in which immigrants are constructed as threats to democracy who have to be constrained in various ways. In such cases, the contracts are unlikely to promote the inclusion of immigrants. In other cases, however, the contracts reflect a genuine effort to think through the requirements of inclusion, giving weight both to what the immigrants can reasonably expect of the society they have joined and to what the receiving society can expect of them. One virtue of this sort of contractual approach is that making the expectations explicit makes it possible to reflect on the compatibility of the stated expectations with liberal democratic principles. We can also ask whether relevant expectations are missing from a proposed contract.

The contracts usually say that they expect immigrants to accept the basic liberal democratic institutional framework of the state. Sometimes they say that immigrants should accept the receiving society's commitment to basic values like gender equality and toleration of different ways of life (though usually without spelling out what these contested concepts entail).

It is certainly correct to think that liberal democracies cannot function only on the basis of formal rules and institutions. They depend also on the values, attitudes and dispositions of the population. Liberal democracies work well only if most of the citizens accept liberal democratic norms, values and principles. A liberal democracy requires a liberal democratic ethos, and it requires citizens with liberal democratic virtues. So, it is reasonable to expect immigrants to accept liberal democratic values and practise liberal democratic virtues, so long as this expectation is suitably qualified in ways that will be discussed below. But an equally reasonable and perhaps more important expectation is that other citizens also accept liberal democratic values and practise liberal democratic virtues. All too often, the assumption in discussions of immigration seems to be that the majority of citizens already possess the dispositions and attitudes that are needed for a liberal democracy to function properly. But that is often not the case. Liberal democratic principles require the inclusion of immigrants, and the inclusion of immigrants requires the majority of citizens to develop attitudes, values and norms that they often do not yet exhibit, at least in the requisite degree. People sometimes speak of the need for a 'muscular' liberalism that is not afraid to assert its worth and to demand the adherence of those living in liberal democratic states. If muscle is indeed what is called for, a lot more of this muscle should be directed at non-immigrant citizens than is usually recognised.

There is one particularly important liberal democratic principle that sets severe limits to the expectations that citizens should face, whether they are immigrants or not, namely the principle that people should be able to live their lives as they choose so long as they are not harming others. This idea was given its classic formulation in Mill's *On Liberty*. As is well known, it is an idea with many internal tensions and contradictions, and I won't attempt to sort those out here. Nevertheless, Mill was certainly right to argue that human freedom will be very limited, especially for minorities, if the majority feels free to impose the informal sanctions of public disapproval on any behaviour that does not conform to the majority's view of what is appropriate or even their view of what is moral. To put the point another way, the respect that people owe one another in a liberal democracy requires a sense for what is nobody's business but that of the person directly involved. This applies not only to what people do behind closed doors but also to how they conduct themselves in the public sphere, at least within

257

very broad limits. People in a liberal democratic state have what is sometimes called in France a 'right to indifference', a moral right to present themselves in the public sphere and to interact with others on a voluntary basis without having to submit to the judgement of others. Everyone should be able to ride the subway and expect that others will ignore them. That is why the Pakistani parents in my opening story should have felt free to speak Urdu without embarrassment. It is why a gay couple should be free to appear in public displaying affection for one another to the same extent as a heterosexual couple without evoking any reaction. And it is why Muslims should be free to appear in public in hijab without drawing attention, much less harassment. The principle applies to all three cases in the same way. So, liberal democratic principles justify all citizens, whether immigrants or not, in expecting (normatively) that other citizens will leave them alone and let them live as they choose.

I don't want to overstate this freedom from the expectations of others, however. Those who think that immigrants should conform to the established rules and norms in the states in which they live sometimes like to cite the old proverb 'When in Rome, do as the Romans do'.[8] There are dangers in relying too heavily on this maxim, as I have just shown, but it is not entirely wrong. Immigrants, especially those who arrive as adults, always do much more changing and adapting than other citizens and it is not unreasonable that they do so. In the vast majority of cases, the rules and the informal expectations that have been established in liberal democratic states will not have to be changed in order to include immigrants. On the contrary, the immigrants will have to adjust to existing rules and expectations in order to include themselves, and it is reasonable that they should do so.

The institutions, practices, and social life of any complex modern society rest upon informal expectations that provide important collective goods, by making it possible for people to coordinate their activities without direct supervision or instruction. Those in the receiving society have a legitimate interest in maintaining the institutions, practices and patterns of social life that they have established. Immigrants usually have to learn about and adapt to these established institutions, practices, and patterns of social life.

Getting a job, finding a place to live, sending kids to school – all these ordinary human activities are enmeshed in a social environment that immigrants must inevitably take largely as given and to which they have to adjust in order to get what they want.

Anyone who has ever lived in another country for an extended period has had this experience. For example, every modern state relies on bureaucracies that are structurally alike in the main respects but different from one another in important ways. Italian public bureaucracies do not function in quite the same way as German ones, which differ in turn from those in France and those in the United States. When in Rome, you have to learn how the Italian bureaucracy works. You cannot expect it to change for you.

Think of the issue of names. If an immigrant comes to the United States or the United Kingdom from Russia or China or Saudi Arabia or Israel, all places with alphabets different from the one used in English, she will have to adjust and write her name using the English alphabet. No one would suggest that that is an unjust or unreasonable requirement. If she comes from China where surnames normally come first, she will have to take into account the Anglo-American practice of listing surnames last in deciding how to communicate when asked her name. Some people may be aware of Chinese practices and ask for clarification, but many will not and she cannot reasonably expect them to do so. If she comes from Spain, where people have two surnames with the first normally taking precedence, she will have to be aware that what she regards as her primary surname is likely to be treated as a middle name. The burden will be on her to adjust to this communication issue, and again this is normally not unreasonable.

It is precisely because immigrants are (reasonably) expected to adjust in so many ways that many immigrants want to live in neighbourhoods with others of similar backgrounds. They will not have to change quite so much all at once, and those who have been present longer can serve as interpreters, not just linguistically but socially. They can explain about the myriad norms and expectations that are not written down, how they should interpret the behaviour and communications of the non-immigrant population, what are likely to be points of conflict or misunderstanding, and so on. They can anticipate difficulties, offer analogies, and, in short, help the newcomers to learn the ropes.

Of course, the kinds of changes and adjustments that I am describing apply to the greatest extent to the original immigrants. Their children normally learn most of these things just by living in the society. They don't usually experience them as the expectations of others to the same extent as their parents did.

I don't mean to say that immigrants or their descendants always accept all of the informal expectations of other members of society, or that they ought to do so. Think about the ways in which social norms govern things like modes of greeting, gestures, tones of voice, body language, physical distance, forms of respect, humour, politeness, acceptable displays of sexuality and countless other aspects of daily life. On the one hand, it helps to understand the dominant norms of the society in all these areas when one is seeking to navigate social interactions. On the other hand, immigrants often stick to their established patterns in such matters, and their children can and often do challenge some of the wider society's norms, holding on to the patterns and practices that they see in their parents and in families of similar backgrounds rather than simply accepting the prevailing norms. Often they blend both in ways that may influence others in society, a pattern that is evident in the areas of food, fashion and art as well as daily life. So, immigrants are not obliged simply to accept whatever social practices they find in place.

Incentives

In the broadest sense of the term an incentive is something that a person finds advantageous (a positive incentive) or disadvantageous (a negative incentive). One could think of the sanctions that are used to enforce rules and expectations as negative incentives, but in the sense in which I want to use the term the key difference between incentives on the one hand and rules and expectations on the other is that incentives are purely about interests. Rules and expectations make normative demands. The 'ought' is built in, as it were. Sanctions enforce rules and expectations but the normative demands are primary, not the sanctions. Incentives, by contrast, are contingent. No one demands that you respond to an incentive (in my sense of the term) or criticises you for failing to do so (unless there is an expectation alongside the incentive). People respond to incentives because they see it as in their interest to do so. Different people may respond to a given incentive differently because they have different interests. In a modern market society economic incentives are usually relatively effective for most people, but not always and not for everyone. Some people care much more about money than others. To say that people *ought* to respond to economic incentives would be to add a normative expectation to the incentive itself.

Most citizens of immigrant origin see themselves as having interests that are similar to the interests of other citizens, at least to a considerable degree, and especially in the economic domain. As a result, social life is filled with incentives for them to accept the way things are usually done in the state where they live, even when there are no rules or expectations requiring conformity. These incentives often emerge spontaneously, as it were, from the interactive effects of people simply pursuing their own interests without much conscious concern for the interests of others (as in the invisible hand of the market). For example, if the vast majority of people in a state speak one language and do not understand yours, your social options will be very limited if you don't learn to speak that language. In the absence of any norm about speaking English, the girl's parents in my opening story will be free to speak Urdu to one another, but if they want to buy something to eat on the train or get information from a fellow passenger, they will probably have to speak English, simply because that is the language most other people in the UK speak. More generally, anyone who wants to have a reasonable range of economic opportunities will have to learn the language that most people speak and use in economic life. This social reality creates powerful incentives for citizens of immigrant origin to learn the majority language.

The same social reality leads in a different direction, however. It creates incentives for citizens of immigrant origin to live in neighbourhoods with others of a similar background. They will then be able to use their native language more in daily life. Most people find it easier to use their native language even when they have learned a new one (as was presumably the case with the parents in the opening story). People who share the same immigrant background often eat similar foods, interact with one another in familiar ways, and so on. There are great advantages to sticking with what is familiar and comfortable. If the education system is working properly, those incentives will be much reduced for subsequent generations who will have learned the dominant language very well and will also have acquired a lot of other informal social knowledge.

For the purposes of this chapter, the crucial question is how to evaluate general patterns of incentives from a normative perspective. Even though incentives themselves (in my sense of the term) carry no normative weight, some patterns of incentives are morally problematic. It matters whether the incentives for citizens of immigrant origin to live in the same neighbourhoods are primarily the advantages of shared social patterns that I described above, or the disadvantages of living elsewhere because of the hostility and discrimination that they would encounter in other neighbourhoods. The former pattern of incentives is completely compatible with liberal democratic principles, but the latter is not. It is one that liberal democratic states have an obligation to try to change.

Immigrants often face incentives to change, as is illustrated by the incentives for immigrants to learn the majority's language, an important form of cultural adaptation. There is nothing morally wrong with incentives to learn the dominant language of the society if they are of the sort that I described above. Most of the existing population has no moral duty to learn the native language of immigrants. So, the incentives that flow from their failure to do so are not unjust.

Other incentives to change are more problematic. For example, in the late nineteenth and early twentieth centuries it was common for immigrants to the United States to change their names to ones that sounded more 'American'.[9] There was certainly no rule and arguably not even a social norm demanding that immigrants change their names, and many did not do so, but many others made the calculation that it would be advantageous to disguise their immigrant origins in this way, that it would make them less likely to be subject to discrimination and more likely to be accepted by the rest of society. This incentive for immigrants to change their names was an indication that the immigrants were not adequately included in society, and not treated equally. By the early twenty-first century, this practice of immigrants to America changing their names had virtually disappeared, again because the incentives had shifted. Immigrants no longer thought that it would be a great advantage in social life to change their names. On the whole, this transformation should be seen as a positive development.[10] The existing population has a moral duty not to discriminate against immigrants. Their behaviour should not generate incentives for immigrants to change their names.

Although most incentives emerge spontaneously, public policies can affect the incentives that people face. Sometimes policies are explicitly designed to change incentives. For example, if a school offers courses in the language of origin of some group of immigrants, that makes it easier for the descendants of the original immigrants to learn their parents' or grandparents' native language and to pass it on to their own children. Hence it increases the incentives for them to do so. Notice that it is possible to offer this on a purely optional basis without either a rule requiring children to take the courses or a social expectation pressuring them to do so. Again, the key question is how the creation of such incentives fits with liberal democratic principles. In my view, liberal democratic states have considerable latitude to create or not create incentives of this sort (for example, to offer or not offer such language of origin courses) but the latitude is not unlimited.

Some people argue that public policies promoting multiculturalism have created incentives for immigrants to live separate lives from the majority population. This is unpersuasive. As I explained above, there are powerful spontaneous incentives for immigrants to cluster together with people from a similar background when they first arrive. These incentives have nothing to do with public policies, multicultural or otherwise.

I am not suggesting that liberal democratic states should be entirely indifferent to patterns of social interaction. There is certainly a responsibility to eliminate discrimination and also a legitimate public interest in overcoming social barriers between immigrants and others, even when these barriers are not the product of discrimination. It is important to find ways to bring citizens together to promote social ties and a sense of common belonging. It matters how states pursue this goal, however. Apart from prohibiting discrimination, it can be wrong to force people together through rules or even through expectations, although it may be morally permissible and desirable to create incentives for people to come together. Indeed, many public policies that have been adopted under the rubric of multiculturalism are designed to do just that.[11] Contrary to what the critics say, these policies often create incentives for immigrants to participate in mainstream institutions and to engage with others.

Identities

Let me turn finally to the issue of identities. An identity involves seeing oneself and being seen by others as a member of a particular social group. Most people have many different identities: political, cultural, religious, ethnic, professional, familial, sexual, personal and so on. For the purposes of this chapter, the most important type of identity is nationality, that is, the feeling that one belongs, along with others, to a self-governing community with a shared history, culture and values. Other identities matter as well, however, because immigrants often have cultural, religious, ethnic and other identities that distinguish them from the majority of the non-immigrant population. The crucial question is whether the national identity is constructed in a way that is open to and compatible with the distinctive identities of the immigrants. Are immigrants seen as members of the nation, and, if so, on what terms?

What does it mean to be Danish or Dutch, German or Greek? Must one have a certain sort of ancestry, belong to a particular religion, adopt certain values and behaviours in order to be accepted as a member of the national community or are all citizens living in the state seen as full members? From a liberal democratic perspective, the answer is clear. It is not morally acceptable for a liberal democratic state to construct its national identity in a way that excludes or marginalises some of its citizens.

264

This does not mean that all political communities must have identical identities, limited to abstract liberal democratic principles. Different political communities will have different national identities, but the identity of any given liberal democratic community must include all of its citizens. That is part of what it means to speak of a self-governing people that respects liberal democratic principles.

Like expectations and incentives, however, a national identity is not something that can be enforced through rules or constructed as a right. While every liberal democratic state is obliged to construct its national identity so that all citizens, including immigrants, will normally see themselves and be seen by others as members of the nation, it is not sufficient to pass a law saying that all citizens are members of the nation. (Recall that I am presuming in this chapter that the immigrants are citizens.) Rules and rights do not govern hearts and minds, at least not directly. Moreover, reducing national identity to the possession of citizenship status would rob national identity of all substantive content. In my view, it is compatible with justice and normatively desirable on other grounds for a liberal democratic state to have a strong and distinctive national identity, so long as it is one that genuinely includes immigrants.[12]

In developing this line of argument, I do not claim to be saying anything new. While talk about expectations and incentives is relatively rare in the literature on immigration and multiculturalism, talk about identities, and especially national identity, is common.[13] My main goal is simply to draw attention to the fact that whatever the specifics of a particular national identity, it must be constrained and shaped by the ethos of inclusion that is required by liberal democratic principles. And, as we saw with the discussion of muscular liberalism, this means that it is not only immigrants who must change to take on the national identity of the political community they have joined but also the non-immigrant members of the community who must often change their own understanding of the national identity to make it open to immigrants, and thus compatible with liberal democratic principles.

This means that morally defensible national identities cannot be tied to ascribed characteristics like race and ethnicity that people cannot change, or to things like religion that it is unreasonable to ask people to change. The history of the nation has to be imagined and recounted in a way that enables citizens of immigrant origin to identify with it. Citizens of immigrant origin have to be visible as representatives of the nation. Both the official images of the nation and the pictures that people carry around in their heads about national membership must include immigrants.

Does constructing a national identity that includes immigrants either entail or preclude recognition of the particular identities of immigrants, the ways in which immigrants differ from most of the long-settled population? In answering this question we should keep in mind that recognition involves both state policies and the behaviour of ordinary citizens and that there are both positive and negative forms of recognition.

Negative recognition often involves stereotyping and prejudice. Negative recognition defines identities in ways that denigrate the holders of these identities and contributes to their exclusion. One example is the negative way in which Islam and Muslim immigrants have been treated in the media and in political discourse, especially over the past decade or so.[14] Sometimes negative recognition takes the form of a public, symbolic act of exclusion. The Swiss law prohibiting the building of new minarets is perhaps the clearest example in recent memory. There is no pretence that the law is serving some general neutral purpose. Its entire goal is to limit the visibility of Islam as a religion in Switzerland and to restrict the access of Muslims (who are usually, though not always, immigrants) to public space. It would be hard to imagine a more direct way of communicating the message that Muslim immigrants are not welcome or that Islam is not part of, and indeed is in conflict with, Swiss national identity. Clearly, this kind of negative recognition is not compatible with an inclusive democratic ethos.

Positive recognition involves acknowledgement and acceptance of the broad ways in which citizens of immigrant origin differ from the majority. This does not entail an endorsement of particular practices or beliefs, but rather an affirmation that this public identity is not incompatible with the political community. If immigrants are to be included, they cannot be expected to conceal or disguise important aspects of their identities. A democratic state and its citizens have to communicate clearly that citizens who have the cultural and religious identities associated with immigration are regarded as full members of the political community.

This does not mean that the state has to impose identities on individual citizens or require them to reveal their identities if they prefer not to do so. What will be publicly visible about any particular individual will depend on the nature of her identity and the character of her commitments. But cultural and religious identities have a collective as well an individual dimension. It is the collective identity that must be acknowledged and affirmed. For example, it is important when leading public officials say that Islam is part of Germany or the United States because this sends the message that the national identity does not exclude Muslims. Whether any individual wears clothing that identifies her as a Muslim will vary, depending on her own understanding of her religious duties, but the ideal of inclusion is that others will regard Muslims as normal citizens and a Muslim citizen will be able to see herself that way, whether others are aware of her identity or not.

Positive recognition can take a number of forms. For example, school curricula can contain information about the histories and background cultures of immigrants, perhaps taking particular account of the composition of the school's population if there are too many sources of immigration to include all in a general curriculum. Information can be provided in schools and in the media about the major holidays that immigrants celebrate, and accommodations offered with respect to school and work schedules. One particularly important form of public recognition is facilitating the access of immigrants to places for collective worship. Another form of recognition is the use of languages of origin in various forms of communication where that seems appropriate, not as a substitute for the official language, especially in school, but as a supplement in contexts where it can help those with particular needs. Still another form of recognition is the provision of models. When citizens of immigrant origin occupy positions of authority in public life, especially in symbolically important fields like law and politics, and when they are visible in positions of responsibility in the media, that also sends a message about the acceptance of identities. I am not suggesting here that this is best achieved through particular targeted programmes like affirmative action, but I am saying that it matters for a sense of inclusion whether or not immigrants see people like themselves in positions of responsibility.[15]

The ways in which positive recognition should be pursued are bound to vary considerably from one state to another. The important point is that the cultural and religious identities of the majority will already be publicly recognised to a very considerable degree. That is simply inevitable in any liberal democracy. I am not arguing that immigrants should aspire to comparable levels of recognition. That is impossible. Rather my suggestion is that some positive recognition is appropriate, enough to make it clear that these differences of culture and identity are compatible with full and equal membership in the political community. What is required is a commitment to even-handedness, a sensitive balancing of different claims, that moves beyond the principles of majority rule and minority rights towards genuine inclusion.[16]

In sum, liberal democratic principles require more than treating immigrants as equal under the law and granting them equal legal rights. They require efforts to include immigrants fully within the political community. This is compatible with expecting immigrants to accept democratic institutions and to adjust to many established social practices, but it does require setting limits to social expectations that interfere with the moral rights that immigrants have to live their lives as they choose and expecting other citizens to live up to liberal democratic principles in their own interactions with immigrants. Further, it entails scrutinising incentives to make sure that they do not reflect discriminatory attitudes and values. Finally, it requires the transformation of national identities wherever these national identities contain elements that exclude citizens of immigrant origin.

Note on text

My contribution to this volume overlaps substantially with Chapter 4 of J. H. Carens (2013), *The Ethics of Immigration* (New York: Oxford University Press), although it was originally written for the conference in honour of Parekh from which the current volume emerges.

Notes

1. B. Parekh (2000), *Rethinking Multiculturalism* (Cambridge: Harvard University Press), p. 204.
2. Parekh (in *Rethinking Multiculturalism*) rightly wonders whether the perceived norm would have applied to another European language like French.
3. Perhaps the girl's behaviour simply reflected her adaptation to British norms about how teenagers should relate to their parents. Nothing is more common than the emergence of conflicts between immigrant parents and their children when the children turn out to be British (or Canadian, American, French, German and so on) in ways that the parents never anticipated when they immigrated.
4. See I. M. Young (1990), *Justice and the Politics of Difference* (Princeton, NJ: Princeton University Press), for a classic discussion of the concerns that are still relevant today.
5. Will Kymlicka's influential book from 1995: W. Kymlicka (1995), *Multicultural Citizenship* (Oxford: Oxford University Press).
6. Parekh, *Rethinking Multiculturalism*, p. 204.
7. See L. Seidle (2008), *Commissions on the Accommodation and Integration of Immigrants and Minorities*, Commission de consultation sur les pratiques d'accommodement reliées aux différences culturelles, January (2008), available at www.accommodements.qc.ca/documentation/rapports/rapport-2-seidle-leslie.pdf (accessed 6 May 2012). One problem with this sort of approach is that the image of a two-party contract between the state and immigrants may implicitly treat the state as an institution that belongs to the rest of the population, rather than as an independent entity with responsibilities for both immigrants and the rest of the population. But I don't want to make too much of this. The language of such contracts varies. I discuss a specific version of this sort of contract with immigrants

in J. H. Carens (1995), *Is Quebec Nationalism Just?* (Montreal: McGill-Queen's University Press), Chapter 2.

8. The proverb, 'When in Rome, do as the Romans do', is variously attributed to St. Augustine and St. Ambrose. When the early Christians would not do as the Romans did (that is, worship Roman gods), the Romans threw the Christians to the lions. Worshiping Roman gods was probably not the sort of conformity to Roman practices that St. Augustine and St. Ambrose (writing in a later era) had in mind. To the Romans who demanded it, however, asking people in Rome to worship Roman gods seemed to be a very reasonable request. The Christians' refusal to do this marked them in Roman eyes as religious fanatics who threatened governmental authority. Even this potted history gives reason to exercise care when invoking this familiar proverb.

9. See S. Roberts (2010), 'New life in America no longer means a new name', *New York Times*, 25 August (accessed 20 August 2014 at www.nytimes.com/2010/08/26/nyregion/26names.html).

10. Why do I not characterise the decline in the practice of changing names as an unambiguously positive development? Because some scholars attribute the reduced incentives to change names not to a reduction in discrimination against those of immigrant origin but to the fact that changing names is simply no longer a very effective strategy for avoiding discrimination because so many more immigrants are now what Canadians call 'visible minorities', that is, people whose physical appearance indicates that they are probably not of European origin. If all that had changed was the effectiveness of the name-changing tactic and not the underlying discrimination, there would be nothing to cheer about. The truth is probably somewhere in between. See S. Roberts, 'New Life in America'.

11. Will Kymlicka has argued forcefully that the point of most multicultural policies is to enable minorities to participate in mainstream institutions, and that it is the refusal to recognize and respect their distinctive concerns and commitments that is more likely to lead them to want to live separate lives. See Kymlicka, *Multicultural Citizenship* and W. Kymlicka (1998), *Finding Our Way* (Toronto: Oxford University Press). I agree with him, although I would add one nuance to his general argument. Some multicultural policies, like permitting Sikhs to wear their traditional headgear rather than the usual headgear required by an official uniform, are designed to make it more likely that immigrant minorities will participate in mainstream institutions. Other multicultural policies, like funding

optional courses in languages of origin (in addition to the required education in the official language) or óther cultural initiatives of that sort serve the interests of immigrant minorities, but do not directly enhance their participation in mainstream institutions. On the other hand, these sorts of policies communicate to citizens of immigrant origin that their identities and cultural commitments are accepted by the wider society. This can make them feel included and so increase the likelihood of their committing themselves in turn to the wider community.

12. The problem of constructing a genuinely inclusive national identity is obviously not limited to the issue of how to include immigrants. Long-settled religious, ethnic and cultural minorities have often been excluded from the dominant conception of national identity in liberal states. Moreover, sometimes states contain more than one national identity, as in multinational states like Canada, the United Kingdom, Spain and so on. In such cases, each of the component nations must construct its national identity in a way that is open to all of those living permanently on the national territory, including immigrants and their descendants. And indeed that is precisely the way in which Quebec, Scottish and Catalonian nationalisms have evolved.

   That still leaves open the complicated question about the relationship between particular national identities and the national identity of the state as a whole, but I won't pursue that complication here.

13. Some advocates of multiculturalism worry that even the aspiration that citizens share a common national identity inevitably carries with it an exclusionary component that is homogenising and incompatible with respect for difference. See, for example, M. Williams (2002), 'Citizenship as identity, citizenship as shared fate, and the functions of multicultural education', in W. Feinberg and K. McDonough (eds) *Collective Identities and Cosmopolitan Values* (New York: Oxford University Press). However, many others think that it is highly desirable for a political community to promote a strong sense of national identity, so long as it is sufficiently open to the distinctive identities of minorities within the community. That is the position I am endorsing here. Bhikhu Parekh has an important and extensive treatment of this issue in B. Parekh (2008), *A New Politics of Identity* (New York: Palgrave Macmillan). T. Modood (2007), *Multiculturalism* (Cambridge: Polity), pp. 146–54 specifically, has a clear and (to me) convincing

explanation of why multiculturalists should favour strong national identities. For other illuminating discussions from different, sometimes conflicting, perspectives that nevertheless share this basic orientation, see Kymlicka, *Multicultural Citizenship*; D. Miller (1995), *On Nationality* (Oxford: Oxford University Press) and D. Miller (2000), *Citizenship and National Identity* (Cambridge: Polity); A. Mason (2000), *Community, Solidarity and Belonging* (Cambridge: Cambridge University Press), and V. Uberoi (forthcoming) *Nation Building through Multiculturalism* (New York: Palgrave Macmillan). Even B. Barry (2001), *Culture and Equality* (Cambridge: Harvard University Press), pp. 77–90, who presents himself as a fierce critic of multiculturalism takes a broadly similar position on national identity to the one outlined here.

14. T. Modood (2007), *Multiculturalism* (Cambridge: Polity), pp. 146–54.
15. For the importance of having minorities visible in the public sphere, see Young, *Justice and the Politics*; A. Phillips (1995), *The Politics of Presence* (Oxford: Clarendon Press); M. Williams (2000), *Voice, Trust, and Memory* (Princeton, NJ: Princeton University Press).
16. For a fuller discussion of evenhandedness as an ideal, see J. H. Carens (2000), *Culture, Citizenship and Community* (Oxford: Oxford University Press).

10

Multiculturalism and the Public Sphere

Andrew Gamble

During the last twenty-five years multiculturalism has been a subversive force in our politics, challenging established ways of understanding the public sphere and the nature of political identity. The political theorists most associated with multiculturalism, including Bhikhu Parekh, have been unlike many other political theorists because of their engagement in public debates. They have been public intellectuals as well as academic theorists, seeking to address the political claims of cultural minorities and suggest changes to the dominant arrangements and understandings of Western societies. For this they have been strongly criticised, but this has not deterred them. They have immersed themselves in the details of policy, and the policy debates have influenced their more scholarly work. It is one of the best examples of sustained engagement by political theorists in practical politics.

The nature of this kind of engagement is seldom explored, and this chapter will attempt to do this by examining the idea of the public sphere and what it means to be a public intellectual in politics. Bhikhu Parekh is an exemplar of one distinct kind of public intellectual (Keynes is another example) who constantly seeks to write both for scholars and for the general public. It is part of the same enterprise. Keynes saw his task to be both persuading his fellow economists and persuading the general public. Some leading scholars seek to persuade only fellow scholars, and it is left to others to communicate what they have to say in more popular and accessible forms. The theorists of multiculturalism are distinctive because they are not prepared to stand on the sidelines. Remarkably for a student of Michael Oakeshott, Bhikhu Parekh has never been content with philosophical contemplation. He has always wanted to be engaged in trying to shape and change the world as well. Many of the distinctions that other political theorists have drawn between knowing and doing, or between ideal and non-ideal theory, are rejected. Multiculturalist theorists believe that from practical engagement with practical problems different kinds of theory can emerge, which are pluralist in character, respecting the diverse needs and beliefs of individuals and communities. I argue that the engagement of the theorists of multiculturalism as public intellectuals has breathed fresh life into the idea of a public sphere and into the idea of the public itself. In doing so they have sparked fierce debate with other public intellectuals, keen to defend the idea of the universal, liberal secular state, and have also unleashed a wave of hostility and crude misrepresentation from populist media and politicians. The debate on multiculturalism tells us much about both the nature of contemporary politics and the health of democracy.

Multiculturalism rejects that strand of theorising about the modern state that is monist and universalist. It belongs to a different strand, which is pluralist and particularist, emphasising difference and diversity in knowledge, interests and beliefs as the inescapable roots of politics. As Bhikhu Parekh has argued so eloquently and compellingly, taking multiculturalism seriously requires all functions of the state to be reconceived, because the constitution of most modern states assumes national and cultural homogeneity.[1] It also assumes that the public sphere in such states has a universalist character. Multiculturalism has been accused of challenging these assumptions, and rejecting fundamental principles of the liberal secular state and of the national identities that are expressed through it. In the case of the United Kingdom this means that it is seen as undermining dominant understandings of Britishness. Multiculturalism is seen as requiring a commitment to pluralism not just in civil society but also in the state itself, which offends unitary conceptions of the state across the political spectrum.

The debate around multiculturalism in recent times has become a debate about the character of the public sphere, in the sense used by Habermas,[2] and whether multiculturalism is compatible with it. The public sphere is a political space, distinct from the both state and economy, which emerged as an aspect of the development of the modern state, and specifically of the liberal state. The public sphere which was once used to glorify the power of rulers became a means by which rulers could be held to account. It became a sphere which encouraged openness, the search for truth, and rational discussion of public issues. Public intellectuals often based in universities or the media have played and continue to play a key role in shaping and organising this space. It is a space concerned with general debate and deliberation on public affairs, such as whether there is a public interest, how it might be known, and in what it consists.[3] Through debate a public ethos is generated, and a public ethic articulated that helps define the nature of the state, and establishes rules and conventions for public discourse, and assumptions that all participants come to share. Independent, critical intellectual work is essential for such a public sphere to exist, and those who perform that work are public intellectuals.

The public sphere conceived in this way is fragile, and vulnerable to erosion. It depends on there being shared norms and values indicating how public affairs should be conducted and how the public interest should be determined. That requires commitment across the political class, of which public intellectuals form a part. Although public intellectuals will have sharply different perceptions and ideals, for an individual to be recognised as a public intellectual there has to be a commitment in some form to the worth and significance of the public sphere itself, and for that individual to be considered independent and disinterested, not beholden to any special interest.

In liberal conceptions of the public sphere a particular importance has been placed on values such as openness, rationality, diversity, clarity and tolerance. There is a marketplace of ideas, in which the good ideas are expected to drive out bad ones. Participating in the public sphere is a process of self-government and education. Where the public sphere begins and where it ends, which activities, institutions and organisations come within its scope, are not prescribed, but vary between democracies and between different national political traditions and cultures. In authoritarian regimes the scope of the public sphere is very restricted and what is allowed to enter it is closely policed, but in liberal and democratic regimes a public sphere of some kind will exist, in the sense that there is a more or less open and unrestricted public conversation about what should be public and what should be considered by all because it affects the interest of all and the identity of all.

Multiculturalism has been understood in different ways, but one claim that has been associated with it is that the state should not merely accommodate and tolerate multiple identities, which all liberal theories of the state seek to do, but should also permit those multiple identities to be reflected in different rules and laws. The state should no longer try to achieve a uniform set of rules for its citizens in all areas. Many liberal accounts of the state accept that the state has a duty to protect group identities, but want those groups to acknowledge their membership of the state, which comes with the obligation to accept its rules, rather than living apart under their own rules. This issue keeps arising in public debate, because many public intellectuals and many in the political class regard any concession on this matter to be a betrayal of the ideal of the secular liberal state, which they regard as the guarantor of the freedom that permits a multicultural society. It has also been seized on by political opponents of pluralism and liberalism as well as defenders of traditional conceptions of national identity, who would prefer to return, if they could, to a monocultural society.

The issue has been posed particularly sharply by Iris Marion Young in her critique of the ideal of universal citizenship. She contends:

> [T]he ideal that the activities of citizenship express or create a general will that transcends the particular differences of group affiliation, situation, and interest has in practice excluded groups judged not capable of adopting that general point of view; the idea of citizenship as expressing a general will has tended to reinforce a homogeneity of citizens.[4]

She rejects the ideals of the civic public in modern political thought, because they assume the possibility and the desirability of a general will that transcends differences. It is, as she puts it, 'a demand for homogeneity among citizens'.[5] It is also gendered, because it contrasts a public realm of 'manly virtue and citizenship as independence, generality, and dispassionate reason' against a private sphere of the family, emotion, sentiment and bodily needs.[6] For Young there can be no impartial general perspective, because the way people think about public issues is necessarily shaped by their particular situations. As she puts it, 'different social groups have different needs, cultures, histories, experiences, and perceptions of social relations which influence their interpretation of the meaning and consequences of policy proposals and influence the form of their political reasoning'.[7] Demanding that everyone abandon their own identities and experiences privileges certain identities and experiences over others, those of the powerful over the powerless.

Liberal theorists have often maintained that to be a citizen is to transcend private interests and sectional identities and embrace the common good. The idea of a public interest has been debunked by public choice theory as disguised private interest, and from a different angle multicultural theorists argue similarly that invoking the public interest is often a mask for private interest, for the supremacy of one group over others. Recognising that there are many different group histories and perspectives means that these can never be dissolved into a single history or a single perspective. A participatory democracy cannot be constructed on the assumption of an undifferentiated humanity, according to Young, but only on the recognition that group differences exist, and that there will always be some groups in any society that are actually or potentially oppressed or disadvantaged.[8] Multiculturalists do not regret the fact of group difference. They celebrate it. Group difference is desirable and has to be protected against oppression and discrimination.

In his conception of a communicative ethic, Habermas retains the idea of a public so constituted that claims can be decided by appeal to a universal and therefore impartial point of view. Young thinks this an unattainable ideal, and advocates instead group representation of difference as the best way to build a democratic polity. She acknowledges however that this creates a dilemma. Multiculturalists and other social movements seek the full inclusion and participation of all disadvantaged groups. They claim that there are no essential differences between individuals that prevent any individual from being included in any particular institution or from aspiring to any particular position. The liberal answer is to adopt the principle of equal treatment of all individuals. But this is not sufficient for multiculturalists. Group-based differences between people, they argue, make the principle of equal treatment unfair. Groups cannot be expected to adopt the same universal norm. Instead there needs to be a dialogue in which the views of groups are respected and it is accepted that groups need to be treated differently. What multiculturalism challenges is the idea that including everyone in public life means devising universal rules that apply to all citizens in the same way.

Sharia law and the Archbishop

A recent example of the disputes that multiculturalism triggers is the controversy over a lecture by the former Archbishop of Canterbury, Rowan Williams, on the question of Sharia law. Williams and Parekh have much in common, not only a personal friendship but also public trajectories on multiculturalism that have followed a similar path. Williams' reflections were taken as implicitly criticising a form of modern liberalism that defines citizenship in terms of a secular state, a single overarching national identity and a set of universal norms. Defenders of the liberal secular state have identified 'multiculturalism' as their main enemy, and were quick to accuse the Archbishop of embracing it. In recent years in Britain and other countries in Europe, 'multiculturalism' has aroused strong passions and its proponents have often been vilified in the popular media. Multiculturalism has been developing both as a theory and as a policy since the 1970s, but its future has become increasingly contentious, because its opponents have come to present it not only as an attack upon the liberal secular state, but also as a threat to the preservation of dominant national identities, and implicitly therefore of the possibility of retaining societies that are predominantly monocultural. Particular anxiety has come to focus on the implications for liberal states of the presence within them of substantial Muslim immigrant communities. These communities have been developing for a long time, but alarm about them has intensified since 9/11 and the declaration of a 'war on terror' by the United States.

This was the context in which Rowan Williams delivered his lecture in February 2008.[9] Without meaning to do so he unleashed a firestorm. He was subjected to a torrent of abuse in the tabloid press, reflecting the sensitivity of issues connected with Islam and the integration of Muslim communities in Western societies. It became a debate about whether the rules of the liberal state needed to be relaxed to accommodate the practices of these communities, whether certain groups should be treated differently to promote their inclusion, or whether all groups should be treated the same.

The argument made by Williams is worth noting in some detail, especially since what he actually said was ignored by many of his critics. He began by arguing that there is uncertainty about the degree of accommodation that the law can and should give to minority communities that have their own strongly entrenched legal and moral codes. What are the rights of religious groups within a secular state? The problem is particularly acute, he argued, in respect of Islam, and can be solved only by 'crafting a just and constructive relationship between Islamic law and the law of the United Kingdom'. Part of the difficulty lies in the complexity of Sharia law, and the Islamic conviction that it is not one set of laws among others, but represents the mind of God. This has to be set against the liberal tradition, which according to Williams, involves the claim that our identities are not necessarily constituted by an exclusive set of relations. He acknowledges that the dominant religious tradition in both Christianity and Islam treats participation in the church or umma as the only possible mode of identity, the supreme identity, all others being considered a betrayal. Such a view however makes a secular state impossible. A secular state is only compatible with these communities of faith if a way can be found for members to live under more than one jurisdiction. The authority of the secular state is accepted in return for the protection of religious rights and religious identity. The practical political question then becomes how far this process should go, and in particular whether some legal functions should be delegated to the religious courts of a community.

Williams' answer is highly qualified. He draws a distinction between what he calls 'cultural habits' and 'seriously rooted matters of faith and discipline'. He also points to the dangers of permitting more than one jurisdiction; it might reinforce 'repressive and retrograde elements' particularly in relation to the role and liberties of women, including issues concerning forced marriages and inheritance. Williams argues that the same law cannot allow rights that it acknowledges as generally valid to be taken away. The law is the law. 'Everyone stands before the public tribunal on equal terms . . . the recognition of corporate identities or supplementary jurisdictions is simply incoherent if we want to preserve the great political and social advances of western legality'.

He then goes on to say, however, that this doctrine of the secular state arose in a particular context as a protest against traditional forms of governance and custom. It ignores the realities of complex modern societies with their multiple affiliations and identities, which cannot be reduced to an abstract form of equal access and accountability. His conclusion is that understanding the complexity of the rule of law in a plural society leads to the search for ways to allow the 'plurality of diverse and overlapping affiliations' to work for a common good.

The lecture was interesting on a number of levels, not least in the reception that it received. This nuanced and measured argument was intended as part of a process of engagement with some extremely complex issues. But that was not how the British tabloids saw it. Shrill headlines denounced the Archbishop for recommending the introduction of Sharia law and the creation of a separate legal jurisdiction for the Muslim community. The coverage dwelt on some of the prescribed punishments in Sharia for particular offences (implying that the Archbishop supported their introduction), and denounced the lecture as a shameful appeasement of Islamists, typical of the defeatist liberal intelligentsia. Williams was treated not as an Archbishop whose views

280

should be treated with respect even if they were not shared, but rather as a misguided liberal intellectual who, instead of defending the secular basis of the state, was advancing suggestions that would fatally undermine it. His views were abhorrent and should be condemned. Taking their cue from the way the tabloids framed the event, political leaders from all the three main political parties stepped forward to criticise the lecture. Gordon Brown, the Prime Minister, declared that British law must be based on British values. The Conservatives said that British law had been developed through Parliament and the Courts and must continue to develop through these channels, while the Liberal Democrats insisted that the principle of equality before the law had to be maintained for all citizens. The majority of the political class wanted to close the debate down and declare the issue off-limits. Nobody wanted to engage with the serious argument that the Archbishop was making.

This reaction was predictable and part of a new trend that has been establishing itself in Britain, which has seen a hardening of attitudes towards both immigration and 'multiculturalism' in all three main political parties. Another expression of this mood is the speech by David Cameron at the Munich Security Conference in 2011. Cameron blamed the attractiveness of the ideology of 'Islamist extremism' to so many young Muslims in the West directly on the mistaken policy of what he called 'state multiculturalism':

> We have allowed the weakening of our collective identity. Under the doctrine of state multiculturalism, we have encouraged different cultures to live separate lives, apart from each other and apart from the mainstream ... We've even tolerated these segregated communities behaving in ways that run completely counter to our values.

The answer he declared was to stop ignoring the extremist ideology and instead to confront it:

> We must build stronger societies and stronger identities at home. Frankly, we need a lot less of the passive tolerance of recent years and much more active, muscular liberalism. A passively tolerant society

says to its citizens, as long as you obey the law we will just leave you alone. It stands neutral between different values. But I believe a genuinely liberal country does much more; it believes in certain values and actively promotes them. Freedom of speech, freedom of worship, democracy, the rule of law, equal rights regardless of race, sex or equality. It says to its citizens, this is what defines us as a society: to belong here is to believe in these things ... Each of us in our own countries ... must be unambiguous and hard-nosed about this defence of our liberty.[10]

Cameron was articulating the new common sense. In rejecting the doctrine of 'state multiculturalism' he gives no clue as to how his favoured policy of 'muscular liberalism' is to be imposed on faith communities that resist it. If people do not share an identity how easily can they be forced to accept it? And if they still resist, what then? The practical difficulties of following through the policy are evident. Is the government planning to close all faith schools, including Christian and Jewish schools, in line with its new muscular liberalism? Plainly not. It is committed to expanding them under its 'free school' programme. But what argument can it then use to deny the faith schools that Muslims want to establish? Hell will freeze over before Muslim schools give their pupils a liberal education, according to the *Daily Mail*, although on other occasions the *Daily Mail* has campaigned vigorously against 'liberal' education in Britain's comprehensives, associating it with low standards, poor discipline and political correctness.[11] What is meant here by 'liberal' education is education based on a monocultural view of what Britishness is and what should be taught in schools.

What this debate highlights is a deep rift in liberalism. Multiculturalism has come to be seen by some, including the Archbishop, as a development that needs to be accommodated by the liberal secular state, and that will thus change the nature of the public sphere and the kind of debates that are appropriate to it. Others see the liberal secular state as a line that must be defended at all costs. If it is breached the specific values of the liberal secular state that permit such a diversity of belief and culture may be lost with it. In questioning the latter position and making the case for a qualified multiculturalism, Rowan Williams was speaking as the senior Archbishop of the Anglican Church, but also as a public intellectual concerned to intervene in the public sphere and to explore how the public interest might be defined in relation to this issue.

The populist media, however, which has long since abandoned its former deference to authority and knowledge and instinctively favours monoculturalism rather than multiculturalism, was not interested in contributing to a debate on what the public interest was in this matter, and whether some changes were appropriate in the way that faith communities were treated, but only in denouncing him for having crossed a line, and revealing himself as an aberrant public intellectual who was questioning fundamental values of the British way of life. They launched an all-out attack on him, both political and personal, for daring even to raise the issue. The crude stereotypes and reductionist arguments, which the modern media deploys habitually,[12] aim to close down the debate, and to make certain things unsayable, because of the ridicule and hostility they attract. Tabloid commentators provide these arguments and seek to police the public sphere. The role of public intellectuals is to challenge received ideas and stand up against mainstream opinion. This has always been difficult, but modern media has made it much harder, because of the way it encourages persecution and ridicule, and the low value it places on critical analysis.[13]

The role of public intellectuals

To explore these questions further it is first necessary to say something more about public intellectuals. The term is in general use, but has no agreed definition. Some doubt that it has any precise meaning, and see public intellectuals as nothing more than media intellectuals, those who acquire a certain prominence and celebrity by appearing regularly in public as pundits on the media. The lists that are compiled of the most influential 'public intellectuals' tend to give most importance to media visibility. It is certainly true that most of the major figures to whom the label 'public intellectual' has been attached tend to be prominent in the media, but public intellectuals are more than media or celebrity intellectuals. To be public intellectuals they have to have a particular relationship with the public sphere and with the public world that sets them apart from many media intellectuals, but also from many other kinds of intellectuals.

A useful starting point in considering the nature of public intellectuals and how they differ from other intellectuals is Gramsci's distinction between traditional and organic intellectuals. Gramsci associated traditional intellectuals with institutions such as the church, the law, and the universities, and argued that it was this institutional base that encouraged intellectuals to think of themselves as an independent and separate social stratum. One expression of this was the English idea of 'men of letters', which developed in the eighteenth and nineteenth centuries. These men of letters were cultivated generalists, who saw their role as preserving and continuing essential aspects of the national culture, national institutions and national identity. 'Organic intellectuals' by contrast were the product of the new bureaucratic organisations of the modern state and the industrialised economy, including political parties and companies but increasingly universities and churches as well. The function of organic intellectuals has been to articulate the interests and shape the ethos of a particular class or group or corporation, rather than to express the public interest or participate in the public sphere. During the twentieth century there was a major expansion in the number of these organic intellectuals. Many sites once the preserve of traditional intellectuals, such as the universities, have been transformed by the increasing needs of the economy and the state. There has been ever-greater demand for specific kinds of expertise, leading to inevitable fragmentation and specialisation of knowledge. As the modern state has become increasingly complex in its structures, networks and governance, and the public interest more opaque, so it has become harder to connect decision-making with the citizens, to imagine alternatives, or to understand the claims of experts and how these are to be reconciled with democratic participation.[14]

Neither traditional nor organic intellectuals are necessarily public intellectuals, since the great majority remain anchored in a particular institution or specialism and do not venture beyond it. Karl Mannheim however observed that many intellectuals come to think of themselves as an independent stratum not tied to any particular class or interest group, the free-floating intelligentsia.[15] The emergence of this consciousness has facilitated the emergence of public intellectuals in the modern era. At first they tended to come from the ranks of traditional intellectuals. Their sense of being relatively detached became allied to certain intellectual norms, such as pursuing the truth wherever it leads, speaking truth to power, developing the power of critical analysis, prizing intellectual integrity, and giving priority to rational enquiry and debate as the best way of finding solutions to problems. Exemplars of this type of public intellectual in the last 150 years include John Stuart Mill, John Maynard Keynes, Bertrand Russell, Noam Chomsky and Jean-Paul Sartre. In their own self-image such intellectuals became guardians and articulators of the public interest. Some of them have seen themselves as tribunes of the people, but a more common self-image is as a disinterested elite above politics and above self-interest, whose opinion can be trusted *because* it is disinterested. The obverse of this is that the existence of such an elite implies that most citizens are either too ignorant or too foolish to decide matters on their own, and therefore should defer to these experts, who are much better placed to determine what lies in the public interest than are the citizens themselves.

So much of what we understand by the term public intellectual has been shaped by these titanic figures, who seem different from other intellectuals because they take on the responsibility of being public voices, defenders of the public sphere, and actors within it. Many of them become known for being outspoken, independent, maverick, highly individualistic, and sometimes eccentric protesters against authority. They are individuals ranged against the state, against the establishment, and against conventional wisdom. They value their intellectual purity, and despise the corruptions of power. Blake's words ring in their heads: 'the strongest poison ever known came from Caesar's laurel crown'. Such public intellectuals have often sought as a result to keep their distance from power to avoid being compromised by it, or succumbing to its temptations. Edward Said expressed this aspect of being a public intellectual when he spoke of the true intellectual as being 'always an outsider, living in self-imposed exile, and on the margins of society'.[16]

This type of public intellectual is however quite rare, and most public intellectuals while preserving a sense of their independence are also often directly involved in policy making and working for the state or for political parties or for other institutions in civil society. But an intellectual does not become a public intellectual because of his or her professional expertise, but rather despite it. Such intellectuals enter the public sphere and become participants in politics. The authority they have rests less on their professional expertise than on the strength of their arguments, their ability to frame new discourses and the moral claims they make. Such public intellectuals have become inseparable from the notion of a public sphere. The struggle to define what is the public interest and how it might be implemented are not trivial questions, but have great significance for any feasible politics of reform and progress. The public sphere becomes a sphere of political and ideological contestation, in which attempts to set agendas and define identities and the public interest, assemble coalitions and alliances, and make interventions become all-important. Public intellectuals are the organic intellectuals for the public sphere, rather than simply for their own specialised area of activity, and that there should be a number of intellectuals prepared to act in this way is crucial for the existence of a public sphere, a space where there can be debate about what is and is not in the public interest.

The liberal secular state

This account of the public sphere has often been associated with a republican tradition of politics, which tends to emphasise the secular character of the state, the separation of church and state, the establishment of the rule of law and the territorial basis of rule and legitimacy. Multiculturalism potentially offers a different account of the public sphere, and poses a challenge to those liberal and republican understandings, which give high priority to preserving the integrity of the public sphere. In the republican tradition in particular, the public is not a residual category, and notions of common good and civic virtue are celebrated. The public sphere is an integral part of the idea of the secular state, a sphere of common norms and common interests in contrast to the private sphere. The strong reaction by British popular press and political opinion to the views attributed to the Archbishop shows how strong commitment to those norms remains in British political culture.

Multiculturalism challenges this traditional republican conception of the state by raising some fundamental issues, such as who can participate, who can speak, and on what terms. It further asks what are the common interests and values that bind people together; how these are to be specified; and how inclusive should the public sphere be? Multiculturalism points to the fact that the boundaries of the public sphere are never fixed but are constantly shifting; they can widen but they can also contract. Traditional ideas of the public sphere in Britain associate it with particular institutions, such as Parliament or the Courts, the BBC, the press, the established churches and other institutions in civil society, as well as the institutions and conventions that make possible the practice of free speech. The argument of those public intellectuals who have developed the idea of multiculturalism is that the coming into being of a multicultural society makes necessary a broader definition of those institutions in civil society that need to be involved in the determination of key questions in the public sphere.

The provision of this broader definition and its implications is a work in progress. It involves adapting the idea of a public sphere to the needs of a multicultural society and this has been undertaken by public intellectuals from a variety of backgrounds, perspectives and locations. The work of such intellectuals has generated considerable resistance, and the political implications of their arguments have been caricatured as 'state multiculturalism'. There is no such unified doctrine, and on close examination most of the public intellectuals who are associated with multiculturalism or sympathetic to aspects of it, such as the Archbishop of Canterbury, do not advocate such a doctrine.

What does exist are the many and varied sources from which

multiculturalism draws. They include the Austro-Marxists such as Otto Bauer and Karl Renner, who advocated cultural autonomy for the nations of the Habsburg Empire, an early formulation of the idea of a community of communities.[17] Another source has been liberal pluralism and the respect for difference, which has become such an important facet of contemporary liberalism.[18] A commitment to pluralism undercuts the kinds of certainty purveyed by the universalist ideas that have nurtured the secular liberal state. As John Gray has argued: 'There is no impartial or universal viewpoint from which the claims of all particular cultures can be rationally assessed. Any standpoint we adopt is that of a particular form of life and the historical practices that constitute it.'[19] This pluralist perspective creates the space for multiculturalism, because it requires that all cultures be accorded respect and understanding as a minimum.

Alongside this has been the political imperative, the need, as Tariq Modood has argued, for the political accommodation of minorities formed by immigration to Western countries from outside the prosperous West.[20] The development of pluralism has pointed towards the reformulation of the public interest and the idea of the public, and of the interests that need to be accommodated within it. Once the idea of a homogenous national society and national culture is abandoned, the need for a dialogue with all communities and all faiths becomes necessary if the public sphere is to remain inclusive, and the state legitimate. This is the idea contained in the Archbishop of Canterbury's speech. He was not seeking to subvert the liberal secular state, indeed he explicitly defended it. He wanted instead to broaden its basis to deal with the reality of a multicultural society.

The reason why the reaction was so fierce is that the issue remains unresolved. The gradual transformation of Britain and other European countries into multicultural societies has been recognised as a fact, and how to respond to it has become an issue in contention within the public sphere. Roger Scruton offers one of the most coherent arguments as to why the liberal secular state should not be changed in the way that the Archbishop of Canterbury and many liberal public intellectuals of different faiths and none now suggest. Scruton argues that Western civilisation has been held together not by religious faith but by a political process and by the rights and duties of the citizen that this process has come to define. In this sense, although Western civilisation is nominally Christian it is profoundly different, in Scruton's view, from Islam, because for Islam the 'gate of ijtihad' is closed, so that the divine law, Sharia, cannot be adjusted or added to, only studied for the meaning it contains.[21] This interpretation is disputed by many Islamic scholars but it is crucial for Scruton's argument, because it allows him to make the case for the uniqueness of the West: its inheritance from Rome. Roman law was fundamentally secular in Scruton's view because it was unconcerned with an individual's religious well-being; its principal purpose was instead to provide an instrument of government. By detaching law from the demands of religion an abstract system of rights and duties was evolved, which was modified but not destroyed by Christianity, and re-emerged in conceptions of the modern state with its secular idea of citizenship and its bounded territorial jurisdiction and conception of sovereignty and law. Scruton argues that it was this inheritance that made the modern nation state in the West the object of a common loyalty, giving rise to the notions of popular sovereignty and national self-determination. The Koran by contrast, he asserts, is fundamentally hostile to the idea of territorial jurisdiction and national loyalty, and this finds expression in the ideas of contemporary groups, such as Hizb ut Tahrir, seeking to unify all Muslims in a unitary Islamic state. For Scruton, the doctrines of radical Islamists emphasise the uniqueness of Islam, and how it is at odds with all other civilisations and ideologies in the modern world, but in particular with the Western understanding of politics.

Scruton's eloquent defence of Western exceptionalism is testament to the passions that multiculturalism arouses in its opponents. They resist any widening or redefinition of the rules governing the liberal secular state to reflect the new realities of a multicultural society. They imply that there can be unity or diversity but not both, and that a Western secular state with its liberal public sphere cannot be reconciled with the principles and practices of Islam in particular, but also with any other faith community that puts aspects of its faith above the claims of citizenship, including certain forms of Christianity. There can be tolerance of religious faith in such a regime, but it can never be allowed to encroach on the laws that define the secular character of the state.

The multicultural state

Jesus himself acknowledged the dilemma for faith communities in deciding the principles that should govern their relationship to the state. When asked whether Jews should pay taxes to the occupying Roman power he prudently advised his questioners to 'render unto Caesar the things which are Caesar's but unto God the things which are God's'.[22] This was an ambiguous reply, presumably intentionally so, which left open the issue of where exactly the line should be drawn between the things of Caesar and the things of God.

The dispute over multiculturalism in Western societies in recent years is in part an attempt to answer that question of where the line should now be drawn. The claim made by the Archbishop of Canterbury and many of the leading political theorists of multiculturalism, including Bhikhu Parekh, is that the liberal tradition is well equipped to find ways to balance unity and diversity.[23] This position from within the liberal tradition does not seek to dispense with the liberal secular state. It recognises that such a state is the most likely to guarantee respect and tolerance for minorities. This means that there are dividing lines that cannot and should not be crossed. Rowan Williams, in his lecture, explicitly warns of the dangers of allowing more than one jurisdiction to operate, since this could mean that rights such as rights for women, which had been accepted as generally valid in one jurisdiction, could be taken away or compromised in another. This exposes the dilemma of liberal multiculturalists. Williams wants to distinguish between cultural habits and matters of faith and discipline. The former must give way to the liberal secular state, but the latter should be accommodated, perhaps even by allowing them to be determined by the religious courts of a community. This implies a complex negotiation since there are almost certain to be some issues which the majority community regards as unacceptable cultural habits, but which some in the minority community regard as essential matters of faith. The presumption for liberal multiculturalists is that the principle of equal treatment, a core principle of the liberal state, will need in many instances to be enforced, but that in others, often to do with dress, certain exceptions are permissible.

Muslim scholars, such as Tariq Ramadan, have sought to address how those compromises might be found. Ramadan argues that the West should be regarded as a land for Muslims, and that the task for Muslim scholars is to explore ways to preserve the vitality of religion in a modern society that is both secular and industrialised.[24] Muslims should find ways to justify participating in the life of the City, and engage in public issues. They should become active citizens. One of the fears of the opponents of state multiculturalism is that it would lead to fragmentation, with minority communities choosing to live apart from the majority community, disengaged from politics or from civic life. Ramadan counters that by arguing that participation in the public sphere and open debate are the ways in which a distinctive Muslim identity can be affirmed, and Muslim voices heard, without threatening other communities.

This is a theme that others have pursued as well. Bhikhu Parekh argues that since no culture is perfect or represents the best life, all can benefit from a critical dialogue with other cultures, and to facilitate this, all cultures should be open, self-critical and interactive. Stuart Hall likewise has been concerned with how to widen and deepen political communication and political education in a liberal state, exploring the way in which identities are constructed, represented, and negotiated, allowing different projects to emerge, and different possibilities to be identified. Ideological struggle and debate are not external reflections on politics, but the heart of politics itself, because they determine the nature of political reality and political possibility, and construct a liberal, open and tolerant public sphere.[25]

Bernard Crick, one of the great defenders of British civic traditions, was another strong advocate of multiculturalism. He challenged the assumption that Britain must have a single national culture to retain its identity, pointing out that there is no incompatibility between Britishness and multiculturalism because

Britain has for so long been a multinational state and a multicultural society, and the idea of Britishness has been correspondingly fluid, and subject to evolution and imaginative reconstruction. The arrival of new communities and new identities can therefore be accommodated through a process of mutual engagement. For Crick the notion of Britishness is embodied above all in the secular character of the British state with its emphasis on law, Parliament, tolerance and rights. Precisely because Britain contains more than one national identity, it can more easily accommodate multiculturalism and develop a model that maintains unity around the acceptance of British values and British institutions while respecting the diversity of faiths and cultures. Crick sought to replace a subject culture with a citizen culture, to recognise the multicultural character of the British state while developing the languages and practice of a common citizenship.[26]

As the backlash in recent years against multiculturalism shows, however, the United Kingdom has a complicated political tradition that is not uniformly positive to multiculturalism. David Marquand has distinguished four separate strands in this tradition – Whig imperialism, Tory nationalism, democratic collectivism and democratic republicanism.[27] Of these Whig imperialism and some strands of republicanism might accommodate multiculturalism, but the Tory nationalist and the democratic collectivist traditions have been predominantly hostile, favouring different kinds of monoculturalism. Tory nationalists tend to hold exclusive notions both of the national territory and the national stock, and to be very hostile to immigration, from the desire of Joynson Hicks in the 1920s to stem 'the flood of filth coming across the Channel', to Enoch Powell being filled with foreboding about the separateness of immigrant communities in the 1960s, and Margaret Thatcher feeling 'swamped' by immigrants in the 1970s. Democratic collectivists also have often proposed restrictions on immigration to protect entitlements of existing citizens, and for those immigrants already here the emphasis has been upon assimilation to a non-negotiable set of rules. Whig Imperialists on the other hand, those key architects of Britishness and the multinational state, have always had a pluralistic view of the British state and British identity, and have been more concerned with promoting institutions and practices that ensure a balance between freedom and order, change and stability, the rulers and the ruled than with a homogenous and uniform society. Democratic republicans are particularly concerned with the public sphere, its protection and enhancement, and therefore with the conditions of citizenship. They favour government by vigorous discussion and mutual learning, active deliberation over passive obedience. Their instinct is to support pluralism and diversity, so it might be thought that democratic republicans would be strong supporters of multiculturalism. Many of them are, but they are divided on whether pluralism should be extended to the organisation of the state itself and the pattern of general rules which define it. Many in the democratic republican camp, such as Brian Barry, have fiercely defended the integrity of the liberal secular state. Episodes like the Salman Rushdie affair and the publication of the Danish cartoons have polarised attitudes among democratic republicans, sparking some ferocious attacks upon Islam from some secularists, and have led to attempts to define the public sphere in ways which exclude Islam, or force Muslims to accept the secular state as the framework which cannot be questioned.

One response from Muslim intellectuals has been to become very critical of liberalism, for its apparent intolerance and lack of pluralism, once its core principles are questioned. Liberalism is very diverse however, just as multiculturalism is, so general denunciations of 'liberalism' often miss the mark. Much more interesting are the attempts by Tariq Ramadan, Iris Marion Young and others to think about the rules which might reconcile diversity and recognition with support for a public sphere.

Multiculturalism is under attack, but as the vitriolic and intolerant response to the Archbishop of Canterbury's lecture shows, the attack is also on the open character of the public sphere itself. In every age public intellectuals are required with the commitment, skills and knowledge to sustain the public sphere and to contribute to the delineation of the public interest. For this to be valuable there has to be conflict and debate, but it has to be conducted in a way that allows as many voices as possible to be heard. There will always be some limits to the views that can be expressed, but a flourishing public sphere keeps these as small as possible.

Democracy is never a finished system, and it can wither as easily as it can grow. It has to be sustained by committed and at times courageous action to preserve a public sphere ruled by the values of tolerance, pluralism and rationality. The discourse of multiculturalism in that sense has made a profound contribution to reinforcing the public sphere, but in the era of the war on terror multiculturalism has now itself come under attack, and its proponents are charged with being gullible, weak appeasers, and at the extreme soft on terrorism, or even complicit in terrorism.

Conclusion

Public intellectuals will seldom agree with one another, and it would be undesirable that they should.[28] But what is needed in every generation is for people in different parts of civil society to commit themselves to be public intellectuals, participants in the public sphere, with all the obligations and standards that this involves. This is however becoming increasingly difficult, because of the sacrifice that is demanded. The idea and the practice of a public sphere are being undermined by the increasingly contested nature of authority and expertise. Old forms of authority have been cast down and new ones struggle to establish themselves. A widespread belief has developed, fanned by the media, that everyone in public life is self-interested, and dishonest about their real motives. Individuals are assumed not to be advocating a course of action because it is right, but only because it will benefit them. Politics is an elaborate charade through which private interests masquerade as the public interest.

In these circumstances multiculturalism represents an attempt to reassert the importance of a public sphere, and to open a genuine debate about the nature of contemporary society and the options open to us. Such attempts have become rare. Modern government has become highly technical, because of the complexity of coordination and organisation required to implement policies. The infrastructural power of the modern state has never been greater, but the nature of that power is very hard to subject to traditional democratic processes of deliberation and consent, and to make government accountable. As complexity increases, and cynicism and scepticism spread, so large numbers of voters become more prone to populist appeals and instant solutions. Modern media has played a large role in this. It once played a crucial role in creating the public sphere, but it has now become more often a way of closing it down. The simplifying of issues such as asylum and immigration, or the MMR vaccine, or multi-culturalism, produces a public discourse that is shaped by scares, prejudices, fears and ignorance rather than reasoned argument. Sections of the media now delight in attacking and discrediting expertise, and the cumulative effect is the discrediting of authority in general, and a steady collapse of trust. The treatment of the Archbishop of Canterbury's rather mild and erudite lecture is an example of this trend.

Outbursts of populist feeling on key issues, including multi-culturalism, have been increasing. Underlying them is the feeling that 'governments don't listen', and that the only way to make them listen is to take direct action. The logical direction of such a democracy would be government by referenda and by tabloid, bypassing representative institutions and forcing instant compliance with the popular will. The media are indispensable to a viable and flourishing public sphere, and are the base for many of its intellectuals, but they have also become a major factor in its current erosion. Parts of the media have always disliked complexity, and recent trends have encouraged a flight to populism. The constant blurring of comment and news, the slanting of headlines, the exaggeration of stories, speculation masquerading as fact, the selection of material according to editorial agendas, the vendettas and campaigns, even the direct corruption and resort to illegality – all have become commonplace, as the revelations about practices at the *News of the World* in 2011 showed.

Tabloid journalists have become one of the least trusted professions, but are still reluctant to acknowledge responsibility for their actions. The relentless anti-government and anti-authority agenda that they pursue has been a major factor in the denigration of politicians and politics and the collapse of trust, and the closing of the public sphere. The constant sneering at politicians and other public figures, the constant questioning of their motives, the constant coverage only of stories that highlight shortcomings in government, have helped to create a deeply cynical political culture and a disengaged electorate.

A degree of scepticism, and even cynicism, is indispensable for critical intellectual work, but if it becomes unbalanced, it can be deeply corrosive of any sense of a public sphere. Substantial numbers of journalists no longer see themselves as public intellectuals with a wider responsibility for the public sphere but as opponents of a corrupt and mendacious political class. Yet journalists are as much part of the political class as politicians, but this journalistic tendency, labelled 'journalistic fascism' by Martin Kettle in its extreme forms,[29] is that no one in authority is to be trusted or believed. If such campaigns were ultimately to succeed the end point would be some kind of authoritarianism, because every intermediate structure that supports the public sphere would have been dismantled, to make way for the undiluted expression of the popular will.

The public intellectuals who have sought to explore multiculturalism have for the last twenty-five years been an important bulwark against this erosion of a public sphere. They have sought to reinvigorate it. This is the reason they have been so attacked. When the Commission on the Future of Multi-ethnic Britain, which was chaired by Bhikhu Parekh, published its Report in 2000, it was the subject of a highly critical article in the *Daily Telegraph* by the Home Affairs editor, which instead of engaging with the argument used tabloid techniques of ridicule and misrepresentation.[30] As Samir Shah, the Chair of the Runnymede Trust, protested, the Report did not say that the UK should be redefined as a community of communities, it did not suggest that the term British should cease to be used to refer to the inhabitants of the UK, nor that the terms 'Britain' and 'British' should be abolished. Nor did it claim that the term 'British' has racist connotations.[31] Yet these claims were all published by the *Daily Telegraph*. Its lead was then followed by the rest of the media, which interpreted the Report through the frame provided by the *Daily Telegraph*, rather than bothering to read what the Report had actually said.[32] A frenzy of abuse was unleashed, in which the Report was condemned variously as wicked, Stalinist and corrupting, for seeking to 'rewrite British history'. The way the Report was treated by the media blunted its impact and closed down the debate.

Can anything be done? What is needed is a change of culture to protect the public sphere, not so that reporting becomes less critical but so that it becomes more balanced and more accurate. The present practices of parts of the media are helping create the basis for authoritarian politics and the suppression of the public sphere. Journalists have a huge responsibility for the health of democratic politics. They create and sustain the narratives through which the citizens obtain political information and their understanding of what is going on, and the basis on which they form their judgements.[33] The best journalists are pillars of the public sphere, because their reporting and commentaries are designed to open up discussion and argument, and they practice respect and tolerance even when they are sharply criticising the behaviour or the opinions of others in the public sphere.

The political theorists of multiculturalism such as Bhikhu Parekh and Rowan Williams are also an example of public intellectuals at their best. They have been active participants in politics in the sense that they seek to advance the political education of citizens, by articulating choices, framing questions, offering alternatives, and challenging orthodoxies and entrenched attitudes. They address themselves to the public, not to coteries of experts, or office-holders. They are essential builders of the public sphere, and their presence is vital if larger numbers of people, and from all the ethnic communities, are to become involved in politics, and to furnish their own public intellectuals. At times the project of an open liberal public sphere appears hopeless, so great are the forces seeking to undermine it, and maintain ignorance, fear and hate as the dominant political responses of citizens. But the need for the public sphere does not diminish, which is why in every generation new public intellectuals come forward to assist in the task of building and defining it, although sometimes at considerable personal cost. The public sphere is always a work in progress, and we have to be clear-sighted about the many obstacles in its path, as well as the institutions that are needed to help form public intellectuals and widen political participation throughout our multicultural society.

Notes

1. B. Parekh, *Rethinking Multiculturalism: Cultural Diversity and Political Theory* (London: Macmillan 2000); Campaign for a Multi-ethnic Britain (CMEB) (2000), *The Future of Multi-ethnic Britain: The Parekh Report* (London: Profile).

2. J. Habermas (1992), *The Structural Transformation of the Public Sphere: an Inquiry into a Category of Bourgeois Society* (Cambridge: Polity); C. Calhoun (ed.) (1997), *Habermas and the Public Sphere* (London: MIT Press).

3. R. Flathman (1966), *The Public Interest: An Essay Concerning the Normative Discourse of Politics* (New York: Wiley).

4. I. M. Young (1989), 'Polity and group difference: a critique of the ideal of universal citizenship', *Ethics*, 99, p. 251.

5. Ibid., p. 252.

6. Ibid., p. 254.

7. Ibid., p. 257.

8. Ibid., p. 261.

9. R. Williams (2008), 'Civil and religious law in England: a religious perspective', Foundation Lecture at the Royal Courts of Justice, 7 February.

10. D. Cameron (2011), Speech to the Munich Security Conference, 5 February (available at https://www.gov.uk/government/speeches/pms-speech-at-munich-security-conference).

11. M. Benn (2011), *School Wars: The Battle for Britain's Education* (London: Verso).

12. W. Lippmann (1922), *Public Opinion* (New York: Harcourt, Brace and Company).

13. J. Lloyd (2004), *What the Media Are Doing to our Politics* (London: Constable).

14. M. Weber (1994), 'Politics as a vocation', in M. Weber, *Political Writings* (Cambridge: Cambridge University Press).

15. K. Mannheim (1991), *Ideology and Utopia* (London: Routledge).

16. J. Jennings and A. Kemp-Welch (eds) (1997), *Intellectuals in Politics: From the Dreyfus Affair to Salman Rushdie* (London: Routledge), pp. 1–2.

17. J. Schwarzmantel (2005), 'Karl Renner and the problem of multi-culturalism', in E. Ninmi (ed.) *National Cultural Autonomy and its Contemporary Critics* (London: Routledge), pp. 63–73.

18. M. Kenny (2004), *The Politics of Identity: Liberal Political Theory and the Dilemmas of Difference* (Cambridge: Polity).

298

19. J. Gray (1995), *Berlin* (London: Fontana).
20. T. Modood (2007), *Multiculturalism: A Civic Idea* (Cambridge: Polity).
21. R. Scruton (2002), *The West and the Rest: Globalisation and the Terrorist Threat* (London: Continuum).
22. Matthew 22:21, *The Holy Bible, New Testament* (Oxford: Oxford University Press edition, 1984).
23. Parekh, *Rethinking Multiculturalism*.
24. T. Ramadan (2004), *Western Muslims and the Future of Islam* (Oxford: Oxford University Press).
25. S. Hall (2001), *The Multicultural Question* (Milton Keynes: Pavis Centre for Social and Cultural Research).
26. B. Crick (2001), *Crossing Borders: Political Chapters* (New York: Continuum).
27. D. Marquand (2008), *Britain Since 1918: The Strange Career of British Democracy* (London: Weidenfeld & Nicolson).
28. This conclusion develops an argument first made in A. Gamble (2004), 'Public intellectuals and the public sphere', *New Formations*, 53, pp. 41–53.
29. M. Kettle (2004), 'The threat to the media is real. It comes from within' *Guardian*, 3 February.
30. P. Johnston (2000), 'Straw wants to rewrite our history', *Daily Telegraph*, 10 October.
31. S. Shar (2000), 'Get your facts right first, please', *Guardian*, 20 October.
32. E. McLaughlin and S. Neal (2004), 'Misrepresenting the multicultural nation', *Policy Studies*, 25:3, pp. 155–74.
33. J. Friedman (2003), 'Public opinion: bringing the media back in', *Critical Review*, 15: 3–4, 239–60.

11

Can Democracy be Multicultural? Can Multiculturalism be Democratic?

Benjamin R. Barber

In the last two decades, multicultural theorists such as Iris Young and Will Kymlicka have been examining the relationship between democratic institutions and multicultural societies in terms of how democracy is reflected by or modifies itself to accommodate multiculturalism. But an underlying question about the fundamental compatibility of democracy and multiculturalism has been somewhat overlooked. In this context, Bhikhu Parekh has been crucial to the debate in ways that need to be accounted for. He has urged that democracy be seen, not hegemonically as 'a paternalist, and even an imperialist project', (although some in the West act as if that is what it is), but as 'an expression of our shared humanity and the duties arising out of it'.[1] He understands multiculturalism as a feature of modern democratic life.

Yet European critics of immigration and of the Muslim inroads into 'European civilisation' it has supposedly occasioned, far from recognising any affinities between democracy and multiculturalism, have generally blamed multiculturalism for democracy's trouble. They have held minorities responsible for their own marginalisation (and radicalisation) in traditional monocultural societies. British Prime Minister David Cameron thus has condemned 'segregated communities' that are conducive to Islamic extremism and a life 'apart from the mainstream'. He excoriated what he called a 'hand's-off tolerance' that permits terrorism to take root inside Britain. Former President Sarkozy of France has also pinned the blame for French problems on unregulated immigration. Such criticisms too often express the biases of power, with traditional majorities indicting those they victimise for exploiting liberal tolerance, blaming them for turning it to the purposes of violence.

I want to acknowledge tensions between multiculturalism and democracy, but go considerably farther and argue that they are more than just a 'Christian civilisation' cultural bias on the part of frightened Europeans. In making this case, I will stipulate that I am using multiculturalism here not just as a normative construct, but rather as a description of sociological realities. It is the fact of multiculturalism to which American critics of multiculturalism such as Samuel Huntington and Arthur Schlesinger Jr. have responded. That Schlesinger has displayed such anxieties demonstrates that it is not only a conservative but also a liberal reaction to multiculturalism with which we must deal. Schlesinger has worried that democratic solidarity cannot withstand the pressure of a fractious, multi-identity society, an identity that appears to undermine consensus and national identity.[2] While some of this critique emanates from ageing American cultural wars (taken up again by some candidates in the 2012 and 2014 American elections), and has an affinity to Europe's cultural battles, signifying an analogous hypocrisy, multiculturalism does pose some genuine and consequential issues for modern democracy that are much more than just reactionary populism. These can complicate the commitment of multicultural democrats like Bhikhu Parekh (and me) to their (and my) ideals at the same time that they enlarge the compass of debates over the meaning of multiculturalism and its relationship to democracy.

I begin then with the controversial claim that democracy and multiculturalism – despite such locutions as 'multicultural democracy', 'democratic diversity' and 'pluralist democracy' – are actually in deep tension with one another and that the democratic idea is more at home in monocultural than multicultural societies. As we will see, this is not an argument for a reactionary return to monocultural democracy (which is out of the question in any case); but it is an argument to take seriously the tensions and seek democratic solutions that recognise them. As Bhikhu Parekh himself has acknowledged in the conference in June 2011 at which these essays were presented and debated, cultural diversity can raise issues of 'moral diversity' that are difficult to address.

The birth of democracy in monoculturalism and nationalism

Democracy was first born in ancient Athens and Sparta, and then flourished again several millennia later in small principalities and river towns and ports in Europe: places like Florence, Venice, Amsterdam and Zurich. Eventually democracy was transposed to the United States in the sixteenth and seventeenth centuries, where it was installed in small towns and village communities as well as several colonial commonwealths, in which, though governed in theory from England, citizens were in fact self-determining in local affairs and acquiring vital experience in local democracy.

In a word, democracy was designed for and emerged in small, intimate, monocultural societies, societies with a shared religion, a shared language, a shared history, a shared ethnicity and a shared set of values. Securing democratic consensus is less daunting then when you have *thick* community among citizens in small-scale polities where citizens speak the same language, practice the same religion and share the same ideals. There was room for dissent and disagreement in such communities because one could count on a fundamental underlying agreement about identity and core values. As Rousseau and Tocqueville were to argue, in order for democracy to work, you need a foundation in community, in solidarity, in fraternity and in the sense of equality that comes out of living with people more or less like you. This kind of foundation privileges consensus and thick community in ways that made possible effective democratic societies and a participatory politics which used their commonality to facilitate self-determination.

Changes that took place in the fifteenth, sixteenth and seventeenth centuries as societies organised into 'nation states' became larger, less monocultural and less consensus-based, called into question the original communitarian foundation for democracy. Participatory systems that thrived in the setting of an intimate and parochial monoculturalism found themselves confronting the new challenges of a vastly enhanced scale. When scaling up their size and compass, such societies quickly outran earlier consensual and participatory models of democracy that depended on monocultural consensus and social uniformity – a citizen body limited both by demography and constraints of race, property and gender.

The political response to the new scale of early modern societies was to focus on and organise around a broad unitary idea, not the tribe or township but the idea of the nation – the *gens, ein Volk, le peuple*, a single coherent people, who can be understood once again to share a language, a history and an ethnicity. A weakened and thinner form of commonality rooted in the idea of 'the French People', the Irish or the German *Volk*, an Italian or an American nation was born. This new nation state communality was largely invented – in Michael Kammen's term, 'imagined'[3] – and even in places like England and France deemed today to be 'unitary', a period of national consolidation (England's War of the Roses, Joan of Arc's campaigns in France) was needed to forge some semblance of national commonality. It took centuries for parochial pieces to coalesce into new and artificial national wholes. Only when that process was completed was democracy again feasible. For despite the large-scale character of the new nation states and the thinness of their imagined national identities, some sense of shared identity had been re-established among what were now millions of men across an expansive territory encompassing towns and cities and rural provinces – a quantum leap in the compass of democracy.

It is important to add that democracy itself helped to stabilise the new multicultural entities (masquerading under the faux unity of the 'nation'). As Charles Taylor and also Will Kymlicka and David Miller have suggested, democratic institutions can themselves alleviate the conflicts that otherwise imperil democratic consensus in divided societies. Nonetheless – turning necessity into a virtue – while democracy has found a way to accommodate and even sustain multiculturalism, it has an easier time with monoculture, as is evident from the new sociology of liberal nationalism advanced in the eighteenth and early nineteenth centuries by Rousseau, Mazzini and Garibaldi, which made the identitarian nation the unifier of the voluntarist liberal state. The goal was to show that a liberal democratic society, much 'thinner' than earlier polities, could nonetheless be held together if rooted in a people representing an artificial but still unified and coherent community.

The new national societies, never strictly monocultural even at the outset, were becoming ever more pluralistic and diverse. The need, as John Dunn has suggested, to work out rules for 'cohabitation among divergent cultures' has become both pressing and problematic. Divergent streams resisted integration even in Europe. The (then) new French nation still comprised northern and southern tiers at odds in France's early days, and was federalised into distinct provinces with their own *parlements* and identities. The United States of America, founded in 1776, tried to forge an American nation from a heterogeneous confederation, and this did not come together, and then only fitfully, until after the Civil War.

Indeed, the United States was perhaps the first real multicultural society that established a nation state. For as far back as 1776 when it was still predominately White Anglo-Saxon Protestant (WASP), there were Scots, Germans, Dutch, English and Irish scattered throughout the colonies, compromising the newly minted 'American' identity, based on the idea of a new American man.[4] Then there was the coercively impressed and numerically impressive population of African slaves brought to the New World in bondage, as well as the expansive Native American Indian population being displaced by the new arrivals. Those natives, though hardly citizens of the new nation, were also 'Americans' even though they would trouble the 'American' national consensus for centuries.

By the end of the nineteenth century, diversity had spread considerably as new waves of Irish, Italian, Polish, then Jewish and other Austro-Hungarian immigrants reached American shores and African-Americans became technically (in terms of law) citizens. More recently, Latino and Asian immigration has continued in diversifying a democracy – so much so that, as we have seen, even liberal observers like Arthur Schlesinger Jr. came to fear that the nation could be split asunder. Today America, with Canada and

Brazil and India too, is one of the impressively multicultural nations on earth that has also managed to become and remain democratic. Yet there are calls to this day (from Texas Governor Rick Perry, for example, a candidate for the Republican nomination in 2011) for decentralisation and states' autonomy based on the incompatibility of local traditions and the dominant 'American' paradigm. Paradoxically, although multiculturalism offers many challenges to democracy, it has been in distinctively multicultural countries that democracy has often been most successful, perhaps because diversity, immigration and pluralism promote and incline towards an open democratic society, but also, as Kymlicka and Taylor insist, because democracy helps enable the multiculturalism that can undermine its communitarian foundations.

Today, most multicultural societies are becoming increasingly diverse, while monocultural societies find themselves under pressure from immigration to become more multicultural. In the United States, demographic projections suggest that by 2050, there will be *no* American ethnic or cultural majority, but only a majority of minorities. Already today the American school-age population has reached that benchmark, and states including California, Florida and New York are on the verge of going 'majority minority'. The American multicultural future promises whites will be a minority among minorities, ditto for blacks, Asians, Latinos and other ethnicities – the only enduring majority, a majority of minorities.

It has hardly just been the United States, however, that has had to face the challenge of *y pluribus unum* – making democracy work in a multicultural society by forging a synthetic unity from the natural diversity of its peoples. After all, the same challenge faced the great empires of the nineteenth century – the Russian, Ottoman and Austro-Hungarian Empires, each of which had managed to integrate many different peoples, *gens*, *peuples*, into imperial wholes, without the benefit of democracy (throwing some doubt on Kymlicka's and Taylor's claims!) In modern India, even after it hived off a majority of its Muslim citizens into Pakistan, multiculturalism remained and remains a potent force within the country. What many think of as Hindu India remains the third largest Muslim nation in the world (see below).

In democratic societies, variety grew not just through immigration but also through the extension of the franchise to ever more diverse populations, above all women. Overnight, the enfranchisement of women could double the size of a society's citizenry. Empowering the other half of the human race brought justice but also created new tensions for democracy. Switzerland resisted offering women the vote until 1971 in part because the men insisted their direct democracy in the cantons could not survive a doubling of the electorate.

In Latin America, another post-colonial continent, democratic societies have long struggled to unify African, European and indigenous Indian populations with the preponderant Iberian-origin immigrants (and erstwhile colonisers). Not only did a variety of European immigrants have to be assimilated, but both the children of the slave trade and indigenous Indian peoples demanded integration in ways that made the successful multicultural societies of Latin America look even more ingenious than the United States. And of course in post-colonial Africa, many multicultural and multi-tribal 'nations' were created by the artificial borders imposed by empire that paid little heed to traditional tribal and territorial boundaries – in some cases, with genocidal results.

Can democracy survive multiculturalism?

This rudimentary political history of the modern world, etched here out of necessity in broad and superficial strokes, suggests that by the end of the nineteenth century the fundamental challenge for democracy had become less about how to establish democratic governance per se than how to make democracy – designed for small monocultural societies – work effectively and justly in large-scale multicultural societies. Today in our age of interdependence, the challenge has become even more daunting; for nations depend not just on themselves and their own populations, whether mono- or multicultural, for their success, but are constrained to depend on one another. Cross-border international organisations – whether the UN system, or the G9 or independent transnational NGOs – are not up to cross-border challenges, so

that democracy's problems with multicultural diversity are com-
pounded globally. The international order often complicates what
are already national quandaries. India, confronting an international (and nuclear-capable) adversary in Muslim Pakistan must
also face the dilemma of being not just the largest Hindu nation
on earth, but also the third largest Muslim nation in the world.
Although Muslims constitute less than 16 per cent of India's
total of 1.2 billion people, India comes behind only Indonesia
and Pakistan. Bangladesh, Turkey, Egypt, Iran each has fewer
Muslims. Indeed, the spread of the Muslim population of nearly
1.6 billion (nearly a quarter of the world's population) around
the world offers dramatic evidence of just how multicultural
our planet has become. There are more Muslims in Nigeria (78
million) than in Egypt (77 million), more in China (21 million)
than in Syria (20 million), more in Russia (16.5 million) than in
Tunisia (10 million), more in the United States (6 million) than
in Palestine (4 million). Multiculturalism, multi-ethnicity and
multi-religious pluralism are no longer exceptions within nation
states, they are the rule. Who would guess that Europe has more
Muslims (38 million) than Saudi Arabia, Jordan and Libya put
together? Or that nearly two-thirds of the world's Muslims are in
Asia and nearly a fifth in sub-Saharan Africa?

Combine these startling demographic realities with the patterns
of diversity associated with colonialism, trade, international education, job mobility, the flow of capital and large-scale immigration and it becomes apparent why democracies must deal with
multiculturalism just about everywhere in the world. There are
a tiny number of countries (Japan? Norway?) that claim enduring monocultural traditions, but even here appearances are not
necessarily what they seem, and change is coming. Finland is
often regarded as isolated and monocultural, yet 17 per cent of
its population is Swedish, and it is subject to increasing immigration from beyond Europe. And gentle Norway was devastated
in the summer of 2011 by a massacre perpetrated by a crazed
Norwegian fearful of immigration.

Moreover, even the traditional European religions are more
disperse than people often recognise. Brazil, with 150 million
Catholics, has three times more than France – and they are far

more ardent in their belief.[5] The United States, with 65 million, has more Catholics than Italy (58 million), and at 34 million, Argentina's Catholics are equal in number to Poland's. It is almost comical to hear fearful Europeans complain about the Muslim 'incursions' into Europe, when Catholicism has so successfully made 'incursions' into other local cultures all over the world.

Two thousand years of growth in the scale of society and the growing mobility and multicultural diversification of nations around the world raise everywhere then the fundamental question that is at the heart of Bhikhu Parekh's twin commitments to democracy and to multiculturalism: can democracy survive multiculturalism? This question has animated an ongoing but frustrating set of so-called 'dialogues of civilisations' – of which the Reset Foundation's Dialogue in India in the autumn of 2010, for which an early version of this chapter was written, is only a recent example. In the balance of this chapter, I want to try to develop an answer to the query. Are there strategies that can help democracy flourish, not in spite, but because, of multiculturalism?

To answer this question, we must first query the easy assumption many commentators make that multiculturalism and democracy go hand in hand, a natural expression of a natural hybrid known as 'pluralist democracy'. However convenient it is to assume democracy's hospitality to diversity, the analysis here suggests the very contrary: if democracy was born for, designed for and works best under monocultural conditions, then the conditions presented by such democratic multicultural societies as India, America, Brazil or even Holland or Denmark (recall the cartoon controversy), let alone by autocracies like China (where the Uighur Muslim minority is playing an increasingly large role and there are 21 million Muslims in all), are anything but hospitable to social capital, solidarity or the idea of common/public goods. We have already noted how prominent social scientists, reflected in the popular literature by the likes of Arthur Schlesinger Jr. and Samuel Huntington, have insisted that diversity is an impediment rather than a catalyst to the conditions of commonality that nurture democracy. The starting point then is tension rather than affinity, a challenge to be met rather than a potential to be realised.

Are there in fact strategies we might develop to respond to the challenge of making democracy work under conditions where communitarianism, solidarity, fraternity and ethnic and historical ties have been eroded, and egalitarianism has had to function in the face of hierarchy, us/them exclusion and a fear of the 'other'?

Strategies that accommodate multiculturalism and democracy

I want to suggest that there are at least three strategies available to democrats to help them accommodate radical multiculturalism. Two of these have been often tried, the first with tragic consequences, the second fitfully and only in part successfully. The third, I will argue, holds out more hope and I want to recommend it here.

The first option is less a strategy than a reactionary response to democracy under conditions of multiculturalism: call it right-wing populism – the *politics of resentment* or the *politics of fear* – and it has had disastrous consequences for democracy. It is the sort of reaction typical of the Tea Party in the United States, the right-wing neo-populist (perhaps neo-fascist), anti-immigrant and anti-Muslim movements found in Holland (the ascendancy of the anti-immigrant party), Switzerland (no more minarets!), Denmark (the cartoons parodying Islam to 'test' the tolerance of Muslims!), as well as in Germany, Italy, France and the UK where anti-Muslim fever, sometimes masquerading as anti-immigrant bias, is alarmingly potent. Even in China, there has been an angry and ugly reaction to the presence of Uighurs and their claims for some autonomy and recognition.

Such reactionary responses try to reverse history's arrow and retreat through time to re-establish supposedly ancient (but never altogether real) conditions of monoculturalism that facilitated the making of early modern democracy. 'We' can rule democratically, when 'we' really means just 'us' shorn of the other; when 'we' is embodied in a consensual community bound together by common history, common religion, common race and – as Rousseau suggested – a common economy and common fraternal values. Compelling in its original historical incarnation as a portrait of what was needed for a democratic community to evolve (what Montesquieu, Rousseau and de Tocqueville regarded as the sociological conditions demanded by democracy), today this perspective enjoins a politics of fear in which a self-professed ur-original population asks 'what has happened to our nation?' and tries then to 'reclaim' its putative heritage – 'take back the country' in effect by excluding the newer immigrants who have tainted the 'purity' of the original. Whether they are Tea Party WASPS or Hindu nationalists or Dutch advocates of the old 'pillars' of society, such reactionaries hold out the promise of fleeing backwards: India for the Hindus! Europe for the Christians! America for the . . . Americans! In Europe, defenders of Euro-purity tried to load Europe's Christian antecedents and character into the failed European constitution several years ago, though this did little to win anti-immigration zealots to the cause since for the most part they were preternaturally anti-European as well.

There is also a stealth version of the politics of fear that blames minorities for their own victimisation (and for the radicalisation that can ensue) because of their putative resistance to integration. This was David Cameron's tactic in his controversial comments alluded to in my opening, and it is typical of racist reactions in once monocultural societies that blame all of the decentring and destabilising tendencies of modernity on minorities and their inability to assimilate. In the United States, the conventional critique says, Muslims happily sink into the melting pot and become 'real' Americans; in Europe they refuse, and so encourage rejection on the basis of their distinctive cultural features.

The problem with this kind of noxious reaction, whether couched in Cameron's 'respectable' terms or in overt racism, is that – morality aside – it flies in the face of the social realities of the modern world and thus sets an impossible course against history. For better or worse, the world today is multicultural, interdependent and mobile. Global markets assure global immigration and global diversity and accelerate the growing irrelevance of national borders, indeed of nationality itself. These realities, dominated by incessant immigration and the mobility of labour and capital alike mean that no country, however monocultural today, is likely to remain so tomorrow. Multiculturalism is the future of nations and relations among nations and assimilation is not likely to work in every society. The American trick was to ameliorate difference by imposing artificial uniformity. Such magic will not work in most places. So diversity must be confronted.

To travel backwards via reactionary politics to a world of relatively isolated, relatively homogeneous, relatively autonomous nation states is a recipe for disaster. It cannot work, but it can exact a terrible price in injustice and economic inefficiency. The politics of violence, the politics of intolerance, the politics of anger and resentment are to be sure easy, and they can win (and have won) some pyrrhic political victories, especially in Europe where the experiment with integration has come to look problematic. But such reactive strategies can only undermine democracy's long-term sustainability.

The real devil's bargain you make when you turn your back on multiculturalism in the name of sustaining democracy is surrendering real democracy in the name of a faux purity. The populist option has been very popular. It has been the first choice of media scaremongers and political charlatans alike, and it has proved a savvy if destructive way to win elections. But it cannot succeed in staving off history's ever more multicultural character or in preserving democracy in the face of the thinning out of is social base. Reactionary populism may impair democracy, but it will not abolish the daunting realities of multiculturalism.

The second option in confronting the tensions with democracy produced by multiculturalism is *liberal tolerance*, a perspective with a long and noble lineage. While it is far more attractive than the politics of exclusion, and has compelling philosophical credibility, it has not been wholly successful in practice (part of David Cameron's complaint). It originates with early liberals like John Locke, concerned with religious differences and their destructive potential in undoing democracy's necessary civic consensus. We need not like others or enjoy difference, but we are constrained by democracy to respect others and tolerate difference. Liberal democracy is nothing if not the politics of difference adjudicated by law and deliberative compromise. Cultural difference conceals human commonality, recognised in the doctrine of human rights.

311

Originally intended to nurture religious comity among warring Christian confessions in the sixteenth and seventeenth centuries, liberal tolerance became the tonic for all difference: ethnic, racial and national. In time, tolerance came to be grounded in the powerful rhetoric of universal human rights. For 300 years this rights approach has been the primary response of liberal democracy to multiculturalism and difference. When in the United States, slaves were emancipated and granted civil and political rights, when subsequently women gained the vote, the idea was not to obliterate difference or even create a common community among different groups. It was only to respect the rights of every group and assure their equal access to civic and political citizenship (see the thirteenth, fourteenth and fifteenth amendments to the US constitution). Rooting an accommodation with difference in universal rights obviously has a powerful and universal appeal independent of particular cultures and political arrangements, and it remains central to the issues we are concerned with. The individual worth of each person that constitutes equality is an effective riposte to the politics of fear, and has played a significant role in India, the United States and other pluralist democracies.

Yet Bhikhu Parekh has helped show the limits of abstract rights talk in addressing concrete diversity in its cultural and religious forms. The human rights approach, so potent and venerable in the abstract, has a practical defect: it is weak sociologically, unrooted in notions of community, fraternity and solidarity that are key preconditions for democracy. Tolerating 'otherness' can protect minorities but does little to forge social capital or community. Nice to 'respect' others, but can we work with them to secure common ground and enact common laws? One man's Sharia is another man's anathema: an encroachment by religious 'fanatics' on a 'reasonable' secular law code. Or, other way round, one man's separation of church and state is another man's rejection of communal religion and of the priority of ethics over politics that religion mandates. There has always been something peculiar about the approach to tolerance that requires that religion be seen as 'private' – as if ethics and religious doctrine have no necessary communal or public character but are another variety of private taste.

Once their public character is acknowledged, however, their

public entailments become evident. One woman's community practice – female 'ritual surgery', for example – is another community's 'genital mutilation', and a clear-cut perversion of rights. Rights give all persons a claim to inclusion, but such claims are abstract and formal and likely to result in a fairly 'thin' form of democracy, where association feels frail. The individual as a rights-bearing person has been a powerful legal construct, and can give courts and constitutions an argument for respecting difference. Yet individuals thus construed contribute little to feelings of common identity, and carry only modest sociological weight. The public domain, as Andrew Gamble points out, is more fragile than we sometimes recognise. Rights have moral force but are not necessarily the best social glue.

Sharing access to rights does not turn members of the majority and members of minorities into neighbours or fellow citizens. Whether you are a Hindu, a Christian, a Sikh, a Muslim, a Jew or a Buddhist, you are equally worthy as a human person with equal rights. But this does not mean you are equally capable of reaching agreement with others outside your religion on prickly policy debates over (say) teaching creationism in the schools, or supporting abortion with state funds, or recognising pacifism as an acceptable value in war time. 'All men are brothers' has a nice ring to it, but from the start it excludes women. Besides any locution starting with 'all men' is unlikely to motivate action by individual men and women who see themselves first of all not as generic humans but as Hindus or Arabs or Burmese or, for that matter, as lesbians or union members or Tories. As Bhikhu Parekh has written:

> [T]he human identity remains abstract unless it is anchored in and enriched by our particular identities ... we are not homogenous instantiations or specimens of the human species. We are French or American, Hindu or Christina, mothers or fathers, and thus human in our mediated and unique ways ... we are similar by virtue of being different.[6]

To put the matter historically, liberal democracy has had the comfort of human rights as an ameliorator of difference from the beginning, and liberal rights thinking has gone some way towards opening the way to greater variety and multiculturalism in democratic societies. But that the challenge remains so formidable today that a British Prime Minister can seemingly abjure Locke's most potent formula, suggests that by itself, the rights approach enjoining tolerance cannot overcome the suspicion of difference that democracies in search of consensus will inculcate. For democracy to flourish, we would seem to require a thicker and 'stronger' form of community than abstract liberal human rights allow for.[7] That it is a firm foundation for legal struggle does not yet make it a sufficient foundation for pragmatic politics or for democratic sustainability.

The third option I wish to consider, and the option that has my enthusiastic support, is variously known as *constitutional patriotism* (Jürgen Habermas' *Verfassungspatriotismus*)[8] or what in the United States have been understood as the practices of *civil religion*. It has some affinities for John Rawls' argument for 'overlapping consensus' as a road to social cohesion in conflicted liberal states, though I will not deal with Rawls here. The promise of this third approach lies both in its actual historical successes, and its capacity to respond to the seeming insufficiency of liberalism's thin sociological premises. This third option works best when it is twinned with a rights strategy, for it can put meat on the bones of that approach's skeletal and formalistic liberalism.

Tellingly, it is a strategy better understood in the United States, where multiculturalism has been relatively successful, than in Europe, where it has created anxiety and an intolerant, reactionary politics, inviting the kinds of foolish reactions we have seen from otherwise respectable politicians in England, Holland, France and perhaps most egregiously, in Germany. We have already cited British Prime Minister Cameron's awkward comments. Compare them with former French President Sarkozy's biting rhetoric about how France is 'suffering the consequences of 50 years of immigration, insufficiently regulated, that have led to a failure of assimilation'.[9]

In Germany, the longtime residency and citizenship of Turkish immigrants and their children has become a source of controversy and bitterness. There, a former federal banker and Social

Democrat named Thilo Sarrazin published a best-selling book in 2010 called *Deutschland Schafft sich ab*. Sarrazin's title, which translates as 'Germany Abolishes Itself', argues with earnest shamelessness that the Turkish immigrant minority in Germany is responsible for 'abolishing' Germany. Aside from the obvious links to racist notions of a 'pure' Germany in danger of being tainted by foreign elements, Sarrazin is indulging in the familiar conceit that 'immigrants' (many actually born in Germany) are responsible for all of Germany's ills – a particularly baleful perspective given Germany's history.

In the United States, such arguments make less headway, not least of all because America has relied on civil religion but also because it is a nation of immigrants. Not to say that anti-immigrant feeling has no traction in a country where up until recently one in five Americans insisted their President was not born in the United States (the number declined by half after the killing of Osama bin Laden under President Obama's executive command), and where from 1925 to 1965 there was a stringent cap on immigration. Although the climate for immigration should have improved, the current reality in the United States sets one party against any change in immigration laws and compels President Obama to try to address the reality of 12 million undocumented workers through executive actions.

Certainly the United States has done better than many other nations in pursuing the integration of 'others' into a national community, although notoriously it locked up Japanese-Americans in detention camps during World War II and currently is considering ways to wall off its long southern border with Mexico. The success, such as it is, may be in part due to the historical fact that other than Native American Indians who have largely been excluded from membership and African-Americans, brought to the New World in chains, Americans are all voluntary immigrants from somewhere else, a fact that not only facilitates but necessitates special strategies of assimilation.

The strategy defined by civil religion allows democrats to marry the thick potential of religious community to the secular values of civic patriotism. Civic patriotism defines a voluntary arena where the rites and rituals of constitutionalism and civic history play the role of unifying norms around which a community of citizens otherwise differentiated by background, religion and economic status can nonetheless be constructed. By focusing on *voluntary* forms of identity that arise out of common activity (military or community service, for example), common civic commitments (jury service, public voting, civic education) and a common civic history with its common civic liturgy (the struggle for rights, a common war effort), a civil religion may evolve that trumps the differences inherent in *ascriptive* identity. Ascriptive identity denotes an identity that is 'given', that is predetermined as a result of such involuntary characteristics as caste, ethnicity, religion or race. (Some will argue that there is nothing 'voluntary' about schooling that can impress opinions on unformed minds, or a faith in constitutional documents taught uncritically from an early age, but the distinction between voluntary and ascpritive as used in sociology and history is widely understood, and is not impacted by the philosophical debate about just how 'free' voluntarism really is.)

The United States in particular has been a country that has prided itself on forging a new American identity. Even in the eighteenth century the French observer J. Hector St. John de Crevecoeur wrote in his *Letters from an American Farmer* about a 'new American man'. This new American found his identity in ideas and civic commitments rather than country of origin or race. One might object that the Americans have had little choice but to forge a 'new man' since the only original American men of old times were the natives they were busy exterminating. Besides, the newcomers enjoyed no singular deep monoculture. But that would be to ignore the power of the majority WASP culture. Which is to say, civil religion has been a choice rather than a consequence of identity, something chosen rather than given.

There was a weak and inauthentic 'natural' identity available founded on Protestantism, and the dominant majority tried to define new American character around it. But the choice for elective identity rooted in common activity and common citizenship was the notion of a civil religion, and it was the wiser choice. It has manifested itself over time in the development of an evolving civic liturgy – a compendium of ideas, declarations, speeches

316

and celebrations to which all citizens can subscribe in common, regardless of their origins. It was this liturgy that came to represent the civic identity of the 'American' or, better, the American citizen.

In the American case, this civic liturgy includes the Declaration of Independence, the Constitution and the Bill of Rights, and other founding and inspirational documents, but also stories about the Founders – about Washington crossing the Delaware in midwinter, about Jefferson composing the Declaration with an eye on John Locke, about Patrick Henry declaring 'Give me liberty or give me death!', and about Ben Franklin battling in Paris for French support for the new American government. Beyond the founding era, the civic liturgy also includes the Emancipation Proclamation, Lincoln's Gettysburg Address, Roosevelt's appeal to the four freedoms, and Martin Luther King's 'I have a dream' speech, and now perhaps President Obama's speech on race when he was a candidate (and in time even the speech of closure for 9/11 that the President made after the killing of Osama bin Laden). But it also embraces stories about the thousands of freed slaves who fought in the Union Army to defeat the slave south in the Civil War, about defeated Confederate soldiers allowed by Lincoln to go home with their rifles and horses thus securing a future union unfettered by the kinds of resentment that stalked Germany after World War I, about Rosa Parks refusing to sit in the back of the bus and sparking the civil rights movement, about a black man with a father from Kenya and a mother from Kansas being elected the first black (and the first multicultural) President of the United States of America, and then being re-elected to a historic second term.

In sum, in America's history it doesn't matter if you are a refugee from the potato famine in Ireland, an Austrian trying to avoid conscription at home in an expiring empire, a Latino in search of a paying job or a Jew fleeing religious persecution in Europe. Claim the American civic stories as your own, embrace these declarations and speeches as the core of your civic value system in place of the narratives of the countries you leave behind, and you are an American.

Commonality here is a matter of what we *do* and what we

believe, not who we *are* and where we *came from*. The voluntary character of this form of identity comes precisely from its *action* component, its focus on the future. For it is about the highway before us, not the road behind us. To be sure, these contrived civic ties are less thick than ascriptive identities like race and ethnicity; yet they remain thicker and more binding than the splendid but abstract idea of 'personhood' or the noble claim to equal rights. They act to bind Americans together and permit them to live with identitarian differences that in other settings might rip a community apart. Racial patriotism stops at the epidermal boundaries of human skin; nationalist patriotism extends only to a people made common by ethnicity and language. But constitutional patriotism crosses all other identities and draws from differences a genuine unity (*y pluribus unum*). Even human rights, abstract and bare-boned as an idea, become binding only when rooted in *action*, in a history of a common *struggle* for rights. What we *do* is ultimately more powerful than who we *are*. The rights component demonstrates the case that civil religion is not merely the result a majority turning its identity into civic patriotism but rather something that minorities help forge through their sturggles. Documents like the thirteenth to the fifteenth amendments, Lincoln's speeches and Martin Luther King's 'I have a dream' speech prove that civil religion is dynamic, and grows out of the struggle of minorities to shape the majority, not just the other way round – an argument Parekh makes in his *Rethinking Multiculturalism*.

This is why another dimension of any civil religion must derive from its association with real practices, sometimes revolutionary practices. As with religion itself, what we believe and what we do, what we say and how we act, reinforce one another. Each demands the other. Action without belief is arbitrary and meaningless. Belief without action is abstract and empty. The Christian idea that God is love enjoins charitable action and such actions and practices support Christian brotherhood. The civic idea that rights define equal citizenship enjoins social struggle and the political pursuit of justice, and the struggle endows rights with substance. Citizenship entails public and community service as well as the right to vote. The liturgy entails action, and action is

318

given meaning by the liturgy. Just as with real religion, which has practices as well as a liturgy, behaviours, as well as ideals, a civil religion must rest on particular practices that inscribe ideals on real people.

Community organisers and advocates of democratic community have long understood that the best way to motivate people divided by identity and background to unite around common ideals is to get them not just to believe things in common, but to do things together: to build or make something, to help or serve some person or group or institution, to realise ideas in action. So powerful is the fraternity forged by fighting a war together – however different individual soldiers may be from one another – that William James, anti-military pacifist though he was, proposed we seek a 'moral equivalent of war' that would create an association of brothers as coherent and fraternal as the army platoon. Some would say we have done just that in the United States with the creation under President Kennedy of a Peace Corps, where Americans of every background served together in overseas lands of every variety on the way to serving others but also to forging their own American identity.

In recent decades, a potent service movement has taken root. Adumbrating that movement, James had written:

If now – and this is my idea – there were, instead of military conscription, a conscription of the whole youthful population to form for a certain number of years a part of the army enlisted against *Nature*, the injustice would tend to be evened out, and numerous other goods to the commonwealth would remain blind as the luxurious classes now are blind, to man's relations to the globe he lives on, and to the permanently sour and hard foundations of his higher life. To coal and iron mines, to freight trains, to fishing fleets in December, to dishwashing, clothes washing, and window washing, to road-building and tunnel-making, to foundries and stoke-holes, and to the frames of skyscrapers, would our gilded youths be drafted off, according to their choice, to get the childishness knocked out of them, and to come back into society with healthier sympathies and soberer ideas. They would have paid their blood-tax, done their own part in the immemorial human warfare against nature; they would tread the earth more proudly, the

319

women would value them more highly, they would be better fathers and teachers of the following generation.[10]

Our modern version of William James' experiment in forging community through common service began with the Peace Corps and then the 'Points of Light' efforts of the first Bush Administration (spearheaded over time by General Colin Powell). It evolved in President Clinton's first term into the National Service Corporation (in whose creation and development I played a modest personal role) as well as a concept of service that, while decentralised (every state had a service commission), was not just about 'voluntarism' and charity but about citizenship and civic service. It culminated in the election of President Barack Obama, an American whose own story has become part of the civic liturgy and hence the civil religion, and whose election was the result of a participatory service ethic on the part of millions of young people who had never been civically involved before. Today, perhaps weary from two wars and the burdens of a pathologically divisive politics in the United States, President Obama seems to have backed away from his own commitment to community organising and national service. While the White House now has an office of 'Civic Participation' devoted to outreach and service, it is no longer a national priority as it was in the late 1980s and 1990s.

Nonetheless, more even than jury service or voting, citizen and community service have become emblematic of what it means, at its very best, to be an American. When (as happened at Rutgers University in the 1990s when I ran a college-wide service learning programme there) a young black man from the slums of Camden joins with a Japanese-American from Princeton and a Cubano from Newark to serve alongside a Jewish girl from Passaic and an Anglo from Montclair whose forebears came to America on the *Mayflower*, a group with a new identity is formed. These young individualists, diverse as they are united, come to service full of the usual panoply of ethnic and racial prejudices, tending to distrust everyone 'foreign' to their own particular background. Yet once engaged together in common service, they became Americans in the richest and most egalitarian civic sense. Not by any means inconsequential, their service also engages them in local communities, few of whose members have gone to university at all, and so also extended the compass of their civic empathy to non-college (uneducated) Americans living in poverty.

Subscribing to common civic ideals and imbibing common civic stories is the way to initiate a civil religion and inaugurate a civic identity. And engaging in common activities and participating in service are how that identity becomes a psychological and socio-logical reality capable of overcoming bias and achieving common ground among people who have little in common other than mutual dislike.

The most recent example of the third approach to dealing dem-ocratically with difference comes from the Arab Spring, in par-ticular Egypt during the tumult of the winter of 2011. There, in the uprising in Tahrir Square, there was hope (later dashed) for a genuinely liberal society. Christians and Muslims who at the start of the revolution had been attacking and killing one another in the name of their rival religions found themselves united in a broad national civic action against President Mubarak's corrupt regime. Astonishingly, these erstwhile enemies not only joined in common protests, but also protected one another from pro-Mubarak thugs inciting violence when Muslims or Christian Copts were at prayer on their respective Friday and Sunday Sabbaths. Almost over-night, an inspiring common civic movement allowed age-old dif-ferences to be challenged.[11] No such abrupt transformation can be complete, of course, and I am not so naïve as to think dif-ference in Egypt is done. New suspicions between Muslims and Copts arose during the transitional democratic process in the spring, and in the next several years an autocratic but democrati-cally elected Muslim Brotherhood regime under President Morsi reasserted fundamentalist rights. This in turn led to a violent over-throw of the Morsi regime during which the military reasserted its power and destroyed the residue of the vanished 'Spring'. Military dictatorship prevails again in Egypt (Mubarak has been released from prison and all charges against him dropped). Yet despite the demise of the revolution, the memory remains of a people united across religion and sect against autocracy able to forge a civic union in spite of deep historical differences.

The final challenge: interdependence

Multicultural difference can be overcome by common civic activity and the unifying norms of a national civil religion – a kind of constitutional patriotism (in the case of Egypt, a 'we demand a constitution' constitutional patriotism) – resolves many of the tensions that make multiculturalism a challenge to sustaining democracy. But it also produces a new and troublesome predicament for democracy: ours is an era of increasing interdependence, when global challenges no longer respond to exclusively national and sovereign state remedies. Under these novel conditions, a recourse to civil religion and constitutional patriotism risks intensifying rather than diminishing nationalism and sovereignty at the very moment when they are standing in the way of new cross-border approaches to citizenship and governance. That is to say, as civil religion helps solve the problem of democracy, as it scales up to the realities of expansive, multicultural nation states, it increases the barriers to overcoming the problems of the next stage, the new global scale of our interdependent planet. For it reinforces the inability of nation states held together by tolerance and civil religion to address the brutal new realities of interdependence.

A successful Indian civil religion that overcomes the rivalries of Hindus, Sikhs, Muslims and others may do so by intensifying the cross-border rivalries with China and Pakistan. An Egypt united around the popular pursuit of a democratic constitution will not necessarily be a more peaceful interlocutor with Israel or Iran or the United States. A United States that has vanquished and liquidated Osama bin Laden in the name of its civic virtues (liberal democracy and pluralism, for example), may nonetheless witness its citizens chanting 'USA! USA!' and 'We're Number One', when they might better be considering the malevolent interdependence that allowed al-Qaeda (call it a 'malevolent NGO') to terrorise the world, precisely because it was part of no nation state and belonged to no sovereign entity.

How baleful nationality can become precisely when strengthened by civic patriotism can be seen from America's unwillingness even to recognise, let alone cooperate with, treaties on land mines or cluster bombs, or be responsive to the International Criminal

Court in front of which it keeps trying to bring the tyrants it helps overthrow. Although the civic norms it embraces may be universal, their impact on the United States seem parochial. When several hundred nation states put their proud sovereignty on view at the annual COP UN meetings meant to deal with global climate change, the result is not cooperation but paralysis, one state after another explaining why their sovereignty does not permit them to do together what must be done if the planet is to be spared. If they are democratic, their plight is even worse, since the most enlightened statesman fully cognisant of why climate change must be controlled despair of being re-elected if they take this cosmopolitan perspective to the parochial polls that legitimise their power.

What a dilemma. There seem to be but two paths to reconciling democratic civil religion with the discomfiting realities of the new interdependence. The first reflects an old truth – that democracies are less likely to make war on one another or refuse cooperation with each other than are autocracies. Civil religion is by definition an expression of democracy, and is unlikely to increase international tensions unless it becomes a rationale for mere nationalism and jingoism (which requires that it be corrupted and trivialised). Now historically we can certainly think of instances where in the face of a war, a national civil religion has been put to the purposes of inciting nationalist fervour and battlefield spirit. Stalin famously turned World War II into a 'motherland' war in which the disparate parts of the Soviet Union and the contentious divisions surrounding communism were put to rest (temporarily) by an appeal to a common Russian mission. But the Soviet Union was hardly a democracy.

Yet American exceptionalism, rooted in America's much more democratic civil religion (its status as a 'beacon of liberty') has also sometimes been a justifier of armed intervention (Vietnam? Iraq? Libya?), although it also nurtured isolationism in the nineteenth century ('no entangling foreign alliances', President Washington had warned). So while a democratic civic constitutionalism can dampen nationalist rivalries, it need not and does not always do so.

There is a need then for a more affirmative approach to interdependence: the cultivation of new forms of interdependent

323

cross-border citizenship; a bottom-up civil society that aspires to universality (think about transnational NGOs like Doctors Without Borders and the Reset Foundation or the cosmopolitan potential of the world-wide web); a global civil religion that embraces a global human narrative; or establish a new democratic governance organisation such as a 'global parliament of mayors', as I suggest in the final chapter of *If Mayors Ruled the World: Dysfunctional Nations, Rising Cities* (Yale University Press, 2013) – an idea being realised in a pilot sitting of the Parliament in London in 2015. Such stories might allude to rights, but must also offer more particular narratives about the human adventure and common activities in which all women and men are invited to participate – a common campaign to explore space for example. Such an affirmative approach will help to extend citizenship and civil society across borders, finding new commonalities in trade, technology and common challenges that allow citizens to recognise what they share with other peoples across the world.

We have little experience in this domain, however, and talking about global civil society and global citizenship is considerably easier than forging them – especially because, as happened in the transition from the small-scale city state to the large-scale nation sate, the transition from national to global forms of governance is likely once again to thin out commonality and identity. If national citizenship is less thick than local citizenship, imagine how much thinner global citizenship will feel compared to national citizenship, even when nationality is voluntary rather than ascriptive.

Yet, as I have contended here, when liberal commitments to rights are combined with the ideas and practices of civil religion, democracy seems capable of responding to scale, even as it approaches its planetary limits. There is no reason democracy has to stop at the frontiers of the nation, any more than it once stopped at the gates of the city. But progress will require that *we develop forms of citizenship rooted in common action, common civic beliefs, and a common civil religion*, both within and among democracies.

What such ideals and practices look like concretely will of course vary from one country to the next, depending on the specific character of the regime. Bhikhu Parekh has made a major contribution to our thinking about interdependence, not just in India but also in the Interdependence Movement, which he worked with me and others in founding ten years ago.[12] Yet the political focus remains on independence and exceptionalism. And not just in the United States. Americans still boast about the exceptionalist destiny associated with their civic ideals and practices. But so does Switzerland, which claims its own unique character – *Sonderfall Schweiz*, the Swiss say – rooted in its rare civic combination of multinationalism, federalism and neutrality, which (along its alpine topography – 'auf den Bergen, Freiheit', wrote Schiller!)[13] – putatively gives Swiss participatory democracy a unique character.[14] India is an exception of another kind, a product of British imperialism. It needs to discover or must forge its own form of civil religion to compensate for its awkward creation. Perhaps it will start from that experience associated with the quest for independence, and, as Parekh's exploration of Gandhi might lead some to think, will be based on Gandhi's unique approach to national liberation based on non-violent resistance (although this ideology seems to have a weaker hold today on the Indian imagination than membership in the nuclear club and enmity with Pakistan). But one way or the other, India will have to come to terms with the inevitable march of interdependence in the world.

Geography can also condition nationality in ways that encourage both parochialism (we can go it alone as an island republic or alpine sanctuary!) and cosmopolitanism (our self-sufficiency makes us unafraid of cooperation and global community). In places like the United Kingdom, where an island constitutional monarchy is defined and protected by the seas and where a potent new Independence Party (UKIP) is railing against Europe, or, to take Switzerland again, an alpine redoubt that makes the nation intransigent in the face of invasion, the civil religion may be both resistant and open to collaboration. Switzerland refused to join the Common Market, but was there ever a more 'European' nation? The peoples who dwell in seaports or river-ports may unite around trade, transportation and social mobility to a degree that suggests cities rather than nations may eventually merge in global networks capable of global governance.[15] What is shared by every nation bedevilled by forms of difference that have been soothed by a civil religion, however, is a willingness of focus on democratic ideals, understood as a *liturgy* and a set of common *behaviours* and *practices*. The same will apply to the quest for global democratic governance, when a civil religion will have to be constructed across borders.

To respond to the politics of fear, then, we need rights and tolerance, but we also need a politics of hope that takes the form of actions and deeds as well as ideals and constitutions, and one that operates across borders. Mutual respect must be converted into common action and civility must issue out of engaged citizenship; but across borders. And parochial national stories must give way to global human stories across borders (the story of women's struggle for equality? The story of the battle for children's rights? The story of the pursuit of Green consciousness?) Common civic identity entails a common struggle: a fight for a sustainable world, or a fight for a peaceful world, or a fight for a just world. Until now the challenge was national: now it is global – aims and goals that offer support for a global civic religion. For unless we can globalise democracy or democratise globalisation, democracy is unlikely to survive. And global democracy demands global community and a global civil religion, something resembling a Global Parliament of Mayors.

For all the difficulties, if democracy is to meet this latest test of scale and conquer its antagonism to multiculturalism, the challenge of interdependence must then be addressed, whether by a struggle for ecological survival, global peace or justice across borders – say fair trade, rather than free trade. Democracy's last frontier will be a world without frontiers, the sort of world in which cosmopolitan political theory of the kind practised over a lifetime by Bhikhu Parekh will flourish not only in the academy but in the practices and behaviours of democratic innovators.

The good news is that as theorists have remained resourceful and inspired, and citizens inventive and dedicated, democracy has to date been able to show a remarkable resilience in dealing with scale. Its survival and flourishing beyond the confines of the unitary township seemed miraculous at the time, yet now, thanks to such innovations as representative government and federalism, we think of large-scale nation states with a once-unthinkable population of hundreds of millions of citizens as natural habitats for self-government. For by overcoming the pressures that diversity places on democracy's capacity in reaching consensus (or at least prudential agreement) when citizens no longer share a common race or religion or language or gender, without succumbing to a reactionary politics of fear, and without relying exclusively on the thin abstraction of liberal rights and tolerance, democracy has proved its potential long-term sustainability. Given the planetary scale of global governance, crossing the final frontier of sovereign borders will be vexing, but by no means beyond the powers of that irrepressible human imagination that created democracy in the first place.

Notes

1. B. Parekh (2008), *A New Politics of Identity* (London: Palgrave/Macmillan), p. 278.
2. S. Huntington (1998), *The Clash of Civilisations* (New York: Simon & Schuster); A. Schlesinger Jr (1998), *The Disuniting of America: Reflections on a Multicultural Society* (New York: W. W. Norton).
3. M. Kammen (1990), *People of Paradox: An Inquiry Concerning the Origins of American Civilisation* (Ithaca, NY: Cornell University Press).
4. For the idea of a new American man, see Hector St. John de Crevecœur's *Letters from an American Farmer*, 1788.
5. Numbers for 2005 from www.Catholic-Hierarchy.org.
6. Parekh, *New Politics of Identity*, p. 3.
7. B. Barber (2004), *Strong Democracy: Participatory Politics for a New Age* (Twentieth Anniversary Edition) (Berkeley, CA: University of California Press).
8. J. Habermas (1991), *The Structural Transformation of the Public Sphere: An Inquiry into a Category of Bourgeois Society* (Cambridge, MA: MIT Press).
9. C. Caldwell, 'Le Pen is mightier', *Weekly Standard*, 14 March, 16:25, p. 23.
10. W. James (1910), 'The moral equivalence of war', *McClure's Magazine*, August, p. 467. There has been some dissent from the

idea that common service contributes to solidarity and civic participation (see for example, S. Segall (2005), 'Participation as an engine
of solidarity: a sceptical view', *Political Studies*, 53: 362–78), but
while I have not the space to take on scepticism here, I believe there
is overwhelming evidence from studies of the Peace Corps and of
the impact of Community Service to show that there are clear effects
of service on civic patriotism and participation.

11. Here is more evidence to refute sceptics about participation as an
engine of solidarity like Segall (2005).

12. The Interdependence Movement, on whose global steering committee Bhikhu Parekh sits, was established initially to commemo-
rate 12 September, the day after 9/11, as 'Interdependence Day',
helping citizens to overcome parochial national identity. In recent
years, after celebrations in Rome, Paris, Casablanca, Mexico City,
Brussels, Istanbul, Berlin and New York, it is morphing into a
global movement. See www.interdependencemovement.org.

13. 'In the mountains, freedom!'

14. B. R. Barber (1971), *The Death of Communal Liberty: The History
of Freedom in a Swiss Mountain Canton* (Princeton, NJ: Princeton
University Press).

15. My latest book focuses on the role of cities rather than states in
global governance, see B. R. Barber (2013), *If Mayors Ruled the
World* (New Haven, CT: Yale University Press). For more on the
Global Parliament of Mayors project, see www.globalparliament
ofmayors.org.

12

Interculturalism, Multiculturalism

Charles Taylor

In this chapter I would like to discuss the term 'multicultural-ism' itself, and some of the misunderstandings that arise around it. These misunderstandings are very important, because they are bound up with the resistances to the policies that (rightly or wrongly) go under this name. I will reflect on some of the many meanings the word has acquired, and the cross-purposes that this multiplicity has engendered.

I

In order to introduce my subject I intend to start off with my own parochial context, which is that of the never-ending Canada–Quebec imbroglio. The fact that I start from is that policies concerned to deal with diversity and integration are grouped in 'English' Canada (Canada outside Quebec) under the rubric 'mul-ticulturalism', whereas in Quebec they are referred to as 'intercul-turalism'. These policies are in fact quite similar when one spells them out. But it has nevertheless been politically imperative to use a different name.

Now part of the explanation lies in the lowest kind of dema-gogic rhetoric. Quebeckers of a very nationalist bent (1) cannot bring themselves to adopt policies having the same name they bear in 'English' Canada; (2) they have created a history in which multiculturalism was introduced in Canada in order to avoid having to deal properly with French–English duality, and they often claim (3) that Canadian multiculturalism is designed to slow down and even defeat integration, that it consists in encouraging immigrants to retreat into their communities of origin, in short that it encourages ghettoisation.

Now (1) is not a valid reason, and (3) is just plain wrong; although it is worth noting that this negative, ghetto-inducing idea of the point of multiculturalism is shared widely in Europe, as Canadians discover to their cost and horror when they discuss these questions with the French, Germans or Dutch.

I remember reading a headline in a German newspaper, 'Multikulturalismus ist gescheitert', where the explanation was that the politics of laisser-aller, which recognises difference with no concern for integration, had brought Europe to a terrible pass, and that now was the time to get tough, and make immigrants conform. In fact, in recent months, the heads of government of the three biggest EU countries – Merkel, Cameron and Sarkozy – have announced the end of this pernicious 'multiculturalism'. In France, 'Communautarisme' has been regularly stigmatised as the same kind of encouragement to retreat into closed cultural communities, *le multiculturalisme* is seen as an endorsement of philosophy of closure. Quebeckers are often just repeating the French rhetoric on this. Canadians find it hard to recognise themselves in this travesty, because multiculturalism in this country has from the beginning been concerned with integration, putting a great emphasis, for instance, on teaching the national languages, English and French.[1]

But the fact that the word has a different sense in Europe and in Canada is not just a harmless semantic shift. Anti-multicultural rhetoric in Europe reflects a profound misunderstanding of the dynamics of immigration into the rich, liberal democracies of the West. The underlying assumption seems to be that too much positive recognition of cultural differences will encourage a retreat into ghettos, and a refusal to accept the political ethic of liberal democracy itself – as though this rush to closure was the first choice of immigrants themselves, from which they have to be dissuaded through 'tough love'. Up to a point, we can understand why politicians with no great experience of the dynamics of immigrant societies fall into this error, because the tendency among immigrants is always at first to cluster with people of similar origins and background. How else can they find the networks they need to survive and move ahead in the new environment? We also see this clustering in globalised cities, like Bombay, where new arrivals seek out people from the same state or village.

But the major motivation of immigrants into rich democracies is to find new opportunities, of work, education, or self-expression, for themselves and especially for their children. If they manage to secure these, they – and even more their children – are happy to integrate into the society. It is only if this hope is frustrated, if the path to more rewarding work and education is blocked, that a sense of alienation and hostility to the receiving society can grow, and may even generate a rejection of the mainstream and its ethic.

Consequently, the European attack on multiculturalism often seems to us a classic case of false consciousness, blaming certain phenomena of ghettoisation and alienation of immigrants on a foreign ideology, instead of recognising the homegrown failures to promote integration and combat discrimination.

This judgement, coming from the western side of the Atlantic may be thought unfair, because for instance, Muslim immigrant populations in Europe are less educated and skilled than are those who have entered Canada or the United States, and this has to do with the selective immigration policies of the Western hemisphere societies. As a result the proportion of those who hold illiberal opinions is higher among immigrants in Europe, and this certainly does create problems and barriers to integration.

It is understandable that populations mainly consisting of long-established ethnic groups can react with a certain unease in face of immigrants of unfamiliar cultures, customs or religions. Will these people change us? How much? Will this change touch our most cherished values? Illiberal attitudes among immigrants can easily play into this fear. But to rationalise this fear in terms of a threat posed by an alien religion is both a mistake of fact and an error in policy.

It is a mistake of fact, because it attributes to most, or at least sizeable numbers of immigrants the intention to overturn the basic values of liberal democracy, whereas in fact these values, along with the prosperity they have helped make possible, are

331

what attracted them in the first place. As I mentioned above, immigrants want mostly to integrate, to find good jobs and education for their children, leading to even better jobs in the next generation. They also appreciate the freedoms they enjoy in their new society, which are often less available in their countries of origin.

But even for that minority that is hostile to liberal values, this fear misinterprets the source of this hostility. It is seen to reside in a religion which is homogenised and essentialised, and is supposed to animate all those who believe in it. Such is, for instance the picture of Islam, which one hears in the Islamophobic discourse of the European Right. Very little account is taken of what people who call themselves Muslims actually believe. There is no allowance that Islam is a religion grouping many cultures, that the line between religion and culture is fuzzy and different from case to case; that many people may be Muslims in a sense that has little to do with piety and religious obligation; that many of the customs that repel us in certain Muslim societies, like female circumcision or honour killings, have no sanction in the religious tradition. Above all no allowance is made for the fact that this tradition is very various and contested.

But this global fear of Islam is not only mistaken in fact, it is supremely damaging as policy. Granted that we want to avoid and even outlaw certain practices, such as the two I have just mentioned; that we want to inculcate certain values, such as those of male–female equality, it would seem to be much wiser to make allies of all those who can be brought to agree, rather than alienating whole communities by stigmatising them as the source of a hideous cultural–moral danger. To talk in a register of high threat of 'Islam' and a threatened 'Islamisation' is not only to invent non-existent dangers, but also to drive a rift between religions and cultures, which cannot but be damaging to a modern democracy.

And when one adds to this that a principal source of hostility to our liberal societies among immigrants comes from their experience of failed integration, the folly of harping on the bogeyman of religion, rather than acting to facilitate integration, and by that stigmatisation to make integration still more difficult, becomes increasingly evident.

But to return to the discussion above of the different grounds for rejecting multiculturalism in Quebec, only in (2) is there some element of truth. This is because at an earlier phase, 'biculturalism' was a term of election for certain Quebeckers who wanted to bring about a serious recognition in Canada of the Quebec difference.[2] Trudeau's negative reaction to this took the form of saying: Canada is bilingual, but not bicultural; rather it is multicultural. But this turned out to be only a minor part of the story. There were serious reasons within English Canada for the multicultural turn, which I will come to shortly.

II

So much for the baser political motivations for this difference in terminology. But there are more serious reasons for the semantic distinction. How could there be, one might ask, if the policies are not all that different? As a first approximation, the answer to this, in a word, might be because the rhetoric is different. What, just rhetoric? one might reply. My answer to this is that anyone who speaks of 'just rhetoric' doesn't understand politics. In fact this difference carries other serious ones in its train, which are crucial to these policies.

Let me explain. Let's agree to use the term 'multiculturalism' on two levels: as a generic term for the ensemble of policies introduced with the combined goals of recognising diversity, fostering integration and producing/maintaining equality; and then as a word designating a subspecies of such policies, to be contrasted with another subspecies, called 'intercultural'. I will go on for a while in a parochial vein, illustrating this difference from the Canadian scene, but then I will try to show that it has wider application.

So what do multicultural programmes and policies hope to effect? They start from the perception that any democratic society has a historically developed and shared culture of interaction. I am gesturing with this term at the ensemble of ways that members of the society relate to each other in a host of contexts, as fellow citizens in the polity, or as fellow members of political or other associations, or as employers and employees of an enterprise, or as merchants and customers, and so on. An understanding comes to circulate of what the normative citizen, members, employee, etc. should be like, of what is expected of him and her, as also of the different footings they should stand on with each other, the modes of intimacy or distance, the assumptions about social distance, and so on. A multicultural challenge arises when this culture defines certain sorts of people as enjoying the status of fully normative citizen, member, economic agent, and so on, enjoying the normal degree of intimacy and recognition in society; and excludes others from this status. This arises, for instance, when people of a certain historical descent are accorded, in virtue of the historical origins of the society, the status of fully normative citizen or member, while people of other origins are viewed differently. But the issue doesn't have to turn on culture in this historical sense. We can also have this imbalance in a society where women are excluded from certain roles, or are treated differently than men when they occupy these roles. Or when people of a certain sexual orientation are discriminated against.

Of course, this kind of inequality can exist for a long time in a society without this being seen as a problem. Hierarchies are often 'normalised' in this sense, even in democratic societies. It may be the general consensus that women have their 'place', and should not aspire to operate outside it; or that this society has as its basic purpose the preservation of a certain historic culture, and that thus full members of this culture have a privileged position within it. For the sense of multicultural challenge to arise, this normalisation has to to be put in question, has to be seen as a denial of equality, which is one of the crucial values of a democratic society.

The age of multiculturalism is in fact the age in which this kind of inequality has come to seem more and more indefensible. The multicultural issue is often posed in terms of natives and immigrants, or people with a long local ancestry versus those who have arrived more recently. But it can also arise because of inequalities suffered by people who have always been there, as with women or historical national minorities, but whose subordination previously seemed normal, and now no longer does so in a fully democratic age.

The challenge of multiculturalism can be met by a range of policies; but these have as a common ultimate goal that they transform the culture of interaction so as to remove the inequalities, and confer the status of normative citizen or member on everyone. But if this is going to happen, we need not only specific policies, conferring skills, like the national language, opening access to various jobs and positions, barring discrimination, and so on. We also need an articulated account of what we are doing: we need to articulate what the new culture of interaction will be, and the way it differs from the old. We need to give some expression to the new footing on which we want to be with each other, having set aside the inequalities and exclusions that characterised the old. We need a narrative of the transition that we are trying to bring about.

Let's call this articulated account, the 'story' that gives the rationale of the policies. This is what I was referring to above in my (admittedly rather flip and provocative) reference to 'rhetoric'. So my point there could be put in these terms: between Canadian multiculturalism and Quebec interculturalism the differences lie less in the concrete policies than in the stories. Admittedly, one can note a semantic distinction between the two terms that seems to point to a different inflexion of policies: if multiculturalism in the generic sense includes policies which aim at recognition of both difference and integration, one might argue that the prefix 'multi-' gives greater weight to the first goal – acknowledging diversity – while 'inter-' invokes more the facet of integration. But why this difference is important will only emerge when we look at the two stories.

So let's look at these. Basically, the story behind Canadian multiculturalism is the following: 'English' Canada, or better, anglophone Canada, used to operate within a culture of interaction in which the normative citizen traced his/her ascent from the British Isles: English and Welsh, Scottish or Irish. And sometimes discrimination was made among these, matching those prevalent in the home islands (where the Irish were emphatically not equal to the others). People of non-British origin were not quite on the same footing. This had a lot to do with the political identity of anglophone Canada, where the relation to the Empire/

Commonwealth bulked very large, and identity was further strengthened by the two world wars. Our armed services were 'royal' (Royal Canadian Air Force, Royal Canadian Navy); the excitement around the coronation of Elizabeth II was intense.

In the post-war period, we gradually moved away from this identity – though we still have the Royal Canadian Mounted Police, our 'Mounties', as a major police force on the federal level and in most provinces. There were many reasons for this, but an important one was demographic. A declining proportion of Canadians share that 'British' origin; I think it's now down to something like a third of the Canadian population. But also there was the inevitable social advance of people of other origins to positions of importance in all walks of life. That, plus the new climate of opinion developing in the West that put increasing importance on the recognition of identities (and also helped power feminist movements, those for gay rights, and so on), made the old 'Anglo-normativity' no longer tenable.

The story around Canadian multiculturalism as it developed in the 1960s and 1970s was essentially the dethroning of this Anglo-normative understanding. It had to be made clear that one was no closer to the heart of the Canadian identity if one was called Jones, than if one's name was Kowalski or Minelli. Culture, in the sense of what one received from one's origins, was sharply distinguished from citizenship. Canada, it said in the legislation, had no official culture (understood here: ancestral culture). This change was not mainly motivated by a concern for immigration policies, although multiculturalism did alter how immigrants were received, and in particular helped greatly in easing the adjustment to an important change in Canada's immigration policy which came in these years, namely, the abandonment of the bias in favour of people of European origin. A multiracial Canada is much easier to build under the philosophy of multiculturalism than it would have been under the older outlook. But in fact the pressure came largely from the older immigration: people of non-British origin had been coming in great numbers since the beginning of the twentieth century. The new definition of Canadian identity was carried through mainly with them in mind, and of course, with their support.[3]

There was, of course, resistance to this identity shift, and some of it remains. But in general, it went through with a surprising degree of support and in an atmosphere of consensus (mainly in the large cities, where most new immigrants settle). Multiculturalism became a marker of the new Canadian political identity, and Canadians often turned into those insufferable preachers, spreading the word internationally about their own success and its status as paradigm and model for everyone (a trait, ironically, that irritates us most in Americans).

III

Multiculturalism could never take in Quebec, because this story just didn't suit. First, demographically, in Quebec upwards of 70 per cent of the population is descended from the original francophone settlers. Second, their language and culture (and for a long time, their religion) have been under powerful threat of assimilation. As far as the language is concerned, there is a triple threat: an anglo majority in Canada, the overwhelming domination of the English language in North America, and on top of that comes the fact that globalisation speaks (a sort of) English. The continuance of this vibrant, creative French-speaking society on the banks of the St Lawrence is something of a miracle, but it has not happened without a long and persistent struggle. I believe that our more extreme nationalists greatly exaggerate the threats to the French language today, and what is more, often instrumentalise this fear to narrow political ends, and even worse, obsessively support restrictive legislation where we should be concerned with the quality of our French education. But nevertheless, this long struggle has left an understandable legacy of concern for the language and the identity that has been woven around it.

I mentioned above that one possible semantic distinction between the 'multi-'and the 'inter-' was that, within the dual goal of recognising difference and achieving integration, 'inter-' places a greater emphasis on the latter. Now we can see that this has to be the case in Quebec – because integration has to be a more complex goal here than in the rest of Canada. It is not just a matter of ensuring that immigrants find jobs, make contacts, join associations, in short find their place within society. Because of our situation, we have to work to ensure that that integration takes place in French rather than English. Up until the 'quiet revolution' of the 1960s, the normal path of immigrants to Quebec (mainly of course, settling in Montreal) was to integrate into the English minority (of course, this meant into the Canadian majority). In the 1960s and 1970s, particularly in face of the declining birthrate in Quebec, efforts were made to reverse this trend, culminating in the major language legislation of the 1970s. And now the tendency is for immigrants' children, schooled in French, to take their place in francophone society. But this didn't happen of itself. By contrast, in Toronto no one has to do anything to ensure that immigrants' children become anglophones. The host language there is also today's universal speech, not to mention its place in American popular culture.

So for all these reasons, the idea that one could simply dethrone the ancestral identity, and declare that Quebec had no official culture, could never take hold in this province. It sounded too close to abandoning the struggle. But does that mean that there is no way that Quebeckers can change their culture of interaction, which has in fact been very much centred on what we call 'Québécois de souche' (old-stock Quebeckers)? Is there no alternative story that can take us towards the recognition of difference, and the creation of a more equal and inclusive society?

We (Quebeckers, I mean[4]) think there is, but the story cannot simply be a carbon copy of the Canadian one. What does it look like? Something like this. Quebec society has been engaged in a long-term project not only to survive as a francophone society, but also to flourish; and indeed, to flourish as a democratic society based on equality and human rights. We invite those who come here from outside to join us (those already there) in this project as full members, which means of course, learning the language and becoming integrated into the society. But we invite them to become full members of this society, with a say like all the others, whose views and contributions count as much as those of native born. We are indeed, eager to benefit from the skills and insights that they bring to us from outside.

So the contrast is clear: the 'multi-' story decentres the traditional ethno-historical identity, and refuses to put any other in its place. All such identities coexist in the society, but none is official-ised. The 'inter-' story starts from the reigning historical identity, but sees it evolving in a process in which all citizens, of whatever identity, have a voice, and no one's input has a privileged status.

Now these stories have a peculiar status. They purport to be about what is happening, but at another level they are setting out what ought to be happening, and at another level again, they highlight one take on the extremely complex congeries of things that are in fact going on. So the contrast between the Canadian and Quebec stories may exaggerate the differences between what is actually happening. The anglo identity is still very important in anglophone Canada, for instance, and the dynamic in some regions is not totally different from what is going on in Quebec. But nevertheless these are the stories that frame debate and define the dominant interpretation of what is happening in each society.

This 'rhetorical' difference helps explain why, despite the simi-larity of policies, so much tension can arise in Canada/Quebec around the distinction 'multi-' versus 'inter-'. Observers from the rest of Canada are sometimes scandalised that Quebecans don't want to dethrone their traditional identity. It appears to outsid-ers to be a refusal to recognise diversity, whereas it can in fact be part of a different way of opening to difference. And on the other side, this insistence that Quebeckers should treat their historical identity as just one among many is often seen by Quebeckers as a refusal of the fundamental duality of Canada, as a country comprising both a francophone and an anglophone society, each integrating immigrants in its own fashion. Those who speak of 'mere' rhetoric fail to see the essential role these stories play. They see them not as interpretive accounts framing the policy decisions, but rather as simple descriptions of them. They thus too easily conclude that not accepting their story means rejecting the basic principles of recognising diversity.

IV

I want now to look more at the 'inter-' story, and the hopes and fears that arise in connection with it. Of course, this story allows that the society will develop in ways that it would not have done if only the native born were in charge. The hopes connected with that are that people coming from outside will contribute new ideas, new skills and new insights that will enrich our society. The obverse of this expectation is the fear that somehow what are considered essential features of our identity will be lost. In the Quebec case, these essential features include, understandably, the French language. After more than 200 years' struggle to maintain the centrality of French, there can be no question of abandoning it. But these are other basic elements as well. Quebec has become a liberal society, sharing the same basic ethic as other similar ones. The central features of this are human rights, equality and non-discrimination, and democracy. But beyond the language and these basic principles, there is an indefinite zone of customs, common enthusiasms (hockey), common reference points, modes of humour, and so on, each cherished to varying degrees, and more by some than by others, whose weakening, abandonment or demise may be feared.

The degree of acceptance of the intercultural story depends on the balance between these hopes and fears, and the public debate centres on them. But this debate is unavoidably imprecise and semi-articulate. As to the fear element, it seems focused disproportionately on the principles, in present-day Quebec. By that I mean that worries about the third element in our list, the customs and common reference points, and so on (let's call these 'folkways' for short) are often articulated as fears for the principles. So Quebeckers will often state their apprehension that immigrants don't want to adopt our way of life; then when asked for examples, they frequently come up with issues of male–female equality.

Now to some extent this arises from the fact that, as in other Western countries, the debate about integrating newcomers has focused disproportionately on Muslims; and fears around Muslims have focused on instances where women have been mal-treated or given inferior status. But to some extent also, the choice of these examples reflects the fact that it is generally considered more acceptable to invoke universal principles in this context of argument, rather than more 'parochial' modes of cultural unease.

The frequent invocation of male–female equality also reflects the sense that our society has made serious strides in this direction only relatively recently, and that the gains may be fragile. Will these newcomers contribute to bringing about a retreat on this front? Lots of people expressed fear on this score during the hearings of our commission.[5] These fears seem quite unfounded, since (1) Muslim Quebeckers themselves generally support these principles (indeed, often came here because of them); and (2) even if they were hostile, they are a relatively small minority. But if we see the invocation of this example as articulating a more unstructured fear about the possible loss or erosion of our way of life in its many facets, an articulation that has the advantage of being more generally acceptable, and more clearly defined, then the anxiety surrounding it becomes more understandable.

The Achilles heel of the 'inter-' story is thus the fears it can arouse that 'they' may change 'us'. The notion that 'they' can be equal collaborators in remaking our common culture rings alarm bells in all who share this anxiety. It seems safer and more sensible to insist that they conform first to what we consider the basics, before we let them become co-deciders. But this easily slides in practice towards imposing assimilation as a condition of integration; that is, towards insisting that they become like us before they can function beside us to shape our future. Logically, of course, the preconditions could be much more limited; we might just say: start learning our language and accept our basic ethic. But where even these demands are made in a spirit of fear and mistrust, and where they are motivated by a larger unstructured fear for our whole way of life, they begin to amount to something like: win back our trust (and we doubt very much that you can) before we can accept you as equals. That is, in any case, how the demands are perceived by their addressees. And we are on the road to creating and entrenching a deep rift in society, which can compromise democratic life.

Or the fear may take an alternative form. 'They' are hostile or recalcitrant to our way of life. But what they want to do is not so much transform 'us', as to set up their own self-contained communities in our midst; in short build a ghetto. In fact, 'they' are carrying out the 'multicultural' programme (as this is widely misunderstood by those who see it as favouring cultural retreat into closed communities). And they are being assisted by naïve liberals who don't realise how disastrous this is. We have to demand that they conform. (And so we come to the same policy: assimilation as a condition of integration.)

Now the push towards assimilation undercuts the intercultural scenario, as indeed, it goes against any form of multiculturalism in the generic sense. But how can one combat fears of the kind that drive this demand?

V

Here let me step beyond the parochial, and say what I have been building up to all along. The intercultural story is not simply made for Quebec. It also better suits the situation of many European countries. The features that make it applicable to Quebec also often apply in Europe. There: (1) many countries have a longstanding historic identity that is still shared by the great majority of their citizens. (2) This identity frequently centres on a language that is not spoken elsewhere, and is under pressure from larger, globalised languages. And (3) the same kind of not-fully-structured fears for the future of its culture and way of life may arise there as I noted in Quebec. Points (1) and (2) make the intercultural story a better fit than the multicultural one. Indeed, they may contribute to fears around the word 'multiculturalism' analogous to those encountered in Quebec, and to the misunderstanding that it amounts to encouraging ghettos. And at the same time, (3) may mean that a policy of openness to difference may trigger off some of the same reactions as we have found in Quebec.

These fears may be aggravated by several factors: (1) European experience as immigrant-receiving societies has been much shorter than that of societies in the Western hemisphere; (2) much of that experience occurred under (what turned out to be) a disastrously wrong story, that summed up in the term *Gastarbeiter*, the idea

342

that outsiders who came to fill the needed jobs would end up returning to their home countries, with the benefit of the funds earned during their time of employment in Europe. As a result, the necessary measures were not taken to integrate them and their children. For instance, programmes to ensure that immigrant children learn the language of the host country were not undertaken, and are only now being introduced. Also (3), as I mentioned above, there is an important difference in the level of education and skills between immigrants to Quebec and those to many European societies. The former are selected on the basis of their skills and competences, which are usually much higher than those entering Europe. They are frequently professionals, or potential occupants of middle-class jobs. They often have a level of education, and hence outlook and way of life that been influenced more by globalised trends, and thus find it easier to integrate into the host society.

The intercultural story thus faces additional obstacles and resistances to those encountered in Quebec (and God knows, they are great enough here). Because the necessary policies were late in coming, immigrant children may find themselves in an underclass where they lack the linguistic and other skills to succeed; and their skill set will probably already have been lower to begin with than their Quebec counterparts. In addition, they may be culturally more distant from the native born than we experience these days in societies in the Western hemisphere. The result can be a growing sense of alienation, especially among younger people in immigrant communities, a conviction that they are not welcomed, not treated as equals, and discriminated against in employment housing and in their treatment by police and other authorities.

This sense of alienation can lead to expressions of revolt and rejection of the host society, of the kind that were dramatically evident in the riots and car-burnings in the 'banlieues' of France in autumn 2005. Such movements obviously increase the fears of the majority, and sharpen their sense that their historic culture is under threat. Indeed, immigrant alienation and host society cultural fear are in a relation of mutual intensification. The fears stoke hostility to immigrants, and intensify demands for stern, even punitive measures of assimilation, or else more radically for

343

an end to immigration, or even a repatriation of those already present. This hostility then entrenches further immigrant alienation, which leads to further expressions of anger, and so on into a dangerous spiral.

How to stop the spiral? The best antidote, perhaps the only one, is successful enactments of the intercultural scenario. That is, leaders and members of the majority mainstream seek out leaders and members of the minorit(ies), together with them work out new ways of resolving the conflicts, and then cooperate effectively to resolve them. (This is, for instance, what Jop Cohen did when he was mayor of Amsterdam.) The ensemble of such collaborative enterprises contributes in effect to the elaboration of a new more inclusive culture of interaction.

So enactment of the scenario eases fears. But people also have to overcome their fears to enter into these enactments. So a catch-22 obstacle threatens to block our way forward. How to convince members of the mainstream to enter this kind of collaboration?

Perhaps what they need is more familiarity with the immigrant situation. And this brings me back to a point made earlier. The vast majority of immigrants to the rich countries of the North are drawn to them because they hope for a better life for themselves and their children. Indeed, millions aspire to this, and sometimes risk their life on the ocean, or crammed into containers, on the outside chance of getting in. A better life, in what sense? For some this means a place of relative freedom, of security, of human rights. But for just about everyone, it means opening possibilities for themselves or their children, particular jobs, with access to higher income, and education for their children, leading to even better occupations and greater prosperity.

Success in these endeavours creates an enormous positive bonding with the host society, a sense of gratitude and belonging that one often hears expressed by immigrants to the USA, and sometimes Canada. And this is what tends to come about, provided the hope is not negated: the avenue to the hoped-for job systematically blocked, by discrimination or other structural factors, avenues to other associations blocked by prejudices; or stigmatisation as an outsider and a danger to society. When this happens the resultant bitterness is proportionate to the dimensions of the antecedent hope, and great alienation can result. But when things go as planned, newcomers can express a patriotism that makes natives blush. (This may be particularly the case in Canada, where such fulsome expressions make people uneasy.)

In our northern societies this kind of positive bonding should not be difficult to create. It takes some special factors to wreck it. These can be geopolitical, as one sees in ex-imperial countries, where relations with the ex-colonised are compromised by a heavy and problematic past. Or hatred and resentment may be mobilised today on the geopolitical level, as with various jihadist movements in the Muslim world, and these may find recruits among immigrants in northern societies. But for the most part these movements have little success without a hefty assist from high levels of hostility and exclusion generated within these northern societies themselves. Alienation within these societies is to a great extent created by the fear and mistrust people in the host country have generated against the new arrivals.

This is a sad fact, but it can be seen as a basis of hope: that more open policies may turn the situation around, and reverse the spiral. Enactments of the intercultural scenario thus inspire further such enactments, and make the story itself come true.

VI

Let me try to draw together some of the threads of this discussion. I started off in section I looking at the distinction that has come to be made in Canada/Quebec between multiculturalism and interculturalism. I argued that beyond the misunderstandings, whether genuine or politically motivated, there is an important distinction here, which touches not so much the description of the detailed policies hatched under these terms, as the overall story of what we are trying to do, and of how things are meant to unfold. In the light of this difference, it is highly understandable that Quebec should have preferred what it calls interculturalism to Canadian multiculturalism, as the scenario it desires to follow.

But I think this is of more than parochial Quebec/Canada interest. Some of the reasons that make interculturalism right for Quebec apply also to some European countries. The issues involved in their situation might be more clearly discernible if seen in the light of this story, rather than the multicultural one. And so I thought that a discussion of the dynamic of fears and hopes that we see arising around Quebec's intercultural story might help shed some light on the parallel situations that we find in Europe. This is what occupied the fourth and fifth sections of my chapter. I am admittedly obsessed by the situation in my own (double) country. But my excuse for dwelling on this at great length is the hope that the concepts worked out here may be somewhat helpful elsewhere.

Acknowledgements

This chapter is a modified version of C. Taylor (2012), 'Interculturalism or multiculturalism?', *Philosophy and Social Criticism*, 38:4–5, 413–23. In writing this chapter, I have been greatly helped by discussions with Gérard Bouchard, both during our time as co-chairs of the Quebec Commission on Reasonable Accommodation, and since. I have also benefited from the comments of and/or discussion with David Miller, Varun Uberoi and Tariq Modood.

Notes

1. See W. Kymlicka (2007), 'Distangling the debate', in J. Stein (ed.) *Uneasy Partners: Multiculturalism and Rights in Canada* (Waterloo, ON: Wilfrid Laurier University Press).
2. This was the term put forward by André Laurendeau, and the commission he co-chaired was called the Royal Commission on Bilingualism and Biculturalism.
3. Of course, the change in policy went along with a reconceptualisation of Canadian history, which made the change seem less striking, by highlighting the aspects of our past that foreshadowed the multicultural era. Like many 'inventions of tradition', this had a kernel of truth, but it also underplayed the scope and the intensity of the change. The scope, because this proto-multiculturalism operated among the Caucasian populations that made up the bulk of the older immigration. Japanese and Chinese immigrants on the West coast certainly were not treated in this spirit. The intensity, because

prior to the change, the spirit of anglo-normativity was still present and active, whereas with the new policy it lost the last thread of legitimacy.

4. The reader may notice that my use of the first person plural pronoun varies in reference. Sometimes I refer to 'us Canadians', and sometimes to 'us Québécois'. I hope the reference is clear in each case. But the slide from one to the other is unavoidable in those with dual identity.

5. I am referring to the 'Commission de Consultation sur les pratiques d'Accommodement Raisonnable reliées aux différences culturelles (CCPARDC)', which the Quebec government set up in 2007 (it was reported in 2008). Gérard Bouchard and I chaired the Commission.

13

Rethinking Multiculturalism, Interculturalisms and the Majority

Tariq Modood

One of the central themes of Bhikhu Parekh's masterpiece, *Rethinking Multiculturalism* (*RM*)[1] is the political importance of intercultural dialogue. While dialogue was present in other statements of multiculturalism, *RM* made it more central; for example in contrast to one, if not the leading, political theory of multiculturalism up to that point, namely that of Will Kymlicka,[2] which prioritised constitutional and legal rights, territorial autonomy and formal representation. Parekh's emphasis on intercultural dialogue has been said to mark the end of multiculturalism and a transition to interculturalism.[3] I see no grounds for this judgement, but it does provoke the question, what is interculturalism and what is its relation to multiculturalism? I suggest that interculturalism does not have one meaning but has two quite different versions that I will refer to as European interculturalism (IC-E) and Quebecan interculturalism (IC-Q).[4] The former, with its exclusive focus on individuals, interpersonal encounters and cultural mixing however, is not at all close to *RM* and because I have discussed it elsewhere with Nasar Meer[5] I will make only a brief reference to it here. Quebecan interculturalism, however, is radically different and is consistent with the ideas of national community and group accommodation that are part of the political core of *RM*, and it is this interculturalism (IC-Q) and its relation to multiculturalism (MC) that I wish to explore here.

Interculturalisms

Let me briefly illustrate what I mean by IC-E by reference to a recent book-length statement published subsequent to the discussion in Meer and Modood (2012). The book I have in mind is Ted Cantle's *Interculturalism: the New Era of Cohesion and Diversity*, 2012. The central argument of Cantle's book is that mass migrations and urban super-diversity are inevitable in an age of globalisation, and so national, ethnic and communal identities will seem irrelevant as individuals, through diverse neighbourhoods, foreign travel, work abroad, global media and online social networks will be in constant interaction across cultural and national boundaries, which inevitably will decompose and individuals come to have, and be comfortable with, hybridic, fluid and multiple identities of their own and of others.[6] I do not think Cantle's book occasions any revision of my previous views. I hope it is quite clear from the very brief summary that I have offered that Cantle's IC is a version of cosmopolitanism, that is to say, the view that people are rightly thinking increasingly of themselves as global citizens and identifying with humanity in a post-national way. As such it has certain normative and sociological strengths but also does not analytically capture the full range of contemporary ethnic, religious and national identities and their legitimate claims, no less than that of cosmopolitans, to be recognised politically.[7] It is not an alternative to MC but a valuable complement to a communitarian multiculturalism and indeed to other modes of integration. Nevertheless, it is antipathetic to *RM*. The moral communities and traditions that in *RM* are seen to be at the centre of multiculturalism, indeed at the centre of human existence, have virtually no presence in Cantle or in European interculturalism generally.

My main interest is to use the occasion of the suggestion that interculturalism is an alternative to multiculturalism to examine the Quebecan version as expressed in two recent publications. One is the preceding chapter in this volume by Charles Taylor[8] and the other is Gerard Bouchard's article 'What is interculturalism?'.[9] While the former deals specifically with some of the distinctive resonances that the terms 'multiculturalism' and 'interculturalism' have in Quebec, the latter is one of the fullest statements and justification of IC-Q, and its contrast to MC, in English, and will be the principal object of my engagement. A preliminary remark is that while it is clear that this version of IC owes considerably, perhaps everything, to a Quebecan struggle for the rest of Canada to recognise it as a founding nation, and a refusal to be defined within the terms of Canadian MC, my interest is not in this provenance.[10] Indeed, one of the striking features of these two texts, especially Bouchard's, is that IC is not defined in terms of its aptness in contexts of minority nationhood, where a nation like Quebec is a minority within a larger state, and while IC is presented as an alternative to and superior to Canadian MC, it is not conceptualised in terms of the relation of one nation to another. Bouchard does not mention minority national identity in his account of IC, which he says distinctively 'concerns itself with the interests of the majority culture'[11] and Taylor explicitly concludes his discussion of the meaning of IC in Quebec by suggesting that it may fit majoritarian anxieties in Europe.[12] My interest in IC is at this level of general applicability, regardless of its origins, though I note that this has a certain real-world logic too. If Quebec were an independent state, its government and publics would presumably continue to subscribe to IC. They would not say that interculturalism was no longer more suited to Quebec than MC just because Quebeckers had a state of their own. Quebecan interculturalism (IC-Q) is thus about integration in relation to a national state and not in relation to a minority nation. It is however worth noting tht while Taylor now uses 'interculturalism' to capture the desire of the Quebecan *majority* to preserve its culture, in his famous essay on multiculturalism, Quebeckers are the central illustration of the right of a *minority* to preserve its culture.[13]

Explicitly drawing on 'authors from Quebec who have a long history of reflecting on the topic', Bouchard considers IC to be a model that 'aims at integration within a single nation',[14] which, as a pluralist model, 'concerns itself with the interests of the majority culture, whose desire to perpetuate and maintain itself is perfectly legitimate, *as much as* it does with the interests of minorities and immigrants'.[15] As an aside, it is worth reflecting upon the highlighted 'as much as'. It seems reasonable but it is not usually how egalitarian perspectives are stated; such perspectives normally assume a starting point where one party's interests need to be highlighted. Feminism, for example, does not normally consist of the view that men do not have legitimate interests but rather that they are in the main already catered for, or over-catered for, or can best be met by considering the interests of women more than hitherto.

Of the various characteristics Bouchard offers of IC I will consider only two, the two that I believe are distinctive to his version of IC: a *diversity/duality distinction* and a *majority cultural precedence*, which presupposes an assumption of duality. My purpose, then, is not to summarise Bouchard's multi-aspected position but to bring out, explore and learn from what I think is distinctive about his IC and challenging for MC as I understand it. While Bouchard's conception of IC is based on a contrast with MC, and this contrast is rooted in his understanding of the discourses and policies of Federal Canada and Quebec, nevertheless he wants to theorise at a more general level, and illustrates his argument by reference to a number of countries. For example, in relation to the first point I am interested in, he holds that MC takes different form in different countries and changes over time (and not just in one direction) but to the extent that it is MC it exists in a 'diversity' model. The central feature of a diversity paradigm is 'there is no recognition of a majority culture and, in consequence, no minorities per se'.[16] Bouchard sometimes refers to the inherently individualistic character of MC;[17] which for a European is very confusing, as in Europe IC is the individual-friendly correction of 'groupist' MC,[18] but that is not the issue. The key idea of diversity is that all individuals and groups are on an equal footing. Without using the same analytical framework or vocabulary, Taylor takes the same view: 'the "multi-" story decentres the traditional ethnohistorical identity and refuses to put any other in its place. All such identities coexist in the society, but none is officialized'.[19] They are both clearly thinking of federal Canadian MC, as put by Pierre Trudeau: 'although there are two official languages, there is no official culture, nor does any ethnic group take precedence over any other'.[20]

IC by contrast, 'as a global model for social integration . . .

takes shape within the duality paradigm':[21] a recognition of 'the majority/minorities duality . . . an us–them divide'.[22] 'More precisely', Bouchard says,

> I am referring to the anxiety that the majority culture can feel in the face of cultural minorities. Indeed, they can create a more or less acute sense of threat within the majority culture not only in terms of its rights, but also in terms of its values, traditions, language, memory and identity (not to mention its security).[23]

This is an interesting contrast but I do not think it does the work that Bouchard wants it to do. First, it is not clear that it adequately distinguishes different states. Bouchard believes that a number of countries have at some time or other during the past fifty years or so, partly or fully, embraced diversity, that is, denied that there are minorities/majorities and have disavowed an official recognition of a (historical) culture: USA, Federal Canada, Australia and Britain are mentioned explicitly. This characterisation of each of these countries can be disputed, though I will not pursue that here. Note, however, that Bouchard thinks that they have been moving away from diversity to duality in recent years – exactly the opposite sense that Cantle and cosmopolitan interculturalists have of where the world is going.[24]

Related to this, and second, the term 'diversity' is often appropriated by certain critics of MC. Bouchard has chosen a term to characterise MC that is the term of choice of those who offer an anti-groupist and individualist alternative to MC.[25] Similarly, its presence in the approach known as 'diversity management' positively expresses an individualistic understanding of 'difference' as an alternative to MC and related egalitarian approaches,[26] and not just in the anglophone sphere, but also in France.[27] So, at a minimum, Bouchard's diversity/duality distinction risks cross-national misunderstandings.

My first reservation about whether any Western country has in practice ever denied the existence of a foundational or official culture in the name of MC might be countered by saying that some intellectuals and politicians have flirted with this idea; and my second point, that Bouchard's vocabulary confuses MC with that of its critics who self-define around a concept of 'diversity', may be regarded as unfortunate but not major objections. But my third point is the one I want to press here. Bourchard does not distinguish IC-Q from MC at a conceptual level.

It is true that an emphasis on majoritiarian anxieties is a radically different starting point from MC. The latter originates in a sensitivity to the condition of minorities: with negative perceptions and treatment of minorities in the form of racist stereotypes, group labels, misrecognition, discrimination, exclusion, marginalisation and various other forms of inequality that are centred around the existence of a public space that reflects the culture of some citizens and not others.[28] Nevertheless, it should be apparent from the last sentence that MC is framed within the majority–minority duality; at the very least its starting point is an 'us–them divide'. My own way of expressing this is that MC begins with 'the fact of negative difference . . . an unequal "'us–them'" relationship'.[29] I begin with 'difference' and speak of minorities (as does *RM* and all the MC positions that I know) and so, once again, it is not MC but IC-E or cosmopolitanism that seems to fit 'diversity' and seems to be Bouchard's unintended target.

Majority precedence

I turn now to the second of Bouchard's two defining ideas of IC: 'While seeking an equitable interaction between continuity and diversity, interculturalism allows for the recognition of certain elements of ad hoc (or contextual) precedence for majority culture'.[30] Lest there is a misunderstanding, he adds immediately: 'I say *ad hoc* because it is out of the question to formalise or establish this idea as a general legal principle, which would lead to the creation of two classes of citizens.'[31] Taylor seems to be making the same qualified claim when he writes: 'The 'inter-' story starts from the reigning historical identity but sees it evolving in a process in which all citizens, of whatever identity, have a voice, and no one's input has a privileged status'.[32]

So, while for Rattansi[33] and other European authors intercultural dialogue and exchange are the key characteristics of interculturalism and the best characteristics of MC,[34] these are not the key features of the IC of Bouchard and Taylor. The idea of majority precedence I believe constitutes a significant difference from most accounts of MC.[35] Moreover, it is different from classical assimilation and liberal individualism, which do not seek a lower status for minorities so much as their gradual dissolution and the confinement of 'difference' to private spaces and weekends. Moreover, while Bouchard contrasts his perspective with liberalism in several places, it could be said that his ideas here are within a touching distance of at least one version of liberal nationalism, namely, that expressed very recently by Tim Soutphommaasane, which includes the claim that 'the liberal nationalist suggests that any minority cultural identity should be subordinated to the national identity',[36] and Geoff Levey has expressly argued that Australian multiculturalism as state policy has always recognised the foundational character of Anglo-Australian majority culture.[37]

Bouchard argues that it is difficult, given that it is emphatically not to be given a legal or official status, to express what this precedence means in the abstract. Hence he gives some examples of legitimate and illegitimate precedence from the Canadian and Quebec context. I do not have the space here to consider such nationally specific examples and to do so would distract from the idea of majority precedence as such and in what way it is different to and a challenge to MC. Bouchard's emphasis on majority precedence, while by no means the only point of interest in his complex position, is most challenging for multiculturalists, as it is fair to say multiculturalists have not addressed the issue about the majority and do need to do so. Of course multiculturalists have written a lot on the remaking of a national citizenship in order to make it more inclusive (on national identity, see Chapter 3 by Varun Uberoi and his forthcoming piece on *The Parekh Report*[38]), as that is central to multiculturalism as I understand it;[39] so perhaps it is not entirely accurate to say that multiculturalists have neglected to note the normative significance of the majority *tout court*. Insofar as multiculturalists distinguish between the majority culture and the public or civic culture, it is about the tendency of the majority culture to dominate and pass itself off as the whole of the national culture. It is assumed that a minority culture can be identified as distinct from what it needs to be included into but much less is said about the majority culture in this respect. I confess to being guilty here. Stimulated by this sense of neglect I would like to reflect on the place of the majority in MC.[40]

Having admitted that multiculturalists have not engaged much with the concept of 'the majority', I think a good way to approach Bouchard's view on this topic and to consider what multiculturalists may learn from it is to ask what might be the current view of the concept of the majority implicit in MC. What I have said to date about minorities in relation to the majority can be summarised in terms of two 'protectionist' statements and two positive statements:

1. There should be protection from racism, cultural racism and Islamophobia (not from the majority culture *per se*).
2. There should be no insistence on assimilation, but nor should anything hinder the uncoercive social processes of assimilation or self-chosen assimilation; different modes of integration should be equally welcomed.
3. There should be multicultural accommodation of minorities within shared public institutions.
4. Minorities should be able to make claims on national culture and identity in their own ways and this remaking of national identity is part of multicultural citizenship and should be welcomed and encouraged by the majority.

So, while multiculturalists may need to think more about 'the majority', it is not the case that existing theories are *negative* about majority culture *per se*, or even that multiculturalism is about protecting minorities from majority culture.

Let me consider what I think are the three main arguments for 'majority precedence'. Bouchard's distinctiveness is not in the arguments as such but in their deployment to support the idea of majority precedence. I accept the starting points of the arguments but not the conclusions. The arguments show that the majority culture has a normative significance, but not normative precedence if that means the majority can make normative claims that minorities cannot make, or that there is always some *prima facie* presumption in favour of the majority culture.

No *neutral space*

Here the idea seems to be that liberal or democratic or secular states, 'beyond their founding principles, values, norms and laws' 'typically incorporate a number of contextual and historical elements'.[41] Such states have a national identity that is not reducible to universal laws and norms or even to a legal–political framework, and also have a cultural aspect – such as a language(s), a specific history, a religion or set of religions, national memories and an official calendar, ceremonies, memorials and other symbols marked by these religions and histories; and this culture is central to what state-funded schools are required to teach. While these national identities should be common to all citizens they are inevitably deeply shaped by 'the majority culture', parts of which may sometimes even be indistinguishable from the 'national culture'. Liberal states may aspire to be culturally neutral but all societies must have a symbolic-normative core that acts as an integrative mechanism, and liberal states are no exception. In short, liberal democratic states are not a neutral public space but have a cultural character in which the majority culture has a legitimate precedence.

I fully endorse the impossibility of a neutral public space but query the implication of precedence. I can see that by the mere fact of what I might call 'sociological privilege', members of the majority culture will enjoy advantages of identification, access, discursive and other capabilities – in short a certain kind of cultural capital or cultural power – over those less steeped in the majority and therefore the national culture. Yet while it does not follow that those advantages are unfair – given that there is not a neutral public space, some will always have some advantages of that kind relative to others. Neither, however, does it follow that some particular normative precedence should be acknowledged by all, in addition to these socio-cultural advantages. If Bouchard means that the sociological precedence, the fact of the power imbalance, the mechanisms by which the majority culture reproduces itself, incorporates minorities and manages change is not illegitimate *per se*, is not necessarily illegitimate, that would be right and is a useful point to make if some multiculturalists and theorists imply that it is necessarily illegitimate. But it is not legitimate in all instances either. In talking of national culture and citizenship we necessarily invoke a concept of equality and therefore have to formulate concepts of intercultural dialogue as Parekh does in *RM*, or of oppression in relation to public culture as Iris Young does,[42] or concepts such as misrecognition as Taylor does[43] in order to identify the ways in which minorities can have their claim to equal dignity and equal respect ignored or compromised. Positive aspects of this equality can include the expunging of racist language and imagery from the public space or widening the register of symbolic prestige to include demeaned and marginal groups. The fact that a polity cannot be culturally void of content or neutral between all cultures does not mean that the concept of equality becomes secondary to majority precedence.

Identity preservation

This argument is that '[i]n order for the majority group to pre-serve the cultural and symbolic heritage that serves as the foun-dation of its identity and helps to ensure its continuity, it can legitimately claim some element of contextual precedence based on its seniority or history'.[44]

Here I query if the right to identity preservation – with which I have no quarrel – depends on 'seniority or history'? If yes, then by definition no new minority has a right to identity preservation, which is a very extreme view, and I do not think there is any-thing to indicate that it is Bouchard's view. If, however, minori-ties do have a right to identity preservation, then such a right depends not on 'seniority or history', but on being a group that is not harming anyone. In which case, the majority does have this (qualified) right, but so do the minorities. Sometimes, there will be clashes and we will have to work out ways to handle them, but automatic precedence of one party over the other does not emerge simply because of seniority or history, as there will be other considerations to take into account, such as individual rights, marginal utility, the vulnerability of a culture and some sense of fairness and even-handedness such that one argument like historical precedence does not unduly trump all others.

Indeed, the relatively secure place of the majority, their enjoyment of 'sociological privilege' and cultural power to reproduce themselves and to extend to minorities what majorities claim for themselves is one of the origins of MC. Every group and not just a majority should have a prima facie right to identity preservation (as long as the rights and interest of others – groups and individuals – are taken into account, the cost is not too high, and so on). Multiculturalists are mindful of how minorities can be under various pressures to assimilate, and can become anxious about their identities and so argue that minorities should be allowed to preserve, change and adapt in their own way and at their own pace. Bouchard usefully alerts us to the fact that under some conditions, which seem to be growing today, the majority may feel anxious about a sense of cultural loss, of losing control over the pace of identity change. Multiculturalists normally assume that the majority already has what the minority is seeking, but suppose it has not? Or parts of it – such as say, parts of the white working class – have not? As a matter of fact, the growing presence and empowerment of minorities, the multiculturalist project, itself may be a cause for identity anxiety among the majority.[45] Where this is the case multiculturalists need to show the same sensitivity to change and identity anxiety in relation to the majority as to the minority. This may lead to some political difficulties at times but there is a theoretical problem as such. After all, one of the fundamental philosophical arguments for minority recognition is based on a dialogical or relational sense of identity, which posits that it is not only members of minorities whose sense of self and self-worth is dependent on the perceptions and treatment of the majority, but also vice versa.[46] So, where appropriate, emphasising mutual recognition, or as Bouchard puts it, reciprocity, and not merely minority accommodation, may be a political adjustment but is not a philosophical difficulty for multiculturalists. Multiculturalists can, therefore, acknowledge that the majority and minorities have a right to be supported through state structures and policies without conceding that the majority has an exclusive right to identity preservation or the precedence of seniority, let alone the right to suppress a minority's right to publicly express and preserve its identity, simply because that would mean the public space is less reflective of majority culture.

National culture as 'useful and necessary'

The last argument I will examine is the suggestion that the fact of non-neutrality, which means that every liberal democratic state has a distinctive national–cultural identity, can be 'useful and necessary even in a liberal democratic state. For example, it allows for the consolidation of national identity, which is at once a source of solidarity and a foundation for responsible citizen participation and social justice'.[47] Bouchard cites a number of authors who hold this view, including several multiculturalists, including me, and also liberal nationalists such as David Miller, who is among those who have argued this most fully.[48] Some of us have utilised this argument without the implication of majority precedence. The argument establishes that a national–cultural identity, because of its linkage with national citizenship, has some political and normative significance but is only acceptable as such if interpreted in a very liberal way: for example, if racist or intolerant aspects of the national culture get dropped. Individuals and groups have some freedom in emphasising different aspects of the national identity, which are differently and freely interpreted and allowed to change over time and through the inclusion of new groups. State-manufactured identities are not imposed on people and there is no expectation that a national identity – shared with minorities but largely reflective of the majority – must be everyone's most important and cherished identity and must always trump all other identities.

In this way the national identity and its component parts, including key aspects of the majority culture, has to be made consistent with democratic values such as liberty, equality and fraternity and can therefore in principle also be consistent with multicultural citizenship. In this formation too, the majority culture does not enjoy a unique position. Minority identities such as that of Catholics or of black people, or specifically in relation to my own work, Muslim civic identities also participate in and thereby both potentially adapt and support the shared citizenship.[49] Of course they may do so in different ways and in the process extend and complexify the relevant conception of national citizenship, giving it a multicultural character. I think that in principle all group identities can and should be encouraged (but not pressured) to support and adapt citizenship in this way. This is best done through dialogues or multilogues in which conceptions of citizenship and corresponding national identities are contested and reworked. Dialogue is indeed an idea central to multicultural citizenship and *pace* certain versions of IC, it is not thought of only in relation to micro, everyday interactions but also in relation to controversies as for example Parekh in *RM* demonstrates in relation to *The Satanic Verses* affair, where the majority have a chance to make their point but often do so in a manner that is not conducive to dialogue or mutual learning.[50] Parekh shows that such dialogues inevitably have a majoritarian or status quo starting point, because even while wanting to express unfamiliar sensibilities and bring in new arguments minorities are primarily trying to persuade the majority that what they are seeking is not so different to what the majority at one time or another has sought for itself and in so arguing the minority must justify itself by appealing to – even while seeking to modify – the existing operative public values that structure public debate and what is thought to be legitimate or reasonable in that polity at the time.[51]

These three arguments (no neutral space; identity preservation; national culture as useful and necessary) then press multiculturalists to acknowledge not just recognition of minorities but also mutual or multilogical recognition, and thereby to be sensitive to anxieties about threats to identity on the part of the majority as well as of minorities. They also remind us that the power of the majority to preserve their culture and to enshrine it within a national identity supported by the state is not necessarily illegitimate, though it does not invalidate multiculturalist concerns about the ways majorities can oppress, misrecognise and marginalise, formally and informally. These arguments that I have been discussing do not establish a majority precedence and are not a basis for repudiating the multiculturalistist project of remaking national citizenships so that all citizens can see themselves in the national identity and achieve a sense of belonging together. A living national identity is a work in progress, a conversation between where we are coming from and where we are going. The past is central to the sense of nationhood today, we have to be able to see it as our past, as how it has formed us, but equally we must appreciate the country we are becoming. It is a story in which the white or ethnic majority is central but it is a developing story, and one in which new minorities too are characters and not just replicas of the majority or mere 'add-ons'.

Given that I do not think that the priority of the majority culture in the national identity and public culture is necessarily illegitimate and Bouchard is explicit that the principle of precedence can be abused, it may well be asked how substantive are our differences? I mentioned that Bouchard draws on some of the controversies today in Quebec and Canada to illustrate what he thinks is legitimate from illegitimate majority precedence. While I do not want to get drawn on the specifics of those cases, nevertheless, I do owe some examples in order to give content to my own position and that is what I would like to do by way of concluding. I take two examples from education.

Two examples

Many liberal democratic countries have a statutory national curriculum for all state schools.[52] That is a legitimate thing for a state to have. It is also legitimate for the nation to be the reference point for most of the curriculum, rather than a region or a locality or the composition of a specific school, though they too may be relevant. Yet that still leaves open the question of the content of the national curriculum. For a start the national curriculum must not be reducible to the majority culture or be a synonym for it: the national curriculum must seek to include aspects of the presence of minorities and their contribution to the ongoing development of the country. So in relation to history it would be illegitimate for it to be just what in the UK, or perhaps mainly in England, we call 'our island story'. A narrative of the various peoples – ancient and modern – who have come to and settled in Britain – mainly violently up to 1066 and peacefully since then, thus continually changing and shaping and being absorbed by what today we may call majority culture. It should in the British case include histories of how the British encountered and conquered various peoples, and something about the histories of those people before and after these encounters and conquests. It should show how the history of the country was changed by the encounter and so how today we have come to have the ethnic composition that we have (as is said: 'we are over here because you were over there'), how the national identity has become multi-stranded and has expanded and contracted over time as one-time minorities, like various waves of refugees, have become part of the nation or as some have sought to leave the union such as most of the island of Ireland and others have sought to change the terms of membership and to adjust majority–minority relations, usually in the direction of greater equality.

The national history will therefore not be simply a history of the majority; indeed it will show how compositions of the majority are themselves a feature of historical evolution. Jews for example were and are a minority when we conceive the majority to be Christians but are part of the majority if we think in terms of white, black, brown, red and yellow. Moreover, each new generation does not simply add a new chapter to an ever-expanding book but it rethinks the whole story; new emphases, under-appreciated themes and storylines, the significance of certain actions, such as the British Empire, emerge and grow. In the absence of the mass migrations from countries like India and Jamaica, certain events of the past – such as the large contribution of Indian soldiers in the two world wars – may seem marginal but should come to be significant in the national narrative today. While a national history will be for the most part what today's majority thinks of as its history, it is legitimate to prescribe it alongside, indeed as part of the national goal of producing citizens for a multicultural nation of tomorrow. It would be illegitimate if the national were simply identified as the history of the majority, if the national identity were presented as less than open to and inclusive of minority citizens, and if no effort was made to revise the history syllabus so that all the citizens-to-be can see how the minorities are part of the national story.

Let me take one other school subject, religion. It is clear that in the present phase of multiculturalism debates, religion has come to have a centrality and is the subject of most of the controversy associated with multiculturalism. Most people accept a distinction between religious instruction (RI), which is the teaching of how to become a member of a certain faith, and religious education (RE), which is the learning of a variety of faith traditions and their past and current effects upon individuals and societies, upon the shaping of humanity, and is taught to classes comprising those of all religions and those of none. It is fairly uncontroversial in many countries that religious education should be part of a national curriculum.[53] So, the main issue in relation to majority precedence is in relation to RI. Broadly speaking there are two majoritarian possibilities. First, we have a society where there is a majority religion and that alone is allowed as RI. Minorities might be exempted from these classes but no alternative RI is provided. Or second, the majority view is that there should be no RI in state schools, as in the USA. Is it fair to impose either of these policies on minorities that do want RI?

That is certainly an appropriate subject for a national dialogue but if after that certain minorities want RI as well as RE, then a truly national system, certainly a multicultural system, must make an effort to accommodate minority RI. In my understanding then, under both the majoritarian possibilities the minorities should have their religions instructed or practised within the national system. On the other hand, minorities do not have the right to stop the majority from including the instruction of their religion. We should not, for example, ask schools to cease Christian RI or worship or celebrating Christmas because of the presence of Muslims or Hindus; rather, we should extend the celebrations to include Eid and Diwali, for example. Muslims and other religious minorities in Europe are seeking accommodation within something resembling the *status quo*, not a dispossession of Christian churches, and so what we are really seeing is an *additive* not a *subtractive* view of inclusivity.[54] The challenge is not

363

how to de-Christianise Western states but how to appropriately add the new faiths alongside the older ones in ways that are faithful to national cultures but also adapting them so they are inclusive in this additive sense. All the evidence suggests that this is what most minorities, especially Muslims, want, certainly in Britain.[55] It is not the case, as a political scientist recently put it, that 'accommodating Muslims in the political sphere certainly requires abandoning a commitment to the Christian norms that have, historically, defined European states.'[56] The challenge is not how to de-Christianise states like ours but how to appropriately add the new faiths alongside the older ones. This indeed is what is gradually happening across much of Western Europe, albeit in an ad hoc and uneven way. What is interesting is that those most uncomfortable with this are not Christians or churches but ideological secularists.

These two examples, then, illustrate what I take to be a multiculturalist recognition of the legitimate claims and limits of majority culture. The majority may insist that the history curriculum centre on how the majority came to be formed as a nation and a polity, but they may not exclude the minorities from that story. The majority may include – in addition to, not as a substitution for an RE, which includes all religions – the instruction of the majority religion(s), or the majority may choose to not have its religion(s) instructed in state schools, but it cannot impose its preference in this regard upon minorities, who must be given the option to have their religion instructed in state schools or not, independently of what the majority may decide for itself. The national, then, must aspire to be more than merely the majority or merely 'difference-blind', it must be genuinely inclusive. If IC-E is for dethroning the inherited national identity and leaving that space blank, and IC-Q is for embracing while opening up the national identity, MC is about opening up and replacing the national identity if closed and for embracing if plural. In the national identity the majority clearly has centrality, but it is only legitimate if we work to make the national identity a true reflection of the citizenship and so to extend 'precedence', not hoard it.

Acknowledgements .

This chapter is a modified version of my 'Multiculturalism, inter-culturalisms and the majority', *Journal of Moral Education*, June 2014. I am grateful for comments on earlier drafts from Joe Carens, Terrell Carver, Nicole Hossan, Geoff Levey, David Miller, Bhikhu Parekh and Varun Uberoi.

Notes

1. B. Parekh (2000/2006), *Rethinking Multiculturalism: Cultural Diversity and Political Theory* (Basingstoke and New York: Macmillan).
2. W. Kymlicka (1995), *Multicultural Citizenship* (Oxford and New York: Oxford University Press).
3. A. Rattansi (2011), *Multiculturalism: A Very Short Introduction* (Oxford and New York: Oxford University Press).
4. G. Bouchard and C. Taylor (2012), *Building The Future: A Time for Reconciliation*, Commission de consultation sur les pratiques d'accommodement reliées aux différences culturelles (Quebec: Government of Quebec), p. 118, states that the first record of the term 'interculturalism' in Quebec is in 1985 and prior to this they could only find two references, a Council of Europe and a Belgian government document, both dated 1981. So, it seems that 'interculturalism' is only about fifteen years behind the emergence of 'multiculturalism', in the late 1960s, and that it originated in Europe, emerging in Quebec soon afterwards. The idea of 'intercultural education' is probably older still.
5. N. Meer and T. Modood (2012), 'How does interculturalism contrast with multiculturalism?', *Journal of Intercultural Studies*, 33:2, 175–96.
6. For Cantle's own summary, see T. Cantle (2012), 'Interculturalism: for the era of globalisation, cohesion and diversity', *Political Insight*, 3:3, 38–41.
7. T. Modood (2012), *Post-Immigration 'Difference' and Integration: The Case of Muslims in Western Europe* (London: The British Academy, February).
8. Originally published as C. Taylor (2012), 'Interculturalism or multiculturalism?', *Philosophy and Social Criticism*, 38:4–5, 413–23.

9. G. Bouchard (2011), 'What is interculturalism?', *McGill Law Journal*, 56:2, pp. 435–68.
10. On which see D. Weinstock (2013), 'Interculturalism and multiculturalism in Canada and Quebec: situating the debate', in P. Balint and S. Guerard de Latour (eds) *Liberal Multiculturalism and the Fair Terms of Integration* (Basingstoke and New York: Palgrave).
11. Bouchard, 'What is interculturalism?', p. 438.
12. Taylor, this volume, pp. 345–6; and 'Interculturalism or multiculturalism?', p. 420.
13. C. Taylor (1994), 'Multiculturalism and 'The politics of recognition'', in A. Gutmann (ed.) *Multiculturalism and 'The Politics of Recognition'* (Princeton, NJ: Princeton University Press).
14. Bouchard 'What is interculturalism?', p. 439.
15. Ibid., p. 438; my emphasis.
16. Ibid., p. 441.
17. Ibid., p. 464.
18. e.g. Council of Europe (2008), 'Living together as equals in dignity', White Paper on intercultural dialogue, Strasbourg.
19. Taylor, this volume, pp. 338–9; and 'Interculturalism or multiculturalism?', 418.
20. House of Commons (1971), *Debates* (Ottawa: The Queen's Printer).
21. Bouchard, 'What is interculturalism?', p. 445.
22. Ibid., p. 443.
23. Ibid., p. 443.
24. These issues are matters of debate in Europe too, but no European country has come close to the view that there is no such thing as a national historic culture, and few MCs are demanding that they do, a position that comes closer to cosmopolitanism than multiculturalism; and actually the same tensions exist within IC-Q too: B. Maxwell, D. I. Waddington, K. McDonough, A.-A. Cormier and M. Schwimmer (2012), 'Interculturalism, multiculturalism and the state funding and regulation of conservative religious schools', *Educational Theory*, 62:4, 427–47.
25. cf. T. Faist (2009), 'Diversity – a new mode of incorporation?', *Ethnic and Racial Studies*, 32:1.
26. J. Kandola and R. S. Fullerton (1994), *Managing the Mosaic: Diversity in Action* (London: Chartered Institute of Personnel and Development); J. Wrench and T. Modood (2001), *The Effectiveness of Racial Equality Employment Policies in the UK* (Geneva: International Labour Office).
27. Charte de la Diversité en Enterprise (2014), *The French Diversity*

Charter, available at www.diversity-charter.com (accessed 17 January 2014).

28. T. Modood (2007), *Multiculturalism: A Civic Idea* (Cambridge: Polity), pp. 37–41, pp. 34–7.

29. Ibid., p. 37, p. 34.

30. Bouchard, 'What is interculturalism?', p. 451.

31. Ibid., p. 451.

32. Taylor, this volume, p. 339; and 'Multiculturalism', p. 418.

33. Rattansi, *Multiculturalism*.

34. Ibid., pp. 152, 160.

35. In a private communication Bouchard has said that he thinks I am 'making way too much of the idea of precedence'. He says that he sees it as 'stemming from a sociological necessity . . . every society, in order to function and to survive, needs a strong symbolic foundation', and his 'point is that it should be preserved not as the culture or identity of the majority . . . but as a necessary social feature'. I have reread his article in the light of this communication and do not feel the need to make any changes to my text.

36. T. Soutphommaasane (2012), *The Virtuous Citizen: Patriotism in a Multicultural Society* (Cambridge: Cambridge University Press), p. 76.

37. G. B. Levey (2008), 'Multiculturalism and Australian national identity', in G. B. Levey (ed.) *Political Theory and Australian Multiculturalism* (New York: Berghahn Books).

38. V. Uberoi (accepted, forthcoming), 'The Parekh Report: national identities without nations and nationalism', *Ethnicities*.

39. Modood, *Multiculturalism*.

40. I appreciate that examples are necessary to understand general propositions, and offer two detailed examples below.

41. Bouchard, 'What is interculturalism?', p. 453.

42. I. Young (1990), *Justice and the Politics of Difference* (Princeton: Princeton University Press).

43. Taylor, 'Recognition'.

44. Bouchard, 'What is interculturalism?', p. 451.

45. O. Jones (2011), *Chavs: The Demonization of the Working Class*, London: Verso Books.

46. Taylor, 'Recognition', pp. 60–3.

47. Bouchard, 'What is interculturalism?', p. 452.

48. D. Miller (1995), *On Nationality* (Oxford: Oxford University Press).

49. Modood, *Multiculturalism*.

50. Dialogue is one of the foundational ideas of MC (*RM*; Taylor, 'Multiculturalism'), in contrast to political and social theories that centre on logics of conflict, abstract rationality, market choices, legal mechanisms, and so on. Multiculturalists have mainly thought of dialogue at the level of public discourses and political controversies; interculturalists have added the micro in terms of interpersonal cultural encounters and group dynamics at the level of youth clubs, neighbourhoods, towns and cities, and so on (Meer and Modood, 'How does interculturalism contrast').

51. *RM*.

52. I accept my two examples run against US practice and sensibilities but nevertheless they are consistent with educational policy and practice in most liberal democratic states.

53. Again, I appreciate that this will read oddly to US readers. They should bear in mind that the US is not typical of how religion is treated in schools in the Western democracies. For example, all states of the European Union give funding either to religious schools or for religious education in state schools.

54. Modood, *Multiculturalism*; T. Modood (forthcoming, 2015), 'State–religion connexions and multicultural citizenship', in J. Cohen and C. Laborde (eds) *Religion, Secularism and Constitutional Democracy* (New York: Columbia University Press, available at https://www.academia.edu/5735585/State-Religion_Connexions_and_Multicultural_Citizenship since 16 January 2014 (accessed 20 August 2014).

55. T. Modood (ed.) (1997), *Church, State and Religious Minorities* (London: Policy Studies Institute).

56. P. T. Lennard (2010), 'What can multicultural theory tell us about integrating Muslims in Europe?', *Political Studies Review*, 8, p. 317.

Index